Malawi

the Bradt Travel Guide

Philip Briggs
Mary-Anne Bartlett

edition 4

www.bradtguides.com

Bradt Travel Guides Ltd, UK
The Globe Pequot Press Inc, USA

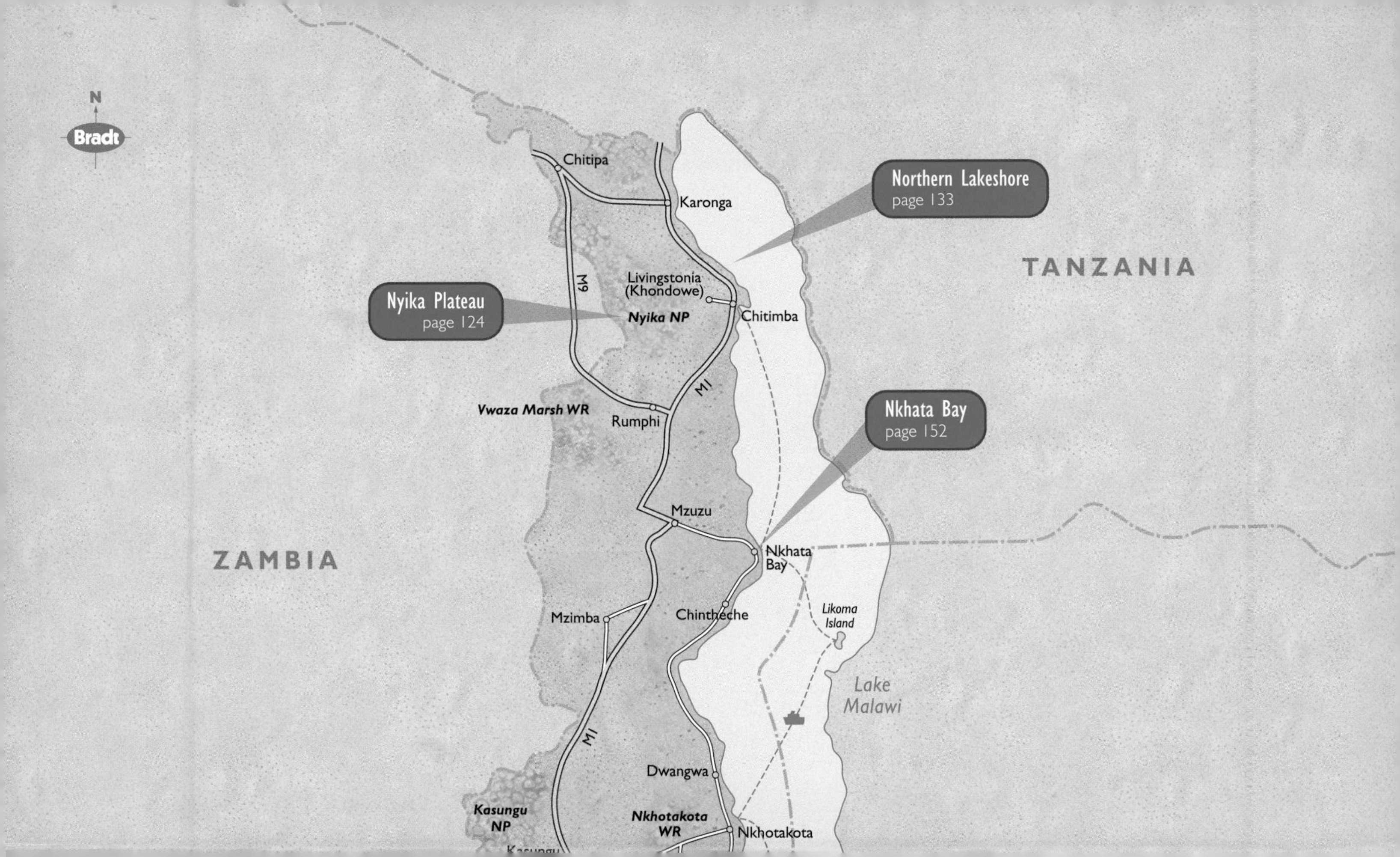
N
Bradt
TANZANIA
ZAMBIA
Northern Lakeshore
page 133
Nkhata Bay
page 152
Nyika Plateau
page 124
Chitipa
Karonga
Livingstonia
(Khondowe)
Nyika NP
Chitimba
M9
M1
Vwaza Marsh WR
Rumphi
Mzuzu
Nkhata
Bay
Mzimba
Chintheche
Likoma
Island
Lake
Malawi
Dwangwa
Kasungu
NP
Nkhotakota
WR
Nkhotakota

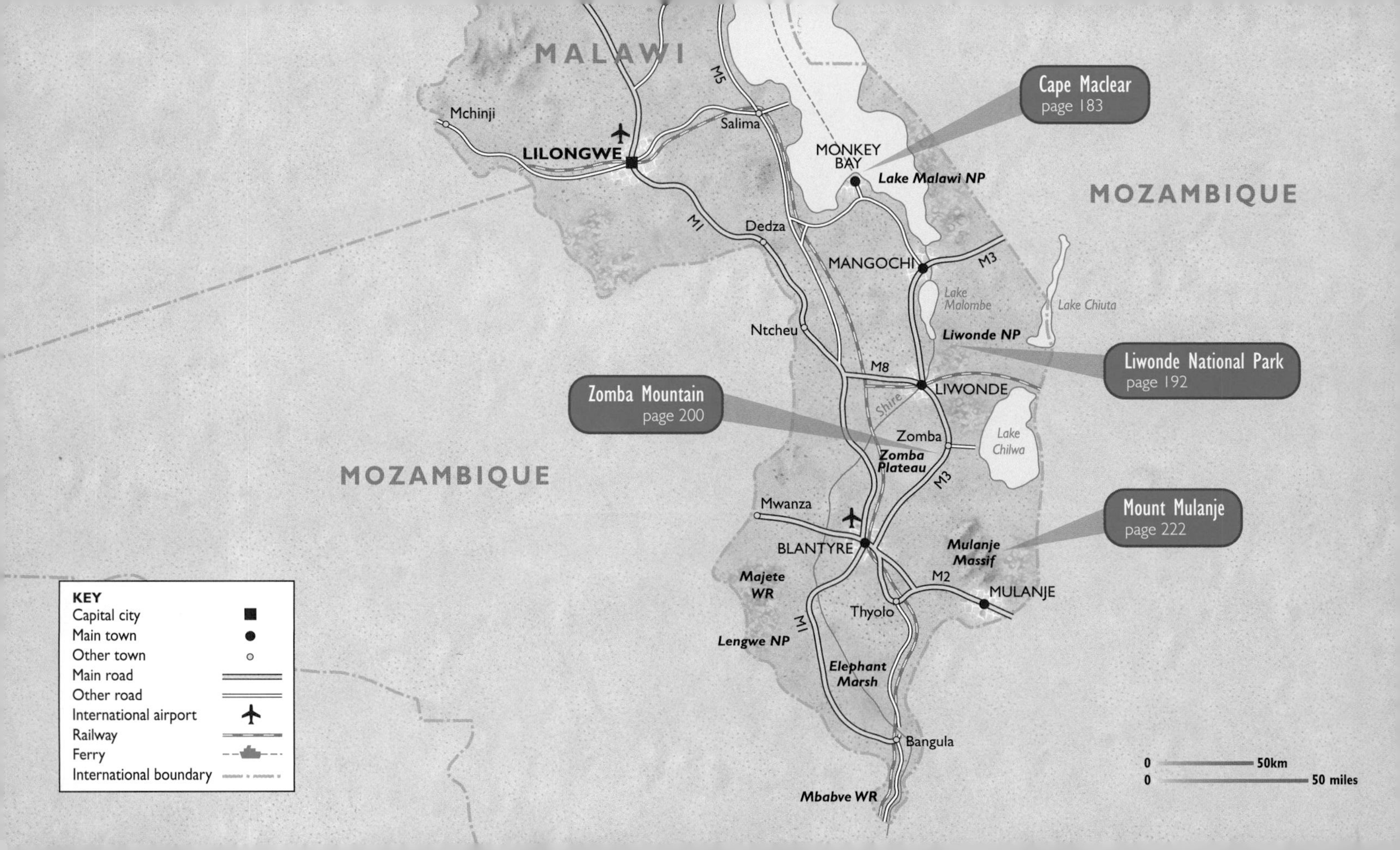

MALAWI
MOZAMBIQUE
MOZAMBIQUE
Cape Maclear
page 183
Liwonde National Park
page 192
Zomba Mountain
page 200
Mount Mulanje
page 222
Mchinji
LILONGWE
Salima
M5
MONKEY BAY
Lake Malawi NP
M1
Dedza
MANGOCHI
M3
Lake Malombe
Lake Chiuta
Liwonde NP
Ntcheu
M8
LIWONDE
Shire
Zomba
Lake Chilwa
Zomba Plateau
M3
Mwanza
BLANTYRE
Mulanje Massif
M2
MULANJE
Majete WR
Thyolo
M1
Lengwe NP
Elephant Marsh
Bangula
Mbabve WR
KEY
Capital city
Main town
Other town
Main road
Other road
International airport
Railway
Ferry
International boundary
0
50km
0
50 miles

Malawi Don't miss...

Liwonde National Park
African elephant, *Loxodanta africana*
(MAB) page 192

Nyika Plateau
Breathtaking vistas
(MAB) page 124

Mount Mulanje
Hiking
(MAB) page 222

Cape Maclear
Kayaking
(MAB) page 183

People and culture
Local musicians, Zomba
(MAB) page 19

top **Buffalo**, *Syncerus caffer*, **Majete** (MAB) page 35

centre **African elephants** *Loxodonta africana* (MAB) page 34

left **Monitor lizard**, *Varanus salvator*, **Domwe Island** (MAB)

top **Warthog**
Phacochoerus africanus
(AZ) page 35

centre **Common eland**, *Taurotragus oryx*, **Majete**
(MAB) page 32

right **Roan antelope**, *Hippotragus equinus*, **Majete** (MAB) page 32

top **Giant eagle owl**, *Bubo lacteus,* **Mulanje** (MAB) page 35
above left **Boehm's bee-eater**, *Merops boehmi,* **Mvuu** (MAB) page 36
above right **White-breasted cormorants**, *Phalacrocorax carbo lucidus,* **Shire River** (MAB) page 36
below **Lesser striped swallow** *Hirundo abyssinicus* (AZ) page 36

top **Likoma Island**
(MAB) page 159

centre **Nkhotakota harbour**
(AZ) page 143

right **Hippo** *Hippopotamus amphibius*
(AZ) page 34

previous page **Tea plantations, Mulanje** (MAB) page 219
above **A local delicacy** (MAB)
below left **Drying chillies in the sun, Lilongwe** (MAB) page 99
below right **Mushrooms for sale, Zomba** (MAB) page 197

left page

above **Malawi chair stall, Nkhata Bay**
(AZ) page 152

below **Reed baskets for sale, Nkopola**
(AZ) page 181

right page

above **Children on shore of Lake Malawi**
(MAB) page 183

below **Tobacco leaves drying, Nkhotakota**
(MAB) page 143

left page

top **Sheltering from the rain, Mulanje** (MAB) page 219

centre **Old mission church, Blantyre** (AZ) page 205

left **Nuns, Karonga** (MAB) page 139

right page

top **Zebra and tourist on horseback, Nyika** (MAB) page 124

centre **Cycling on the Nyika Plateau** (MAB) page 124

right **Riding along Kande Beach** (MAB) page 148

above **Nyika Plateau** (MAB) page 124

below **Liwonde National Park** (MAB) page 192

Authors

Philip Briggs is a travel writer specialising in Africa. Raised in South Africa, where he still lives, Philip first visited east Africa in 1986 and has since spent an average of six months annually exploring the highways and back roads of the continent. His first Bradt Guide, to South Africa, was published in 1991, and he has subsequently written Bradt's guides to Tanzania, Uganda, Ethiopia, Malawi, Mozambique, Ghana, and east and southern Africa; he has also co-authored the first travel guide to Rwanda. Philip has contributed sections to numerous other books about Africa. He writes a column for independent travellers for the magazine *Travel Africa*, and also contributes regular features to several specialist travel and wildlife magazines.

Mary-Anne Bartlett is a travel artist inspired by Africa. She has been visiting Malawi regularly since she joined a university expedition in 1991 to survey the Elephant Marsh and to walk the length of the Shire River from Chikwawa to Monkey Bay. The expedition followed the footsteps of Dr David Livingstone and her great-great-grandfather Sir John Kirk who was botanist and doctor on the Zambezi expedition. Since then she has got to know the rest of Malawi in depth. Rarely to be found travelling without a paintbox, Mary-Anne started a creative travel company, Art Safari, encouraging others to view Africa with an artist's eye too. She now brings groups to Malawi and neighbouring countries to sketch and paint and to experience the wonder and inspiration of Africa. Writing is one of those interesting diversions in life. She would encourage any traveller to take a small art kit to Malawi, as there are times when a camera just doesn't do it.

PUBLISHER'S FOREWORD

Hilary Bradt

The first Bradt travel guide was written in 1974 by George and Hilary Bradt on a river barge floating down a tributary of the Amazon. In the 1980s and '90s the focus shifted away from hiking to broader-based guides covering new destinations – usually the first to be published about these places. In the 21st century Bradt continues to publish such ground-breaking guides, as well as others to established holiday destinations, incorporating in-depth information on culture and natural history with the nuts and bolts of where to stay and what to see.

Bradt authors support responsible travel, and provide advice not only on minimum impact but also on how to give something back through local charities. In this way a true synergy is achieved between the traveller and local communities.

* * *

I visited Malawi 30 years ago, in 1976. The political scene has changed (thank goodness!) but the extraordinary natural world of lake and mountain is still the same. The hiking we enjoyed on the Mulanje Plateau rivalled the best in Africa, and the lakes provided the perfect post-hiking relaxation. We also loved the warmth and friendly self-confidence of the people. It is a pleasure to know, through the descriptions of Philip Briggs and Mary-Anne Bartlett, that in this respect Malawi hasn't changed. You're in for a treat.

Fourth edition September 2006
First published 1996

Bradt Travel Guides Ltd, 23 High Street, Chalfont St Peter, Bucks SL9 9QE, England.
www.bradtguides.com
Published in the USA by The Globe Pequot Press Inc, 246 Goose Lane,
PO Box 480, Guilford, Connecticut 06475-0480

British Library Cataloguing in Publication Data
A catalogue record for this book is available from the British Library
ISBN-10: 1 84162 170 6 ISBN-13: 978 1 84162 170 8

Photographs Mary-Anne Bartlett (MAB), Ariadne Van Zandbergen (AZ)
Front cover Images of Africa Photo
Back cover Elephant in Liwonde (MAB), Mother and child at Lake Malawi (AZ)
Title page Aloe vera (MAB), Malawian lady (MAB), Lizard (MAB)
Illustrations Annabel Milne **Maps** Terence Crump

Typeset from the authors' disc by Wakewing
Printed and bound in Italy by Legoprint SpA, Trento

Acknowledgements

Mary-Anne Bartlett

There's often a generosity of spirit in Africa that you feel you can never repay, whether it's a winning smile and wave from a child in a village, the sudden appearance of a herd of elephants on the Shire River or of a nonchalant baboon on a mountain road, or the sight of a carmine bee-eater on a telephone wire, or whether it's those boys who guided me through the floods across a half-collapsed road near Mangochi or the genuine welcome and hospitality of friends and strangers in the villages, towns, national parks, forest reserves and lakeside lodges.

I would like to thank some of those who helped and advised me while I was researching and writing this fourth edition and who made the whole process a wild amount of fun, nevermind the rains: Ronald Bowyer from Zomba Forest Lodge whose Land Rover coped where my valiant Toyota Corolla from SS Rent A Car might have stuck for ever, Mark Sprong, Macdonald and Godfrey at Land & Lake Safaris whose enthusiasm has got me this deep, the Wardlows at Luwawa Forest Lodge, Mick and Josie Mitchell from the Mushroom Farm at Livingstonia, John 'Horse' at Kande Horse and his colleagues at Kande Beach, Chris and Charity Stevens from Dedza & Nkhotakota Potteries, Carl Bruessow and Nathalie from Mulanje Conservation Trust, Colin Gange-Harris at Game Haven, Amos and Ida Chimseu, Mr Dzimba, Robert Bita and Lakina Mtekama as well as many others in National Parks & Wildlife, Darren Bruessow at Chinguni Hills and Christopher at Mvuu Camp, not to mention Chris and Pam Badger and all the staff at Wilderness Safaris, Ulendo Safaris, and Jambo Africa, Ken and Charlotte Smith at Barefoot Safaris, Harry from Harry's Bar and Ian Musyani from Malawi Tourism Board. My thanks also to Lois Losacco from La Caverna Gallery.

Malawi specialists John Douglas and Kelly White from the Malawi Tourism Marketing Consortium always offer brilliant advice, as does Catherine Mungoni from the Malawian Embassy in London. Thanks too to the Bradt team, principally to Hilary and my editor Tricia Hayne.

I have met many dedicated people involved in inspiring organisations, all crucially linked to the conservation of Malawi's survival as one of the most beautiful and unspoilt places in Africa, not only for us as visitors, but for Malawi's population as a whole. These include: the regional Wildlife Societies of Malawi, Mulanje Conservation Trust, African Parks, Project African Wilderness, Chinguni Trust, J&B, Children in the Wilderness, Peace Parks Foundation and Nyika Vwaza Conservation Trust.

Contents

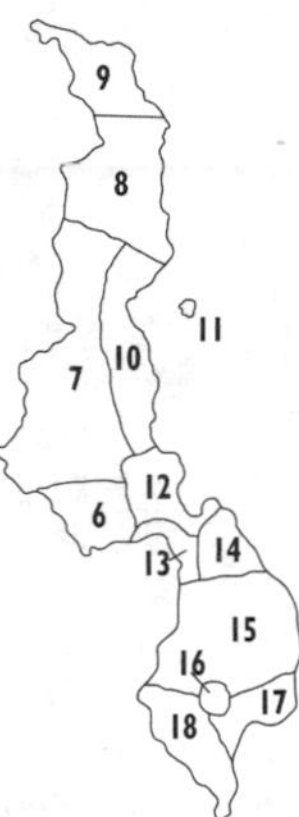

LIST OF MAPS

Introduction

'The Land of the Lake', 'The Warm Heart of Africa', 'Africa for Beginners' ... Malawi certainly attracts its share of snappy catchphrases, and these three sum up much of what makes this small African country so well liked by all who visit it.

Few countries are so dominated by a single geographical feature as the Land of the Lake. Lake Malawi follows the dramatic contours of the Great Rift Valley for a distance of 585km; it is up to 100km wide in parts, and it covers more than 15% of Malawi's surface area. Enclosed by sheer mountains and edged by seemingly endless palm-fringed sandy beaches, Lake Malawi is the most beautiful of Africa's great lakes, and the indisputable focal point of Malawi's tourist industry.

There is much truth in the phrase 'The Warm Heart of Africa'. Not only do the climate and lush vegetation of the lakeshore conform effortlessly to every stereotype image of tropical Africa, but the people of Malawi exude a warmth and friendliness that make most visitors feel instantly at home. Malawi may well be the most laid-back nation on earth.

And 'Africa for Beginners'? Well, certainly, Malawi would lie near the top of any list of African countries I'd recommend to a nervous novice traveller. Although crime is on the increase, Malawi remains as safe as anywhere on the continent, and it is one of a handful of African countries where English is widely spoken. The country's small size, relatively well-maintained roads and unusually nippy public transport combine to spare visitors from the arduous all-day bus trips that are part and parcel of travel elsewhere on the continent. Malawi is remarkably compact, cheap and hassle-free – with one qualification: the high incidence of malaria on the lakeshore.

Tourism in Malawi has developed along rather unusual lines. The country lacks the vast game reserves of east Africa and the world-class tourist facilities of southern Africa; as a result, it sees little in the way of fly-in tourism. Instead, Lake Malawi has become the ultimate venue for backpackers crossing between east and southern Africa. It also relies on being included in the itineraries of tourists visiting neighbouring countries, and has suffered in recent years as Zimbabwe's troubles have kept visitors away from the region.

Within Malawi, tourist patterns are oddly schizophrenic. Travellers gather in their hundreds at lakeshore retreats like Cape Maclear and Nkhata Bay, yet away from the lake there are many attractive and accessible destinations which regularly go weeks on end without seeing a non-resident visitor. There is more to Malawi than a lake, and with the publication of this guide, I hope to draw attention to several exciting destinations which have previously been overlooked by visitors.

Malawi boasts a wealth of forest and mountain reserves, ranging from the relatively well-known Mulanje and Zomba plateaux to the little-visited but highly accessible mountains around Dedza, Ntchisi and Mzimba. Malawi's wildlife reserves may not compare with the very best in Africa, but several – Nyika, Vwaza, Nkhotakota and Liwonde – are easy and cheap to visit, and they have an untrammelled and unpretentious appeal, which, combined with the opportunity to watch big game on foot, should make them popular fixtures on the overland travel circuit. Add to this such currently obscure gems as Lake Chilwa and the Elephant Marsh and you realise it is one of the anomalies of African travel patterns that a country which attracts such consistently heavy traveller traffic has so much unrealised travel potential.

Perhaps the greatest of Malawi's attractions is a low-key charm that most visitors find thoroughly addictive. Many travellers fly into Africa barely aware that Malawi exists; by the time they return home, a high proportion have come to regard it as their favourite African country.

Whether you're content to relax at the lake or prefer actively to explore little-visited mountains, forests and game reserves, it is difficult to think of a more agreeable place for easy, unstructured travel than Malawi.

NOTE ON TELEPHONES Telephone numbers are still rare commodities in Malawi, and have not been reliable means of communication for long. This means that advance booking is rare for small guesthouses and lodges. Individuals and smaller businesses and lodges may change their cell-phone numbers several times over the years, so that unfortunately there's a high possibility that some of the phone numbers we've supplied may soon be out of use – Malawi is full of unused, lost, forgotten and stolen numbers. Oh, and don't forget that if you do ring you might have to try three times before you get through ...

FEEDBACK REQUEST

Every effort has been made to ensure that the details contained within this book are as accurate and up to date as possible. Inevitably, however, things move on. Any information regarding such changes, or relating to your experiences in Malawi – good or bad – would be very gratefully received. Such feedback is priceless when compiling further editions, and in ensuring pleasant stays for future visitors.

Bradt Travel Guides, 23 High Street, Chalfont St Peter, Bucks SL9 9QE, England; **e** info@bradtguides.com.

Part One

GENERAL INFORMATION

MALAWI AT A GLANCE

Area 118,484km^2
Population 13,013,926 (June 2006)
Location Southern Africa, east of Zambia
Border countries Zambia, Tanzania and Mozambique
Type of government Democratic republic
Head of state Dr Bingu wa Mutharika (president)
Ruling party Democratic Progressive Party
Independence (from the UK) 6 July 1964
Capital Lilongwe (population 646,750, June 2006)
Other main towns Blantyre, Mzuzu, Zomba and Karonga
Climate November–March, hot and wet; April–August, moderate and dry; September–October, hot and dry
National parks Lake Malawi, Liwonde, Nyika, Kasungu and Lengwe
Game reserves Vwaza, Nkhotakota, Majete and Mwabvi
Forest reserves Viphya, Ntchisi, Dzalanyama, Tuma, Chongoni, Dedza, Mua-Livulezi, Phirilongwe, Namizimu, Zomba Mountain and Mulanje Mountain
Currency Malawian kwacha (MK)
Rate of exchange US$1=MK140; £1=MK260; €1=MK180 (August 2006)
Economy Predominately agricultural. Depends on substantial inflows of economic assistance from the IMF, the World Bank, and individual donor nations. Performance of the tobacco sector is key to short-term growth.
Inflation 16.1% (June 2006)
People About 11 groups. Chewa in central region, Yao along lakeshore districts of central and southern regions, Lomwe mainly in Shire highlands, Nkhonde, Lambya, Nyanja, Tonga and Tumbuka in northern region. Ngoni in north and centre, Sena in Chikwawa, Nsanje in south as well as Asian and European.
Language English (official) widely spoken by most Malawians. Chichewa 57.2% (national language), Chinyanja 12.8%, Chiyao 10.1%, Chitumbuka 9.5%, Chisena 2.7%, Chilomwe 2.4%, Chitonga 1.7%, other 3.6%.
Religion Approximately 50% Christian, 12% Muslim; remainder a selection of other faiths and sects
Time GMT +2
International dialling code +265
Electricity AC 240V
Flag Three equal horizontal bands of black (top), red and green with a radiant, rising, red sun centred in the black band.
Public holidays 1 January, 16 January, 3 March, 1 May, 14 June, 6 July, 2nd Monday in October, 2nd Monday in December, 25–26 December

1

Background and History

HISTORY

History has scant regard for the arbitrary political boundaries of modern Africa, and the history of Malawi in particular throws up several problems of definition. Malawi took its modern shape only in 1907, for which reason it is misleading to think of it as a discrete entity prior to the 20th century, and it's questionable whether one can write meaningfully about the history of Malawi in isolation of events that took place outside its modern boundaries.

Between 1907 and 1964 Malawi was known as Nyasaland and Lake Malawi was called Lake Nyasa (the name that is still in use today in Tanzania). In the history that follows, we have used the name Nyasaland where appropriate, but we have referred to Lake Malawi by its modern name throughout.

At different times we refer to Malawi as a part of southern Africa, east Africa and central Africa. This is simply because Malawi doesn't fit convincingly into any of these regions. Geographically, the country follows the southern end of the east African Rift Valley, and in prehistoric and geographical terms it seems to us to be a part of east Africa. In the 19th century, northern Malawi was most often influenced by events further north, and southern Malawi by events further south. During the colonial era, the term central Africa was generally applied to the grouping of Nyasaland and Northern and Southern Rhodesia (ignoring any geographical reality). In modern Malawi, you sense a society and economy that looks south to Johannesburg rather than north to Nairobi, and we would thus tend to think of Malawi as part of southern Africa.

For the sake of clarity, when we refer to east Africa we generally mean Kenya, Uganda, Tanzania, Malawi and Mozambique north of the Zambezi River; when we refer to central Africa, we generally mean Zambia, Zimbabwe and Malawi; and when we refer to southern Africa we generally mean Malawi, Zambia, Mozambique and those countries south of the Zambezi River.

PREHISTORY It is widely agreed that the entire drama of human evolution was enacted in the Rift Valley and plains of east Africa. The details of human evolution are obscured by the patchy nature of the fossil record, but the combination of DNA evidence and two recent 'missing link' discoveries (the fossils of a 4.4-million-year-old hominid in the Ethiopian Rift Valley and a 5.6-million-year-old jawbone unearthed in the Turkana Basin in northern Kenya) suggest that the ancestors of modern humans and modern chimpanzees diverged roughly five to six million years ago.

Malawi has not thrown up hominid remains of a comparable antiquity to those unearthed in Kenya, Tanzania and Ethiopia. Nevertheless, it is reasonable to assume that Malawi has supported hominid life for as long as any other part of east Africa, an assumption which is supported by the discovery near Karonga in 1993 of a 2.5-million-year-old hominid jawbone of the species *Homo rudolfensis*.

Stone Age implements over one million years old have been discovered throughout east Africa, and it is highly probable that this earliest of human technologies arose in the region. For a quarter of a million years prior to around 8000BC, Stone Age technology was spread throughout Africa, Europe and Asia, and the design of common implements such as the stone axe was identical throughout this area. Little is known about the early Stone Age hunter-gatherers who occupied central Africa, but the only known skull of this period, found at Broken Hill in Zambia, suggests they were of completely different stock from the modern peoples of the region.

The absence of written records means that the origin and classification of the modern peoples of east and southern Africa is a subject of some academic debate. Broadly speaking, it is probable that east and southern Africa have incurred two major human influxes in the last 3,000 years, on both occasions by people from west Africa.

The first of these influxes probably originated somewhere in modern-day Democratic Republic of Congo, about 3,000 years ago. The descendants of these people, remembered locally as the Akafula or Batwa, are thought to have been similar in appearance to the pygmies of west Africa and the Khoisan of southwestern Africa. In other words, they were slightly built hunter-gatherers, much shorter in stature than the modern occupants of the region. The rock paintings that are found throughout east and southern Africa are generally credited to people whose social customs derived from this early human influx. By the time the first Europeans settled, it is probable that the Batwa had already been exterminated in Malawi, although rumours that a few still lived on the Mulanje Massif suggest that they may have survived in small numbers into the 19th century.

The second human influx started in roughly AD100, and it apparently coincided with the spread of Iron Age technology in the region. The earliest-known Iron Age site in Malawi, dated to AD300, is on the South Rukuru River near Phopo Hill. There is good reason to suppose that the people who brought iron-working techniques into the region were the ancestors of the Bantu-speakers who, by AD500, probably occupied most of sub-equatorial Africa with the major exception of the arid southwest, which was still occupied by the Khoisan when the Cape was settled by Europeans in 1652.

EAST AND CENTRAL AFRICA BEFORE THE 19TH CENTURY It is impossible to discuss events in Malawi prior to European colonisation without first having a general grasp of the regional history.

The eastern coast of Africa has been a hub of international trade for millennia. It is not known when this trade started, but the region was certainly known to the Phoenicians at around the time of Christ. By AD1000, trade between east Africa and the Shirazi Arabs of Persia was well established; by AD1300, more than 30 Swahili city-states had been established along the coast between Mogadishu in Somalia and Sofala in Mozambique. The most important of these cities was Kilwa, which lay on a small island 2km off the shore of what is now southern Tanzania.

The cornerstone of Kilwa's medieval trading empire was gold, and the source of this gold was the powerful Shona Kingdom of Great Zimbabwe. The nature of trade between Great Zimbabwe and Kilwa is obscure, but the absence of Arabic influences on Shona architecture suggests it was the Shona who organised trade as far as the coast. Great Zimbabwe alone is evidence enough that this was a well-organised and technologically impressive society. Founded in around AD1250 and abandoned 250 years later (when its inhabitants moved into the Zambezi Valley to form the Mwene Matupa Empire), the old Shona capital near Masvingo (in modern-day Zimbabwe) remains the most compelling and impressive ruin anywhere in sub-equatorial Africa.

The amiable trading relationship between the Shona, the Swahili and the Shirazi was shattered by the arrival of the Portuguese in the early 16th century. Portugal's interest in east Africa was driven to some extent by the desire to check the spread of Islam, which had become the predominant religion on the coast. But this motive was rapidly sublimated to simple greed: Portugal wanted to control the gold trade, not only on the coast (which it did by razing Kilwa and moving the main trading centre to Sofala near the Zambezi mouth) but also at the source of the Zambezi in the interior.

After the Portuguese captured Sofala in 1505, they decided to seek out the gold fields of Mwene Matupa, which they believed to be the fabled mines of King Solomon. In 1513, a Portuguese emissary called Antonio Fernandez was sent inland up the Zambezi Valley to locate the source of the gold. By 1540, Portugal had established official trading posts at Tete and Sena, the result of which was that the Zambezi Valley rapidly became a hotbed of religious tensions, with the Christian Portuguese and Islamic Swahili vying for trade with Mwene Matupa, and for converts. King Sebastian's first military incursion into the Zambezi Valley in 1569 met with dismal failure – only one-fifth of the 1,000 soldiers sent inland returned to the coast alive. A second attempt at colonisation in 1574 was only marginally more productive.

In 1596, Portugal took control of the Zambezi Valley by placing a puppet king on the Shona throne. This led to a brief flourishing of coastal trade, but also to civil war in Mwene Matupa and the eventual split of the Shona in 1665. The Portuguese were never prepared to pay fair prices to local gold traders and so production slowly dropped. Up until 1680, the Zambezi Valley produced around 16,000 ounces of gold annually. By 1800, this figure had dropped to less than 200 ounces per year. Portuguese expansion into the plateau south of the Zambezi was halted in the 1590s by the Changamire Empire, a Shona offshoot, but the Portuguese remained in control of the Zambezi Valley right up until Mozambique's independence in 1974. The net result of Portuguese interference in east Africa was the destruction of a trade network that had existed for centuries.

Coastal trade probably prompted the change in Malawi's social structures from loosely related clans to more centralised kingdoms. The process of centralisation started in the 14th century, as Malawi became an increasingly important source of ivory to coastal traders, and it gathered momentum under Portuguese influence. The most important kingdom, Maravi (from which the name Malawi derives), was formed in around 1480 and covered much of what is now southern Malawi, northern Mozambique and eastern Zambia. It was an agriculture- and trade-based empire, ruled by a dynastic king or Kalonga from a capital in central Malawi. The Kalonga dynasty reached its peak under Chief Masula, who ruled from about 1600 to 1650. Masula formed a strong alliance with Portugal, at one time sending 4,000 warriors to help quell a rebellion in Mwene Matupa, and by the time of Masula's death, the empire extended all the way to the coast near Mozambique Island. This vast kingdom was feared and respected by the Portuguese, but it gradually collapsed after 1650, and by 1700 it had split into several less powerful groups united under a breakaway Kalonga known as Undi. Many of Malawi's modern ethnic groups, most notably the Chewa, share a common Maravi heritage.

Centralisation was less of a feature in northern Malawi, where the Tumbuka people lived in loosely related clans, united by language and culture rather than politics. In around 1775, a group called the Balowoka established a major trading post in Tumbuka territory, but they had no imperial ambitions and were regarded by the Tumbuka as fair and honest in their dealings. The Balowoka were probably

Swahili people from the Kilwa area, whose main interest was to maintain the ivory trade between northern Malawi and the coast.

Although Portugal had no sustained physical presence in what is now Malawi, a Portuguese trader called Gaspar Boccaro was probably the first European to enter the country. In 1616, Boccaro marched the 1,000km stretch between Tete and Kilwa in seven weeks, a remarkable if now largely forgotten feat of exploration. Boccaro crossed the Shire River near Chiromo and he also passed close to Lake Chilwa. His journals mention 'a lake which looks like the sea, from which issues the river Nhanha, which flows into the Zambezi below Sena and there it is called the Chiry', a clear reference to Lake Malawi and the Shire River. It is uncertain whether Boccaro ever saw the lake, and, rather oddly, the Portuguese showed no apparent interest in his report, though after his journey Lake Malawi appeared on several of their maps.

THE SLAVE TRADE The 19th century was a period of rapid and destructive change in Malawi, as the previous relative stability of the region was shattered by brutal incursions from all sides.

In 1824, Sultan Said of Muscat captured Mombasa and effectively ended Portugal's dominance of the east African coast north of Mozambique. By 1840, when the sultan moved his capital from Muscat to Zanzibar, coastal trade and commerce was dominated by newly arrived Omani Arabs, who established trade routes deep into the interior: most significantly from Bagamoyo to Lake Tanganyika and from Kilwa to Lake Malawi.

Slavery had always played a role in east Africa's coastal trade, both under the Shirazi-Swahili and later under the Portuguese, but prior to the 19th century it was subservient to the trade in gold and ivory. Under Omani rule, which coincided not only with the abolition of slavery in Europe and America but also with the decline of gold output from Zimbabwe, the slave trade took on fresh and quite horrific dimensions. By 1839, over 40,000 slaves were sold annually at Zanzibar's slave market, and perhaps five times as many Africans died every year in slave raids and on the long march from the Rift Valley lakes to the coast.

Several coastal slave traders established themselves in what is now Malawi. The most important was Jumbe, who moved to Nkhotakota in around 1845, founding a dynasty which ruled over the local Tonga for three generations. Under the Jumbe dynasty, Nkhotakota became the main slave terminus out of Malawi, shipping thousands of slaves annually across the lake to Kilwa.

The Omani slavers were methodical and ruthless. Their night raids, known as *chifwamba*, were initiated by letting off a volley of gunshots around the targeted village. The slavers would then wait outside hut entrances to club or spear to death the village's men, who would rush from their huts to see what was happening. The fittest and healthiest women and children were selected as captives and tethered together using iron neck bracelets; the rest were killed on the spot. The captives would be herded to the nearest slave stockade until they numbered around 1,000, when they were shipped across the lake. After crossing Lake Malawi, the captives were forced to march for three or four months to Kilwa, generally carrying heavy loads of ivory and other goods. If any of the captives became ill or expressed tiredness along the way, they were instantly beheaded so that their neck bracelet could be reused. At Kilwa, males were castrated, because eunuchs fetched higher prices. Eventually, the captives would be shipped to Zanzibar in conditions so crowded and dirty that a cargo of 300 people might be reduced to fewer than 20 on arrival.

The devastation that was caused to east African societies by the Omani slave trade cannot be underestimated. For Malawi, it was exacerbated by the arrival of the Yao, an itinerant group who originally came from the Ruvumu River Valley east of the lake. In the 1840s, the Yao were converted to Islam by Zanzibari Arabs, who also gave them weapons and agreed to buy any slaves they could capture. From 1850 onwards, many Yao settled in southern Malawi operating as a kind of fifth column, repaying the hospitality shown to them by the local Maganja and Chewa by capturing and killing them in their hundreds, and in a manner only slightly less ruthless than that of their mentors. The Yao also sold their captives to the Portuguese, whose trade in slaves grew greatly after about 1850.

THE MFECANE Nineteenth-century Malawi was further rocked by the aftermath of events in what is now the Zululand region of the KwaZulu-Natal province of South Africa. Prior to the turn of the 19th century, Zululand was populated by around 20 small, decentralised Nguni-speaking clans. Between 1800 and 1830, the nature of this society was transformed by the cataclysmic series of events which became known as the *mfecane* – 'The Crushing'. The roots of the *mfecane* remain a subject of debate, but modern theorists believe they had more to do with the influence of the Portuguese slave and gold trade in what is now Mozambique than with the more distant European settlement in the Cape. For whatever reason, there is no doubt that the first few years of the 19th century saw Nguni society become highly militarised, the result of which was the formation of three centralised kingdoms: Ngwane, Mdwandwe and Mthethwe.

In 1816, the Mthethwe Kingdom fell under the rule of Shaka, a member of the previously insignificant Zulu clan. Shaka revolutionised Nguni warfare by replacing the traditional throwing spear with a shorter stabbing spear, and instructing his troops to surround their foes in a U-formation and stab them to death. The result was an extended massacre which reverberated across the country and depopulated vast tracts of the southern African interior. As many as two million people died in the *mfecane*, and those who were not killed by Shaka's marauding army either joined its ranks or fled, taking with them the Zulus' frenzied militarism and deadly tactics.

In 1818, the Mdwandwe Kingdom collapsed beneath Shaka's military onslaught. Under the leadership of Zwangendaba, a Jere chief, various Mdwandwe clans fled north into Mozambique, where they attacked and co-opted the local Tonga people to form a mighty migrating army known as the Jere-Ngoni. Northwards they marched, into the Zambezi Valley, where they ran riot over the Portuguese settlements at Tete and Sena, and destroyed the powerful Changamire Empire. The Ngoni raided every village they passed through, killing everybody but young men (who were drafted into their army) and women of marriageable age. Their methods of killing were without mercy: men were bludgeoned to death and unwanted women had their breasts lopped off and were left to die of blood loss.

The Jere-Ngoni crossed the Zambezi in November 1825, settling for many years in the area west of Lake Malawi, where they terrorised the Tumbuka of the highlands and the Tonga of the lakeshore. This period is still remembered by the people of northern Malawi as 'The Time of Killing'. In 1845, Zwangendaba died on the southern tip of Lake Tanganyika. After his death, the Ngoni split into several factions, two of which returned to what is now Malawi. The most significant of these, the Mombera-Ngoni, subjugated the Tumbuka, Tonga and Nkonde people of northern Malawi, killing their chiefs and massacring huge numbers of people at the first sign of rebellion.

LIVINGSTONE AND THE ZAMBEZI EXPEDITION By the middle of the 19th century, the combined efforts of the Ngoni, the Yao, and the Omani and Portuguese slave traders had turned Malawi into something of a bloodbath. And so it might have remained but for the arrival in 1859 of David Livingstone, a Scottish missionary turned explorer who, perhaps more than any one man until Banda, was to shape the future course of events in Malawi.

David Livingstone was born at Blantyre, Scotland in 1813. He trained as a medical doctor at Glasgow University and then as a missionary at the London Missionary School. In 1840, he joined Robert Moffat's mission station at Kuruman in South Africa, where he married Moffat's daughter Mary. While at Kuruman, Livingstone came to perceive his role in Africa as something grander than merely making a few more converts: his ambition was to open up the African interior so that other missionaries might follow in his wake.

Between 1853 and 1856, Livingstone became the first European to cross Africa from west to east, starting at Luanda in Angola and then following the course of the Zambezi to its mouth in Mozambique. Livingstone was a first-hand witness to the suffering caused by the brutal slave trade; he became convinced that the only way to curb slavery was to open Africa to Christianity, colonisation and commerce. Livingstone's faith in the so-called 'three Cs' was not untypical of Victorian attitudes to Africa, but, more unusually, Livingstone was fuelled neither by greed nor by arrogance, but by plain altruism.

In 1858, Livingstone convinced the British government to finance an expedition to search for a navigable river highway upon which European influences might be brought to the African interior. This was the second 'Zambezi Expedition'; it lasted for six years, with the diverse crew of botanist and physician Dr John Kirk, navy officer Captain Norman Bedingfield, geologist Richard Thornton, Livingstone's younger brother Charles as evangeliser, the artist Thomas Baines and the engineer George Rae.

Livingstone's firm belief that the Zambezi would prove to be this highway was crushed by the end of 1858, when the Kebrabasa Rapids west of Tete proved to be impassable by steamer. In 1859, Livingstone turned his attention to the Shire, a tributary of the Zambezi and, though he did not know it at the time, the sole outlet from Lake Malawi. Livingstone's steamer made several trips up the river, but his projected highway to the interior was again blocked, this time by the Kapichira Rapids. Nevertheless, Livingstone, together with his companion John Kirk, explored much of southern Malawi on foot in 1859, including mounts Mulanje and Zomba, as well as Lake Chilwa and the southern part of Lake Malawi.

In 1861, Livingstone was sent a new boat by the British government. It arrived at the Mozambican coast carrying a party of clergymen, who had been sent by the Universities' Mission to Central Africa (UMCA) at Livingstone's request to establish the first mission in central Africa. Livingstone deposited the party, led by Bishop Mackenzie, at Magomero near Chiradzulu Mountain (between the modern towns of Blantyre and Zomba).

On 2 September 1861, Livingstone sailed up Lake Malawi in a local boat, a trip that John Kirk was to describe as 'the hardest, most trying and most disagreeable of all our journeys'. Livingstone stopped at Jumbe's slaving emporium at Nkhotakota, which he called 'an abode of bloodshed and lawlessness'. Further north, the lakeshore was 'strewed with human skeletons and putrid bodies', victims of the marauding Ngoni. By the time he reached Nkhata Bay, the depressed and exhausted doctor feared for his life, and he decided to turn back south, thus underestimating the length of the lake by 100km.

From hereon, the Zambezi Expedition went from disaster to disaster. Disease claimed the lives of several of the Magomero missionaries, including Bishop Mackenzie himself in late 1861, and the UMCA eventually withdrew the mission to Zanzibar. Days after Bishop Mackenzie's death, Mary Livingstone, who had only shortly before joined her husband in central Africa, died of malaria. In 1863, the last time Livingstone sailed up the Shire, the river was described by a member of the expedition as 'literally a river of death'. The boat's paddles had to be cleared of bloated corpses every morning. Livingstone realised that in attempting to open the Shire to the three Cs, he had unwittingly opened the way for Portuguese slave raids. The British government withdrew their support for the expedition in 1864, and Livingstone returned to Britain.

Livingstone is now best remembered as the recipient of Henry Stanley's immortal greeting, 'Doctor Livingstone I presume', and as one of the many explorers of his era obsessed with the search for the source of the Nile. Neither memory does him justice: Livingstone had been exploring Africa for more than two decades before he turned his thoughts to the Nile (on his last African trip between 1867 and 1874), and the posthumous reward for his earlier efforts was indeed the abolition of slavery through the influence of the three Cs. Somewhat ironically, it was only after Livingstone's death near Lake Bangweula in 1874 and his emotional funeral at Westminster Abbey that Britain finally made serious efforts to end the slave trade around Lake Malawi.

CHRISTIANITY, COMMERCE AND COLONIALISM Livingstone's Zambezi Expedition was, on the face of it, an unmitigated disaster. In time, however, it was to prove the catalyst that put an end to the slave trade. Livingstone's published descriptions of the atrocities he had witnessed in Malawi heightened public awareness in Britain. In the year that Livingstone died, John Kirk, a leading member of the Zambezi Expedition and now Consul General of Zanzibar, succeeded in convincing the Sultan of Zanzibar to close Zanzibar's slave market and ban the highly lucrative slave trade.

The UMCA returned to Malawi in 1875, establishing a chain of missions, the most important of which was on Likoma Island. In 1874, the Free Church of Scotland established the Livingstonia Mission at Cape Maclear under the leadership of Dr Robert Laws, but due to the high incidence of malaria at Cape Maclear the mission moved to Bandawe in 1881, where Dr Laws made the significant breakthrough of persuading the Ngoni to cease their endless harassment of the more peaceable Tonga. The Livingstonia Mission moved to its current position on the Rift Valley Escarpment above the lake in 1894. The other important mission established in 1875 was the Blantyre Mission in the Shire Highlands, eventually to become the site of Malawi's largest city.

As a rule, the arrival of missionaries in Africa was at best a mixed blessing. Many were unbelievably arrogant in their handling of Africans. Often they collaborated with would-be colonisers against the interests of their purported congregation, and the use of violence to create converts was commonplace. The Scottish Missions in Malawi were a happy exception. Inspired by Livingstone's humanitarian values and his respectful attitude towards Africans, they made great efforts to end local wars and to curb slavery, often risking their lives in the process.

The Scottish missionaries offered education to thousands of Africans. Malawi's northern province had at one time the highest educational standards anywhere in central Africa, and Likoma Island boasted the only 100% literacy rate on the continent. The missionaries introduced new crops and farming methods as well as passing on practical skills such as carpentry and tailoring. Reverend Scott, who ran the Blantyre Mission for 30 years from 1881, said that 'Africa for the Africans has been our policy from the first'. And it is true that many of the graduates of the mission schools at Blantyre and Livingstonia played a significant role in the eventual rise of Malawian nationalism, as well as in the struggles for equality in Zambia, Zimbabwe and South Africa. Banda himself once referred to Livingstonia as the 'seed-bed' of his Malawi Congress Party.

Livingstone's prediction that legitimate trade might slow the slave trade encouraged two Scottish brothers, John and Frederick Muir, to form the African Lakes Company (ALC) in 1878. The ALC not only provided an important source of materials for the missions, but it rapidly became a major trading force on Lake Malawi and the Shire River, and was to prove instrumental in controlling and eventually killing Mlozi, the sultan of a vast slaving empire around Karonga.

The so-called 'Scramble for Africa' (1885–95) was precipitated by Germany's unexpected claim to a vast portion of east Africa, firstly Tanganyika (what is now mainland Tanzania) and then parts of Malawi, Uganda, Kenya and Zanzibar. In 1890, Germany relinquished all its claims (except for Tanganyika) in exchange for Heligoland, a tiny but strategic North Sea island. In 1891, the vast British territory north of the Zambezi and south of Tanganyika was given the rather unwieldy name of the British Central African Protectorate, and Harry Johnston was appointed as its first commissioner.

Johnston's overriding concern was to stamp out the slave trade, which, despite its abolition on Zanzibar, was still operating between Lake Malawi and Kilwa. In 1891, Fort Johnston was built near the village of the dominant Yao slave trader, Mpondo. Mpondo's village was destroyed and 270 slaves were released from imprisonment. The Yao slave traders hit back several times, but Johnston was eventually able to stop their shipments across the lake. The south of Malawi was finally freed of slave raids when the last two Yao traders were defeated in 1895, and Fort Lister was built near Mulanje to block the last usable route to the coast. In northern Malawi, Johnston persuaded Jumbe, the overlord of Nkhotakota, to give up the slave trade in exchange for British protection. His attempts at negotiating with Mlozi, the self-styled Sultan of Nkondeland (near Karonga), were less successful. After several battles, Mlozi was captured by Johnston in 1895 and sentenced to death.

Twenty-one years after his death, Livingstone was proved to have been correct – Christianity, commerce and colonialism had ended the slave trade. They had also brought inter-tribal peace to Malawi, as the Yao and Ngoni abandoned their spears for the education offered by the Scottish Missions. Colonialism in Malawi was eventually to take on the more nefarious character it did elsewhere in Africa, though never perhaps to the same degree. Again, the paternalistic Scottish missionaries must take much credit for this: in the words of one of the most fondly remembered missionaries, William Johnson, they 'did not come here necessarily to subjugate [but] to protect and instruct'. Ultimately, it is difficult to argue with the assertion that British intervention was the best thing that happened to Malawi in the troubled 19th century.

NYASALAND In 1907, the British Central African Protectorate was divided into two separate territories: Northern Rhodesia (now Zambia) and Nyasaland (the colonial name for Malawi). Throughout the colonial era, there were strong ties between Nyasaland, Northern Rhodesia and Southern Rhodesia (now Zimbabwe), culminating in the federation of the three colonies in 1953.

Nyasaland was the least developed of the three colonies, due to the absence of any significant mineral deposits and also because the region was so densely populated that large-scale cash-crop farming was not a realistic option. A coffee boom at the turn of the 20th century turned out to be short lived when production fell by 95% between 1900 and 1915. Tea was the only settler-dominated agricultural product that really took off, but its production was restricted to the hills around Thyolo and Mulanje.

Together with this lack of development went a low level of alien settlement. By 1953, the settler population, comprised mainly of European administrators and

Indian traders, numbered little more than 10,000. The indigenous population, on the other hand, had by this time grown to 2.5 million, creating a population density six times greater than that of Southern Rhodesia, and ten times greater than that of Northern Rhodesia.

The lack of development had its good and bad sides. At no point in the colonial era was more than 15% of the land under colonial or settler ownership, in large part due to the unusually scrupulous attitude of early governors such as Johnston and his successor Sharpe in ratifying settlers' claims to having 'bought' land from local chiefs. By 1953, a series of government actions had guaranteed that 90% of the land was for the communal use of Africans, while the remaining 10% was protected in forest reserves or occupied by cities or settler farms. This meant that, unlike many other British colonies where the majority of good land was used by settlers to produce cash crops, Africans in Nyasaland were in theory free to continue their traditional subsistence lifestyle.

The obstacle that prevented theory from becoming reality was the system of taxation introduced by the colonial administration. This was called a poll tax: something of a misnomer as there was no related poll. It was not good enough for the people of Nyasaland merely to subsist; they were forced by the colonial administration to pay for the privilege. A small number of local farmers got around the need to earn money by growing cash crops such as tobacco and cotton. Far more Africans entered into the migrant labour system: they were in effect forced to leave their homes and to work for paltry wages and in miserable conditions in the copper mines of Northern Rhodesia and at the gold and coal reefs of South Africa and Southern Rhodesia. In the 1930s, it was estimated that 20% of the men of Nyasaland spent a part of any given year working outside of the country. Villages were thus robbed of their most able workers for months at a stretch, while traditional family structures collapsed under the stress of long periods of separation. Worse still, in 1938 it was estimated that 5% of the men of Nyasaland had been lost permanently to migrant labour – either victims of the filthy living conditions on the mines, or seduced by the big cities.

ETHIOPIANISM AND THE RISE OF NATIONALISM Protest against colonial rule surfaced in Nyasaland even before World War I, in large part due to the influence of Scottish missionaries, notably Dr Robert Laws, who presided over the Livingstonia Mission for half a century, and the Reverend Joseph Booth, a noted denomination hopper whose outspoken pro-African politics forced him to leave Nyasaland in 1902.

The early protests in Malawi were strongly linked to the Ethiopianist churches which emerged in America and South Africa in the wake of Ethiopia's victory over Italy at Adwa in 1896 (the victory which resulted in Ethiopia remaining independent for all but five years of the colonial era). Ethiopianist Churches attempted to reconcile Christianity with traditional African customs and beliefs, producing a distinctly African brand of religion with a strongly Baptist flavour. By taking a pro-African stance at a time when few people of African descent had political power, Ethiopianism was an inherently political movement, and it became strongly aligned with the 'Africa for the Africans' philosophy of the Jamaican visionary Marcus Garvey.

The first indigenous Nyasa to challenge colonial rule was Edward Kamwama, a product of Laws's Mission School in Bandawe. Kamwama worked in the gold fields of South Africa for several years, where he met Rev Booth, who introduced him to the Ethiopianist Watch Tower Church. Kamwama returned to his home in Bandawe in 1908, and formed his own Watch Tower Church, organising the first public protests to forced taxation. He was driven into exile by the colonial administration, but the Watch Tower Church grew all the same. Growing out of this movement, and with the encouragement of Dr Laws, the first of a number of Native Associations was formed in 1912. In alliance with so-called 'Tribal Councils', the Native Associations made repeated demands to government to improve educational levels and end taxation.

Reverend John Chilembwe is now heralded as Malawi's first fighter against colonial rule and was yet another product of the mission schools. Chilembwe was born near Chiradzulu in 1871 and worked as a kitchen boy for Reverend Joseph Booth for several years. He was baptised by Booth in 1893 and then travelled with him to the USA, to Lynchburg in Virginia. Here he studied in a Baptist seminary and where he became influenced by Ethiopianism of which the creed is 'Africa for the Africans'. On his return to Chiradzulu in 1900, Chilembwe bought land close to the original site of the Magomero Mission, where he founded the Provident Industry Mission (PIM). By 1912, over 800 converts lived in the mission grounds.

Adjoining the PIM were the Bruce Estates, owned by the daughter and son-in-law of Dr David Livingstone. One of the estates, Magomero, was managed by another member of the clan, William Jervis Livingstone. Chilembwe had come into conflict with the adjoining estate over the traditional labour laws and what he felt was the oppressive system of *thangata*, or work in lieu of rent. Chilembwe's full indignation at colonial rule was further exacerbated when many African soldiers died in what he saw as the white man's cause of World War I – the Battle of Karonga, northern Malawi, between Britain and Germany. In his final correspondence, which was censored, from *The Nyasaland Times*, Chilembwe asserted:

> Let the rich men, bankers, titled men, storekeepers, farmers and landlords go to war and get shot. Instead we, the poor Africans who have nothing to own in this present world, who in death, leave only a long line of widows and orphans in utter want and dire distress are invited to die for a cause which is not theirs.

On 23 January 1915, three armed columns set out from the PIM. One went to Magomero on the Bruce Estate where Chilembwe ordered them to kill all the European men they found. Another column went to the Nguludi Mission and clubbed – nearly to death – Father Svelsen. A third column headed to Blantyre in order to raid the arsenal for weapons.

The raid on the Bruce Estate was fatal, with William Livingstone and two other Scottish men killed. Livingstone was decapitated in front of his wife and small children in his bedroom at 21.00 as they were retiring to bed. Livingstone's wife Kitty, her two lady houseguests and their five children were then captured and forcibly marched off by Chilembwe's men into the night. The raid on Blantyre failed, with the colonial troops descending on the PIM. Kitty Livingstone and the women and children were found alive after a three-day manhunt by the King's African Rifles. Chilembwe and his rebels were still on the run, but on 3 February he was shot dead near Mulanje, resisting capture. Many of his supporters were jailed or executed and his church was blown up. The PIM, along with several other Ethiopian Churches, was revived at the end of World War I, but the ensuing decades saw little in the way of organised protest.

After the end of World War II, protests against colonialism in Nyasaland and elsewhere in Africa became more militant. Thousands upon thousands of African conscripts had been shipped around the world to fight for the freedom of their colonisers; those who returned found their own liberty as restricted as ever. The first major uprising against colonialism took place in February 1948 in the Gold Coast, when a group of returned war veterans started a riot in Accra. As a result, Britain granted the Gold Coast self-government in 1953 and full independence in 1957, when the country was renamed Ghana.

Kwame Nkrumah, Ghana's first president, declared the moment of independence to be 'the turning point on the continent' and indeed it was. In 1957, Ghana joined Ethiopia and Liberia as one of only three African countries with black rule. A decade later, this picture had been reversed. By 1968, only three of Africa's 50 countries (those colonised by Portugal) remained European dependencies, and three others (South Africa, South West Africa, and UDI Rhodesia) remained under white rule.

HASTINGS KAMUZU BANDA During the heady years from 1953 to 1957, the Ashanti town of Kumasi in the Gold Coast housed the practice of the Nyasa-born Dr Hastings K Banda. In the year that the Gold Coast became Ghana, Banda returned to the land of his birth after more than 40 years abroad; despite being only a year shy of his 60th birthday, he was destined to dominate every aspect of his homeland's politics for nearly four decades.

Hastings Kamuzu Banda was born at Chiwenga near Kasungu. The most likely year of his birth was 1898, a mere three years after the Chewa chief of Kasungu signed a treaty of protectorateship with Britain. Banda was educated in the mission schools; by 1914 he had passed his Standard Three examinations. In 1915, after being accused of cheating in an examination, Banda decided to leave Nyasaland. He walked 800km via Mozambique to Southern Rhodesia, where he worked for a year as a sweeper in a hospital at Hartley. He then obtained a contract to work at a colliery in Natal, the only way he could legally gain entrance to South Africa, but after three months he deserted his job to live in Johannesburg.

It was in Johannesburg that Banda first took an interest in politics. Like many educated Africans of his era, he fell under the influence of the Ethiopianists, joining the AME Church in Johannesburg in 1922. In 1925, the AME sent Banda to the USA to receive further education. For three years he studied at the AME's Wilberforce Institute in Ohio. From 1928 to 1929 he studied at the University of Indiana, then in 1930 he moved to the University of Chicago, where he obtained a Bachelor of Philosophy degree. Finally, in 1932, Banda fulfilled his dream by enrolling at the Mihary Medical College in Nashville, Tennessee, where he was awarded his Doctorate of Medicine in 1937.

Banda's dream was to return to Nyasaland to serve his compatriots as a doctor; in 1938 he moved to Edinburgh where he studied for a licence to practise medicine in the British Empire. But when, in 1941, he tried to find medical work in Nyasaland, his applications were repeatedly snubbed. The nurses at Livingstonia refused to serve under a black doctor, while the colonial administration in Zomba, after much deliberation, would offer him work only if he agreed not to attempt to seek social contact with white doctors. Banda declined the offer and instead set up in private practice in Liverpool.

In 1945, Banda moved his practice to London. The benevolence of spirit that was noted by his patients in London also stretched back to his homeland. He made generous donations to the Nyasaland African Congress (NAC), and he financed the education of 40 Africans over a period of seven years. His Harlesden home became a meeting ground for African nationalist leaders based in London; regular visitors included Kwame Nkrumah and Jomo Kenyatta, the future leaders of independent Ghana and Kenya respectively. It seems likely that Banda would have stayed in London indefinitely had it not been for the humiliation of being named as the co-respondent in a divorce suit filed by Major French against his wife Margaret. In August 1953, the respected Dr Banda of Harlesden closed his practice, packed his bags, and, at the urging of Nkrumah, the newly installed prime minister of the Gold Coast, Banda and Mrs French moved to Kumasi.

THE FEDERATION SAGA The idea of federating Nyasaland with Northern and Southern Rhodesia surfaced as early as the 1890s and it was raised several times before World War II without ever coming to anything. After the war, however, the white settlers of Southern Rhodesia made a more concerted appeal for federation, knowing that it would give them practical sovereignty over the other two colonies in the face of growing African nationalism. The Africans of Nyasaland and Northern Rhodesia were opposed to federation for precisely the same reason that the white settlers favoured it. As Banda pointed out, under a colonial government 'the relationship between [Africans] and the authorities [was] one of ward and warden', but under a government provided by Southern Rhodesia it would become 'one of slaves and masters'.

The issue of federation became the focal point of protest in Nyasaland. The Nyasaland African Congress (NAC), formed in 1943, became the most vocal opponent of Rhodesian rule, and in alliance with Banda in London it entered into negotiation with Britain and Southern Rhodesia to prevent federation. Yet, despite the clear opposition of the African people of Nyasaland and Northern Rhodesia, Britain agreed to federation in 1953 (ironically, the same year in which the Gold Coast was granted self-government), thereby placing the future of Nyasaland under the overtly racist and, to all intents and purposes, self-governing settlers of Southern Rhodesia. Banda described this enshrinement of white dominance in central Africa as a 'cold, calculated, callous and cynical betrayal' and he vowed not to return to Nyasaland until the federation was dissolved.

In August and September of 1953, a series of spontaneous protests against federation took place in Nyasaland, starting in Thyolo and spreading to Chiradzulu, Mulanje and Nkhata Bay. Eleven Africans were killed in these protests and a further 72 were injured. The relatively conservative NAC leadership responded to the protests with some ambiguity, and as a result the organisation fell increasingly under the influence of a group of radical young leaders, the most prominent of whom were Henry Chipembere and the Chisiza brothers, Dunduzu and Yatutu. In 1957, Chipembere asked Dr Banda to return to Nyasaland. After some vacillation, Banda agreed.

Chipembere and his cohorts built Banda up as a messianic symbol of resistance. However, they saw him not as the potential leader of an independent Nyasaland, but as the figurehead through which their more radical views could dominate NAC policy. Banda had rather different ideas. On his return to Nyasaland in 1958, he took over the NAC presidency and urged its 60,000 members to non-violent protest. The first official riot took place in Zomba on 20 January 1959, when 400 people spontaneously rushed the police station after an NAC rally. They were fired on with tear gas and forced to disperse, but the incident marked the start of a spate of riots during which 48 Africans were killed in police fire. The most serious of these incidents took place at Nkhata Bay, where 20 rioters were killed by police reservists.

On 3 March 1959, a State of Emergency was declared, and the NAC was banned. Banda and over 1,000 of his most prominent supporters were arrested. Immediately the NAC was banned, one of its more prominent members, Orton Chirwa, founded the Malawi Congress Party (MCP). Banda became MCP president on his release from jail in April 1960. By releasing Banda, Britain had signalled recognition of the need for change. At the Lancaster House conference of August 1960, Britain disregarded the protests of the Southern Rhodesians and allowed Nyasaland greater autonomy within the federation. And significantly, the colonial administration awarded a selective vote to Africans, so that in the election of August 1961 the MCP won 94% of the national vote and all but six of the 28 seats in parliament.

In January 1962, Banda became Minister of Natural Resources and Local Government in a government headed by the colonial governor, Glyn Jones. In November 1962, at the Marlborough House talks in London, Britain agreed to a two-phase plan for self-government in Nyasaland, and on 19 December the House of Commons announced that Nyasaland could withdraw from the federation. On 1 February 1963, Banda was sworn in as the Prime Minister of Nyasaland; on the final day of the same year, the federation was formally dissolved, and on 6 July 1964, Nyasaland was granted full independence and renamed Malawi.

MALAWI UNDER BANDA Even before independence, Banda had demonstrated to his cabinet a reluctance to accept constructive criticism and other people's ideas. His autocratic tendencies were emphasised when, at the Organisation of African Unity (OAU) summit in Cairo exactly three weeks after independence, he announced that Malawi had 'one party, one leader, one government and no nonsense about it'. It was this sort of statement, as well as a sudden reversal on foreign policy (in 1960, Banda had issued a joint statement with the future president of Tanzania, Julius Nyerere, to the effect that both countries would boycott white-ruled African states, but after independence he showed an unexpected enthusiasm to strike a trade deal with Portuguese Mozambique) that prompted the fateful 'Cabinet Crisis' little more than a month after independence.

On 16 August 1964, following Banda's return from the OAU conference, a group of cabinet members, led by Orton Chirwa, confronted Banda regarding his inflexible leadership and foreign policy. Banda offered to resign, but the cabinet asked him to continue as president on the condition that he would consider their grievances. Instead, Banda dismissed Chirwa and two other ministers from his cabinet. Three other ministers resigned in protest, including Henry Chipembere and the surviving Chisiza brother (in 1961, Dunduzu Chisiza, widely regarded as the most intellectually capable and far-sighted politician of his generation, had become the first of many Malawian politicians to die in a suspicious car 'accident'). The highly talented independence cabinet was overnight transformed into a bunch of yes-men.

Banda faced two more challenges to his rule. In February 1965, Henry Chipembere led a rebellion which was foiled by the army at Liwonde. Chipembere escaped to America, but many of his supporters were killed. In 1967, Yatutu Chisiza, another of the Cabinet Crisis discards, led several supporters into Malawi from a base in Tanzania. Chisiza was killed by soldiers. Remnants of Chipembere's rebels used guerrilla tactics to destabilise Banda's government for several years, but by the end of 1970 they had all been rounded up. After the Chipembere rebellion, Banda formally declared Malawi to be a one-party state, and on 6 July 1971, he made himself Life President.

It is often said that Banda was a benign dictator. True enough, he was not in the murderous class of somebody like Amin; nevertheless, he was entirely ruthless in his quest to obtain and maintain absolute power. It is conservatively estimated that 250,000 Malawians were detained without trial during his rule. Prisoners were underfed and in many cases brutally tortured. Banda's perceived political opponents, if they were not killed by the security police in jail, were victims of suspicious car accidents, or else – as Banda was proud of boasting – became 'meat for crocodiles' in the Shire River. Several exiled Malawians died in explosive blasts strikingly reminiscent of those used by the South African security police.

To say that Banda was intolerant of criticism is an understatement. Critics were jailed, and not just political critics: it was, for instance, a detainable offence to discuss the president's age or his past relationships and medical activities. Gossip was not tolerated regarding his relationship with the MCP's 'Official Hostess',

Cecelia Tamanda Kadzamira, who became Banda's mistress in 1958. Other illegal subjects included family planning (Malawi's population tripled under Banda) and, naturally enough, politics of any variety. Jehovah's Witnesses were persecuted (20,000 fled the country and many who remained or returned were detained or tortured to death) and Muslims were only barely tolerated, probably because they were so numerically strong in areas like Mangochi that even Banda wasn't prepared to stoop to the required scale of genocide.

Censorship was rife under Banda. Thousands of films, books and periodicals were banned, often for absurd reasons. Banda's whimsical dictates even covered personal dress – from 1968 to 1993, Malawian women were banned from wearing mini-skirts or trousers. Perhaps no other episode illustrates the absurd vanity, megalomania and paranoia of Banda as his banning of an innocuous Simon & Garfunkel song: its release coincided with a rocky patch in Banda's love life and the lyrics ('Cecilia, you're breaking my heart...') were more than he could bear.

That Banda was perceived as benign is partly because so little information about Malawi reached the outside world. Most of all, though, it is because it was in Western interests to support the status quo in Malawi. In a climate of socialist-inspired African nationalism, Banda was an arch-conservative, openly Anglophilic, and cynical enough to deal openly with the South African government throughout the apartheid era. Banda was acceptable simply because he was co-operative. As recently as 1989, Margaret Thatcher and the Pope both visited Malawi, praising Banda's achievements and uttering not one public word of criticism of what had become the longest-lived dictatorship of its sort in Africa.

What did Banda achieve during his rule? Peace and stability, for one – though it can be argued that his ruthless dictatorship allowed for little else, and that Malawians are not a people given to civil disorder. Economic growth, for another – but again, Malawi was so underdeveloped at the time of independence that the growth rate he achieved (around 5% per annum on average) might easily have occurred under a genuinely benign leadership. Banda built Malawi its new and more centrally positioned capital at Lilongwe – a capital city funded almost entirely by the South African government. He improved the infrastructure and in particular the road system immeasurably – using Western aid given in exchange for his pro-Western policies. In short, Banda achieved little that might not have been achieved by a more consensual government. And, in 1993, Malawi remained as it had been at the time of independence: one of Africa's poorest countries.

Banda did much to stir latent ethnic conflict in Malawi. His dream was to restore the ideal of the Maravi Empire, to which end he dressed his speeches in traditional Chewa symbolism and made Chichewa the official language, despite the fact that less than 30% of Malawians spoke it as their mother tongue. At the same time, he used the messianic build-up to his return to Malawi and the authority which Africans traditionally invest in a man of his age to create a powerful personality cult. He carried with him at all times a fly-whisk, the traditional symbol of the *sangoma* (witchdoctor). On his return to Malawi, he insisted on using a name which he had reduced to a middle initial in Britain and Ghana – Hastings K Banda became Kamuzu (meaning 'the little root', roots being the primary source of traditional Malawian medicines). By using this traditional symbolism, and by emphasising his background as a Western doctor, Banda set himself up, especially in the eyes of village elders, as the new Kalonga of a revived Maravi Empire. Banda was a dictator; he was no fool.

THE ROAD TO DEMOCRACY In the last decade or so of his rule, Banda's was increasingly a puppet presidency, largely due to his advanced years (Banda turned 80 in 1978 and he was 95 when he finally relinquished power). From the mid

1980s onwards, Malawi was to all intents and purposes ruled by Banda's shadowy official hostess and her much-reviled uncle, John Tembo.

John Tembo was born in Dedza in 1932. He went to university in Lesotho and worked as a schoolmaster before he was appointed to Banda's cabinet as Finance Secretary in 1963, an appointment which was unpopular with other cabinet members for its strong air of nepotism. In the early years, Tembo played a sycophantic role in parliament, using his position primarily to acquire a personal fortune (by 1990, he was a director of a major firm in practically every business sector that dealt with government, including Malawi's main bank). Tembo came to be seen as Banda's natural successor, and in January 1992 he finally became, in name, the Minister of State in the Office of the President. In effect, John Tembo was appointed the executive president of Malawi.

One of the reasons why Malawians tolerated Banda for so long was that, for all his failings, he commanded respect, particularly from the rural population. Another was that nobody could have predicted how long he would live: there was always hope that his replacement would have more democratic inclinations. Tembo neither commanded respect (he was widely seen as the mastermind behind Banda's greatest excesses) nor, at 60, was he particularly old, and his appointment in 1992 made it clear that he was Banda's chosen successor.

Even without Tembo, it is probable that Banda's days as Life President of Malawi were numbered. The end of the Cold War meant that supporting the West was no longer enough to ensure Banda a good international press and generous aid packages. In 1989, the British prime minister praised Banda for his 'wise leadership'; two years later, Britain made the belated and hypocritical gesture of withdrawing all non-humanitarian aid to Malawi in protest at Banda's abuse of human rights. The neighbourhood, too, was changing. By the end of 1992, Kenya and Zambia had held their first multi-party elections, Tanzania and Uganda were talking about them, South West Africa had become independent Namibia, and in South Africa the previously unthinkable was fast becoming an eventuality. Banda had become a man out of time.

But despite the change in the external climate, Tembo's appointment was probably the main impetus behind the Catholic bishops' galvanising *Lenten Letter*, which documented in graphic detail the failings and abuses of power of the Banda administration. The *Lenten Letter* was read aloud simultaneously, in churches across the country, on 3 March 1992 and then faxed to the BBC. Banda's response to the letter was to place the bishops under house arrest. But for once the world was watching. Banda was condemned by governments and Church bodies worldwide, and within Malawi, for the first time since independence, there was a climate of open dissent. May 1992 saw Malawi gripped by strikes and protests, culminating in the Lilongwe Riot of 7 May in which 40 people were shot dead by police. In October 1992, Orton Chirwa, the founder of the MCP and a leading member of the short-lived independence cabinet, died in suspicious circumstances in the Zomba Prison where he had been detained since 1981.

Banda's growing unpopularity left him with little option but to announce a referendum on the question of a multi-party election. The referendum took place in March 1993, and it drew an overwhelming majority of votes in favour of change, a popular pro-referendum slogan being 'Votey smarty, votey multi-party'. Two new parties of note emerged: AFORD and the UDF, the latter led by Bakili Muluzi, a Muslim businessman who had once briefly served in Banda's cabinet before resigning.

Polling took place on 17 March 1994. The election was declared substantially free and fair, which in the strict sense it probably was, though the final results were a reflection less of policies and popularity than of regional and ethnic differences.

The MCP won by a landslide in the central region, AFORD achieved a similar result in the northern region, and the UDF won overwhelmingly in the south. The southern region being the most populous part of Malawi, the overall election was won by the UDF. Bakili Muluzi was made the second president of Malawi.

The general election of 1999 was again won by the UDF and Dr Muluzi was installed for a second presidential term. Although Muluzi has proved to be a democratic ruler, in 2002 he and his party attempted to alter the constitution to allow him a third term as president, a move that caused controversy and dissent. Freedom of speech is still a reality, as is a free press, and many Malawians were openly critical of Muluzi's leadership, something that would never have been allowed under Banda.

Banda himself died of natural causes in 1997, aged somewhere between 97 and 101, depending on which of the several possible dates given for his birth you believe. In 1995, the former Life President was tried for the alleged murder of three cabinet ministers and an MP who died in a 'car accident' near Mwanza in 1983. Both he and his co-defendants, John Tembo and Mama Cecelia, were acquitted on all charges. This alone says much about the new Malawi: a legal trial was a privilege given to few opponents in the despotic days of Banda and Tembo.

MODERN POLITICS *Nicholas Wright*

The general election of 1999 was again won by the UDF and Dr Muluzi was installed for a second presidential term. Gwanda Chakuamba, who had surprised John Tembo and the rest of Malawi by being chosen by Banda to succeed him as leader of the MCP, was declared the close second in a much-disputed ballot. Whereas Muluzi's first term might be interpreted in terms of the consolidation of Malawian democracy and constitutionalism, his second, which followed this election, was very seriously compromised by high-level corruption and the intimidation of political opposition by the UDF Youth Wing, the Young Democrats. Such was the hold Muluzi had established over Malawian politics that, although he narrowly failed to have the constitution altered to allow himself a third term, he managed, in 2004, to impose upon a reluctant UDF and a suspicious electorate, a presidential candidate who was heartily disliked by the one and virtually unknown to the other. His name is Bingu wa Mutharika, President of Malawi since May 2004.

Mutharika has transformed Malawian politics since 2004 by dumping UDF, the party which carried him to power, and by forming a new governing party of political opportunists, called the Democratic Progressive Party. His government has been characterised by a vigorous anti-corruption rhetoric, which is inevitably targeted at the old UDF bigwigs, including Muluzi, and by an appeal to some of the 'old-fashioned values' of the Banda era which, in his own case at least, manifests itself in a certain personal integrity and a deep suspicion of the institutions of the budding Malawian democracy: its extraordinarily free press and its extremely rowdy National Assembly. His government is becoming the darling of the international community because of its relative financial responsibility and trade liberalisation policies. The ordinary Malawian is still prepared to give it the benefit of the doubt, in the hope that its anti-corruption net will one day catch some really big fish and that its 'pro-poor' election promises will be honoured. The Malawian intelligentsia is the most fearful of this government, sensing in it a drift back towards authoritarianism, and a poisonous culture of secretiveness at the centre of power.

ISSUES FACING MALAWI TODAY Perhaps the greatest crisis facing Malawi is continual poverty. Crime, too, has increased dramatically, and allegations of government corruption are rife. During the years after the elections in 1994, many seemed to query the benefits of democracy, and you may still come across nostalgia for the relative prosperity, apparent national self-sufficiency and the safety and social stability of the Banda era.

Malawi is an endangered but magical place, seeming to be part of a long process of constant decline and regeneration, hope and perseverance. Its people still manage to greet strangers and smile, despite poverty and family losses due to AIDS, even though prices rise and income drops. Deforestation is just one dire indication of the pressure on land and fuel supplies of a crowded nation. It's a country where change is never far beyond the present, though often out of reach and where self-sufficiency has diminished.

GOVERNMENT AND ADMINISTRATION

Malawi is a democratic republic, with elections every five years. In 1970, Hastings Kamuzu Banda, Malawi's president since independence in 1964, amended the constitution to declare himself Life President, a position he retained until 1994. During these years Malawi was a one-party state, and the only people who were allowed to stand for election were members of Banda's Malawi Congress Party (MCP). The first truly democratic election took place in May 1994, bringing the United Democratic Front (UDF) to power, with Dr Bakili Muluzi as president. Re-elected in 1999, President Muluzi attempted to change Malawi's constitution to allow him to seek re-election for a third term but prior to the election of May 2004 he installed Dr Bingu wa Mutharika as the UDF presidential candidate. As president of Malawi, Mutharika established a new party, the Democratic Progressive Party, in March 2005.

ADMINISTRATIVE REGIONS Malawi is divided into three administrative regions: southern, central and northern provinces, the capitals of which are respectively Blantyre, Lilongwe and Mzuzu.

PEOPLE AND CULTURE

POPULATION The population of Malawi is estimated to stand at close to 13 million people, making it one of the most densely populated countries in Africa, especially in the south. Despite this, most of the population lives in rural areas. The most populous city in Malawi is Blantyre, followed by Lilongwe, Zomba and Mzuzu.

LANGUAGES The official language of Malawi is English and the national language is Chichewa. The indigenous languages of Malawi all belong to the Bantu group. The most widely spoken of these, especially in the southern and central regions, and the joint official language until 1994, is Chichewa. In the north, the most widely spoken language is Chitumbuka. There are many other linguistic groups in the country, some of the more important being Yao, Ngoni and Nyanja.

RELIGION Organised religion has played a major role in the history of Malawi. Its influence started with the slave-trading Yao tribe that settled in southern Malawi after being converted to Islam by Zanzibari Arabs, and picked up when the Christian Portuguese arrived on the scene in the first half of the 19th century to share in the spoils of this evil trade. The arrival of the Scottish explorer, Dr David Livingstone, in 1859 was the catalyst that put an end to the slave trade and the string of mission stations that followed opened up the country for trade and colonisation. The missionaries were a strict bunch and offered a high standard of education to all, a tradition which, to this day, ensures that Malawians are well educated and well disciplined.

The modern Malawi government allows freedom of religion and believes in co-operation between the state and religious organisations for assistance in the socio-economic uplifting of the people – the missions are still very involved in education. It is estimated that about half the country's population is Christian and 12% Islamic; various other faiths and sects make up the remaining 38%. There is a high degree of religious tolerance between all religions, which contributes to the generally peaceful state of affairs in Malawi.

CULTURE With about ten different ethnic groups in the country, Malawi has a mosaic of cultural norms and practices. Unique traditional dances and rituals as well as arts and crafts identify the groups. The Museum of Malawi recognises the importance of these traditions, and promotes appropriate activities in schools and other public places. Mua Mission's KuNgoni Art Centre and Museum has embraced the cultures and religions of the Central region, which is also seen clearly in the approach to the mission's work. Above all though, it is the tradition of hospitality, friendship and courtesy that permeates the entire country and warrants Malawi's epithet 'the Warm Heart of Africa'.

Art *Mary-Anne Bartlett*

The life, colours and contours of Malawi lend themselves to painting. Sometimes everywhere you look there is another picture.

I rarely travel anywhere without a sketchbook, pencil and watercolours, even if I have a camera in my bag too. The most rewarding times I have had in Malawi have been when painting – it causes an interaction that is seldom found between tourists and Malawians. It's also thoroughly absorbing and addictive. Trying to record a sunset or a market scene in colour, or a moving elephant in line can be the most intense experience as you observe and allow the feeling of the environment to combine into image through your hand on to paper.

If you don't want to create art yourself, you can buy it. The art scene in Malawi is not limited to the stylised paintings that you will be tempted to buy on the beaches and streets. Amongst the street art are paintings, batiks and drawings that encapsulate some of the wit, striking looks and movements of many Malawians.

Malawi has only very few internationally recognised artists. Amongst them are two who keep their feet straddled between the Western world and Malawi. Both are based in the UK, and have work that reflects both halves of their lives. The 'new contemporary' Samson Kambalu is currently winning awards for his conceptual work, while painter David Kelly uses his deep knowledge and understanding of the African bush to make canvases come alive with the wildlife of the national parks.

In Blantyre, artists to look out for include Aaron Banda and David Matoto (both highly collectable for birds and village scenes respectively) as well as Brian Hara, Jomwe, Innocent Willinga, Lovemore Kankhwani, Ellis Singanu and Boston Mbale, all of whom exhibit at La Caverna at Mandala House. A selection of artists also exhibit at Central Africana Bookshop in Uta Waleza Shopping Centre.

Lilongwe's galleries include Mtendere Art Gallery in Mbico House along Chilambula Road, Arthouse Africa, behind the Hong Kong Restaurant in Capital City as well as La Galeria in Old Town Mall. La Galeria champions all the top names including amongst others Nyangu Chodola, William Mwale, Elson Kambalu, Peter Mtungi and Hughson Mbawa, Noel Bisai and Nixon Malamulo and Peter Chikondi. The Nyanja Art Studio on the Salima Road out of Lilongwe

MALAWI MUSIC SCENE: BELIEVE IT

Harry Gibbs, Harry's Bar

Malawi music is currently enjoying an explosion of styles and genres which are showcased in bars, clubs and taverns throughout the country every weekend. Whether it be a traditional band with homemade instruments or a budding Hip Hop or Ragga artist, the standards of music have noticeably improved over the last five years.

Bands such as Wambali Mkandawire and Manyasa and the Black Missionaries have impressed audiences across southern Africa while Lucius Banda, Wendy Harawa Joseph Tembo and others have toured as far afield as England, France, Australia and Nigeria.

2006 was a special year for young musician John Chibade, who sold over 100,000 copies of his first album within Malawi, while Billy Kaunda and Ben Mankhamba (previously Ben Michael) continued to maintain their standing with strong album releases.

In Blantyre the Blue Elephant and Cappineros are hosting several bands including a very exciting duo of Rappers Marvel and Dominant 1. A home-produced Hip Hop album released in June of 2006 hit Malawi like a storm with its strong implementation of local beats and dialect into the Hip Hop genre.

Lilongwe's live music scene has been prominent at Chameleon where acts such as Kenny Gilmour, Ifeyo and Mitchell Moss with Kalimba have all had well-attended shows. Harry's Bar continues to promote new talent such as Elias Kadwala and King Yellow, while Friday and Saturday nights are kept busy with DJ Duzzle and DJ Prince William playing music to move to.

No mention of Lilongwe would be complete without Chez Ntemba, the pinnacle of Malawi nightlife: a night at Chez Ntemba will often give you the opportunity to watch the sun rise.

In Mzuzu there are two main venues: Paris and Villa Kagwenta, while the Mzoozoozoo is a pub and place to stay of great character and also home to Souls of the Ghetto, acoustic winners of the 2005 Kuche Kuche Music Awards.

There are two major festivals in Malawi: Lake of Stars Festival and Mango Festival. Lake of Stars Festival is held at Chintheche Inn in September and has hosted such giants as Andy Cato from Groove Armada and Felix B of Basement Jaxx (*www.lakeofstarsfestival.co.uk*). The Mango Festival is held in November in Lilongwe and is a street party held at Harry's Bar to celebrate the Mango. Both events are organised by Umunthu Consulting (e *Umunthu@eomw.net*).

Radio stations such as Zodiac, Power FM, Capital and MBC Radio 1 and 2 play a vast amount of music from all over the world and also do their part to showcase Malawian musical talent. So when in Malawi turn on the radio, buy the tape or CD and go out to the clubs and bars to see what is happening.

is worth stopping at for unframed works. The highlight of the visual arts calendar is without doubt the Wildlife Society Art Fest in Lilongwe each November, where over 300 artists and craftspeople exhibit.

Malawi has long been famous for its hardwood carvings, which have been exported all over the world. Very few of Malawi's carvers have been credited by name, until, through Mua Mission and a couple of the galleries including African Habit and La Caverna, some of the master carvers are now achieving a recognised status of excellence.

Pottery and ceramics are less common now that plastic has arrived, however clay pots of all sizes are still made in many areas. Dedza and Nkhotakota Potteries are the key places to buy glazed stoneware and where traditional clay pot and ceramics workshops take place.

Malawi attracts more than its share of artistic visitors through Art Safari, a unique travel company which lays an equal emphasis on art and travel, with adventurous itineraries combining art tuition and safari guiding. Many of Malawi's artists have also benefited from its artist-in-residence scheme (e *info@artsafari.co.uk; www.artsafari.co.uk*).

2

The Natural World

If we do not do something to prevent it, Africa's animals and the places in which they live will be lost to our world and her children – forever.

Nelson Mandela

GEOGRAPHY

LOCATION Malawi is a landlocked country in south central Africa falling between 33° and 36° E and 9° and 18° S. It is bordered by Tanzania to the north, Zambia to the west and Mozambique to the east and south.

SIZE Covering an area of only 118,484km², Malawi is one of the smallest countries in Africa, smaller even than England. It is 840km long from north to south, and is nowhere more than 160km wide.

CAPITAL In 1975, the centrally situated city of Lilongwe replaced Zomba as the capital of Malawi. Until recently Blantyre was the unofficial capital and its population is similar to Lilongwe's. Blantyre still remains the financial centre of Malawi. However most other businesses, government bodies and non-government organisations have their headquarters in the capital of Lilongwe.

The Malawian landscape is dominated by the Great Rift Valley, which runs through the eastern side of Africa from the Red Sea in the north to the Zambezi Valley in the south. Lake Malawi is the most southerly of the great lakes of the Rift Valley; at 585km long and up to 100km wide, it is the third-largest lake in Africa and the 11th largest in the world. The only outlet from Lake Malawi is the Shire River, which flows out of the southern tip of the lake near Mangochi and then follows the course of the Rift Valley southwards, descending to an altitude of 38m above sea level near Nsanje, before it crosses into Mozambique where it drains into southern Africa's largest river, the Zambezi.

In addition to Lake Malawi, there are three other sizeable lakes in Malawi. Lake Malombe lies in the Rift Valley south of Mangochi along the Shire River, and it can thus be seen as part of the Lake Malawi system. Lakes Chilwa and Chiuta are shallow bodies of water east of the Rift Valley near the border with Mozambique. Altogether, some 20% of Malawi's surface area is covered by water.

The Rift Valley Escarpment rises sharply to the west of the lake, in some areas reaching altitudes of above 1,500m (about 1km higher than the lakeshore). The highest and most extensive mountain range in northern Malawi is Nyika, protected in the national park of the same name, followed by the Viphya Plateau around Mzimba. Southern Malawi is also rather mountainous. Mulanje and Zomba are the most important mountains in the south, but there are also several smaller peaks in the Dedza and Thyolo areas. The highest peak in central Africa, Sapitwa (3,002m), is part of the Mulanje Massif in southeastern Malawi.

There are three distinct altitude levels in the country, the highest being the Nyika Plateau in the north, dropping down to the highlands of the central region and dropping again to the Shire Valley in the south

CLIMATE

Malawi's climate is tropical, with hot days and balmy nights. However, within Malawi, temperature variations are influenced greatly by altitude. The hottest parts of the country are Lake Malawi and the Shire Valley, which lie below 500m. Highland regions such as Mulanje, Zomba, Nyika, Dedza and Viphya are more temperate, and they can be very chilly at night.

There are three seasons in Malawi. The months between November and March are hot and wet, those between April and August are moderate and dry, while September and October are hot and dry. July and August can be very cold at night. Despite the large amounts of surface water in Malawi, much of the country is prone to drought; the absence of any irrigation schemes means that local famines are a serious threat in years of low rainfall.

VEGETATION

The dominant vegetation type in Malawi is *brachystegia* woodland (also known as *miombo* woodland), which naturally covers around 70% of the country's surface area, though it has been degraded in many areas. *Brachystegia* woodland is found at altitudes up to 1,500m in areas with an average annual rainfall of over 1,000mm. In areas of higher rainfall, such as the Viphya Mountains, the *brachystegia* woodland often has a closed canopy and consists of tall trees, while in areas with a rainfall between 1,000mm and 1,300mm, trees are more stunted and the canopy is open.

Brachystegia woodland is, as the name suggests, dominated by trees of the *brachystegia* family. These trees are highly resistant to fire and, although they are technically deciduous, they lose their leaves only briefly in September and October. Several other woodland types (again named after the most common type of tree) occur in Malawi, mostly at altitudes below 500m. Mopane woodland is dominant in the Liwonde area, while *terminalia* woodland is common in the area east of Zomba and west of Lake Chilwa. The mixed woodland of the Shire Valley and Lilongwe area holds trees of the *brachystegia*, *acacia*, *combretum* and *bauhinia* families.

The unmistakable baobab tree (*Adansonia digitalia*) is a characteristic feature of low-lying parts of Malawi, particularly the Lake Malawi shore and the Shire Valley. The unusual, bulbous shape of the baobab tree makes it one of the most photogenic features of the African landscape, and it has given rise to the belief in many parts of Africa that the tree was planted upside down by God. It is thought that some baobab trees grow to be over 3,000 years old. The spongy wood of the baobab (it is related to the balsa tree) is rich in calcium, making it an important food source for elephants in times of drought.

Palm trees are characteristic of low-lying and well-watered parts of Malawi, and together with the baobabs they give places like Liwonde National Park and the Elephant Marsh much of their character. Four types of palm occur naturally in Malawi. The borassus palm (*Borassus aethiopum*) is a tall tree growing up to 20m in height, and is characterised by a distinctive swelling halfway up its stem, and by fan-shaped leaves. It is common along rivers in northern Malawi, such as in Vwaza Marsh Wildlife Reserve, and on the southern lakeshore around Salima and Monkey Bay.

The doum palm (*Hyphaene benguallensis*) grows to a similar height as the borassus, but it has a thinner stem without a swelling, and more frond-like leaves. Doum palms are common on the Lake Malawi shore and in the Shire

Valley, particularly in Liwonde National Park and around the Elephant Marsh.

The much smaller wild date palm (*Phoenix relinata*) occurs along rivers, where it may take one of two forms: that of a dense bush, or of a tree hanging over the water. The wild date palm can be recognised by its feathery fronds. It is common along the Shire River (you'll see plenty in Liwonde National Park) and in highland areas such as Thyolo, Viphya and Nyika.

The raffia palm is noted for its large leaves: at up to 18m in length, they are the largest found on any plant in the world. The raffia may have a stem of up to 10m in height, or its leaves may grow straight out of the ground in a cluster. Raffia palms are generally found along streams to an altitude of 1,500m; they are common in the Shire Highlands and in Nkhotakota Wildlife Reserve.

Evergreen forests, though they have been reduced to covering a mere 1% of the country's surface area through deforestation, provide Malawi's most biologically diverse habitat in terms of plants, birds and insects. Evergreen forest is distinguished from woodland by having a high interlocking canopy and by being composed mostly of non-deciduous trees. What evergreen forest still occurs in Malawi is confined to remnant pockets in montane areas. Among the more accessible areas of evergreen forest are those on Ntchisi, Mulanje, Viphya, Nyika, Dedza and Zomba mountains.

Semi-evergreen forest covers around 2% of Malawi's surface area. The canopy of this forest is generally formed by *Brachystegia spiciformis* trees, underneath which lies a dense undergrowth of herbs and shrubs. Forest of this type is found on the slopes of Mulanje and Zomba mountains, as well as in the Thyolo and Nkhata Bay areas. It is also common along some rivers.

The most common type of forest in Malawi is probably exotic plantation forest, comprised mainly of pine and eucalyptus trees. Though such plantations play an important role in preventing the further loss of indigenous forest, they have little aesthetic appeal and generally hold few birds and mammals. Many plantations are interspersed with areas of indigenous riverine forest and fringing scrub, which can be very rewarding for seeing wildlife.

Montane grassland and moorland covers about 5% of Malawi's surface area. It is the predominant vegetation type on the plateaux of Nyika, Mulanje and Viphya mountains. These plateaux support a mixture of grasses, heathers and heaths, and are particularly rich in wild flowers, especially after the rains.

A notable feature of Malawi's flora is the high number of orchid species. Around 280 terrestrial and 120 epiphytic orchid species have been recorded in Malawi, with the greatest variety to be found in Nyika National Park and on Mulanje and Zomba mountains. The best time for seeing orchids in bloom is between November and March, though exact flowering times vary from year to year and area to area, depending on local rainfall.

CONSERVATION AREAS

NATIONAL PARKS AND WILDLIFE RESERVES Malawi has five national parks and four wildlife reserves, all except Majete fall under the jurisdiction of the Department of National Parks and Wildlife (*01 752671*; *tourism@malawi.net*).

Nyika National Park This is the largest and most northerly of the reserves at 3,132km^2. The national park protects the vast Nyika Plateau and its northern slopes, the main water catchment area for Lake Malawi. Nyika is primarily a scenic reserve, big sky country with never-ending landscapes, always deliciously cool when the rest of the country is hot. It offers some good game viewing, with the advantage that it can be explored on foot or horseback from Chinguni Camp or Lodge. Access to the reserve is a problem for those without private transport.

Vwaza Marsh Wildlife Reserve lies a short way south of Nyika. Access to the camp at Lake Kazuni couldn't be simpler, and there is excellent game viewing from the camp. All in all, an independent traveller's dream come true.

Kasungu National Park lies along the Zambian border, only about two hours north of Lilongwe. It is the largest 'bush' reserve in the country, with some staggering views. Kasungu supports depleted numbers of large mammals and game viewing is highly seasonal. The lodge at Lifupa has accommodation for all tastes and budgets, which combined with ease of access makes it a good target for independent travellers.

Nkhotakota Wildlife Reserve, near the town of the same name, is the oldest reserve in Malawi. A wide variety of game species is present, including lion and elephant, but animals are seldom seen due to the rough terrain and the limited road network. There is excellent birding. The best way to explore is by foot with an armed game ranger, with adventurous camping at Bua and Chipata Camp, or stay at a lodge by the lake.

Lake Malawi National Park protects Cape Maclear's shores and its islands on the southern lakeshore. Established in 1980 it was the first freshwater, underwater national park in Africa, declared a UNESCO World Heritage Site in 1984. The park is mostly of interest for its marine and birdlife, the waters protecting the breeding grounds of the mbuna rock fish (cichlids). Lake Malawi National Park is highly accessible to independent travellers with plenty of accommodation options from which to choose.

Liwonde National Park, which lies along the Shire River south of Liwonde, is richly atmospheric and well stocked with animals; one of the most attractive parks in Africa. Hippo and elephant are abundant and the birds are simply fantastic. In the centre of the park, Mvuu Camp and Lodge offers bush luxury at reasonable rates, and it allows camping at a price most budget travellers will be able to afford. In the south of the park, not too far from Liwonde town, Chinguni Hills offers affordable accommodation, ideal for exploring the southern section. Unless you're seriously short of cash, Liwonde is not to be missed.

Majete Wildlife Reserve southwest of Blantyre is undergoing an astounding regeneration through the work and management of African Parks Foundation, after having been severely poached in the 1980s. African Parks has been working on the conservation of the park since 2002 (*www.africanparks-conservation.com*). Majete is one of the secret gems of Malawi, with a 15km stretch of rapids in the Kapichira Falls and an increasing game count every year. There is only one short road into the reserve from Chikwawa and no accommodation or camping facilities yet.

Lengwe National Park lies in the Shire Valley, south of Majete. Game viewing on long walks through the grass and trees is a real pleasure, with sightings of antelope species and buffalo, and superb birding. Access can be a problem without private transport. Once there, however, there's good accommodation at Nyala Lodge.

Mwabvi Wildlife Reserve lies in the far south of the country and is currently being given extra conservation support by Project African Wilderness (PAW) through Barefoot Safaris. It is rarely visited by tourists and the rough terrain makes wildlife viewing difficult, but the wilderness atmosphere makes up for that. It feels like a place forgotten by the rest of the world. There is a small, basic camp. Access is a problem without private transport.

FOREST RESERVES Malawi has about 70 forest reserves, the foremost of which are Mulanje and Zomba. The Department of Forestry (☎ *01 771000/ 01 773462;* **f** *+265 1 774268;* **e** *dirfor@sdnp.org.mw*) plays a valiant conservation role by preserving many of Malawi's evergreen and semi-evergreen forests in protected forest reserves. Entrance to these forest reserves is free and there are no restrictions on walking within them. In addition, some of the reserves have accommodation in the form of privatised forest lodges and forestry resthouses, most of which also allow camping in their grounds.

These are areas which are stunning for their scenery and for the freedom of the outdoors. Adventure and activities now include everything from hiking, climbing and mountain biking to birdwatching and fishing. Animals characteristic of Malawi's forest reserves include leopard, bushbuck, red, blue and grey duikers, klipspringer, bushpig, samango and vervet monkeys, baboon, and a variety of secretive nocturnal small predators. The forests are also notable for insects (most visibly butterflies). They are of special interest to birdwatchers. Except for Zomba and Mulanje, Malawi's forest reserves have in the past received little attention from tourists. This is a shame, as several other forest reserves (most notably Viphya, Ntchisi, Dzalanyama, Chongoni, Dedza, Mua-Livulezi, Chiradzulu, Michuru and Thyolo) are in varying degrees accessible to independent travellers, and either have accommodation or else are close enough to a town to visit as a day trip.

Mulanje Forest Reserve in the southern part of Malawi almost bordering Mozambique boasts central Africa's highest peak, Sapitwa, at 3,002m. It is a 550km^2 reserve where no less then nine major rivers originate and is home to numerous endemic species. Mulanje is a dream destination for hikers, climbers and walkers. This granite massif is enormous, its prominent rockface rising 1.5km high from the surrounding emerald green tea gardens. The plateau lies mostly at 1,830m but contains 20 distinct peaks and exceptional scenery containing a variety of climatic and vegetative areas. There are now nine mountain huts on the plateau.

Zomba Forest Reserve covers Zomba Mountain, a place of incredible views and rising to a height of 2,085m. Innumerable footpaths lead routes up indigenous and pine forests to waterfalls, trout streams and precipitous cliffs. A stylish hotel and a homely forest lodge perch on the flanks of this impressive mountain whilst a campsite nestles on the plateau.

Viphya Forest Reserve contains 53,000ha of pine plantation (the largest in Africa outside Lesotho) as well as pockets of indigenous forest and montane grassland.

Ntchisi Forest Reserve has a small rainforest of trees more akin to those found amid the mists of Uganda or the Congo. It is easily accessible from Lilongwe.

Dzalanyama Forest Reserve is on the border with Mozambique southwest of Lilongwe, with forested hills culminating in peaks of 1,600m and 1,700m. This is the watershed for Lilongwe, with many streams and waterfalls for cold dips after walking.

Tuma Forest Reserve is between Lilongwe and Salima, a dramatic reminder of deforestation elsewhere. It is seldom visited and not too easy to get to.

Chongoni Forest Reserve is only 10km north of Dedza and is home to the Forestry College of Malawi. It has its own resthouse and the reserve holds many excellent walks, some of which leading to rock paintings (now defaced, sadly). The nearby

Dedza Mountain Forest Reserve is a lovely spot for walking after a visit to Dedza Pottery. **Mua-Livulezi Forest Reserve** can be accessed from halfway down the Golomoti Pass from Dedza. With a guide and camping equipment it should be possible to walk though these three reserves for several days. The nearest accommodation is at Mua Mission.

Phirilongwe Forest Reserve, northwest of Mangochi, is an area of thick vegetation and lost valleys where elephants still hide from the world and lions are said to visit. Camping is the only option here.

Namizimu Forest Reserve near Malindi is to the east of Lake Malawi and Mangochi on the Mozambican border. Elephants move great distances through this general area; they spend time in Liwonde National Park and migrate through the forests up to the hills of Mozambique.

OTHER CONSERVATION AREAS There are many other parts of Malawi which are of interest for their wildlife and scenery.

The **Lilongwe Nature Sanctuary** divides the Old Town and the city centre of Lilongwe with dense bush and whooping hyenas. The sanctuary currently has a small dusty zoo area but also has plans to become a rehabilitation centre for European zoo animals in the next few years.

The **Elephant Marsh** in the Shire Valley is an area of serene wilderness, about 500km^2 of marshland inhabited and visited by over 300 bird species as well as crocodile and hippo and fished by silently punted dugouts. There's no accommodation and no official tourism network, and is so far off the beaten track that it has the feel of a place that time forgot.

Sucoma Sugar Estate's small private **Nyala Park** is situated close to the sugar estate cottages and to Lengwe National Park and holds a high density of game, including giraffe and wildebeest. In Vumbwe, only a few kilometres out of Blantyre towards Tchyolo, is a game-stocked conservation area, **Game Haven**, part of a new luxury lodge, a superb area for walking for day visitors or guests.

Kuti Game Reserve near Salima is a gentle conservation area which is undergoing huge policy changes; there are plans for it to become a hunting reserve in the future.

Lake Chilwa is a prime area for birding, and like the Elephant Marsh has a timelessness about it, despite large numbers of fishing villages around its shores and on Chisi Island.

WILDLIFE

Malawi boasts as wide a variety of large mammals as most African countries, and all the so-called 'big five' – buffalo, elephant, lion, leopard and rhinoceros – are present in the country. However, human population pressures mean that most big wildlife species are now restricted to reserves, none of which is really large enough to justify comparison with the best in other African countries. That said, some parts of Malawi offer excellent game viewing, and it will be of particular interest to independent travellers that reserves such as Liwonde, Vwaza Marsh, Nyika and Nkhotakota are among the most easily and cheaply visited on the continent.

LARGE MAMMALS Several useful field guides to African mammals are available for the purpose of identification. What most such guides lack is detailed distribution details for individual countries, so the following notes should be seen as a Malawi-specific supplement to a regional or continental field guide.

THE CONSERVATION CHALLENGE

Carl Bruessow, Mount Mulanje Conservation Trust

With a landscape that varies from as low as 35m rising to over 3,000m above sea level, and that includes large freshwater bodies and high mountain plateaux, Malawi has a diverse range of ecological habitats and a rich plant and animal biodiversity. To conserve these habitats and wildlife, the country has proclaimed five national parks, four wildlife reserves and over 80 forest reserves – an impressive commitment of over 20% of the total land area. An indication of the valuable natural heritage here is the 1,000 plus cichlid fish species in Lake Malawi and over 500 plant and animal montane species, all of which are unique to Malawi.

The large mammals of the national parks and wildlife reserves have experienced a continued serious threat to survival over the past 30 years. An under-funded government management authority has battled to carry out its responsibilities and the current status of each protected area reflects the level of involvement of other support agencies. Big mammals have been hunted illegally for their meat and other traditional products ever since these conservation areas were set up and this conflict continues, even where law-enforcement efforts are adequate. All the conservation areas have tourist accommodation, while facilities in the national parks are concessioned out to commercial operations and are of a high standard. There is little doubt that tourists have a direct benefit on the status of wildlife as their presence acts as a deterrent to poachers, and the income generated from tourism supports both local management and community-improvement activities.

Donor assistance to support the country's parks and reserves, and the environment in general, has waned over the past decade as there is a widespread perception that caring for the nation's wildlife and natural resources is a low political priority. In this desperate situation, a number of concerned organisations and individuals have rallied to raise support in a variety of ways. The Wildlife & Environmental Society of Malawi, the original conservation agency formed in 1947, continues to maintain an essential advocacy and support role in the country. Since then a number of other trusts have been established specifically to support activities across most of these parks and this broader public interest is slowly waking up the government. The most significant improvement has been the private sector management takeover by the philanthropic African Parks organisation, which is making a major investment to reinvigorate the Majete Wildlife Reserve.

Malawi's environment and natural resources face an immense sustainability challenge. The majority of Malawians are smallholder farmers but most available arable land is now intensely farmed and the need for local natural resources for livelihood use and sale has also sharpened. The recent increase in the country's already high population has intensified this problem to the point where conservation areas are being encroached in a bid to find more land and forest products. Many of the forest reserves in the southern region originally established for watershed protection have now been completely deforested and opened up for growing crops. The fish stocks of the lakes are depleted and many of the beautiful endemic cichlid fish are threatened by illegal fishing around their island habitats. Motivating a broad public response to reverse this degradation through the adoption of improved approaches and practices is now an essential part of much of the project work being spearheaded by the many local and international non-governmental organisations working in Malawi.

Predators The **lion** is the largest African cat, and the animal that every visitor to Africa hopes to see. Lions are sociable animals which live in family prides of up to 15 animals. They tend to hunt by night, favouring large and medium-sized antelopes. By day, lions generally do little but find a shady spot and sleep the hours away. In Malawi, lions are now extremely rare. If at all, they are most likely to be seen in Mwabvi Wildlife Reserve, and are recorded from time to time in Kasungu, Vwaza Marsh, Nyika, Nkhotakota and Liwonde.

Leopards are compact cats, marked with rosette-like spots, whose favoured habitats are forests and rocky hills. Leopards are still widespread in Malawi: they live in all the national parks and game reserves, most forest reserves and even in some hilly or wooded regions outside of conservation areas. The success of leopards in modern Africa is due largely to their secretive, solitary nature; they are very rarely seen even where they are common. Nyika National Park is said to have the greatest concentration of leopards in central Africa, and sightings are quite commonplace in the vicinity of Chelinda Camp.

Leopard

Cheetahs are creatures of the open plains, normally seen either on their own or in small family groups. They are superficially similar in appearance to leopards, but easily distinguished by their more streamlined build, the black 'tear marks' running down their face, and their simple (as opposed to rosette) spots. Cheetahs were once resident in Kasungu National Park, though they have not been seen there for several years.

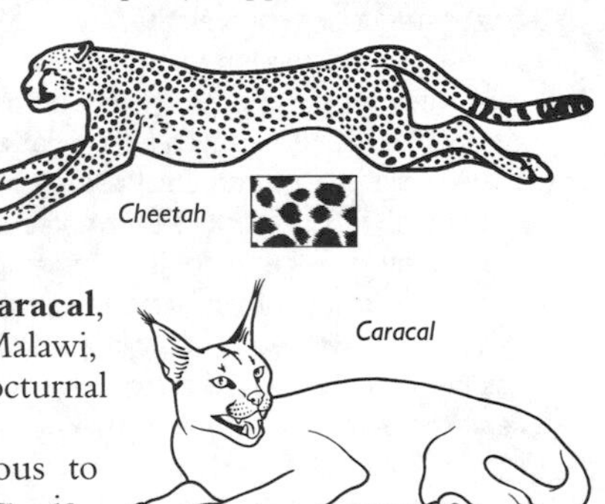

Cheetah

Caracal

Several smaller species of cat, such as **caracal**, **serval** and **African wild cat**, occur in Malawi, but they are rarely seen due to their nocturnal habits.

The largest canine species indigenous to Malawi, the **African hunting dog**, is unmistakable on account of its cryptic black, brown and cream coat. Hunting dogs live and hunt in packs, normally about ten animals strong. The introduction to Africa of canine diseases such as rabies has caused a severe decline in hunting dog numbers in recent years, and this endangered species has been on the IUCN Red List of Threatened Animals since 1984. The status of hunting dogs in Malawi is uncertain; they have been recorded from time to time in several reserves, but so infrequently that it is unlikely they are resident. Significantly, most records come from reserves on the Zambian or Mozambican borders, with sightings in Vwaza Marsh and Kasungu, though it is likely that the wild dog is now extinct in Malawi.

African hunting dog

Jackals are lightly built dogs, mostly nocturnal in habit and generally solitary by nature. Several species are recognised, but only one – the side-striped jackal – is present in Malawi, and can be recognised by its grey or sometimes yellowish coat, indistinct black side stripe, and white-tipped tail. The side-striped jackal has been recorded in Nyika, Liwonde and Lengwe national parks, and in Vwaza Marsh and Nkhotakota wildlife reserves.

The **spotted hyena** is a large, bulky predator with a sloping back, black-on-brown lightly spotted coat and dog-like face. Contrary to popular myth, hyenas are not a type of dog, nor are they exclusively scavengers (when you see hyenas hanging around a 'lion kill', it may well be that they are waiting to reclaim what the lions have hijacked), but rather they are opportunistic feeders whose complex social structure and innate curiosity makes them perhaps the most fascinating creatures to watch in the wild. Spotted hyenas are widespread throughout Africa, often living near human habitation, and can be found in all of Malawi's national parks and wildlife reserves, as well as in many forest reserves and even outside conservation areas. The spotted hyena is nocturnal in habit, but because it is not as retiring as most night hunters, it is often seen around dusk and dawn. Probably because the Old and New towns are separated by a wildlife sanctuary, Lilongwe is probably the only African capital where you can regularly hear hyena at night.

Spotted hyena

The *viverridae* is a group of small predators that includes **mongooses** and the cat-like **civets** and **genets**. At least nine mongoose species have been recorded in Malawi, most of which can be readily observed in the right habitat. The African civet, tree civet and large-spotted genet are all present in Malawi, but they are rarely seen because of their nocturnal habits. The best chance of seeing these animals is on a night game drive in Liwonde National Park.

Four representatives of the *mustelidae* occur in Malawi: the **ratel**, **Cape clawless otter**, **spotted necked otter** and **striped polecat**. Otters are occasionally seen at Otter Point in Lake Malawi National Park.

Primates The most common primate in Malawi is probably the **vervet monkey**, a small, grey animal with a black face and, in the male, blue genitals. Vervet monkeys live in large troops in most habitats except desert and evergreen forest. They are frequently seen outside of reserves.

The closely related **samango** or **blue monkey** is a less common species, with a darker, more cryptic coat. Samango monkeys are always associated with evergreen and well-developed riverine forests and are highly vocal. They are commonly found in Zomba, Mulanje and Majete.

Vervet monkey

Blue monkey

The **yellow baboon** is common throughout Malawi. Like vervet monkeys, baboons are highly sociable animals with a wide habitat tolerance. They are most frequently seen in the vicinity of rocky hills. The greyer **chacma baboon** exists alongside the yellow baboon south of Lake Malawi.

The nocturnal bushbabies (or *galagos*) are small arboreal primates more often heard than seen. The **thick-tailed bushbaby** generally occurs in true forest, and it can be distinguished from the **lesser bushbaby**, a species of woodland and

savannah habitats, by its much larger size and bushy tail. The best way to see a bushbaby is to follow its distinctive, piercing call to a tree and then shine a torch to find its large eyes.

Lesser bushbaby

Antelope

Large antelope All the antelope described below have an average shoulder height of above 120cm, roughly the same height as a zebra.

The **eland** is Africa's largest antelope, with a lightly striped fawn-brown coat, short spiral horns and a slightly bovine appearance accentuated by its large dewlap. In Malawi, eland are most likely to be seen on the Nyika Plateau, where they are seasonally common, but they occur in most of Malawi's reserves and parks.

Common eland

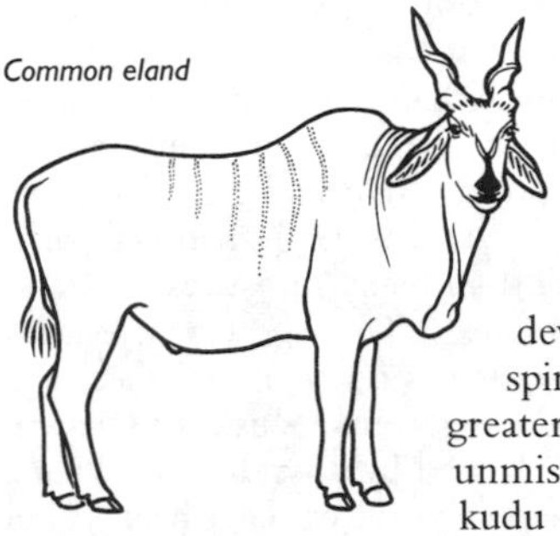

The **greater kudu** is another very large antelope, with a greyish coat marked by thin, white stripes and large pink ears. The small dewlap and immense spiralling horns of the male greater kudu render it unmistakable. Greater kudu are generally found in small groups in woodland habitats. They are present in all of Malawi's national parks and wildlife reserves. Note that the similar but smaller lesser kudu of east Africa does not extend its range as far south as Malawi.

Greater kudu

Sable antelope

The male **sable antelope** is unmistakable with its large, backward-curving horns and black coat. The equally graceful female has smaller horns and is chestnut-brown in colour. Both sexes have a well-defined white belly and rump. The sable antelope is now thriving in large herds in Liwonde National Park, and it has been recorded in all of Malawi's national parks and wildlife reserves.

Roan antelope

The related **roan antelope** is an equally handsome animal, with a uniform reddish-brown coat and short backward-curving horns. The roan is the most common large antelope on the Nyika Plateau, and it also occurs in Liwonde, Majete, Kasungu, Vwaza Marsh and Nkhotakota.

The **common waterbuck** has a shaggy coat and a distinctive white horseshoe on its rump. It is always associated with water, and is particularly common along the Shire River in Liwonde National Park. It also occurs in Kasungu, Majete, Vwaza Marsh and Nkhotakota.

Liechtenstein's hartebeest is an ungainly antelope, closely related to the wildebeest (which, incidentally, does not occur naturally in Malawi, though it has been introduced to Nyala Park and Game Haven), with a red-yellow coat and short stubby horns. It is seen occasionally on the Nyika Plateau and is doing well in the

Rhino Sanctuary in Liwonde National Park. It can sometimes be seen in Kasungu and more frequently in Vwaza Marsh.

Medium-sized antelope All the antelope described below have a shoulder height of between 75cm and 95cm, except for the male nyala, which has a shoulder height of slightly over 1m.

The most widespread medium-sized antelope in Malawi is the **bushbuck**. The male bushbuck has a dark chestnut coat marked with white stripes and spots, while the female is lighter with similar markings to the male, giving it an appearance much like a European deer. The bushbuck is very shy, and mostly nocturnal, but it can be found singly or in pairs in most forested habitats and in thick woodland near water. It can be seen in all Malawi's wildlife reserves and national parks, as well as in many forest reserves and is preyed upon by leopard and python.

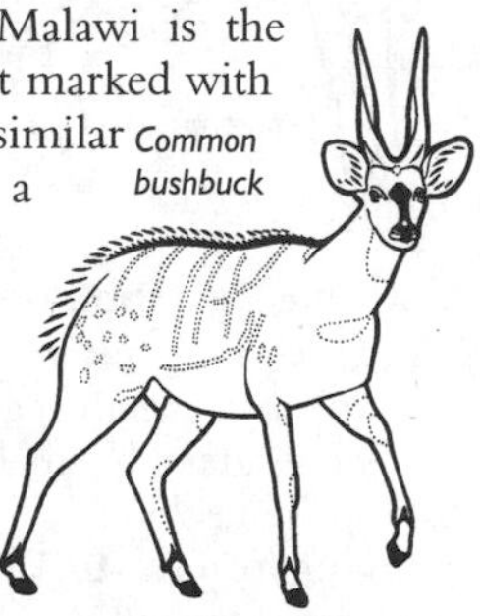

Common bushbuck

The closely related **nyala** is a southern African species that reaches the northern extreme of its range in Mwabvi, Majete Wildlife Reserve and Lengwe National Park, where it is common. The nyala can easily be confused with the bushbuck, though the exceptionally handsome male is much larger and shaggier in appearance, with a distinctive white crest running along its spine and elegant curving horns.

The most successful breeder of all Malawi's antelopes, the **impala** is a highly gregarious and photogenic resident of most woodland habitats. It has a bright chestnut coat, distinctive white and black stripes on its rump, and the male has large lyre-shaped horns. The impala has acute hearing and other animals often stay with impala herds so they can listen for the loud snort alarm call. In the mating season males fight (sometimes to the death) to take a herd of females, with the losers rejoining the bachelor groups. The impala is present in Vwaza Marsh, Liwonde, Lengwe, Majete, Mwabvi and Kasungu.

Impala

The **southern reedbuck** is a lightly coloured, rather nondescript antelope almost always associated with water. It is present in small numbers in most of Malawi's reserves and national parks, as well as on other mountain plateaux, but it is only common in Kasungu and Nyika national parks.

Reedbuck

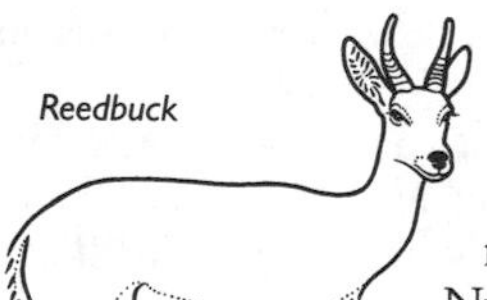

The related **puku**, a woolly golden-brown antelope with no distinguishing features, is found in marshy habitats. Similar in size to the impala it differs in its habits and likes to sit in the sun to chew the cud. It is essentially an animal of Zambia and southern Democratic Republic of Congo, but it occasionally strays into those Malawian reserves which border Zambia, and is more common in Kasungu than the impala.

Small antelope All the antelope described below have a shoulder height of below 60cm.

The **klipspringer** has a grey, bristly coat which gives it a mildly speckled appearance. Klipspringers live exclusively on rocky outcrops and have adapted to the habitat by a phenomenal ability to jump and climb up almost vertical rockfaces.

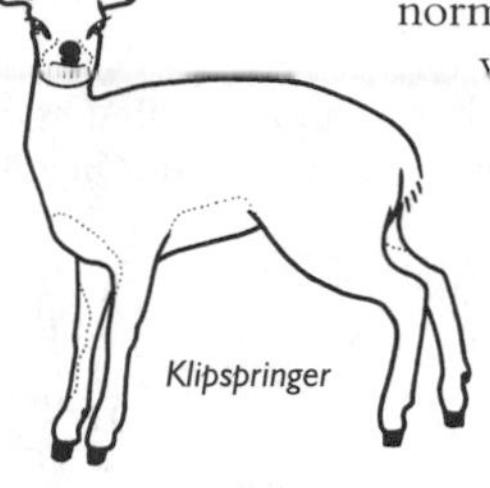
Klipspringer

They are seldom seen on account of their size and colouring, and are normally found in pairs. They occur throughout Malawi wherever there are suitable habitats, which include all the national parks and wildlife reserves except Lengwe, as well as most rocky mountains outside of national parks.

The **oribi** is a tan-coloured antelope with a white belly, black tail and a diagnostic black patch beneath its ears. It generally occurs in open woodland and grassland, but it is rare, swift and secretive in Malawi, where it has been recorded only in Kasungu and Liwonde national parks.

Sharpe's grysbok is widespread in Malawi, occurring in all national parks and wildlife reserves, but it is rarely seen due to its retiring nature and nocturnal habits. It is similar in overall appearance to an oribi, though it lacks any distinctive features and is considerably smaller. Sharpe's grysbok occurs in thicket and scrub rather than open grassland.

Livingstone's suni is a tiny and rather nondescript grey antelope, which in Malawi occurs only in Lengwe and other reserves in the Shire Valley south of Blantyre. In this area, it is only likely to be confused with the significantly larger and more robust grey duiker.

Three duiker species occur in Malawi. The most widespread is the **grey** or **common duiker**, a greyish antelope with a white belly and a tuft between its small horns. The grey duiker is common in almost all woodland habitats. The other two duiker species are forest animals and are thus very rarely seen. The **Natal red duiker** is a tiny antelope with a reddish coat and no distinguishing markings. The even tinier **blue duiker**, one of the smallest antelope found in southern Africa, is grey with a white tail.

Common duiker

Other herbivores Back with animals you're unlikely to have much trouble identifying, **elephants**, despite the heavy poaching of the 1980s, are still reasonably common in many of Malawi's reserves. The largest elephant herds occur in Liwonde, Kasungu and Vwaza Marsh, but there are also elephants in Nkhotakota and Nyika and they are soon to be reintroduced to Majete.

Black rhinoceros, too, are easy enough to identify – if you can find one. The last indigenous black rhinos were poached from Mwabvi in 1992, and not long before they were a common sight in Kasungu. Black rhino from South Africa were reintroduced into Liwonde National Park's Rhino Sanctuary in 1997, and are breeding successfully. Two males were transferred to another safe area in Majete in 2003.

Hippos have also suffered from poaching. Over the past 15 years numbers have dropped dramatically, as they are killed by more efficiently armed villagers affected by famine or protecting their crops or by meat traders. Nonetheless, hippo are still common on most major rivers and lakes, particularly on the part of the Shire River that runs through Liwonde National Park, where well over 1,000 individuals are present. Outside of reserves, hippo can be seen in the Salima area, in the Elephant Marsh, and in the Shire River near Sucoma Sugar Estate.

Black rhino

Of relevance here is the other common large aquatic creature in Malawi, the **crocodile** (not, of course, a mammal or a herbivore, but a reptile). Crocodiles are

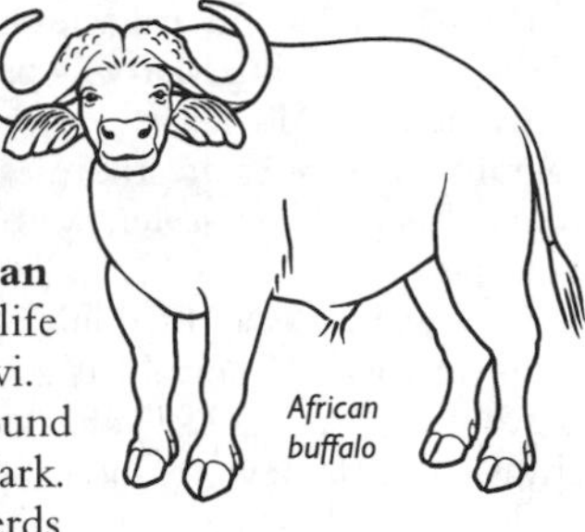
African buffalo

very common along the Shire River, particularly in Liwonde National Park and in the Elephant Marsh. They are also present in many other rivers and lakes, including Lake Malawi.

Another unmistakable large animal is the **African buffalo**, which occurs in all Malawi's wildlife reserves and national parks except for Lake Malawi.

Burchell's zebra is the only equine species found in Malawi. It is common in Nyika National Park. Many survive in Kasungu despite poaching. Herds translocated from Kasungu to Liwonde and Majete are doing very well. Zebra occur in small numbers in all the wildlife reserves except Mwabvi.

Two swine species occur in Malawi. The **warthog** is a diurnal swine with a uniform bristly grey coat and the distinctive habit of holding its tail erect when it runs. Warthogs are normally seen in pairs or family groups in savanna and woodland habitats. They are common in all Malawi's wildlife reserves and national parks. The nocturnal **bushpig** has a red-brown coat and a hairier appearance than that of the warthog. It is widespread in forest and riverine woodland, and occurs in all Malawi's national parks and wildlife and forest reserves, but it is very rarely seen due to its retiring nature.

Warthog

Several other nocturnal animals are widespread in Malawi, but unlikely to be seen by tourists. The **porcupine**, for instance, occurs in every national park and wildlife reserve and most forests, but the most you are likely to see of a porcupine is a discarded quill on a forest path. The insectivorous **aardvark** occurs in most reserves and national parks, but if you see one you can rank yourself among the luckiest people on the planet.

Hyraxes (dassies) are small mammals which have a guinea pig-like appearance, though they are considered to be more closely related to elephants than any other living animal. The rock hyrax is commonly seen on koppies (small hills) and other rocky areas throughout Malawi. The tree hyrax is a less common animal, and strictly nocturnal. It is more likely to be heard than seen – it has a quite outrageous shrieking call.

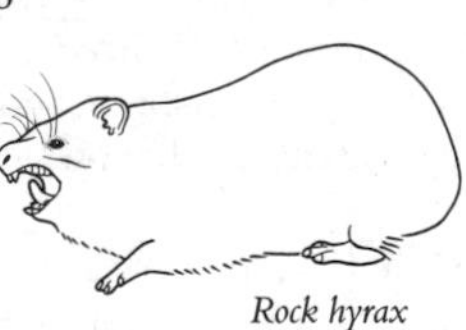
Rock hyrax

One characteristic African mammal which was never indigenous to Malawi is the **giraffe**. It is not the policy of the wildlife authorities to introduce animals into areas where they have never been recorded. The only record of wild giraffe in Malawi within living memory was when an individual strayed over the Zambian border in Karonga district where it was killed by terrified villagers. However, herds of **Thornicroft's giraffe** from the Luangwa Valley in Zambia have been translocated into three private reserves in Malawi: Nyala Park, Kuti Game Ranch and Game Haven.

BIRDS A total of 649 bird species have been recorded in Malawi, a highly impressive total for a country smaller than England. Though Malawi does not boast the diversity of birds of east African countries like Kenya and Uganda, serious birdwatchers who visit Malawi are likely to find it a less frustrating country, for no reason other than that it is served by excellent and comprehensive field guides (see *Appendix 2, Further Reading*, page 240), which means that identification is rarely the problem it can be in east Africa.

Roughly 10% of the species recorded in Malawi are not found on the southern African list, making Malawi a particularly rewarding destination for South African birdwatchers. Also, several birds which appear on the southern African list as vagrants or rarities are more easily seen here – African skimmer, racquet-tailed roller, Boehm's bee-eater, wattled crane and green-headed oriole being obvious examples.

National parks and wildlife reserves are the best places to see a good variety of birds. Liwonde National Park in particular is excellent – the birdlife along the river is stunning, and guided morning walks from Mvuu Camp or Chinguni almost always yield a few localised species. The forests in Nyika National Park are probably the best place to see birds which occur in Malawi but not in southern Africa: many east African species extend their range no further south than Nyika, Vwaza or the nearby Viphya Plateau.

Evergreen forest is a particularly rich bird habitat, and, unlike game reserves, many of Malawi's forest reserves can be explored on foot. Among the more accessible forest habitats in Malawi are the Viphya and Zomba plateaux, Mulanje Massif, and Ntchisi, Chiradzulu and Thyolo mountains.

Brachystegia woodland also holds several characteristic birds, many of which are found in no other type of woodland, for instance Stierling's woodpecker, *miombo* pied barbet, white-winged starling, red-and-blue sunbird, pale-billed hornbill and chestnut-mantled sparrow weaver. As *brachystegia* woodland is the dominant vegetation type in Malawi, most *brachystegia* birds are widespread in Malawi.

Malawi boasts an exceptional range of water habitats. Lake Malawi can impress with its kingfishers, cormorants and fish eagles, while Lake Chilwa has a far greater number of birds. The marshes that form around several rivers during the rainy season (known in Malawi as *dambos*) are also excellent for birds – one of the best and most accessible is Mpatsanjoka Dambo near Salima. For waterbirds in general, few places I've visited compare to the Elephant Marsh in southern Malawi, where you're likely to see such unusual species as purple heron, African skimmer and pygmy goose.

Really, though, in a country as rich in birdlife as Malawi, almost anywhere is likely to prove rewarding to birdwatchers. Don't ignore the obvious – even a morning walk through Lilongwe Nature Sanctuary can throw up a variety of robins, kingfishers and the gorgeous Schalow's turaco, while, over a ten-year period, more than 100 species were recorded in one garden in Blantyre.

FISH Each of Africa's three great lakes (Victoria, Tanganyika and Malawi) contains more species of fish than any other lake in the world. It is not yet known which of the three lakes is home to the greatest number of species, because more species are discovered every year and large parts of all three lakes have still to be explored. The most conservative estimate for the number of fish species in Lake Malawi is 500 – a greater number of freshwater species than are found in Europe and North America combined – and the real total may well be closer to 1,000. No less remarkable is the fact that only a handful of fish species are known to occur in all three of the great lakes – most of them are endemic to one particular lake.

The vast majority of Lake Malawi's fish belong to the cichlid group, one of the few types of fish that cares for its offspring – all but one of Malawi's cichlids are mouth brooders, meaning that the eggs and fry are held in the mother's mouth until they are large enough to fend for themselves. The Lake Malawi cichlids are divided into four major groups: the small plankton-eating *utaka*, the large, pike-like and generally predatory *ncheni*, the bottom-feeding *chisawasawa*, and the brightly coloured, algae-eating *mbuna*.

The *mbuna* are the best known of Lake Malawi's cichlids, not least for their spectacular colours, a source of constant delight to snorkellers and scuba divers. Of more biological importance, however, is that the *mbuna* formed the subject of Dr Geoffrey Fryer's classic study of adaptive radiation in the 1950s. Adaptive radiation is when one species 'explodes' into a variety of closely related species, each of which evolves different modifications to allow it to specialise in some or other aspect of its lifestyle (it is adaptive radiation that occurred among the finches of the Galapagos Islands which led Charles Darwin to propose the Theory of Evolution through Natural Selection). Interestingly, such species explosions have occurred independently among the cichlids in all three of Africa's great lakes, and even within each lake – the *mbuna* of Lake Malawi stick so closely to the rocks on which they feed that two rocky stretches of shore separated by a sandy beach may hold completely different *mbuna* species filling identical ecological niches.

A group of *ncheni* cichlids, belonging to the *oreochromis* genus of tilapia, are known collectively in Malawi as *chambo*, and are regarded as the finest eating fish to be found in the lake.

Although cichlids are by far the most important fish in the lake, both in terms of species and actual fish tonnage, and the *mbuna* specifically are the family that is of most interest to snorkellers and divers, several other fish families occur in the lake.

The *usipa* is a small sardine-like fish that occurs in large shoals, and which forms the backbone of the local fishing industry. Dried *usipa* are sold in bulk at practically every market in Malawi.

The carp family is well represented in Lake Malawi. The *ngumbo*, a type of barbel, is a large silvery fish reaching up to 60cm in length and occurring in shoals on rocky stretches of shore such as Otter Point at Cape Maclear. Another well-known carp is the *mpasa* or 'lake salmon', which is common in the northern part of the lake, where it is an important source of food.

The African catfish is probably the most widespread fish in Africa. It occurs in practically all freshwater habits, largely due to its ability to move across land during wet conditions. The African catfish is common in Lake Malawi. The genus of catfish known collectively as *bombe* or *sapuwa* are all evolved from the African catfish but, since they have lost the ability to cross land, they are endemic to the lake. The *bombe* catfish are the largest fish found in the lake, measuring up to 1.5m in length and weighing up to 30kg. Belonging to a separate genus of catfish, the predatory *kampango* is a popular eating fish throughout Malawi.

Overfishing in Lake Malawi is becoming a major problem. Fish like *chambo*, once plentiful and a crucial source of food, are now becoming scarce. In addition, overfishing is thought to be responsible for the presence of bilharzia in the lake. For treatment of bilharzia, see *Chapter 4*, *Health*, page 68.

3

Planning and Preparation

This chapter covers most practical aspects of planning a trip to Malawi, with the exception of things like vaccinations and medical kits, which are covered in *Chapter 4, Health*, page 59.

WHEN TO VISIT

Malawi is a pleasure to visit at any time of year. Lake Malawi's attractions are unaffected by seasons (though the water is cooler in July and August). Game viewing is good throughout the dry season, and best from June to November. The main hiking and walking areas in Malawi are good throughout the year.

Most people visit between May and October during the long, dry African 'winter', from April to October. Malawi is also stunning during the green season: high-lying areas are much warmer at night, the countryside is lusciously green and full of flowers, and a greater variety of fruits and vegetables is available. Birdwatchers may well want to visit during the rainy season; between November and April the variety of species present is boosted considerably by Palearctic and intra-African migrants.

That said, there are several disadvantages to travelling in Malawi during the hot, wet months between November and the end of March. Malaria is more widespread during this period. Game viewing is never as good during the rainy season, as the vegetation is high and animals tend to disperse away from perennial water sources. In addition, many roads in reserves and national parks are closed after heavy rain, and you might need to be flexible enough to plan around flooding, as roads and bridges are often taken out by rivers during the heavy rains (usually in February). Even though rain in most parts of Malawi tends to take the form of swift storms rather than protracted drizzle, hiking and camping are generally more pleasant in dry weather.

PLANNING AN ITINERARY Any individual itinerary through Malawi is likely to be highly personal, based on your means of transport, your interests and budget, the season, as well as the amount of time you have available. Most readers of this guide will either be making personalised arrangements in advance through a recognised tour operator, or will be travelling independently. In both cases, my advice is the same: go through this book picking out the places that are of greatest interest to you, and then base your itinerary around these, working out a rough route and adding other activities or stops of interest along the way.

In the case of making prescribed travel arrangements, any reliable tour operator based in Malawi will be able to advise you on what is and isn't realistic, and to come up with an itinerary that suits your requirements. As a rule, you'll have a more relaxing holiday if you settle on a relatively compact itinerary rather than one that tries to cram in the whole country over a couple of weeks. In three to four weeks you can enjoy many of the different areas of Malawi. That said, a lifetime there would not be enough to get to know it properly.

Generally, independent travellers have the flexibility to adjust their itinerary as they go along, so that the obvious way of planning their travels is to pick out a rough circuit and follow it at a pace dictated by events. Even more than those visitors who are on organised tours, travellers using public transport shouldn't attempt to take on too much in a limited space of time, or their dominant memory of the country will be of sitting in buses. As a rule of thumb, travellers using public transport are advised to allow themselves at least one day 'off' between travelling days. It is a matter of preference, I realise, but if I had only two weeks or so in which to explore Malawi using public transport, I would prefer to spend a few nights at any one lake resort than to attempt visiting several for one or two nights each.

In my opinion, the sort of itineraries reproduced in most travel guides are somewhat restrictive and serve little practical purpose, since there are so many variables for which they cannot allow, not only regarding the interests of the individual traveller, but also the manner in which they intend to travel.

What follows is not a suggested itinerary, then, but an annotated list of some of Malawi's most alluring spots, some well known, others more obscure, all of them worth visiting.

Cape Maclear (pages 177–87) Once a legendary backpackers' hangout, it still offers good affordable facilities as well as more luxury options; it has plenty of watersports to keep you busy as well as good food, bars and a relaxed beach atmosphere despite the beachboys.

Chintheche (page 149) The long white sands and rocky bays of the northern lakeshore might make you stop longer than you'd planned. There's accommodation and activities for all tastes, from diving to horseriding and from fine eating to lazing on the beach.

Dedza and surrounds (pages 171–5) Hikers could spend a cheap week exploring this underrated area.

Elephant Marsh (pages 233–5) Inexpensive, little-visited, atmospheric, prolific waterbirds, ideal for adventurous backpackers with some days spare to achieve the journey there.

Kasungu National Park (page 112) Seasonal game viewing, a majestic lodge and good camping facilities, easy access, great stopover for those heading north on the M1 from Lilongwe.

Lake Chilwa (page 203) A great and surprisingly accessible off-the-beaten-track excursion for backpackers on a tight budget.

Likoma Island (page 159) A good place to get away from it all, with a friendly atmosphere, attractive scenery, and some historical interest.

Liwonde National Park (page 189) Best game viewing in Malawi, stunning birds, wonderful atmosphere, and excellent facilities ranging from campsites to one of the country's finest game lodges.

Livingstonia (page 133) Site of a turn-of-the-20th-century mission on the Rift Valley Escarpment, overlooking the lake and close to the beautiful Machewe Falls.

ANNUAL EVENTS

If you have a special interest, it might be worth considering any of the following events that take place in Malawi during the year.

JUNE

Luwawa International Charity Mountain Bike Marathon (see page 116) A 42km race through the south Vipyha Forest Reserve on good dirt roads.

JULY

Lake Malawi International Yachting Marathon (see page 179)

Mulanje Porters' Race (see page 226) An international event in which Mulanje porters and other participants race up and down 25km of steep mountain.

Hippy Festival (see page 194) A small and blissful festival with bands and DJs from Malawi.

SEPTEMBER

Lake of Stars Festival (see page 21) Combines the best of UK and African live acts and DJs for a three-day charity event, raising money for Children in the Wilderness.

NOVEMBER

Wildlife Society Art Fest (see page 21) A mammoth exhibition of the visual arts, held in Lilongwe each November in aid of the Wildlife & Environmental Society of Malawi.

Mango Festival (see page 21) Held in Lilongwe to celebrate the new mango season; a great excuse to get all of Malawi's musical talent playing in one place.

Majete Wildlife Reserve (page 230) A relatively obscure reserve, with decent game viewing and excellent hiking; a good excursion from Blantyre in private transport.

Mulanje Massif (page 217) The best montane hiking in Malawi, accessible and affordable to those on a limited budget.

Mwabwi Wildlife Reserve (page 233) This is wonderful hiking country, with very few roads though an unspoilt wilderness.

Nkhata Bay (page 152) A thriving backpackers' scene, cheap dive courses, and a habit of transforming short visits into extended stays.

Nkopola (page 181) Here you'll find the major cluster of tourist-class hotels on the southern lakeshore.

Nkhotokota (page 157) An area ready for discovery, with the idyllic combination of lakeside lodges and a thick wildlife reserve suitable only for the adventurous.

Ntchisi (page 109) The main town on one of the country's least used and most rewarding back roads.

Nyika National Park (pages 124–30) Malawi's largest national park, offering walking and horseriding excursions in fantastic scenery. Good game viewing, too.

Senga Bay (page 165) Plenty of choice from simple, homely lodges with delicious food, to stylish hotels for all tastes and group sizes. Hippo and breeding colonies of birds; very close to Lilongwe.

Viphya Plateau (page 115) Hiking and birding not as good as in some other montane areas, but a lovely spot, infrequently visited by travellers, and very accessible and affordable, great for mountain biking and climbing.

Vwaza Marsh Wildlife Reserve (pages 130–2) The most underrated game reserve in the country – plenty of animals, very accessible and affordable, and a new upmarket lodge.

Zomba Plateau (page 197) The most accessible of Malawi's large mountains, with good walking, camping facilities, and views that stretch to the edge of the world.

TOUR OPERATORS

ORGANISED TOURS Malawi is still a well-kept secret and has not really caught on as a major package-tour destination, however there is a number of companies in the UK and elsewhere offering guided tours, often in conjunction with neighbouring countries, bringing out some of the country's special aspects.

UK

Aardvark Safaris ☎ 01980 849160; f 01980 849161; e mail@aardvarksafaris.com; www.aardvarksafaris.com. Uses mostly small, owner-run properties, to tailor trips that take in the best of the wildlife and scenery on offer.
Abercrombie and Kent ☎ 0845 070 0611 (for UK reservations); e info@abercrombiekent.co.uk; www.abercrombiekent.co.uk. A specialist in luxury and adventure travel with over 40 years of experience.
Art Safari ☎ 01394 382235 or 07780 927560; e info@artsafari.co.uk; www.artsafari.co.uk. Tailor-made trips for those who want to spend time observing nature and learn the skills which will help them paint and draw what they see; ideal for creative travellers of all ages. Also organise trekking safaris. Run by Mary-Anne Bartlett.
Cazenove and Loyd Safaris ☎ 020 7384 2332; f 020 7384 2399; e info@cazloyd.com; www.cazloyd.com. Specialists in tailor-made private travel in Africa and the Indian Ocean.
Cox and Kings Travel Ltd ☎ 020 7873 5000; e cox.kings@coxandkings.co.uk; www.coxandkings.co.uk. Comprehensive tours for both groups and individuals, taking in wildlife and culture.
Expert Africa ☎ 020 8232 9777; e info@expertafrica.com; www.expertafrica.com. Flexible trips for all travellers.
Gane and Marshall ☎ 020 8445 6000; f 020 8441 7376; e holidays@ganeandmarshall.co.uk; www.ganeandmarshall.co.uk. Tailor-made itineraries including cycling.
In the Saddle ☎ 01299 272997; e rides@inthesaddle.com; www.inthesaddle.co.uk. Specialises in horseriding safaris on Nyika Plateau.
Okavango Tours & Safaris ☎ 020 8343 3283; e info@okavango.com; www.okavango.com. Small, friendly company based in north London, offering tailormade trips.
Roxton Bailey Robinson Worldwide ☎ 01488 689700; f 01488 689730; e info@rbrww.com; www.rbrww.com. Specialises in top-end safaris to east and southern Africa.
Safari Bookers ☎ 0870 333 2150; f 0870 333 2151; e henry@safarilink.com; www.safarilink.com. A one-stop website covering all things 'safari' in Africa. Does not sell safaris – provides links to the best resources to help plan a safari.
Safari Consultants Ltd ☎ 01787 228494; f 01787 228096; e bill@safariconsultantsuk.com; www.safari-consultants.co.uk Established in 1983, a specialised safari company dealing with tailor-made and small group departures to east and South Africa.
Wildlife Worldwide ☎ 0845 130 6982; e sales@wildlifeworldwide.com; www.wildlifeworldwide.com. Specialising in tailor-made and small group wildlife holidays worldwide.

Germany

Livingstone Tours Muhlwiesenstr 3, D-72555 Metzengen, Germany; ☎ +49 07123 920943; f +49 07123 920944; e livingstone.tours@t-online.de; www.livingstone-tours.de. A German-based company specialising in set departure 2- and 3-week camping tours for small groups of German speakers. The owner has worked in Malawi for several years and leads the tour himself.

South Africa

South Africans developed a taste for Malawi during the apartheid years when Banda was very welcoming and it was one of the few African countries that they could visit. It's still a popular destination and there is a number of tour operators.

Animaltracks ☎ + 27 11 454 0543; f +27 11 454 0544; e info@animaltracks.co.za; www.animaltracks.co.za
Getaway Travel ☎ +27 0860 43 82 92; e info.getaway@galileosa.co.za; www.getawaytravel.co.za
Pulse Africa ☎ +27 11 325 2290; f +27 11 325 2226; e info@pulseafrica.com; www.pulseafrica.com. Specialises in tailor-made safaris/holidays to Lake Malawi's mountains, lakes and national parks.
Thompsons Tours ☎ +27 11 770 7677; e africaj@thompsons.co.za; www.thompsons.co.za
Touraco Travel Services ☎/f +27 12 803 8585; e travel@touraco.co.za; www.touraco.co.za

OVERLAND TRUCK COMPANIES An ever-increasing number of people experience Malawi for the first time when they're on an overland journey visiting a staggering number of countries and sites on one short holiday. Many return to spend longer in Malawi. Some of the overland companies include:

Absolute Africa ☎ 020 8742 0226; f 020 8995 6155; e absafr@absoluteafrica.com; www.absoluteafrica.com
Africa Overland Company ☎ +27 21 853 7952; f +27 21 853 0153; e info@africanoverland.co.za; www.africanoverland.co.za
African Trails ☎ 020 8969 1538; e web@africantrails.co.uk; www.africantrails.co.uk
Bukima ☎ 0870 757 2230; f 0870 757 2231; e adventure@bukima.com; www.bukima.com
Dragoman ☎ 0870 499 4475; f 01728 861127; e info@dragoman.co.uk; www.dragoman.com
Drifters ☎ +27 11 888 1160; f +27 11 888 1020; e drifters@drifters.co.za; www.drifters.co.za
Exodus ☎ 020 8673 0859; f 020 8673 0779; e info@exodus.co.uk; www.exodus.co.uk
Kumuka ☎ 020 7937 8855; f 020 7937 6664; e adventuretours@kumuka.com; www.kumuka.com
Which Way Adventure Company ☎ +27 21 481 4915; f +27 21 426 5339; www.which-way.com

IN MALAWI Several good tour companies operate out of Lilongwe and Blantyre. It is possible to contact them direct to organise personalised travel arrangements. These companies are also listed within the guide, with full addresses.

Barefoot Safaris ☎ 01 707346/09 307359; e info@barefoot-safaris.com; www.barefootsafaris.com or www.projectaftricanwilderness.org
Danforth Yachting ☎ 09960077; e danforth@malawi.net; www.danforthyachting.com
Jambo Africa Tel 01 623709; e jamboafrica@africa-online.net; www.jambo-africa.com
Kiboko Safaris ☎ 01 754978; e camp@kiboko-safaris.com; www.kiboko-safaris.com
Land and Lake Safaris ☎ 01 757120; e info@landlake.net; www.landlake.net
Nyika Safari Company ☎ 01 330180; www.nyika.com
Soche Tours and Travel ☎ 01 620777/01 772377; e sochetoursbt@sochetoursmw.com; www.sochetourmalawi.com
Ulendo Safaris ☎ 01 754950; e info@ulendo.net; www.ulendosafaris.com
Wilderness Safaris ☎ 01 771153; e info@wilderness.mw; www.wilderness-safaris.com

ECO-TOURISM AND COMMUNITY INVOLVEMENT

John Douglas, Malawi Tourism Marketing Consortium (www.malawitourism.com)

Both the government and the private sector in Malawi are committed to the principles of eco-tourism. The intention is that tourism developments shall be sustainable, with an avoidance of problems which tourism might impose on the environment or on socio-cultural aspects of the country. Tourism resources are to be preserved so that they satisfy the current demands but are also maintained for the future.

Malawi has the advantage that it has no mass tourism; it is small scale and intimate. Most of the lodges, whether on the lakeshore, in the game parks or in the forest reserves are, by regional standards, modest in size. A great deal of care has been taken to avoid visual intrusion. Outside Lilongwe, Blantyre and Mzuzu it is rare to see tourist buildings that rise above a single storey and none is more than two storeys. Even where there is something of a concentration of lodges and hotels, as along the southern shore of Lake Malawi, it is virtually impossible to see one lodge from its nearest neighbour which might be no more than 1km away. It is hoped that some plans currently being mooted for substantial hotel construction at Cape Maclear remain unrealised in favour of small-scale developments.

Seclusion is considered to be an asset worth preserving, with most lodges blending with their surroundings. A majority are built from local materials by local labour and care has been taken to reduce environmental impact to a minimum. For example, Nkwichi Lodge, which has won international awards for its eco-friendly policies, rightly claims that if it closed, the area would easily be returned to its natural state in a matter of months. In Vwaza Wildlife Reserve, Kazuni Safari Camp could be closed down and dismantled in days and there would be little evidence of its previous existence. Outside the cities, electricity is often the product of solar power or back-up generators. Attention is paid to sewage disposal and water conservation.

None of this commendable attention to eco-tourism tenets would be possible without an established working relationship with local communities. Tourism in Malawi means far more than a source of employment. In a country with one of the world's highest unemployment rates and a desperate over-reliance on agriculture, it is estimated that for every worker in the tourism sector there are another dozen reliant on the income achieved. But there is more to it than a revenue source. Very many of the lodges are active in supporting their neighbouring villages by purchasing foodstuffs, by assisting with school building, developing health clinics or establishing charities which help, for example, the appalling number of AIDS orphans.

The particularly good community relations of members of the private sector Tourism Marketing Consortium enables many lodges to offer their tourists visits to local villages and, in some cases, overnight stays.

For Malawi, the future of tourism is not only bright, it is green.

RED TAPE

PASSPORT A valid passport is required to enter Malawi. The date of expiry should be at least six months after you intend to end your travels; if your passport is likely to expire before that, get a new one.

VISAS At the time of writing, visas are required by everyone except passport holders of the following nationalities: Bahamas, Bangladesh, Barbados, Belgium, Botswana, Brunei, Canada, Cyprus, Denmark, Fiji, Finland, Gambia, Germany, Ghana, Grenada, Iceland, Ireland, Israel, Jamaica, Kenya, Lesotho, Luxembourg,

Malaysia, Malta, Mauritius, Netherlands, New Zealand, Nigeria, Norway, Portugal, San Marino, Sierra Leone, Singapore, South Africa, Sri Lanka, Swaziland, Sweden, Trinidad and Tobago, UK, USA, Zambia and Zimbabwe. Such rulings are always subject to change, so even those people who are currently exempt from visa requirements are advised to confirm that this is still the case before embarking for Malawi.

E EMBASSIES AND HIGH COMMISSIONS Malawi has an embassy or high commission in the following countries:

Belgium Third fl, 15 rue de la Roi, Brussels; ☎ 231 0960; f 231 1066
Ethiopia PO Box 2361, Addis Ababa; ☎ 129 4440/1
Germany Mainzert Strasse 1234, Bonn; ☎ 34 3016; f 34 0619
Mozambique 75 Kenneth Kaunda Av, Maputo; ☎ 1741 468
South Africa PO Box 11172, Brooklyn, Pretoria; ☎ 47 7827
Tanzania PO Box 7616, Dar es Salaam; ☎ 51 37260/1
UK 70 Winnington Rd, London N2 0TX; ☎ 020 8455 5624 ; f 020 8455 5624
malawihighcom@btconnect.com
USA 1400 20th St, NW, Washington DC; ☎ 223 4814
Zambia PO Box 5025, Lusaka; ☎ 121 3750
Zimbabwe PO Box 231, Harare; ☎ 70 5611; f 70 5604

IMMIGRATION AND CUSTOMS

Arriving by air Provided that you have a valid passport (and a visa if required) and an onward ticket out of Malawi, you should whiz through the entrance formalities with no hassle. The only reason that fly-in visitors would be likely to arrive in Malawi without an onward ticket is if they were using Malawi as a starting point for broader African travels, which is fairly uncommon (I've yet to meet anyone who has done this).

Nevertheless, if you are arriving in Malawi on a one-way ticket, there is a possibility (my gut feeling is that it is only a slight possibility) that you will be given a rough time. Basically, what immigration officials are worried about is that you won't have funds to buy a flight out of the country. Obviously, the more money you have, the less likely they are to query your finances. And a credit card will almost certainly convince them to let you in. Finally, assuming that you do intend to travel to neighbouring countries, you can underline this intention by arranging a visa or visitors' pass for the next country you plan to visit *before* you land in Malawi.

The very worst that will happen if you arrive in Malawi without an onward ticket is that you will have to buy a ticket back to your home country before being allowed entry. Assuming you intend to leave Malawi overland, it is important you check with the relevant airline that this ticket will be refundable once you have left Malawi, and also that you buy it for a date that will give you time to get to a country where you can organise the refund.

Arriving by land Malawi's land borders are generally very relaxed. Provided that your papers are in order, you should have no problem, nor is there much likelihood of being asked about onward tickets or funds. At one point, the Malawian customs workers had a slightly draconian reputation, mainly for enforcing Banda-era restrictions such as the ban on the travel guide *Africa on a Shoestring*, skirts for women and a haircut for men with hair over their shoulders. These regulations went out with Banda; these days, about the worst you can expect at Malawian customs is a cursory search of your luggage.

If arriving in your own vehicle, you will need its registration documents and, if it's not registered in your name, an official letter giving you permission to drive the

NOTES FOR DISABLED TRAVELLERS

Gordon Rattray

Malawi is known for its Great Rift Valley mountains, sandy beaches and pot-holed roads. It therefore sounds like a thoroughly unattractive destination for somebody with mobility problems. However, the truth is that with enough preparation in advance and the ability to 'rough it' if need be, a trip through Africa's warm heart is quite feasible. The Malawians' innate friendliness, coupled with the ability of Africans to improvise should ensure that you have as varied and rewarding an itinerary as an able-bodied traveller.

TRANSPORT

Air travel I flew with Air Malawi into Blantyre and found the disabled assistance service to be slow, but relatively well managed in comparison with some other African countries' airlines. Blantyre airport has an aisle chair, allowing a dignified exit from the plane for non-ambulant travellers, and although there is no designated disabled toilet, the rest of the building is level and accessible.

By car Distances are great and roads are often bumpy, so if you are prone to skin damage you need to take extra care. Place your own pressure-relieving cushion on top of (or instead of) the original car seat and if necessary, pad around knees and elbows.

It is possible to hire self-drive vehicles, but I know of no company providing cars that are adapted for disabled drivers. If you're not sticking to the main roads, you may need to use a 4x4 vehicle, which will be higher than a normal car, therefore making transfers more difficult. Drivers/guides are normally happy to help, but are not trained in this skill, so you must thoroughly explain your needs and always stay in control of the situation.

Buses and trains There is no effective legislation in Malawi to facilitate disabled travellers' journeys by public transport. If you cannot walk at all then both of these options are going to be difficult. You will need to ask for help from fellow passengers to lift you to your seat, it will often be crowded and it is unlikely that there will be an accessible toilet. If you can

vehicle and cross borders with it. It will cost US$1 for a temporary import permit (TIP) and US$15 per car for insurance for one month (US$30 for light trucks). If you add this to what it costs to bring a vehicle through Mozambique, it might make you wish you'd taken the bus instead.

GETTING THERE AND AWAY

BY AIR There are no direct flights to Malawi from Europe. Flights go via Nairobi with Kenya Airways, via Johannesburg with South African Airways or British Airways, via Addis Ababa with Ethiopian Airlines or via Harare with Air Zimbabwe. Air Malawi operates some of these connections. Almost all international flights land at Lilongwe International Airport, 26km from Lilongwe, the exception being some flights from Johannesburg (South Africa), which land at Chileka Airport, 16km north of Blantyre.

An airport tax of US$30 is charged to all non-residents upon flying out of Malawi. This must be paid in cash, in US dollars. If you don't have dollars cash to hand, you can exchange travellers' cheques for cash at the foreign exchange kiosk at the airport or use the ATM. Domestic departures tax is MK200. Passengers transiting through Lilongwe and Blantyre airports are exempt from departures and pass through the transit routes at international airports.

Getting a good deal on a flight may seem easier on the internet but flight cope with these difficulties, then travelling by bus is quite feasible and is a much more affordable option than hiring a car.

ACCOMMODATION In general, it is not easy to find disabled-friendly accommodation in Malawi. Only top-of-the-range lodges and hotels will have 'accessible' rooms and even then, I've yet to hear of anywhere sporting grab handles, roll-under sinks and a roll-in shower. Occasionally (more by accident than through design), bathrooms are wheelchair accessible, but where this is not the case, you should be prepared to be lifted, or do your ablutions in the bedroom.

HEALTH Doctors will know about 'everyday' illnesses, but you must understand and be able to explain your own particular medical requirements. African hospitals are often basic, so if possible, take all necessary medication and equipment with you. It is advisable to pack this in your hand luggage during flights in case your main luggage gets lost.
Lakeside Malawi can be hot. If this is a problem for you, be careful to book accommodation with fans or air conditioning, and a useful cooling aid is a plant-spray bottle.

SECURITY The usual security precautions apply, but it is also worthwhile remembering that, as a disabled person, you are even more vulnerable. Stay aware of who is around you and where your bags are, especially during car transfers and similar. These activities often draw a crowd, and the confusion creates easy pickings for an opportunist thief.

SPECIALIST OPERATORS There are, as yet, no operators running trips in Malawi who specialise in disability. Having said that, most travel companies will listen to your needs and try to create an itinerary suitable for you. For the independent traveller, it is possible to limit potential surprises by contacting local operators and establishments by email in advance.

specialists still have a part to play. Below is a list of operators who give good service at a reasonable price. Getting the lowest price will require several calls and may result in some rather complicated routing.

Flight specialists

From the UK

BP Tours ☎ 0870 890 7900; www.bptours.com. Competitive prices for Africa and other destinations.
Flight Centre ☎ 0870 499 0040; www.flightcentre.co.uk. Offices in the UK, Australia, New Zealand, South Africa and Canada. An independent travel retailer with more than 1,200 outlets worldwide. The UK head office is located in New Malden, Surrey.
STA Travel ☎ 0870 160 0599; e enquiries@statravel.co.uk; www.statravel.co.uk. STA has 12 branches in London and 25 or so around the country and at university sites. Also has several branches and associate organisation around the world.
Trailfinders ☎ 0845 058 5858; www.trailfinders.com. Provides a one-stop travel service including visa and passport service, travel clinic and foreign exchange.
Travel Bag ☎ 0870 814 4441; www.travelbag.co.uk. 7 UK offices, offering flights, holidays and travel services.

From the US

Airtech ☎ +1 212 219 7000; e fly@airtech.com; www.airtech.com. Standby seat broker that also deals in consolidator fares, courier flights and a host of other travel-related services.
STA Travel ☎ +1 800 781 4040; www.statravel.com

OVERLAND Malawi lies on the most popular backpackers' route between South Africa and Kenya, and so it is highly likely that more tourists arrive in Malawi overland than by air. For this reason, it's worth going into some detail on the main overland routes to Malawi from South Africa and east Africa.

If you are heading to Malawi as part of a larger trans-African trip, read the Bradt Travel Guide *East and Southern Africa: The Backpackers' Manual*, by Philip Briggs (although it's out of print, it remains a useful resource), or Bradt's *Africa Overland* by Bob Gibbons and Sian Pritchard-Jones. Also look out for Getaway's publication, *Cape to Cairo*, by Mike Copeland.

From South Africa Several routes can be used to get between South Africa and Malawi. The quickest route is to head for Blantyre via Harare in Zimbabwe and the Tete Corridor in Mozambique, but from Harare it is equally possible to head directly to Lilongwe via Zambia.

If you literally just want to get to Malawi as quickly and cheaply as you can, there are several bus operators:

City To City ☎ 01 621346 or 09 958499. Daily service for MK8,500.
Ingwe ☎ 01 667045 (formerly **Linking Africa**). Thrice-weekly service for MK11,500.
Munorama Twice-weekly service for MK8,300.
Shire Bus Company ☎ 01 671388; e fcshirebus@africa-online.net. Twice-weekly service between Blantyre and Johannesburg for approx US$85.
Vaal Africa ☎ 01 821265. Twice-weekly service between Blantyre and Johannesburg for MK11,000.

Most bus services also stop in Harare.

Otherwise, if working your way up slowly, getting from **Johannesburg to Harare** couldn't be more straightforward. Trains run once a week, leaving Johannesburg every Monday at 18.15 and arriving in Harare roughly 24 hours later. Tickets cost approximately US$90/60 first/second class (*www.spoornet.co.za*). Greyhound buses run every night between Johannesburg and Harare, leaving from Johannesburg Rotunda (opposite the railway station) at 22.30 and arriving in Harare 16 hours later. A ticket costs around US$35 (*www.greyhound.co.za*). It is also reasonably easy to hitch between Johannesburg and Harare. There are several backpackers' hostels from which to choose in Harare, with dormitory rooms costing around US$4 per person – among the best are Wayfarers (☎ *+263 14 572125*), Backpackers and Overlanders (☎ *+263 14 575715*), The Rocks (☎ *+263 14 576371*) and It's a Small World (☎ *+263 14 335341*). You can call any of these places from the city centre for a lift.

The route from **Harare to Blantyre via the Tete Corridor** is currently seldom used by travellers despite being reasonably safe. Several bus services do the run every day, leaving Harare at 06.00 and arriving in Blantyre at nightfall, though timings are dependent on the border crossings, which, if your bus is the last to arrive at the border, can take several hours. Express buses have the reputation of being the quickest – and thus the first to reach every border. A ticket between Harare and Blantyre will cost around US$16. Note that you will need a Mozambique transit visa to cross through Tete. These are very expensive in South Africa, and take several days to issue, so it's better to do it in Harare.

The alternative to using the Tete Corridor is to travel from **Harare to Lilongwe via Lusaka** in Zambia. Despite being slower, this is a very popular route as it avoids Zimbabwe and gives the opportunity to stop at Victoria Falls and South Luangwa National Park en route through to Malawi. Another advantage, at least for citizens of some Commonwealth states, is that you don't need a visa to travel through Zambia (British citizens should take note that they do now require a visa to enter Zambia, and this costs US$25 transit or single-entry visa, US$40 double entry and US$80 multiple-entry visa – see www.zambiatourism.com).

The trip between Harare and Lusaka takes around ten hours by bus, depending on how busy the border is. In fact, although there are buses all the way to Lusaka, there is a strong case for bussing only as far as the border and either hitching or else boarding another bus once you've crossed into Zambia – you could cut two hours off your travelling time by doing this.

Rather than go all the way to Lusaka – a capital with few charms, even fewer affordable accommodation options, and an abundance of pickpockets – you might think about spending the night in **Kafue**, a small town about 50km south of Lusaka. The Bayi Hotel in Kafue is a reasonable place with self-contained single/double rooms for US$12/20 and there are regular minibuses between Kafue and Lusaka when you're ready to move on. A popular alternative is to stay at Eureka Farm, 7km out of Lusaka on the Kafue road, where you can pitch your own tent, or hire one. In Lusaka itself, the recently moved and reopened Chachacha Backpackers (*161 Mulombo Close;* ↘ *02 222257;* **e** *cha@zamtel.zm; www.zambiatourism.com/chachacha*) provides a much-needed base for backpackers passing through the Zambian capital. The owner will pick up travellers from anywhere in town at no charge; just give him a ring when you arrive. Camping costs US$3 per person, dorms are US$6 per person, and single/double private rooms cost US$12/14. Meals are available all day, and there is a kitchen for self catering. Other facilities include a bar with cold beers, email, and a public phone. Trips can be arranged to an African village outside Lusaka, and there is cultural dancing three nights a week.

Buses from Lusaka to Chipata (the nearest town to the Malawian border) leave until around midday, though buses leaving much after 08.00 are unlikely to reach Chipata before nightfall. If you're still trundling along after dark, you might think about stopping over at Patauke or Betete, both of which have basic hotels for around US$4 per room. It is easy enough to pick up local transport from these towns on to Chipata. For good accommodation at the Petauke turn-off, try Zulu's Kraal – camping is US$3 and chalets cost US$4 per person. Great accommodation is available 10km out on the Malawian side of Chipata at **Mamarula's** out towards the Mfuwe road (**e** *mamarula@iwayafrica.com; www.mamarulas.com, dinner, b&b sgl/sharing zk318,750/255,000 pp, b&b only sgl/sharing zk255,000/191,000 pp*). Mamarula's also has a campsite with permanent tents (*dinner, b&b sgl/sharing zk255,000/191,000 pp*).

The Malawian border is 30km from Chipata. The best way to get there is by shared taxi. It's at least 5km between the Zambian and Malawian border posts, so do try for a lift. Both border posts are very relaxed. Once you cross into Malawi, it's only a few minutes' walk to **Mchinji**, where there are several basic resthouses, and Joe's Motel (↘ *01 242334/01 242409*) has good, self-contained rooms with hot showers for US$5/7 single/double

Many people who travel between South Africa and Malawi will prefer not to go directly via Harare but instead to travel **via Bulawayo and the Victoria Falls**. This, again, is straightforward enough: there is a train once a week and a Greyhound bus every night between Johannesburg and Bulawayo, from where you can either catch the overnight train or else bus on through to Victoria Falls. From Victoria Falls you have the option of returning to Bulawayo and then continuing to Blantyre via Harare and Tete. It is probably easier to head on through Zambia to Lilongwe: first cross the border at the falls into Zambia, then hitch through to Livingstone, 14km away. From Livingstone there are trains to Lusaka (notoriously unreliable) and also buses leaving at around 06.00, but it's as easy as anything to hitch; you should get through in a day. The roads to Lusaka from Livingstone and Harare connect just south of Kafue. There is plenty of choice when it comes to budget accommodation in Bulawayo, Victoria Falls and Livingstone, where one of the best options is Jollyboys (e *enquiries@backpackzambia.com; www.backpackzambia.com*).

If you are driving yourself, be warned that officials along the Tete Corridor have a reputation for fining drivers for transgressing a variety of obscure or non-existent road regulations, though the danger of being attacked or hijacked has diminished considerably since Mozambique's civil war quietened down. Zimbabwe is still going through a bad time, and while many travellers now avoid the country altogether, it is still possible to go through it with care and good planning. Greed, opportunist theft and corruption are factors to consider. You cross into Mozambique and the Tete Corridor from Zimbabwe at the Nyamapanda border post 240km from Harare. Mozambique charges you an outrageous US$2 just to stamp your passport, another US$10 to issue a temporary import permit, and US$30 for one month's vehicle insurance (even though you can traverse the corridor in a few hours). You'll save a lot if using a *carnet de passage*. The 145km to Tete is a good road and fuel, food and accommodation are available there. Pay US$0.50 toll to cross the bridge over the mighty Zambezi, but watch out for the traffic police and other scam artists there. The remaining 120km to the border at Zobue and on into Malawi is also a good road.

The trip up from South Africa to Malawi requires several currency changes. There are no banks or forex bureaux (bureaux de change) at any of the border crossings, but it is easy enough to exchange currency with private individuals. This is quite open at most borders and there is no real danger of being queried by a customs official. A bigger threat (though not great) is that you will be short changed or pickpocketed in the process. To get around this, keep whatever notes you expect to change separate from the rest of your money.

Don't expect to get particularly good exchange rates at borders. The money changers at such places are not black market dealers, but small businessmen performing a service to people crossing in both directions. Understandably, they need to exchange money below the official rate to make a livelihood. In my opinion, it's worth changing money at a slightly lower rate simply to avoid the hassle of arriving in a city without local currency. My advice is to change as much as you think you'll need to get you through your first night in the country you are entering, or through to Monday if you arrive over the weekend.

Note that if you are bussing through the Tete Corridor, there is absolutely no need to carry any Mozambican currency. You'll have no call to use it.

From east Africa By far the most popular route from east Africa to Malawi is from Dar es Salaam on the Tanzanian coast straight through to Mbeya in southern Tanzania, then to the Malawian border at Songwe via Tukuyu and bypassing Kyela. The best way to cover the long haul between Dar es Salaam and Mbeya is by rail: trains run five days a week. There are also plenty of buses, though you are advised not to take overnight buses because of the high risk of theft.

If you arrive in Mbeya late in the day, there is no shortage of cheap hotels to choose from. Otherwise, you could continue straight on towards the Malawian border by boarding a bus heading to Kyela (you could break the trip to Kyela at the beautifully positioned town of Tukuyu, where the Langiboss Hotel offers cheap and congenial accommodation). Ask the bus to drop you at the turn-off to the border, which lies a few kilometres before Kyela. From the turn-off, you can either walk or else hire a bicycle-taxi to cover the 6km to the border post. Bear in mind, though, that transport on the Malawian side of the border is quite thin on the ground; if you get to the turn-off towards mid afternoon, it's probably a better idea to find a hotel in Kyela (there are plenty) and cross into Malawi the next day.

Once you've crossed into Malawi, you'll find that there are no hotels at the border. Fortunately there is now a good number of *matola* pick-up trucks and buses running between the border post and Karonga, so unless you arrive ridiculously late in the day, the chance of getting stuck at the border is minimal.

There are several direct buses operating between Zambia, Malawi, Tanzania and Kenya, including:

Kobs Coach Service Devil St, Lilongwe. Operates twice-weekly coaches between Lusaka, Chipata and Lilongwe.
Mohammed Coach Line Devil St, Lilongwe. Operates a weekly round-trip service between Dar es Salaam and Lusaka via Tunduma and from Lusaka to Dar es Salaam via Lilongwe.
Taqua Devil St, Lilongwe; ☎ 09 334299. 3-times weekly service between Nairobi and Lilongwe, with stops in between, taking 36hrs Nairobi–Lilongwe, MK8,500; 24hrs Dar es Salaam–Lilongwe, MK5,000; 22hrs Morogoro, MK4,800; 20hrs Mukumi, MK4,500; 18hrs Iringa, MK4,000; 17hrs Makambaka, MK3,400; 10hrs Mbeya, MK2,400 and 7hrs to the border at Songwe, MK2,200.

Although the overwhelming majority of overland travellers come from east Africa via Dar es Salaam and Mbeya, a small number use the more obscure route via Lake Tanganyika and Zambia. The Lake Tanganyika ferry runs once a week between Bujumbura in Burundi, Kigoma in Tanzania and Mpulungu in Zambia. If you're heading south, it leaves Bujumbura at 16.00 every Monday and Kigoma at 16.00 every Wednesday, and it arrives in Mpulungu at roughly 10.00 every Friday. From Mpulungu, it is roughly 320km via Mbala and Makonde to the Malawian border post at Nyala. This is rough road and transport is erratic, so it's wise to allow at least two days to get through. From the Nyala border post it's easy to find a vehicle to Chitipa, the first major town in Malawi.

Crossing to Mozambique Owing to its extensive Indian Ocean coastline, noted for numerous idyllic beaches and atmospherically crumbling colonial ports, the former Portuguese colony of Mozambique has generated a great deal of interest among adventurous travellers since the protracted civil war ended in 1994. And, while the relatively developed part of Mozambique lying south of the Zambezi River can be visited with ease from several countries, the more remote and rewarding northern half is readily accessible only from Malawi.

Of the four options open to travellers who intend to visit northern Mozambique from Malawi, the most straightforward is the road crossing between Mangochi and Mandimba. Regular transport to the border leaves Mangochi from the bus station a few hundred metres from the PTC supermarket, stopping en route at Namwera, a small town with plenty of resthouses. If you can't get a lift along the 7km road between the two border posts, your options are either walking or hiring a bicycle-taxi – and if you opt for the latter you won't regret splashing out on a separate bike for your luggage. The Mozambican border post at Mandimba lies on the main road between Lichinga and Cuamba – arrive before 14.00 and you should find transport in either direction – but there is a basic resthouse in Mandimba if you get stuck.

Also worth considering is the train service connecting Liwonde to Cuamba via the Nayuchi border, but you must check that it is running. When in service, trains to Nayuchi leave Liwonde at 06.00 Monday to Friday and take about three hours. In Interlagos on the Mozambican side of the border there's a restaurant and resthouse, though if everything runs to schedule you should pick up the train to Cuamba on the same day, a four-hour trip which might take twice as long on a bad day.

More remote is the crossing between Likoma Island and Cobue on Lake Malawi (or Lago Niassa as Mozambicans call it). The ferry, MV *Ilala* of the Malawi Lake Services, calls in at the ports of Cobue and Metangula on its way up and down the lake (see page 158 for timetable and details). There's a good hostel and campsite in Cobue, but it's easier to get transport out of Metangula.

The Milange border between Mulanje and Mocuba is worth considering only if you're determined to visit Quelimane. It's easy to get a bus from Mulanje to Milange, where there's basic accommodation at Pensão Esplanada, but transport on to Mocuba is more erratic.

Those who are confining their Mozambican travels to the south can use the Zobue border post between Blantyre and Tete. Buses to Harare (in Zimbabwe), which leave Blantyre at 07.30–09.30 daily, will drop you in Tete, no problem, though they do charge the full fare of roughly US$40 to Harare. Alternatively, local buses connect Blantyre to the border town of Mwanza, and at Zobue on the Mozambican side, there are regular *chapas* (the Mozambican equivalent of *matola* vehicles) on to Tete.

Visa requirements are liable to change without notice. The Mozambican government has advised that all persons travelling to the country are to **obtain visas prior to departure**, as certain entry visas will not be issued upon arrival at any border post or airport.

Most backpackers get a visa at the Mozambican Consulate in Blantyre, and there is also an embassy in Lilongwe. Tourist and transit visas cost US$40. It's worth knowing that a transit visa is valid for seven days after issue and there is nothing stopping you from entering Mozambique on the first of those days and exiting it on the last!

For comprehensive travel information about Mozambique, see Philip Briggs's *Mozambique: The Bradt Travel Guide*, the fourth edition of which will be published early in 2007.

WHAT TO TAKE

CARRYING YOUR LUGGAGE If you intend using public transport or hiking up hills, you will want to carry your luggage on your back. There are three ways of doing this: with a purpose-made backpack, with a suitcase that converts to a rucksack, or with a large daypack. The choice between a convertible suitcase or a purpose-built backpack rests mainly on your style of travel. If you intend doing a lot of hiking, you're definitely best off with a proper backpack.

My own preference is for a large daypack or a 45-litre rucksack. The advantages of keeping your luggage as light and compact as possible are manifold. For a start, you can rest it on your lap on buses, thus avoiding complications such as extra charges for luggage, arguments about where your bag should be stored, and the slight but real risk of theft if your luggage ends up on the roof. A compact bag also makes for greater mobility, whether you're hiking or looking for a hotel in town when even a short journey by foot leaves you dripping.

Even in a 45-litre pack you have room to carry lightweight camping gear. Accommodation is cheap in Malawi but you can make significant savings by camping. For most purposes, a light sheet sleeping bag is as useful as the real thing (a sheet sleeping bag still performs the important role of enclosing and insulating your body; it is only in really cold conditions that it will fail you – and if you plan this right you will have bought or hired an extra blanket). I hate travelling with twice as many clothes as I will ever wear so I halve them before I leave home, especially as clothes are cheap to buy on the markets. Without camping gear I aim to take everything I need as well as a few luxuries in a 35l daypack weighing around 8kg, but normally I travel with a 45l pack weighing a few kilos more.

If you find that your luggage won't squeeze into a daypack, a sensible compromise is to carry a large daypack in your rucksack. That way, you can carry a tent and other camping equipment when you need it (for instance, the Zomba Plateau), but at other times you can reduce your luggage to fit into a daypack and leave what you're not using in storage.

CLOTHING If you're carrying your luggage on your back, you will want to restrict your clothes to the minimum. In my opinion, this is one or two pairs of trousers and/or skirts, and one pair of shorts; three shirts or T-shirts; at least one sweater (or similar) depending on when you are visiting the country and where you intend to go; enough socks and underwear to last five to seven days; and one or two pairs of shoes. After all there's not much that you can't buy out there at little expense, except perhaps decent underwear.

Trousers Bring light cotton or microfibre trousers (jeans are bulky and heavy to carry, hot to wear and take ages to dry). If you intend spending a while in montane regions, you might prefer to carry tracksuit bottoms rather than bring a second pair of trousers. These can serve as extra cover on chilly nights, and they can also be worn over shorts on chilly mornings. There is no longer a law against women wearing trousers in Malawi.

Skirts Like trousers, these are best made of a light fabric. For reasons of protocol, it is advisable to wear skirts that go below the knee: short skirts will cause needless offence to many Malawians (especially Muslims) and, whether you like it or not, they may be perceived as provocative in some quarters. Chitenje cloth can be bought at any market to wear over shorts or trousers as a skirt, or as a sarong on the beach.

Shirts Any fast-drying, lightweight shirts are good; pack at least one with long sleeves in case you need extra sun protection. Men favour shirts with top pockets (particularly if the pocket buttons up) so they can keep an eye on their spending money more easily.

Sweaters Those parts of Malawi at an altitude of 1,500m or higher tend to be cold at night. In winter, even places at more moderate altitudes (Lilongwe and Blantyre, for instance) can be surprisingly cool after dusk. For general purposes, one warm sweater or fleece should be adequate in Malawi. If you intend hiking in Mulanje and other highland areas, you'll be grateful for a second one, particularly during winter – and a woolly hat. During the rainy season, it's worth carrying a light waterproof jacket or an umbrella.

Socks and underwear These *must* be made from natural fabrics, and bear in mind that re-using them when sweaty will encourage fungal infections such as athlete's foot, as well as prickly heat in the groin region. Socks and underpants are light and compact enough to make it worth bringing a week's supply.

Shoes Unless you're serious about off-road hiking, bulky hiking boots are probably over the top in Malawi. They're also very heavy, whether they are on your feet or in your pack. A good pair of walking shoes, preferably with some ankle support, is a good compromise. It's also useful to carry sandals, flip-flops or other light shoes.

CAMPING EQUIPMENT As with most countries in southern Africa, there is a case for carrying a tent to Malawi, particularly if you are on a tight budget. Campsites exist in most of Malawi's national parks and reserves, and camping is permitted at most lakeside resorts, backpackers' hostels and forestry resthouses. Travellers who

PHOTOGRAPHIC TIPS

Ariadne Van Zandbergen

EQUIPMENT Although with some thought and an eye for composition you can take reasonable photos with a 'point-and-shoot' camera, you need an SLR camera if you are at all serious about photography. Modern SLRs tend to be very clever, with automatic programmes for almost every possible situation, but remember that these programmes are limited in the sense that the camera cannot think, but only makes calculations. Every starting amateur photographer should read a photographic manual for beginners and get to grips with such basics as the relationship between aperture and shutter speed.

Always buy the best lens you can afford. The lens determines the quality of your photo more than the camera body. Fixed fast lenses are ideal, but very costly. A zoom lens makes it easier to change composition without changing lenses the whole time. If you carry only one lens, a 28–70mm (digital 17–55mm) or similar zoom should be ideal. For a second lens, a lightweight 80–200mm or 70–300mm (digital 55–200mm) or similar will be excellent for candid shots and varying your composition. Wildlife photography will be very frustrating if you don't have at least a 300mm lens. For a small loss of quality, tele-converters are a cheap and compact way to increase magnification: a 300mm lens with a 1.4x converter becomes 420mm, and with a 2x it becomes 600mm. Note, however, that 1.4x and 2x tele-converters reduce the speed of your lens by 1.4 and 2 stops respectively.

For wildlife photography from a safari vehicle, a solid beanbag, which you can make yourself very cheaply, will be necessary to avoid blurred images, and is more useful than a tripod. A clamp with a tripod head screwed on to it can be attached to the vehicle as well. Modern dedicated flash units are easy to use; aside from the obvious need to flash when you photograph at night, you can improve a lot of photos in difficult 'high contrast' or very dull light with some fill-in flash. It pays to have a proper flash unit as opposed to a built-in camera flash.

DIGITAL/FILM Digital photography is now the preference of most amateur and professional photographers, with the resolution of digital cameras improving the whole time. For ordinary prints a 6 megapixel camera is fine. For better results and the possibility to enlarge images and for professional reproduction, higher resolution is available up to 16 megapixels.

Memory space is important. The number of pictures you can fit on a memory card depends on the quality you choose. Calculate in advance how many pictures you can fit on a card and either take enough cards to last for your trip, or take a storage drive onto

intend doing a fair bit of off-the-beaten-track hiking will find a tent a useful fallback where no other accommodation exists.

That said, there are few parts of Malawi where a tent is an absolute necessity, and the costs saved by camping are only sometimes substantial. For travellers using public transport, the disadvantage of carrying a tent (and other camping equipment) is that it adds considerably to the weight, bulk and unmanageability of your luggage. There are plenty of interesting off-the-beaten-track places in Malawi where affordable rooms exist and which involve a walk of anything up to 15km to reach. In such circumstances, the extra bulk and 4–5kg added by carrying camping equipment can turn a pleasant walk into a real slog. If you decide to carry camping equipment, the key is to look for the lightest available gear.

MAPS The 1:900,000 International Travel Map of Malawi published in 2003 by ITMB is available from Malawi Tourism Marketing Consortium (*www.malawitourism.com*) for US$13 (+p&p outside UK) or from Stanfords in London (*www.stanfords.co.uk*).

which you can download the content. A laptop gives the advantage that you can see your pictures properly at the end of each day and edit and delete rejects, but a storage device is lighter and less bulky. These drives come in different capacities up to 80GB.

Bear in mind that digital camera batteries, computers and other storage devices need charging, so make sure you have all the chargers, cables and converters with you. Most hotels have charging points, but do enquire about this in advance. When camping you might have to rely on charging from the car battery; a spare battery is invaluable.

If you are shooting film, 100 to 200 ISO print film and 50 to 100 ISO slide film are ideal. Low ISO film is slow but fine grained and gives the best colour saturation, but will need more light, so support in the form of a tripod or monopod is important. You can also bring a few 'fast' 400 ISO films for low-light situations where a tripod or flash is not an option.

DUST AND HEAT Dust and heat are often a problem. Keep your equipment in a sealed bag, stow films in an airtight container (eg: a small cooler bag) and avoid exposing equipment and film to the sun. Digital cameras are prone to collecting dust particles on the sensor which results in spots on the image. The dirt mostly enters the camera when changing lenses, so be careful when doing this. To some extent photos can be 'cleaned' up afterwards in Photoshop, but this is time-consuming. You can have your camera sensor professionally cleaned, or you can do this yourself with special brushes and swabs made for the purpose, but note that touching the sensor might cause damage and should only be done with the greatest care.

LIGHT The most striking outdoor photographs are often taken during the hour or two of 'golden light', after dawn and before sunset. Shooting in low light may enforce the use of very low shutter speeds, in which case a tripod will be required to avoid camera shake.

With careful handling, side lighting and back lighting can produce stunning effects, especially in soft light and at sunrise or sunset. Generally, however, it is best to shoot with the sun behind you. When photographing animals or people in the harsh midday sun, images taken in light but even shade are likely to be more effective than those taken in direct sunlight or patchy shade, since the latter conditions create too much contrast.

Ariadne Van Zandbergen is a professional travel and wildlife photographer specialising in Africa. She runs The Africa Image Library. For photo requests, visit www.africaimagelibrary.co.za or contact her by email at ariadne@hixnet.co.za.

This is the second edition, and it has useful text and pictures, with town plans of Lilongwe and Blantyre. It is the most up-to-date map of the country, covering tar and dirt roads as well as principal tourist destinations and lodges. It is also available from Central Africana Bookshops in Lilongwe and Blantyre.

The best map sales office in Malawi is in Blantyre, where you can buy the excellent 1:50,000 and 1:25,000 maps produced by the Department of Surveys, covering the whole country. If you are lucky to locate the map office and find it open, these may also be available at any map sales office around the country for US$3 per sheet. Good town plans of Blantyre, Lilongwe, Mzuzu and Zomba can be bought for the same price at any map sales office.

OTHER USEFUL ITEMS A torch is essential as electricity is never a guarantee. Another perennial favourite is the Swiss knife or multi-purpose tool.

Binoculars are essential for birdwatching and to get a good look at animals in wildlife reserves. Compact binoculars have a crisper image than the traditional variety, they are much more backpack-friendly, and these days you can find adequate brands that are not significantly more expensive than traditional binoculars. The one drawback of compact binoculars is their restricted field of vision, which can make it difficult to pick up birds and animals in thick bush. For most purposes, 7x35 traditional binoculars or 7x21 compact binoculars are fine, but birdwatchers might find a 10x magnification more useful.

A mobile phone (unlocked or get it unlocked in any city) will be useful. You can buy a local SIM card for US$5 and top-up cards are readily available and inexpensive (Celtel have perhaps a slightly better coverage than Telcom). This is then your alarm clock for any early starts.

If you stay in local hotels, it is best to carry your own padlock – many places don't supply them. You should also carry a towel, soap, shampoo, toilet paper and any other toiletries you need (all of which are now available in Shoprite and some other supermarkets, including tampons). Contact lens solutions may not be available, so bring enough to last the whole trip and bring glasses in case the intense sun and dry African climate irritates your eyes.

Even in the cities you'll find the range of fiction books is limited and very expensive. There are few secondhand bookstalls around, so bring reading books with you. It's impossible to buy sketching equipment so you would need to pack that if you illustrate your diary or plan to paint. Local newspapers give a fascinating insight into Malawi and there are world pages too (the *Nation* and the *Times* are the main papers), but you might think about carrying a short-wave radio to hear more about the outside world.

If travelling in your own vehicle, make sure you have a good set of tools, a selection of wire, string and rope, your driver's licence and the vehicle's registration papers (and a letter of permission to use the vehicle if not registered in your name). Depending on how far, where and when you're driving, you might also consider spare engine oil, a jerry can for fuel, a fan belt, spare fuses and a fluorescent light that plugs into the cigarette lighter.

Medical kits and other health-related subjects are discussed in *Chapter 4, Health*.

PHOTOGRAPHY

Digital cameras have taken so much of the hassle out of photography. You can even download photos onto disks or onto your email. Both compacts and SLRs give fantastic results, but be sure to bring more memory than you think you need. Most modern digital cameras have good zoom lenses: for wildlife you will ideally want at least a 240mm zoom. For further details, see the box on pages 54–5.

Except in Muslim areas, most Malawians apparently love having their photograph taken, so there is really very little risk of giving offence. All the same, you should always ask permission before taking a photograph of a person, and be prepared to pay in the unlikely event that payment is asked. Try to be sensitive about taking casual street shots in Muslim towns like Salima, Nkhotakota and Mangochi.

$ MONEY MATTERS

ORGANISING YOUR FINANCES Bring the bulk of your money in the form of travellers' cheques, as these can be refunded if they are lost or stolen. The most widely recognised currency is the US dollar, followed by the euro, the pound sterling and the South African rand.

It is advisable to bring a small amount of money (say around US$250) in cash, preferably small denominations, in case you need to change money when banks are closed. Note that US$100 notes are not accepted by some hotels and banks due to the large number of forgeries in circulation in Malawi.

There are Visa ATMs in all major towns at National Bank where you can withdraw up to MK20,000. You can also use your visa at the foreign exchange desks of most banks, though this can be time-consuming. Credit cards are not always readily accepted in shops, hotels and restaurants, though some in Blantyre and Lilongwe will take them with a handling fee. Outside major cities, credit cards are close to useless, except at upmarket game lodges and resorts.

CARRYING YOUR MONEY AND VALUABLES It is advisable to carry all your hard currency and credit cards, as well as your passport and other important documentation, in a money-belt. The ideal money-belt for Africa is one that can be hidden beneath your clothing. Externally worn money-belts are as good as telling thieves that all your valuables are there for the taking.

Use a money-belt made of cotton or another natural fabric, bearing in mind that such fabrics tend to soak up a lot of sweat, so you will need to wrap plastic around everything inside the money-belt.

BUDGETING A budget is a personal thing, dependent on how much time you are spending in the country, what you are doing while you are there, and how much money you can afford to spend.

If you use facilities that are mainly geared to locals, Malawi is a very inexpensive country, even by African standards. You can generally find a room in a local hotel for around US$3–4 per person and you can normally buy a meal for less. But be warned that accommodation standards in local resthouses are not what they once were, and are not always advisable, depending on the town and the location. Buses are cheap, as are drinks. Rigidly budget-conscious travellers can probably keep costs down to US$15–20 per day per person, but US$25 gives you considerably more flexibility. At US$40–60 per day, you can live royally in the low to mid range, especially if you keep some money aside for treats such as horseriding, safari, climbing, trekking, kayaking or diving in Lake Malawi etc. Such activities are what make time in Malawi even more special, and you might budget on keeping US$400–500 aside for these.

4

Health

with Dr Felicity Nicholson and Dr Jane Wilson-Howarth

People new to Africa often worry about tropical diseases, but if you take the appropriate precautions, it is accidents that are more likely to carry you off. Road accidents are very common in many parts of Malawi, so be aware and do what you can to reduce risks: try to travel during daylight hours and refuse to be driven by a drunk. Listen to local advice about areas where violent crime is rife, too.

PREPARATIONS

TRAVEL INSURANCE Don't think about travelling without a comprehensive medical travel insurance policy, specifically one that will fly you home in an emergency. There are innumerable policies available, and many of the travel clinics listed below (see page 63) sell their own versions, so do shop around for the best deal for you.

IMMUNISATION Preparations to ensure a healthy trip to Malawi require checks on your immunisation status: it is wise to be up to date on tetanus (ten-yearly), polio (ten-yearly), diphtheria (ten-yearly), and for many parts of Africa immunisations against yellow fever, meningococcus, rabies and hepatitis A are also needed. Yellow fever is not required for Malawi alone, but may be necessary if you are travelling through other African countries further north.

Hepatitis A vaccine (Havrix Monodose or Avaxim) comprises two injections given about a year apart. The course costs about £100, but protects for 20 years. It is now felt that the vaccine can be used even close to the time of departure and has replaced the old-fashioned gamma globulin. The newer **typhoid** vaccines (eg: Typhim Vi) last for three years and are about 85% effective. They should be encouraged unless the traveller is leaving within a few days for a trip of a week or less, when the vaccine would not be effective in time. **Meningitis** vaccine (containing strains ACW and Y) is also recommended, especially for trips of more than four weeks (see *Meningitis*, page 69). Immunisation against cholera is no longer required for Malawi. Vaccinations for **rabies** are advised for travellers visiting more remote areas (see *Rabies*, page 70). **Hepatitis B** vaccination should be considered for longer trips (two months or more) or for those working with children or in situations where contact with blood is likely. Three injections are needed for the best protection and can be given over a three-week period if time is short. Longer schedules give more sustained protection and are therefore preferred if time allows. A BCG vaccination against **tuberculosis** (TB) may be advised for trips of two months or more.

Ideally you should visit your own doctor or a specialist travel clinic (see pages 63–5) to discuss your requirements about eight weeks before you plan to travel. You will also need to make sure you don't catch malaria by taking the appropriate malaria prophylaxis.

SAFE SEX

Remember that the risks of any sexually transmitted infection are high, whether you sleep with fellow travellers or locals. And let's face it, it's easy to fall for someone when you're travelling. About 40% of HIV infections in British heterosexuals are acquired abroad. If you have any doubt about your partner, it's better to wait for a test before you sleep together. Use condoms or femidoms; spermicide pessaries help reduce the risk of transmission. If you notice any genital ulcers or discharge, get treatment promptly since these increase the risk of acquiring HIV.

Most main towns in Malawi have health clinics where you can ask for advice. On your return home, there are AIDS helplines in every country if you are worried about anything.

PERSONAL FIRST-AID KIT The more I travel, the less I take. My minimal kit contains:

- A good drying antiseptic, eg: iodine or potassium permanganate (don't take antiseptic cream)
- A few small dressings (Band-Aids)
- Suncream
- Insect repellent; malaria tablets; impregnated bednet
- Aspirin or paracetamol
- Antifungal cream (eg: Canesten)
- Ciprofloxacin antibiotic, 500mg x 2 (or norfloxacin) for severe diarrhoea
- Tinidazole (500mg x 8) for giardia or amoebic dysentery (see page 66 for regime)
- Antibiotic eye drops, for sore, 'gritty', stuck-together eyes (conjunctivitis)
- A pair of fine pointed tweezers (to remove hairy caterpillar hairs, thorns, splinters, coral etc)
- Condoms or femidoms
- Maybe a malaria treatment kit and thermometer

While you are in Malawi, the most common causes for concern are sunstroke and sunburn, the common cold, infected cuts or bites, diarrhoea and malaria. HIV should also be added to this list.

MALARIA Along with road accidents, malaria poses the single biggest serious threat to the health of travellers in Malawi. Initial symptoms are enormously varied, but it always starts with a high fever (over 38°C). Other symptoms could include headache, general feeling of disorientation, rash, diarrhoea and flu-like symptoms (mostly without the cold-like symptoms one might associate with flu, such as running nose, sore throat etc). Mosquitoes transmit malaria from person to person in blood by bites. Once it is in your bloodstream it multiplies, destroying your red blood cells.

The key times to be bitten by mosquitoes are between dusk and dawn. The cities, the lake and the Lower Shire are the most common places to catch malaria, with the risk reduced above 1,800m above sea level. For further details, see box *Malaria in Malawi*, page 62.

Malaria prevention There is no vaccine against malaria, but there are other ways to avoid it; since most of Malawi is very high risk for malaria, travellers must plan their malaria protection properly. Seek current advice on the best antimalarials to take. If mefloquine (Lariam) is suggested, start this two-and-a-half weeks (three doses) before departure to check that it suits you; stop it immediately if it seems to cause depression or anxiety, visual or hearing disturbances, severe headaches, fits or changes in heart rhythm. Side effects such as nightmares or dizziness are not medical reasons for stopping unless they are sufficiently debilitating or annoying. Anyone who is pregnant, has been treated for depression or psychiatric problems, has diabetes controlled by oral therapy or who is epileptic (or who has suffered fits in the past) or has a close blood relative who is epileptic, should avoid mefloquine.

Malarone (proguanil and atovaquone) is a new drug that is as effective as mefloquine. It has the advantage of having few side effects and need only be continued for one week after returning. However, it is expensive and because of this tends to be reserved for shorter trips. Paediatric Malarone is now available for children weighing 11–40kg, with the number of tablets given depending on the child's weight. To make life simpler, know the weight in kilograms of your child before you go to the doctor.

The antibiotic doxycycline (100mg daily) is a viable alternative when either mefloquine or Malarone are not considered suitable for whatever reason. Like Malarone it can be started two days before arrival. Unlike mefloquine, it may also be used in travellers with epilepsy, although certain anti-epileptic medication may make it less effective. Users must be warned about the possibility of allergic skin reactions developing in sunlight, which can occur in about 1–3% of people. The drug should be stopped if this happens. Women using the oral contraceptive should use an additional method of protection for the first four weeks when using Doxycycline. It is also unsuitable in pregnancy or for children under 12 years old.

Chloroquine and proguanil are no longer considered to be very effective for Malawi. However, they may still be recommended if no other regime is suitable.

Should you lose your malaria pills, most pharmacies in Malawi will sell a range of different prophylaxes over the counter. They also sell malaria treatment drugs, though they may not be the most effective.

All prophylactic agents should be taken with or after a meal, washed down with plenty of fluid and with the exception of Malarone (see above) continued for four weeks after leaving.

Every so often I run into travellers who prefer to acquire resistance to malaria rather than take preventive tablets, or who witter on about homoeopathic cures for this killer disease. That's their prerogative, but they have no place expounding their radical views to others. Travellers to Africa cannot acquire any effective resistance to malaria, and those who don't make use of prophylactic drugs risk their lives in a manner that is both foolish and unnecessary.

Extra protection It is important to protect yourself from mosquito bites (see page 67 and *Malaria prevention*, above), so keep your repellent to hand at all times. Be aware that no prophylactic is 100% protective but those on prophylactics who are unlucky enough to catch malaria are less likely to get into serious trouble so rapidly.

You also need either a permethrin-impregnated bednet or a permethrin spray so that you can 'treat' bednets in hotels. Permethrin treatment makes even very tatty nets protective and prevents mosquitoes from biting through the impregnated net when you roll against it; it also deters other biters. Putting on long clothes at dusk means you can reduce the amount of repellent you need to put on your skin, but be aware that malaria mosquitoes hunt at ankle level and will bite through socks, so apply repellent under socks too. Travel clinics usually sell a good range of nets, treatment kits and repellents.

MALARIA IN MALAWI

Philip Briggs

The *Anopheles* mosquito which transmits the malaria parasite is most abundant near marshes and still water, where it breeds, and the parasite is most prolific at low altitudes. Parts of Malawi lying at an altitude of 2,000m or higher (Zomba, Nyika and Mulanje plateaux) are regarded to be free of malaria. In mid-altitude locations such as Lilongwe, Blantyre and Mzuzu, malaria is largely but not entirely seasonal, with the highest risk of transmission occurring during the hot, wet summer months of November to April. The low-lying Lake Malawi hinterland and Shire Valley are high risk throughout the year, but the danger is greatest during the summer months. This localised breakdown might influence what foreigners working in Malawi do about malaria prevention, but since tourist activity in Malawi is focused around the lake, all travellers to Malawi must assume that they will be exposed to malaria and should take precautions throughout their trip (see pages 60–1).

It is unwise to travel in malarial parts of Africa, which includes most of Malawi, whilst pregnant or with children: the risk of malaria in many parts is considerable and these travellers are likely to succumb rapidly to the disease.

Treatment Even those who take their malaria tablets meticulously and do everything possible to avoid mosquito bites may contract a strain of malaria that is resistant to prophylactic drugs. Untreated malaria is likely to be fatal, but even strains resistant to prophylaxis respond well to prompt treatment. Because of this, your immediate priority upon displaying possible malaria symptoms is to establish whether you have malaria. In some parts of Malawi it is easy and inexpensive to arrange a malaria blood test. A positive result means that you have malaria. A negative result doesn't necessarily mean that you don't have malaria, bearing in mind that the parasite doesn't always show up on a test, particularly when the level of infection is mild or is 'cloaked' by partially effective prophylactics. For this reason, even if you test negative, it would be wise to stay within reach of a laboratory until the symptoms clear up, and to test again after a day or two if they don't. It's worth noting that if you have a fever and the malaria test is negative, there are many other possibilities that could be treatable.

In more remote places in Malawi, for instance at some of the more remote lakeshore resorts, and in national parks and montane areas, you will be unable to test for malaria. Travellers to such parts would probably be wise to carry a course of treatment to cure malaria, since it is normal enough to go from feeling healthy to having a high fever in the space of a few hours (and it is possible to die from falciparum malaria within 24 hours of the first symptoms). Experts differ on the costs and benefits of self-treatment, but agree that it leads to over-treatment and to many people taking drugs they do not need; yet treatment may save your life. Discuss your trip with a specialist to determine your particular needs and risks, and be sure you understand when and how to take the cure. If you are somewhere remote in a malarial region you probably have to assume that any high fever (over 38°C) for more than a few hours is due to malaria (regardless of any other symptoms) and should seek treatment. Diagnosing malaria is not easy, which is why consulting a doctor is sensible: there are other dangerous causes of fever in Africa, which require different treatments. Presently Malarone or Co-artemether are the favoured regimes, but check for up-to-date advice on the current recommended treatment.

In severe cases of malaria, the victim will be unable to hold down medication, at which point they are likely to die unless they are hospitalised immediately and put on a drip. If you or a travelling companion start vomiting after taking your malaria medication, get to a hospital or clinic quickly, ideally a private one. Whatever concerns you might have about African hospitals, they are used to dealing with malaria, and the alternative to hospitalisation is far worse. And remember, malaria may occur anything from seven days into the trip to up to one year after leaving Africa.

PROTECTION FROM THE SUN Give some thought to packing suncream. Most of Malawi is at a medium to high altitude, which means that the sun has a stronger effect than it would in much of Europe. The incidence of skin cancer is rocketing as Caucasians are travelling more and spending more time exposing themselves to the sun. Keep out of the sun during the middle of the day and, if you must be exposed to the sun, build up gradually from 20 minutes per day. Be especially careful of sun reflected off water and wear a T-shirt and lots of waterproof SPF25 suncream when swimming; snorkelling often leads to scorched backs of the thighs so wear bermuda shorts. Sun exposure ages the skin and makes people prematurely wrinkly; cover up with long, loose clothes and wear a hat when you can. The glare and the dust can be hard on the eyes, too, so bring UV-protecting sunglasses and, perhaps, a soothing eyebath.

TRAVEL CLINICS AND HEALTH INFORMATION A full list of current travel clinic websites worldwide is available from the International Society of Travel Medicine on www.istm.org. For other journey preparation information, consult www.tripprep.com. Information about various medications may be found on www.emedicine.com. For information on malaria prevention, see www.preventingmalaria.info.

UK

Berkeley Travel Clinic 32 Berkeley St, London W1J 8EL (near Green Park tube station); ☎ 020 7629 6233

British Airways Travel Clinic and Immunisation Service 213 Piccadilly, London W1J 9HQ; ☎ 0845 600 2236; www.ba.com/travelclinics. Walk-in service (no appointment necessary) Mon, Tue, Wed, Fri 08.45–18.15, Thu 08.45–20.00, Sat 09.30–17.00. As well as providing inoculations and malaria prevention, they sell a variety of health-related goods.

Cambridge Travel Clinic 48a Mill Rd, Cambridge CB1 2AS; ☎ 01223 367362; e enquiries@cambridgetravelclinic.co.uk; www.cambridgetravelclinic.co.uk. Open Tue–Fri 12.00–19.00, Sat 10.00–16.00.

Edinburgh Travel Clinic Regional Infectious Diseases Unit, Ward 41 OPD, Western General Hospital, Crewe Rd South, Edinburgh EH4 2UX; ☎ 0131 537 2822; www.link.med.ed.ac.uk/ridu. Travel helpline (0906 589 0380) open weekdays 09.00–12.00. Provides inoculations and antimalarial prophylaxis and advises on travel-related health risks.

Fleet Street Travel Clinic 29 Fleet St, London EC4Y 1AA; ☎ 020 7353 5678; www.fleetstreetclinic.com. Vaccinations, travel products and latest advice.

Hospital for Tropical Diseases Travel Clinic Mortimer Market Bldg, Capper St (off Tottenham Ct Rd), London WC1E 6AU; ☎ 020 7388 9600; www.thehtd.org. Offers consultations and advice, and is able to provide all necessary drugs and vaccines for travellers. Runs a healthline (0906 133 7733) for country-specific information and health hazards. Also stocks nets, water purification equipment and personal protection measures.

Interhealth Worldwide Partnership Hse, 157 Waterloo Rd, London SE1 8US; ☎ 020 7902 9000; www.interhealth.org.uk. Competitively priced, one-stop travel health service. All profits go to their affiliated company, InterHealth, which provides healthcare for overseas workers on Christian projects.

MASTA (Medical Advisory Service for Travellers Abroad) London School of Hygiene and Tropical Medicine, Keppel St, London WC1 7HT; ☎ 0906 550 1402; www.masta.org. Individually tailored health briefs available for a fee, with up-to-date information on how to stay healthy, inoculations and what to take. There are currently 30 MASTA pre-travel clinics in Britain. Call 0870 241 6843 or check online for the nearest. Clinics also sell malaria prophylaxis memory

LONG-HAUL FLIGHTS

Dr Felicity Nicholson

There is growing evidence, albeit circumstantial, that long-haul air travel increases the risk of developing deep vein thrombosis (DVT). This condition is potentially life threatening, but it should be stressed that the danger to the average traveller is slight.

Certain risk factors specific to air travel have been identified. These include immobility, compression of the veins at the back of the knee by the edge of the seat, the decreased air pressure and slightly reduced oxygen in the cabin, and dehydration. Consuming alcohol may exacerbate the situation by increasing fluid loss and encouraging immobility.

In theory everyone is at risk, but those at highest risk are shown below:

- Passengers on journeys of longer than eight hours' duration
- People over 40
- People with heart disease
- People with cancer
- People with clotting disorders
- People who have had recent surgery, especially on the legs
- Women on the pill or other oestrogen therapy
- Women who are pregnant
- People who are very tall (over 6ft/1.8m) or short (under 5ft/1.5m)

A DVT is a clot of blood that forms in the leg veins. Symptoms include swelling and pain in the calf or thigh. The skin may feel hot to touch and becomes discoloured (light blue-

cards, treatment kits, bednets, net treatment kits.

NHS travel website www.fitfortravel.scot.nhs.uk. Provides country-by-country advice on immunisation and malaria, plus details of recent developments, and a list of relevant health organisations.

Nomad Travel Store/Clinic 3–4 Wellington Terrace, Turnpike Lane, London N8 0PX; ☎ 020 8889 7014; travel-health line (office hours only) 0906 863 3414; e sales@nomadtravel.co.uk; www.nomadtravel.co.uk. Also at 40 Bernard St, London WC1N 1LJ; ☎ 020 7833 4114; 52 Grosvenor Gardens, London SW1W 0AG; ☎ 020 7823 5823; and 43 Queens Rd, Bristol BS8 1QH; ☎ 0117 922 6567. For health advice, equipment (eg: mosquito nets and other anti-bug devices), and an excellent range of adventure travel gear.

Trailfinders Travel Clinic 194 Kensington High St, London W8 7RG; ☎ 020 7938 3999; www.trailfinders.com/clinic.htm

Travelpharm The Travelpharm website, www.travelpharm.com, offers up-to-date guidance on travel-related health and has a range of medications available through their online mini-pharmacy.

Irish Republic

Tropical Medical Bureau Grafton St Medical Centre, Grafton Bldgs, 34 Grafton St, Dublin 2; ☎ 1 671 9200; www.tmb.ie. A useful website specific to tropical destinations. Also check website for other bureaux locations throughout Ireland.

US

Centers for Disease Control 1600 Clifton Rd, Atlanta, GA 30333; ☎ 800 311 3435; travellers' health hotline 888 232 3299; www.cdc.gov/travel. The central source of travel information in the US. The invaluable *Health Information for International Travel*, published annually, is available from the Division of Quarantine at this address.

Connaught Laboratories PO Box 187, Swiftwater, PA 18370; ☎ 800 822 2463. They will send a free list of specialist tropical-medicine physicians in your state.

IAMAT (International Association for Medical Assistance to Travelers) 1623 Military Rd, 279, Niagara Falls, NY14304-1745; ☎ 716 754 4883; e info@iamat.org; www.iamat.org. A non-profit organisation that provides lists of English-speaking doctors abroad.

International Medicine Center 920 Frostwood Drive, Suite 670, Houston, TX 77024; ☎ 713 550 2000; www.traveldoc.com

red). A DVT is not dangerous in itself, but if a clot breaks down then it may travel to the lungs (pulmonary embolus). Symptoms of a pulmonary embolus (PE) include chest pain, shortness of breath and coughing up small amounts of blood.

Symptoms of a DVT rarely occur during the flight, and typically occur within three days of arrival, although symptoms of a DVT or PE have been reported up to two weeks later.

Anyone who suspects that they have these symptoms should see a doctor immediately as anticoagulation (blood thinning) treatment can be given.

PREVENTION OF DVT General measures to reduce the risk of thrombosis are shown below. This advice also applies to long train or bus journeys.

- Whilst waiting to board the plane, try to walk around rather than sit
- During the flight drink plenty of water (at least two small glasses every hour)
- Avoid excessive tea, coffee and alcohol
- Perform leg-stretching exercises, such as pointing the toes up and down
- Move around the cabin when practicable

If you fit into the high-risk category (see above) ask your doctor if it is safe to travel. Additional protective measures such as graded compression stockings, aspirin or low molecular weight heparin can be given. No matter how tall you are, where possible request a seat with extra legroom.

Canada

IAMAT Suite 1, 1287 St Clair Av W, Toronto, Ontario M6E 1B8; ☎ 416 652 0137; www.iamat.org

TMVC Suite 314, 1030 W Georgia St, Vancouver BC V6E 2Y3; ☎ 1 888 288 8682; www.tmvc.com

Australia, New Zealand, Singapore

TMVC ☎ 1300 65 88 44; www.tmvc.com.au. TMVC has 31 clinics in Australia, New Zealand and Singapore, including:
Auckland Canterbury Arcade, 170 Queen St, Auckland; ☎ 9 373 3531
Brisbane 6th fl, 247 Adelaide St, Brisbane, QLD 4000; ☎ 7 3221 9066
Melbourne 393 Little Bourke St, 2nd fl, Melbourne, VIC 3000; ☎ 3 9602 5788
Sydney Dymocks Bldg, 7th fl, 428 George St, Sydney, NSW 2000; ☎ 2 9221 7133

IAMAT PO Box 5049, Christchurch 5, New Zealand; www.iamat.org

South Africa and Namibia

SAA-Netcare Travel Clinics P Bag X34, Benmore 2010; www.travelclinic.co.za. Clinics throughout South Africa.

TMVC 113 D F Malan Drive, Roosevelt Park, Johannesburg; ☎ 011 888 7488; www.tmvc.com.au. Consult website for details of other clinics in South Africa and Namibia.

Switzerland

IAMAT 57 Chemin des Voirets, 1212 Grand Lancy, Geneva; www.iamat.org

IN MALAWI

TRAVELLERS' DIARRHOEA Travelling in Malawi carries a fairly high risk of getting a dose of travellers' diarrhoea; perhaps half of all visitors will suffer and the newer you are to exotic travel, the more likely you will be to suffer. By taking precautions against travellers' diarrhoea you will also avoid typhoid, cholera, hepatitis, dysentery, worms etc. Travellers' diarrhoea and the other faecal-oral diseases come

TREATING TRAVELLERS' DIARRHOEA

Dr Jane Wilson-Howarth

It is dehydration which makes you feel awful during a bout of diarrhoea and the most important part of treatment is drinking lots of clear fluids. Sachets of oral rehydration salts give the perfect biochemical mix to replace all that is pouring out of your bottom but other recipes taste nicer. Any dilute mixture of sugar and salt in water will do you good: try Coke or orange squash with a three-finger pinch of salt added to each glass (if you are salt-depleted you won't taste the salt). Otherwise make a solution of a four-finger scoop of sugar with a three-finger pinch of salt in a 500ml glass of water. Or add eight level teaspoons of sugar (18g) and one level teaspoon of salt (3g) to one litre (five cups) of safe water. A squeeze of lemon or orange juice improves the taste and adds potassium, which is also lost in diarrhoea. Drink two large glasses after every bowel action, and more if you are thirsty. These solutions are still absorbed well if you are vomiting, but you will need to take sips at a time. If you are not eating you need to drink three litres a day plus whatever amount is pouring into the toilet. If you feel like eating, take a bland, high-carbohydrate diet. Heavy greasy foods will probably give you cramps.

If the diarrhoea is bad, or you are passing blood or slime, or you have a fever, you will probably need antibiotics in addition to fluid replacement. A single dose of ciprofloxacin (500mg) repeated after 12 hours may be appropriate. If the diarrhoea is greasy and bulky and is accompanied by sulphurous (eggy) burps, the likely cause is giardia. This is best treated with tinidazole (four x 500mg in one dose, repeated seven days later if symptoms persist).

from getting other people's faeces in your mouth. This most often happens from cooks not washing their hands after a trip to the toilet, but even if the restaurant cook does not understand basic hygiene, you will be safe if your food has been properly cooked and arrives piping hot. The maxim to remind you what you can safely eat is:

PEEL IT, BOIL IT, COOK IT OR FORGET IT.

This means that fruit you have washed and peeled yourself, and hot foods, should be safe but raw foods, cold cooked foods, salads, fruit salads which have been prepared by others, ice cream and ice are all risky. And foods kept lukewarm in hotel buffets are often dangerous. If you are struck, see the box above for treatment.

It is much rarer to get sick from drinking contaminated water but it happens, so try to drink from safe sources. Water should have been brought to the boil (even at altitude it only needs to be brought to the boil), or passed through a good bacteriological filter or purified with iodine; chlorine tablets (eg: Puritabs) are also adequate although theoretically less effective and they taste nastier. Mineral water has been found to be contaminated in Malawi but should be safer than contaminated tap water.

DENGUE FEVER This mosquito-borne disease is rare in Malawi, but it does still occur. It may mimic malaria but there is no prophylactic medication available to deal with it. The mosquitoes that carry this virus bite during the daytime, so it is worth applying repellent if you see any mosquitoes around. Symptoms include strong headaches, rashes and excruciating joint and muscle pains and high fever. Dengue fever lasts only for a week or so and is not usually fatal. Complete rest and paracetamol are the usual treatment; plenty of fluids also help. Some patients are given an intravenous drip to keep them from dehydrating. It is especially important to protect yourself if you have had dengue fever before, since a second infection with a different strain can result in the potentially fatal dengue haemorrhagic fever.

INSECT BITES It is crucial to avoid **mosquito bites** between dusk and dawn; as the sun is going down, don long clothes and apply repellent on any exposed flesh. This will protect you from malaria, elephantiasis and a range of nasty insect-borne viruses. Otherwise retire to an air-conditioned room or burn mosquito coils (which are widely available and cheap in Malawi) or sleep under a fan. Coils and fans reduce rather than eliminate bites. During the day it is wise to wear long, loose (preferably 100% cotton) clothes if you are pushing through scrubby country; this will keep ticks off and also tsetse and day-biting *Aedes* mosquitoes which may spread dengue and yellow fever. Tsetse flies hurt when they bite and are attracted to the colour blue; locals will advise on where they are a problem and where they transmit sleeping sickness.

Minute pestilential biting **blackflies** spread river blindness in some parts of Africa between 190° N and 170° S; the disease is caught close to fast-flowing rivers since flies breed there and the larvae live in rapids. The flies bite during the day but long trousers tucked into socks will help keep them off. Citronella-based natural repellents do not work against them.

Mosquitoes and many other insects are attracted to light. If you are camping, never put a lamp near the opening of your tent, or you will have a swarm of biters waiting to join you when you retire. In hotel rooms, be aware that the longer your light is on, the greater the number of insects will be sharing your accommodation.

Tumbu flies or ***putsi*** are a problem where the climate is hot and humid. The adult fly lays her eggs on the soil or on drying laundry and when the eggs come in contact with human flesh (when you put on clothes or lie on a bed) they hatch and bury themselves under the skin. Here they form a crop of 'boils' which each hatches a grub after about eight days, when the inflammation will settle down. In *putsi* areas either dry your clothes and sheets within a screened house, or dry them in direct sunshine until they are crisp, or iron them.

Jiggers or **sandfleas** are another flesh-feaster. They latch on if you walk barefoot in contaminated places, and set up home under the skin of the foot, usually at the side of a toenail where they cause a painful, boil-like swelling. They need picking out by a local expert; if the distended flea bursts during eviction the

MEDICAL FACILITIES IN MALAWI

Philip Briggs

Private clinics, hospitals and pharmacies can be found in most large towns, and doctors generally speak fluent English. Consultation fees and laboratory tests are remarkably inexpensive when compared with most Western countries, so if you do fall sick it would be absurd to let financial considerations dissuade you from seeking medical help. Commonly required medicines such as broad spectrum antibiotics and Flagyl are widely available and cheap throughout the region, as are malaria cures and prophylactics. Fansidar and quinine tablets are best bought in advance – in fact it's advisable to carry all malaria-related tablets on you, and only rely on their availability locally if you need to restock your supplies.

If you are on any medication prior to departure, or you have specific needs relating to a known medical condition (for instance if you are allergic to bee stings or you are prone to attacks of asthma), then you are strongly advised to bring any related drugs and devices with you.

QUICK TICK REMOVAL

Dr Jane Wilson-Howarth

African ticks are not the prolific disease transmitters they are in the Americas, but they may spread Lyme disease, tick-bite fever and a few rarities. Tick-bite fever is a non-serious, flu-like illness, but still worth avoiding. If you get the tick off whole and promptly, the chances of disease transmission are reduced to a minimum. Tick removers are now available (eg: Tick Twister) which remove the tick without damaging the mouthparts. If you do not have one then the next best thing is to manoeuvre your finger and thumb so that you can pinch the tick's mouthparts, as close to your skin as possible, and slowly and steadily pull away at right angles to your skin. This often hurts. Jerking or twisting will increase the chances of damaging the tick, which in turn increases the chances of disease transmission, as well as leaving the mouthparts behind. Once the tick is off, dowse the little wound with alcohol (local spirit, whisky or similar are excellent) or iodine. An area of spreading redness around the bite site, or a rash or fever coming on a few days or more after the bite, should stimulate a trip to a doctor.

wound should be dowsed in spirit, alcohol or kerosene, otherwise more jiggers will infest you.

BILHARZIA OR SCHISTOSOMIASIS

With thanks to Dr Vaughan Southgate of the Natural History Museum, London

Bilharzia or schistosomiasis is a disease that commonly afflicts the rural poor of the tropics who repeatedly acquire more and more of these nasty little worm-lodgers. Infected travellers and expatriates generally suffer fewer problems because symptoms will encourage them to seek prompt treatment and they are also exposed to fewer parasites. However, it is still an unpleasant problem that is worth avoiding.

The parasites digest their way through your skin when you wade, bathe or even shower in infested fresh water. Unfortunately, many African lakes, including Lake Malawi, and also rivers and irrigation canals, carry a risk of bilharzia. In 1995, two-thirds of expatriates living in Malawi had evidence on blood testing of having bilharzia, and 75% of a group of people scuba diving off Cape Maclear in Lake Malawi for only about a week acquired the disease.

The most risky shores will be close to places where infected people use water, wash clothes etc. Winds disperse the cercariae, though, so they can be blown some distance, perhaps up to 200m from where they entered the water. Scuba diving off a boat into deep offshore water, then, should be a low-risk activity, but showering in lake water or paddling along a reedy lakeshore near a village is risky.

Although absence of early symptoms does not necessarily mean there is no infection, infected people usually notice symptoms two or more weeks after parasite penetration. Travellers and expatriates will probably experience a fever and often a wheezy cough; local residents do not usually have symptoms. There is now a very good blood test which, if done six weeks or more after likely exposure, will determine whether you need treatment. Since bilharzia can be a nasty illness, avoidance is better than waiting to be cured and it is wise to avoid bathing in high-risk areas.

Avoiding bilharzia

- If you are bathing, swimming, paddling or wading in fresh water which you think may carry a bilharzia risk, try to get out of the water within ten minutes
- Dry off thoroughly with a towel; rub vigorously

- Avoid bathing or paddling on shores within 200m of villages or places where people use the water a great deal, especially reedy shores or where there is lots of water weed
- If your bathing water comes from a risky source try to ensure that the water is taken from the lake in the early morning and stored snail-free, otherwise it should be filtered or Dettol or Cresol added
- Bathing early in the morning is safer than bathing in the second half of the day
- Covering yourself with DEET insect repellent before swimming will protect you
- If you think that you have been exposed to bilharzia parasites, arrange a screening blood test (your GP can do this) MORE than six weeks after your last possible contact with suspect water

SKIN INFECTIONS Any mosquito bite or small nick in the skin gives an opportunity for bacteria to foil the body's usually excellent defences; it will surprise many travellers how quickly skin infections start in warm humid climates and it is essential to clean and cover even the slightest wound. Creams are not as effective as a good drying antiseptic such as dilute iodine, potassium permanganate (a few crystals in half a cup of water), or crystal (or gentian) violet. One of these should be available in most towns. If the wound starts to throb, or becomes red and the redness starts to spread, or the wound oozes, and especially if you develop a fever, antibiotics will probably be needed: flucloxacillin (250mg four times a day) or cloxacillin (500mg four times a day). For those allergic to penicillin, erythromycin (500mg twice a day) for five days should help. See a doctor if the symptoms do not start to improve in 48 hours.

Fungal infections also get a hold easily in hot moist climates so wear 100% cotton socks and underwear and shower frequently. An itchy rash in the groin or flaking between the toes is likely to be a fungal infection. This needs treatment with an antifungal cream such as Canesten (clotrimazole); if this is not available try Whitfield's ointment (compound benzoic acid ointment) or crystal violet (although this will turn you purple!).

EYE PROBLEMS Bacterial conjunctivitis (pink eye) is a common infection in Malawi; people who wear contact lenses are most open to this irritating problem. The eyes feel sore and gritty and they will often be stuck together in the mornings. They will need treatment with antibiotic drops or ointment. Lesser eye irritation should settle with bathing in salt water and keeping the eyes shaded. If an insect flies into your eye, extract it with great care, ensuring you do not crush or damage it otherwise you may get a nastily inflamed eye from toxins secreted by the creature.

PRICKLY HEAT A fine pimply rash on the trunk is likely to be heat rash; cool showers, dabbing (not rubbing) dry, and talc will help. Treat the problem by slowing down to a relaxed schedule, wearing only loose, baggy, 100% cotton clothes and sleeping naked under a fan; if it's bad you may need to check into an air-conditioned hotel room for a while.

MENINGITIS This is a particularly nasty disease as it can kill within hours of the first symptoms appearing. The telltale symptoms are a combination of a blinding headache (light sensitivity), a blotchy rash and a high fever. Immunisation protects against the most serious bacterial form of meningitis and the tetravalent vaccine ACWY is recommended for Malawi. Other forms of meningitis exist (usually viral) but there are no vaccines for these. Local papers normally report localised outbreaks.

DANGEROUS ANIMALS

Philip Briggs

The dangers associated with African wild animals are frequently overstated by hunters and others trying to glamorise their way of life. In reality, most wild animals fear us far more than we fear them, and their normal response to seeing a person is to leg it off as quickly as possible. But while the risk posed to tourists by wild animals is very low, accidents do happen, and commonsense should be exercised wherever they are around.

The need for caution is greatest near water, particularly around dusk and dawn, when hippos are out grazing. Responsible for more human fatalities than any other large mammal, hippos are not actively aggressive to humans, but they do panic easily and tend to mow down any person that comes between them and the safety of the water, usually with fatal consequences. Never cross deliberately between a hippo and water, and avoid well vegetated riverbanks and lakeshores in overcast weather or low light unless you are certain no hippos are present. Be aware, too, that any path leading through thick vegetation to an aquatic hippo habitat was most probably created by grazing hippos, so there's a real risk of a heads-on confrontation in a confined channel.

Crocodiles are more dangerous to locals but represent less of a threat to travellers, since they are unlikely to attack outside of their aquatic hunting environment, That means you need to swim in crocodile-infested waters to be at appreciable risk, though it's wise to keep a metre or so from the shore, since a large and hungry individual might occasionally drag in an animal or person from the water's edge. Near a human settlement, any crocodile large enough to attack an adult will most likely have been consigned to its maker by its potential prey, but the rule of thumb is simple: don't bathe in any potential crocodile habitat unless you have reliable local information that it is safe.

There are parts of Malawi where hikers might stumble across an elephant or a buffalo, the most dangerous of Africa's terrestrial herbivores. Elephants almost invariably mock charge and indulge in some hair-raising trumpeting before they attack in earnest. Provided that you back off at the first sign of unease, they seldom take further notice of you. If you see them before they see you, give them a wide berth, bearing in mind they are most likely to attack if surprised at close proximity. If an animal charges you, the safest course of action is to head for the nearest tree and climb it. And should an elephant or buffalo stray close to your campsite or lodge, do suppress any urge to wander closer on foot – it may well react aggressively if surprised!

An elephant is large enough to hurt the occupants of a vehicle, so if it doesn't want your vehicle to pass, back off and wait until it has moved off. Never switch off the engine

A severe headache and fever should make you run to a doctor immediately. There are also other causes of headache and fever; one of which is typhoid, which occurs in travellers to Malawi. Seek medical help if you are ill for more than a few days.

RABIES Rabies is carried by all mammals (beware the village dogs and small monkeys that are used to being fed in the parks) and is passed on to man through a bite, scratch or a lick of an open wound. You must always assume any animal is rabid (unless personally known to you) and seek medical help as soon as possible. In the interim, scrub the wound with soap and bottled/boiled water, then pour on a strong iodine or alcohol solution. This helps stop the rabies virus entering the body and will guard against wound infections, including tetanus.

If you intend to have contact with animals and/or are likely to be more than 24 hours away from medical help, then pre-exposure vaccination is advised. Ideally three doses should be taken over a minimum of three weeks. Contrary to popular belief these vaccinations are relatively painless!

around elephants until you're certain they are relaxed, and avoid allowing your car to be boxed in between an elephant and another vehicle (or boxing in another vehicle yourself). If an elephant does threaten a vehicle in earnest and backing off isn't an option, them revving the engine hard will generally dissuade it from pursuing the contest.

Monkeys, especially vervets and baboons, can become aggressive where they associate people with food. Feeding monkeys is thus highly irresponsible, especially as it may lead to their being shot as vermin. If you join a tour where the driver or guide feeds any primate, tell him not to. Although most monkeys are too small to be more than a nuisance, baboons have killed children and maimed adults with their vicious teeth. Unless trapped, however, their interest will be food, not people, so in the event of a genuine confrontation, throw down the food before the baboon gets too close. If you leave food (especially fruit) in your tent, monkeys might well tear the tent down. Present only in handful of African countries, chimps and gorillas are potentially dangerous, but only likely to be encountered on a guided forest walk, where you should always obey your guide's instructions.

Despite their reputation, large predators generally avoid humans and are only likely to kill accidentally or in self-defence. Lions are arguably the exception, though they seldom attack unprovoked. Of the rest, cheetahs represent no threat to adults, leopards seldom attack unless cornered, and hyenas – though often associated with human settlements and potentially dangerous – are most likely to slink off into the shadows when disturbed. Should you encounter any other large predator on foot, remember that running away will almost certainly trigger its 'chase' instinct and it *will* win the race. Better to stand still and/or back off very slowly, preferably without making eye contact. If (and only if) the animal looks really menacing, then noisy confrontation is probably a better tactic than fleeing. Where large predators are still reasonably common, sleeping in a sealed tent practically guarantees your safety – but don't sleep with your head sticking out or you risk being decapitated through predatorial curiosity, and *never* store meat in the tent.

As for the smaller stuff, venomous snakes and scorpions are present but unobtrusive, though be wary when picking up wood or stones. Snakes generally slither away when they sense the seismic vibrations made by footfall, though be aware that rocky slopes and cliffs are a favoured habitat of the slothful puff adder, which may not move off in such circumstances. Good walking boots protect against the 50% of snakebites that occur below the ankle, and long trousers help deflect bites higher on the leg. Lethal bites are a rarity (see below).

When all's said and done, Africa's most dangerous non-bipedal creature is the malaria-carrying mosquito. Humans, particularly when behind a steering wheel, come a close second!

If you are exposed as described, treatment should be given as soon as possible, but it is never too late to seek help as the incubation period for rabies can be very long. Those who have not been immunised will need a full course of injections together with rabies immunoglobulin (RIG), but this product is expensive (around US$800) and may be hard to come by: another reason why pre-exposure vaccination should be encouraged in travellers who are planning to visit more remote areas.

Tell the doctor if you have had pre-exposure vaccine, as this will change the treatment you receive. And remember that, if you do contract rabies, death from rabies is probably one of the worst ways to go!

SNAKES Snakes rarely attack unless provoked, and bites in travellers are unusual. You are less likely to get bitten if you wear stout shoes and long trousers when in the bush. Most snakes are harmless and even venomous species will dispense venom in only about half of their bites. If bitten, then, you are unlikely to have received venom; keeping this fact in mind may help you to stay calm. Many so-called first-aid techniques do more harm than good: cutting into the wound is harmful; tourniquets are dangerous; suction and electrical inactivation devices do not work. The only treatment is antivenom. In case of a bite which you fear may have been from a venomous snake:

- Try to keep calm – it is likely that no venom has been dispensed
- Prevent movement of the bitten limb by applying a splint
- Keep the bitten limb BELOW heart height to slow the spread of any venom
- If you have a crêpe bandage, bind up as much of the bitten limb as you can, but release the bandage every half hour
- Evacuate to a hospital which has antivenom

And remember:

- NEVER give aspirin; you may offer paracetamol, which is safe
- NEVER cut or suck the wound
- DO NOT apply ice packs
- DO NOT apply potassium permanganate

If the offending snake can be captured without risk of someone else being bitten, take this to the doctor – but beware since even a decapitated head is able to bite.

FURTHER READING

Self-prescribing has its hazards so if you are going anywhere very remote consider taking a health book. For adults there is *Bugs, Bites & Bowels: the Cadogan Guide to Healthy Travel* by Dr Jane Wilson-Howarth; if travelling with the family look at *Your Child Abroad: A Travel Health Guide* by Dr Jane Wilson-Howarth and Dr Matthew Ellis. See page 241.

5

Travelling in Malawi

TOURIST INFORMATION

There are tourist offices in Lilongwe, Blantyre and Mzuzu. Each has incredibly helpful staff, despite having few resources and no apparent funding. The Blantyre office is the best equipped to help visitors with advice and pamphlets and also sells several books useful to visitors. Lilongwe's office has a more limited range. The Mzuzu staff have a superb knowledge of their area, but little in the way of literature. To contact the head office from outside the country, contact the Malawi Department of Tourism, PO Box 402, Blantyre (*01 620902*; e *tourism@malawi.net*).

Tour companies, other travellers and notice boards at various backpacker hostels are often the most useful and up-to-date source of practical travel information.

Before you travel you might look at the various websites and email letters also offering information, eg: www.malawitourism.com, www.go2malawi.com, www.guide2malawi.com, www.tourismmalawi.com, and any of the safari companies listed in this book.

PUBLIC HOLIDAYS

Visitors to Malawi should be alert to the fact that banks, government offices and many shops and businesses close on public holidays, and also that when a holiday falls on a Saturday or Sunday it is taken on the subsequent Monday. Malawi's relatively small Muslim population celebrates the normal Muslim holidays, but this will have no significant practical effect on travellers. In addition to Easter, which falls on a different date every year, the following public holidays are taken in Malawi:

New Year's Day	1 January
John Chilembwe Day	16 January
Martyrs' Day	3 March
Labour Day	1 May
Freedom Day	14 June
Independence Day	6 July
Mothers' Day	Second Monday in October
National Tree Planting Day	Second Monday in December
Christmas Day	25 December
Boxing Day	26 December

GETTING AROUND

INTERNAL FLIGHTS Air Malawi runs domestic flights connecting Lilongwe to Blantyre, Karonga, Mzuzu and Club Makokola on the southern Lake Malawi shore. Several air charter companies operate in Malawi, including Nyika Air

Services, Jakamaka and Executive Air Charters. Regional airlines offering charter and scheduled planes include Nyassa Express, Proflight, Avocet, Star of Africa and Zambian Airways. Any travel agent or tour operator can give further information about these flights, and there are Air Malawi offices in all three main cities.

SELF DRIVE Malawi is easy to drive around. Speed limits on main roads are 80km/h for big trucks, and 90–100km/h for other vehicles, and 60km/h in towns.

There are many car-hire companies operating out of Blantyre and Lilongwe, and some of the more reputable firms are listed in the respective chapters on these cities. If you decide to rent a vehicle, take a good look under the bonnet before you drive off, and check the state of all tyres including the spare. One reader has recommended you bring an aerosol puncture repair kit with you, for added security should you have to drive on your spare tyre on a poor road.

If arriving with your own vehicle, you've probably made sure it's tough and well kitted out, as driving *to* Malawi is worse than driving *around* Malawi. You don't need a 4x4, especially in the dry season, but a robust vehicle with high ground clearance is best.

The state of the roads in mid 2006 was generally very good, with good new tar on many of the main arteries. The worst roads in the country include the new but unfinished Mtakataka–Golomoti road between the M5 and Monkey Bay (the T326 was to connect with this but this road has also spent several years under construction) and the M26 between Karonga and Chitipa. The road up to Livingstonia will probably be a challenge to most vehicles even though its many hairpin bends are currently being concreted. The Rumphi T305 back road to Livingstonia, though stunning, is impassable in the rainy season. The M3 between Zomba and Blantyre is currently too narrow and uneven for the volume of traffic using it. The M10 is due for resurfacing in 2006/7.

Remember though that roads can deteriorate fast – good tarred roads develop horrendous pot-holes with no maintenance and dirt roads become impassable if not graded regularly. Rain washes roads and bridges away, causing delays and worry even if recently repairs and emergency bridges have not taken too long to put up (only days or weeks, not months or years as in the past). This is Africa, not Europe or the States, and it's what you came for. So take care and, if in doubt, ask local advice.

Those who have never before driven in rural Africa will need to adjust their driving style for Malawi. Basically, this means driving more slowly than you might on a similar road in a Western country, and slowing down when you approach pedestrians or cyclists on the road or livestock on the verge. Drunken driving is a serious problem in Malawi, and minibus drivers tend to drive as if they might be drunk even when sober. Be extra alert to vehicles overtaking in tight situations, driving on the wrong side of the road (especially where there are pot-holes), pulling out behind you without warning, and generally behaving as if it's their last day on earth. Don't drive at night – night driving is extremely hazardous, largely because so many vehicles in Malawi don't have functional headlights.

As in most former British colonies, driving is on the left side of the road, an additional adjustment for visitors from North America and mainland Europe. Petrol is widely available and costs US$0.98 per litre. It is, however, blended with ethanol and has a low octane rating. Diesel is now higher in price than petrol at US$1 and is as freely available.

One final tip – generally Malawians expect everyone to be driving from south to north, and position all signs to lodges and places of interest to face south. Frustrating if you're coming from the north.

CYCLING IN MALAWI

Taken from a letter by Wim van Hoom

We found that most parts of Malawi are very suitable for riding a bicycle. Since one of our bikes didn't arrive in Malawi, we had to buy a local mountain bike. This wasn't up to the standard of a European or American bike, but it was adequate and very cheap at around US$100. Generally, a mountain bike will cost a bit more than this (around US$120–150 including rear pannier and mudguards) and you will be able to arrange to sell it back to the shopkeeper at the end of your trip, so there's a good case for buying your bike after you arrive rather than flying one over to Malawi.

For long hauls, bicycles can easily be transported on the roof of a bus or minibus for a small fee, but you can expect minor damage to the paintwork, and should ask for help when you load and unload them. Suitable straps are available in the main bus stations, and we preferred to let a Malawian fasten the bike, because they are more aware of the dos and don'ts of handling baggage.

We did some cycling on surfaced roads, but we preferred not to, especially in the vicinity of large towns, because they can be very busy and some people drive like madmen. Drivers in Malawi expect a cyclist to make way for them by pulling over to the verge, a reflex we hadn't developed, and a habit that wastes time when you are trying to cover a lot of distance.

The dust roads were more interesting and enjoyable, and allow you to explore areas inaccessible to travellers dependent on public transport. We passed through many small villages where travellers are a relative novelty, and were always met with great enthusiasm and hospitality. It was always easy to organise somewhere to pitch a tent, and often local people would help us find food. We normally paid the villagers the equivalent to what we would have paid for a room or meal in a basic local resthouse. The small resthouses along the way were also an unforgettable experience (not least because we regularly bumped our heads against the low door frames!).

The 1:250,000 maps we bought in Lilongwe and Blantyre proved to be excellent for route finding. Contrary to what we had been told (and to our own experiences in other countries), we were never pointed in the wrong direction by somebody who didn't want to 'disappoint' us. It happened more than once that somebody we stopped to ask for directions walked with us to show us a good short cut. The only navigational problem we had was that some village names are incorrect on the maps, but asking for another village in the same direction always solved this.

PUBLIC TRANSPORT AND HITCHING Malawi has a useful network of public transport, and we have always found the buses in particular to be well organised and quick by African standards. The rail network is limited to the south, and it is too slow and unreliable to be a practical alternative to bus transport. In practical terms, much the same can be said of the ferry which plies up and down Lake Malawi every week, but this is certainly worth using if you enjoy boat transport or you want to visit one of the islands which cannot be reached any other way.

Rail The only railway lines in Malawi connect Lilongwe to Blantyre via Salima, Blantyre to Nsanje (near the Mozambican border in the south of the country) via Luchenza, and Liwonde to Nayuchi (on the Mozambican border northeast of Blantyre). Services are very slow, overcrowded and erratic, and offer no practical advantages over road transport. Some travellers use the train east from Liwonde to cross into Mozambique (see *Chapter 3, Crossing to Mozambique*, page 51).

Lake ferry The MV *Ilala* is a popular means of travelling around the lake and to Likoma and Chizumulu islands; see *Chapter 11, The Lake Ferry and the Islands*, pages 157–9, for details. Constantly threatened with unseaworthy certification it remains in service to date, with the MV *Mtendere* as backup.

Buses There are four main types of bus travel in Malawi. The minibuses work as *matolas* (effectively shared taxis) and leave only when full from the minibus stations which are often close to the main bus depots. The three main line bus services are run by Shire Bus Lines; the Coachline and express services, and the stop-everywhere country service. There is a world of difference between the different services. There are also some private bus companies between major routes. Shire have offices in most major towns.

Coachline is luxurious travelling with air conditioning, waitresses bringing a snack and a cold drink, seatbelts and a toilet on board. It's a fast efficient service between Lilongwe and Blantyre, running four-times daily non-stop at US$18 per person, and taking little more than three hours in either direction. There is also a daily coach service between Lilongwe and Mzuzu, and international services connecting Blantyre to Johannesburg (South Africa) via Harare (Zimbabwe), while other coach companies cover routes to Zambia, Tanzania and Kenya. They leave from the Capital Hotel, the Mzuzu Hotel and Ryalls Hotel, stopping at the normal bus station before leaving town. It is advisable to check current departure times in advance, when you can also reserve or buy your tickets.

By African standards, bus travel in Malawi can be an unqualified pleasure, provided you stick to the Coachline and express services. Buses are generally well maintained and driven with a relatively high level of sobriety, and most main roads are in good condition. Even on slower routes, you can expect Express buses to cover between 40km and 50km per hour. Some routes are much quicker, for instance the express bus between Lilongwe and Blantyre can take as little as four hours to cover 311km. Express buses are inexpensive (in 2006, fares were typically in the region of US$4 per 40–50km) and overcharging tourists is most unusual. Express buses almost always work on fixed departure times, as opposed to the fill-up-and-go system that is common in some other African countries, so it's always advisable to ask about your next day's travel in advance.

Express buses covering the 311km between Lilongwe and Blantyre stop only at Dedza, Ntcheu, Balaka, Liwonde and Zomba, and typically they take four to five hours and cost US$8. Other useful Express services include Lilongwe to Karonga (via Kasungu, Mzimba, Chikengawa, Mzuzu, Rumphi and Chilumba), Nkhata Bay to Blantyre (via Chintheche, Nkhotakota and Salima), Blantyre to Mulanje (via Thyolo) and Blantyre to Monkey Bay (via Zomba, Liwonde and Mangochi). As a rule, the Express buses are fast and efficient, but they do sometimes break down or suffer from problems that slow them down. A country (or 'local') bus may come to the rescue when an Express bus covering the same route breaks down, at which point you have to accept that it's not your day and that you've effectively paid an Express bus fare to be on a country bus.

Shire Bus Company country buses follow the same routes as Express buses, as well as several more obscure routes, but they are much slower because they stop at every bus stage (there's a stage every 2km or so in some parts of the country). As a rule of thumb, expect a country bus to take twice as long as an Express bus covering the same route. The difference in timing between Express and country buses is not normally significant over short distances, so my policy when hopping between nearby places was simply to take the first bus that left. Over longer distances, I'd wait for an Express bus wherever possible. Further details of country bus routes are given in the *Getting around* and *Getting there and away* sections throughout the regional part of this guide.

An increasing number of private buses operate main routes through Malawi. Based on our experience, these are generally even slower than country buses, stopping wherever anybody wants them to.

As a final note, a few people have told me horror stories about slow bus rides and breakdowns in Malawi, and some have moaned that this and other guides to Malawi haven't prepared them for this happening. Our general experience has been that buses are reliable in Malawi, but things can go wrong. Short of adding the clause 'but it could take longer if the vehicle breaks down' after every bus timing, there's not much that any travel guide can do about it.

On most routes in Malawi, and especially where there is no official public transport, bus services are replaced or supplemented by an informal *matola* system of paid lifts. The majority of *matola* vehicles are minibuses, which cover a route for the specific purpose of carrying passengers, making them the Malawian equivalent of the *matatu* and shared taxi transport you find elsewhere in Africa. *Matola* lifts may also come from private individuals who want to make a bit of extra cash from a journey that they're undertaking anyway. In both cases, there is normally a fixed fare for *matola* rides along any given route, and on routes where there are buses, this is generally the same as the bus fare. The main advantage of a *matola* lift is not that it is cheaper than a bus, but that you will get to your destination more quickly. In my opinion, this is outweighed by the reality that many private vehicles are in poor repair and minibuses in particular are frequently driven by drunken lunatics. Our policy in Malawi and elsewhere in Africa is to use buses where we can, and to hop in the death traps only where we have no other option.

Hitching Hitchhiking is generally slow in Malawi and now not advisable, and in any case, many of the lifts you will be offered will expect payment. I met a few travellers who were quite indignant about this, so I should clarify that paying for lifts is the accepted custom in Malawi. The line between hitching and *matola* rides is at best blurred, and it is reasonable to expect that practically any lift you get with a Malawian will be on a paying basis.

Unless it's a point of pride that you hitch everywhere, the sensible policy in Malawi is to flag down whatever vehicle passes your way, take the odd free lift when fortune favours you, but otherwise be prepared to pay.

$ MONEY AND BUDGETING

The unit of currency is the Malawi kwacha, divided into 100 tambala. Notes are printed in denominations of MK500, MK200, MK100, MK50, MK20, MK10 and MK5, while smaller denominations are coins only. Coins are, however, seldom used. The rate of exchange to major international currencies has dropped steadily in recent years; in mid 2006, the rate against the US dollar was approximately US$1 = MK140.

FOREIGN EXCHANGE ATMs have reached Malawi, so it is now easy to withdraw money on both Visa and MasterCard outside National Bank offices. Other banks may soon follow suit. Note, however, that National Bank branches are not in every town, and that there are often long queues. Other bank cards can be used at the foreign exchange desks of most banks.

Foreign currency can be converted to kwachas at any branch of Stanbic Bank, First Merchant Bank or National Bank of Malawi, NBS Bank as well as at many upmarket hotels and at any of several private bureaux de change (generally called forex bureaux) in Lilongwe or Blantyre. The most widely recognised international currency is the US dollar, followed by the South African rand and British pound sterling, but most major currencies will be accepted by banks. Banks are open Monday–Friday 08.00–15:00, Saturday 08.00–11.00; they are closed on Sundays and public holidays.

Changing money is generally a reasonably swift and straightforward transaction in Lilongwe, Blantyre and other large towns such as Mzuzu, Mangochi and Zomba. It may be more tedious in small towns, especially those which see few tourists. It is important to note that there are no facilities for foreign exchange (not even a black market) in many popular tourist spots, most notably Nkhata Bay, Cape Maclear and Monkey Bay, so it's advisable to change what you expect you'll need while you're still in a large town. In any case, the best exchange rates are generally available in Lilongwe and Blantyre. As a rule, private forex bureaux offer a better rate than upmarket hotels and banks. This does vary, however, and you may come across forex bureaux that offer very poor rates, so it's worth shopping around, especially when you want to change a large sum. When comparing rates, allow for the commission that is charged by banks but not by forex bureaux and hotels.

There are scarcely any black-market street touts in Malawi (I have never been approached apart from at border posts, though apparently there are still a few furtive money changers around) and even upmarket hotels may be reluctant to change money for non-residents, so plan your finances carefully.

PRICES QUOTED IN THIS BOOK With a handful of exceptions, mostly some of the upmarket hotels, everything from national park fees to meals in upmarket restaurants can be paid for in local currency. Nevertheless, given the instability of African currencies in general and the devaluation of the kwacha in particular, it is more reliable in the long term to quote prices in the US dollar equivalent. Most mid- to top-range hotels and safari companies base accommodation prices on the dollar (then converted to kwacha) whereas restaurant meals are quoted in kwacha. For this edition, I've used an approximate exchange rate of US$1 to MK150, and rounded up where necessary.

Prices quoted in this book were collected in mid 2006, and may be subject to inflation during the lifespan of this edition.

Here are some supermarket prices of common commodities, but please note that prices vary:

Bread, loaf	US$0.45
Rice, 1kg	US$0.85
Corned beef, can	US$2.50
Mangos (with seasonal price variation)	US$0.25–75
Beer, 375ml bottle	US$0.45
Soft drink	US$0.40
Bottled water, 1 litre	US$0.75
Petrol, 1 litre	US$0.98
Diesel, 1 litre	US$1.00

Some of Malawi's best chips are from roadside stalls. Typically chips and cabbage relish (delicious!) will cost US$0.40, or US$0.80 with a small piece of chicken, sprinkled with salt and *piri-piri*. Freshly cooked gizzards or kidneys, as well as goat and beef, are often available at the market.

BARGAINING AND OVERCHARGING Tourists to Africa may sometimes need to bargain over prices, but this need is often exaggerated by guidebooks and travellers. In Malawi, there are very few situations where bargaining is necessary. Hotels, restaurants, supermarkets and buses charge fixed prices, and cases of overcharging are too unusual for it to be worth challenging a price unless it is blatantly ridiculous.

The main instance where bargaining is essential is when buying curios. What should be understood, however, is that the fact a curio seller is open to negotiation does not mean that you were initially being overcharged or ripped off. Curio sellers will generally quote a price knowing full well that you are going to bargain it down – they'd probably be startled if you didn't – and it is not necessary to respond aggressively or in an accusatory manner. It is impossible to say by how much you should bargain the initial price down (some people say that you should offer half the asking price and be prepared to settle at around two-thirds, but my experience is that curio sellers are far more whimsical than such advice suggests). The sensible approach, if you want to get a feel for prices, is to ask the price of similar items at a few different stalls before you actually contemplate buying anything.

Even when buying curios, it is possible to take bargaining too far. In Nkhotakota, I watched two travellers bargain with a Malawian who was selling a couple of statues he had almost certainly carved himself. The initial price asked (around US$1) was not unreasonable and the Malawian eventually settled on a much lower price. Still, the travellers weren't happy and they spent a full quarter of an hour beating him down by a further kwacha. It was evident to me that the carver's reluctant agreement to sell the statue at the lower price was motivated by desperation for cash. When dealing with individuals, as opposed to large curio stalls, I don't think it hurts to see the situation for what it is (somebody trying to scrape a living in difficult circumstances) and to be a little generous in your dealings.

It is normal for Africans to negotiate prices for market produce, though less so in Malawi than in most African countries. My experience in markets outside Lilongwe and Blantyre is that I was normally asked the going rate straight off. This doesn't mean you can't bargain prices down a little, but I would query whether it is really worth the effort – the general mentality in Malawi (unlike that in some other African countries) is not to overcharge tourists, and it seems appropriate to respond to this by being reasonably trusting.

Malawian hotels, like those in so many other countries these days, have a local residents' rate, a non-residents' rate and, sometimes, an in-between one for residents of other African countries. I found that these rates are often negotiable, especially if the hotel is almost empty.

ACCOMMODATION

Detailed accommodation listings for specific places of interest are given in the regional part of the guide, but the following overview should help readers to be prepared for what to expect.

HIGH-CLASS HOTELS The hotel and tourism industry has boomed in recent years, there are now plenty of high-quality holiday hotels and resorts as well as high-class tourism and business hotels. There are great differences in price between them, which sometimes is not always indicative of the standard they offer. For the classiest tourist hotels in the country (about 30 of them) the best are shown on www.malawitourism.com and are listed throughout this book. All the main travel agencies in Malawi (see page 43) will book into these lodges. All high-class hotels accept the major credit cards.

MID RANGE In most larger towns, you'll find one or two motels which offer self-contained rooms with hot showers for around US$10–20 (sometimes a lot cheaper). All the way along the Lake Malawi shore, there are lodges and resorts with rooms of a similar standard and at a similar price to motels in towns though sometimes higher if including breakfast and dinner (US$20–50). These are often much more geared to Western aesthetics.

CHEAPER ACCOMMODATION There are now affordable backpacker hostels and lodges in most of Malawi's main tourist destinations, including the cities and major towns, offering accommodation for US$3–8. Most of them are owned or managed by former travellers and overland truck drivers. Among the more popular hostels are Doogle's in Blantyre and Kiboko in Lilongwe. There are also many backpacker-oriented hostels and resorts along the length of the Lake Malawi shore. So rapidly have these places sprouted up that a great many backpackers now manage to travel through Malawi using them exclusively. Most of these places offer a combination of private rooms and dormitories for around US$5 per person.

In the towns, there is usually a choice of private resthouses aimed primarily at the local market. These used to be the only choice, and have declined in standard over recent years. Typically, such resthouses offer cell-like rooms for around US$2–4, and as a rule they are rather scruffy and run-down, though perhaps no more so than similar accommodation elsewhere in Africa. Many local resthouses double as brothels, renting rooms not only by the night, but also by the hour (under the delightful euphemism of bed-resting). That said, a bit of grime and noise aside, there is no reason why travellers should have any qualms about staying in local resthouses: the risk of theft or catching sanitation-related diseases is negligible.

CAMPING Almost every national park, backpackers' hostel and lakeshore resort in Malawi allows camping, typically at a cost of around US$2–4 per person.

PRICES AND TERMS

AI all-inclusive: breakfast, lunch, dinner, snacks and drinks are included in the room rate. Usually available only as part of a package at a resort hotel.
FB full board: breakfast, lunch and dinner are included in the room rate.
HB half board: breakfast and dinner are included in the room rate.
BB bed and breakfast is included in the room rate.
s/c self-contained room (with en-suite bathroom).

EATING

The staple diet in Malawi is *nsima*, a stiff porridge made from pounded maize meal boiled in water. Most local people do not feel they have eaten unless they have had a couple of lumps of *nsima*. *Nsima* will be familiar to visitors from east Africa under the name of *ugali*, and to people from southern Africa as *mieliemeal*. Few travellers develop a taste for *nsima*, so it is fortunate that most local restaurants also serve rice and potato chips (or occasionally cassava or sweet potato chips).

RESTAURANTS At tourist-class hotels and restaurants in the major towns, you can eat food that is of international standards at a very reasonable price – there are few upmarket restaurants in Malawi where you can't eat well for under US$8 for a main course. Many of the resorts, lodges and forest lodges also run a restaurant service. There is a marked improvement in the range and quality of food available in Malawi's tourist destinations.

Otherwise, eating out in Malawi is a predictable and somewhat dull affair. The good thing about this is that meals are very inexpensive (at a local restaurant you'll rarely pay more than US$3), the bad thing that food is generally very bland and there is little in the way of variety.

Restaurants serve *nsima* or rice with a small serving of stew. This is most often made with chicken (*mkuku*) or beef (*nyama ngombe*). If you are hungry, you can ask for an extra serving of stew, though this will often double the price of the meal. Along with the meat stew, you will often get a sharp-tasting dollop of stewed cassava or pumpkin leaves (*chisisito*), or a heap of stewed beans.

Along the lake and in some larger towns, the monotony of bland chicken and beef stews is broken by fresh fish (*nsomba*), which may be served either in a stew or else fried whole. Popular fish include *chambo* (a type of tilapia), *kampango* (a type of catfish) and *mpasa* (a large cichlid with dark flesh that is often referred to as lake salmon). The most widely available fish in Malawi is *usipa*, a tiny fish which is generally sun-dried after it is caught. Few visitors to Malawi like the bitter taste of *usipa*.

COOKING FOR YOURSELF The alternative to eating at restaurants is to put together your own meals at markets and supermarkets. The variety of foodstuffs you can buy varies from season to season and from town to town, and sudden shortages of items which are normally readily available are to be expected. In most towns, you can buy fresh bread at the People's or Superette or other supermarkets, or at a bakery if you're lucky. Supermarkets also normally stock a variety of spreads: the locally manufactured jams are generally abysmal, but the peanut butter and honey are good, and you can also buy small sachets of Stork margarine. Other ready-to-eat food you can buy in most supermarkets includes yoghurt, potato crisps, biscuits and sometimes cheese and cold meat.

Fruits and vegetables are best bought at markets, where they are very cheap. Potatoes, onions, tomatoes, bananas, sugar cane and some citrus fruits are available in most markets around the country. In larger towns and in agricultural areas a much wider selection of fruits and vegetables is available, for instance avocados, peas and beans, paw-paws, mangoes, coconuts and pineapples.

At most markets you can buy freshly fried potato chips for next to nothing. It is customary to try a couple of chips before you buy: do so, as sometimes they are very greasy. Grilled meat kebabs and chicken pieces are also cheap and tasty.

Fresh meat is very cheap in Malawi. A kilogram of beef costs around US$2–3 at most markets, and a whole chicken costs around US$4–5 depending on its size. Many PTC supermarkets sell frozen chickens and sausages, while supermarkets in larger towns sell high-grade meat at very reasonable prices (eg: fillet steak at around US$5/kg). A limited range of tinned goods (typically baked beans, soups and vegetables) is also available.

For hikers, packet soups are about the only dehydrated meals that are available throughout Malawi. I occasionally saw packets of dehydrated soya mince, which is tastier than the soups and makes for a more substantial meal. Dried staples such as rice, maize meal and pasta can be bought in supermarkets and markets.

DRINKING

Brand-name soft drinks such as Pepsi, Coca-Cola and Fanta are widely available in Malawi and cheap by international standards. If the fizzy stuff doesn't appeal, you can buy imported South African fruit juices at most large supermarkets. Frozen fruit squashes are sold everywhere in Malawi for a few *tambala*; they're very sweet but otherwise quite refreshing on long walks and bus trips. Tap water is generally safe to drink in towns, providing the chlorine hasn't run out, but bottled mineral water is available if you prefer not to take the risk.

Traditional African beer is made of fermented maize or millet. It is brewed in villages for private consumption, and also brewed commercially to be sold in litre cartons. The most popular brand of traditional beer is the wonderfully titled Chibuku Shake-Shake (the latter half of the name refers to the need to shake the carton before opening), and special Chibuku bars can be found in most towns and villages. A carton of Chibuku is very cheap and, with its gruel-like texture, surprisingly rich in nutrients when compared with most alcoholic drinks. Unfortunately, African beer is something of an acquired taste: most travellers can't stand it.

The most favoured drinks are the MGT, the Green and the Brown. An MGT is a Malawi Gin and Tonic, with neither the gin nor the tonic being quite what you're used to, but without the depressing effect of real gin.

The Carlsberg 'green' is the most popular drink in the country (after Chibuku) and all the Carlsberg beers are inexpensive. Most visitors to Malawi settle on a Green as first choice (named, like most Malawian beers, after the colour of its label), a light lager with 5% alcoholic content or the Brown which has a sweeter taste. A Carlsberg beer which is proving popular is called Kuche Kuche (which means 'all night long'). It has a lower alcohol content of 3.7%, is sold in 500ml bottles and is cheaper than Green. There is now also Carlsberg Light at only 2.4%. Other visitors prefer the stronger Carlsberg Special Brew.

Spirits such as cane, brandy and gin are manufactured locally, while a good variety of imported spirits is available in supermarkets and better bars.

Wines are widely available in hotels, bars and supermarkets at high import prices.

HASSLES

CRIME In 1995, when the first edition of this guide was researched, Malawi was one of the friendliest and most crime-free countries in Africa. It may remain the friendliest, but now, like anywhere else in the world, travellers need to be alert to the risk of armed crime and casual theft.

It is difficult to strike the right balance when discussing crime in a country such as Malawi. I firmly believe that an analytical understanding of how and where you are most likely to become a victim of crime in any given country serves not only to help you prevent being becoming a victim yourself, but also – and no less important – lets you relax in situations where crime really isn't a serious concern. It is important to recognise that African cultures are inherently honest, more so perhaps than ours, and that to the average Malawian theft is unspeakably wrong, to the extent that petty thieves are regularly killed by mob justice. The reason why tourists are often robbed is not because Malawi has a large criminal element, but because *wazungu* (white person, or foreigner) are easily identified as targets (and that includes backpackers, who habitually tell Africans that they are 'poor' travellers, oblivious to the simple truth that their extended travels are beyond the financial reach of practically every Malawian they meet, and that their backpack alone probably cost more money than would pass through the hands of many Malawians in a year). The point is that small-town and rural Malawi remains safe for travel, because Malawians in general wouldn't think of robbing a tourist, and that crime is largely restricted to large towns (where petty thieves often work the markets and bus stations targeting locals and tourists alike) and at a handful of places where large numbers of tourists congregate.

Unlike most African countries, crime against tourists doesn't yet seem to be a major problem in urban areas. Residents of Lilongwe and Blantyre say there has been a notable rise in house burglary and car hijacking in these cities, and the market area of Lilongwe is definitely dodgy. Otherwise, everybody we spoke to agreed that there was no significant risk attached to walking around the city centres by day, and we felt perfectly comfortable doing so. This will probably change, however, so ask local advice, and don't tempt fate by wandering alone along unlit streets or going out at night with more money than you need. In African cities generally, tourists are robbed and hassled on the streets far more often than expatriates; you are far less likely to draw attention by wearing trousers or a skirt with a button-up shirt or blouse than by donning the traveller 'uniform' of shorts and a T-shirt. And if you can, leave that give-away daypack in your hotel room – when we spend a few days in one African city, we are repeatedly struck by how much more hassle we attract on the days when we need to carry a daypack. Finally, when in doubt, *use a taxi* – they are very cheap in the cities.

In Malawi, crime against tourists occurs mostly in a few particular 'trouble spots' in the cities and along the lakeshore. The pattern appears to be a sudden outbreak of mugging and snatch thefts in one particular resort, followed by a quiet period, indicating that these robberies are largely the work of one particular gang which is eventually arrested or moves on. Lilongwe, Blantyre, Nkhata Bay, Cape Maclear and Salima have all experienced problems of this sort in the last year or two, so your best course of action is to be cautious when you first arrive at one of these places, and to ask local advice once you are settled in. Camping wild on parts of the lakeshore is no longer advisable anywhere in Malawi, and we've heard of several instances of tents being broken into at 'proper' campsites.

You should be cautious of people who befriend you on buses and offer you food or drink, because it appears that the practice of doping travellers in this manner has spread into Malawi. It's worth noting that con tricks are most likely to be perpetrated by a smartly dressed, smooth-talking guy who can easily build up a rapport with a traveller.

During our travels in Malawi, we've not heard of many incidents of casual theft, bag snatching and pickpocketing, but it does happen. Casual theft of this sort is largely confined to busy markets and bus stations, where you should keep a close watch on your possessions at all times and avoid having valuables or large amounts of money loose in your daypack or pocket. In any public area, it is advisable to carry all your valuables and the bulk of your money in a *hidden* money-belt. In order not to show your money-belt in public, remember to keep whatever spare cash you are likely to need elsewhere on your person. It is also a good idea to keep a small amount of hard currency hidden away somewhere in your luggage so that you have something to fall back on if your money-belt is stolen.

Many travellers carry their money-belt on their person at all times, even when they walk around a city at night. I must admit that I find this strange behaviour, and where I have the choice I generally feel safer leaving my valuables in a locked room than carrying them on me. Why? Because over the years I've been travelling in Africa, I've met hundreds of people who've been mugged or had their valuables snatched on the streets or on a beach, but I've heard of very few instances of a locked room being broken into. Obviously, an element of judgement comes into this, and if a room strikes me as being insecure or the hotel has a bad reputation, then I wouldn't leave anything of importance in it. When you leave stuff in a room, do remember to check that the windows are sealed and the door is properly locked. One factor to be considered here is that some travellers' cheque companies will not refund cheques which were stolen from a room. Finally, don't bring any jewellery of financial or sentimental value with you.

The last thing I would want is for the above to strike terror or evoke paranoia in travellers to Malawi. Malawi remains a remarkably friendly and honest country, but anybody can be unlucky when it comes to crime. On the whole, so long as you conduct yourself sensibly and listen to local advice, you have little to fear. What most often gets travellers into trouble is one moment of recklessness – walking around Nkhata Bay at night with a money-belt on, wandering around Lilongwe market with a daypack dangling off your shoulder, dithering in a city bus station with a map in your hand and puzzled expression on your face, arriving in a city at night and not using a taxi to get to a hotel. Our policy, developed over years of African travel, is to focus our energy on recognising high-risk situations, particularly those where our valuables are at stake, and doing all we can to avoid them. The rest of the time, we don't worry about crime!

WOMEN TRAVELLERS Sub-equatorial Africa as a whole is probably one of the safest places in the world for women to travel solo. Malawi in particular poses few, if any, risks specific to female travellers, provided that you apply the same sort of common sense you would at home. Women travelling alone may have to put up with some unwanted flirtation and the odd direct proposition, especially if you mingle with Malawians in bars, but a firm 'no' should defuse any potentially unpleasant situation. Men in Malawi probably constitute less of a sexual hassle than men in many Western countries, and for that matter than other male travellers.

Years ago, it was forbidden for women to wear trousers or short skirts in Malawi, and even today most Malawian women dress conservatively. We're not certain how much Malawians expect these dress customs to apply to tourists. Some foreigners working in Malawi feel that it would give offence for a woman to walk around in anything but a skirt or sarong. We tend towards the unfashionable but less patronising view that most Malawians, certainly those who are used to tourists, have better things to worry about than how we choose to dress ourselves. On the other hand, it would be insensitive for a woman traveller to wear shorts or a revealing top in an area where there is a strong Muslim presence, or in villages where tourists are still relatively unusual. The difference is that to many Africans (and to Muslims in particular), exposing your knees or shoulders is indecent and offensive, in much the same way as displaying your breasts publicly would be in a Western society. By contrast, wearing trousers may go against custom, and may even raise a few eyebrows where people are unused to seeing it, but it doesn't amount to indecent exposure.

Any women readers (or men, for that matter) who are concerned about travelling alone in Malawi, but who can't find a travel companion, might be reassured by the thought that there are plenty of places in Malawi where it will be easy to meet with other travellers. You'll find plenty of kindred spirits at the hostels in Blantyre and Lilongwe, or at any of the lakeshore resorts, and there's a lot to be said for hooking up with people along the way – better, by far, than making an advance commitment to travelling with somebody who you don't know well enough to be sure they'll be a suitable travel companion.

BRIBERY, BUREAUCRACY AND THE LAW For all you hear about the subject, bribery is not the problem for travellers that it's often made out to be. The travellers who are most often asked for bribes are those with private transport; and even they only have a major problem at some borders and from traffic police in some countries (notably Mozambique and Kenya). If you are travelling on public transport or as part of a tour, or even if you are driving within Malawi, I wouldn't give the question of bribery serious thought.

There is a tendency to portray African bureaucrats as difficult and inefficient in their dealings with tourists. As a rule, this reputation says more about Western prejudices that it does about Malawi. Sure, you come across the odd unhelpful official, but then such is the nature of the beast everywhere in the world. The vast majority of officials in the African countries I've visited have been courteous and helpful in their dealings with tourists, often to a degree that is almost embarrassing. In Malawi, I encountered nothing but friendliness from almost every government official I had dealings with, whether they were border officials, policemen or game reserve staff. This, I can assure you, is far more than most African visitors to Europe will experience from officialdom.

A factor in determining the response you receive from African officials will be your own attitude. If you walk into every official encounter with an aggressive, paranoid approach, you are quite likely to kindle the feeling held by many Africans that Europeans are arrogant and offhand in their dealings with other races. Instead, smile, try to be friendly and patient, accept that the person to whom you are talking does not speak English as a first language and may thus have difficulty following everything you say. Treat people with respect rather than disdain, and they'll tend to treat you in the same way.

From a traveller's point of view, then, the simple truth about dealing with the law in Malawi is that so long as you don't break it, you're highly unlikely to fall foul of it or to have to worry about it. It should be emphasised, however, that it is highly illegal to possess or smoke marijuana (*chamba*), and that the government has recently cracked down on travellers who smoke the stuff by raiding several backpacker hostels and placing police informants to act as dealers. Very few hostels risk allowing you to smoke openly and the reality is that travellers who are caught in the act or in possession risk at best paying a hefty 'fine' or being deported, at worst being prosecuted and jailed. Travellers who carry marijuana across international borders, no matter what their intention, are, legally speaking, drug smugglers, in Africa as elsewhere, and they will be treated as such if they are caught.

As is the case in many African countries, homosexuality is officially illegal in Malawi, but not something that local people are greatly aware of. It would take an act of overt exhibitionism for it ever to become an issue for travellers.

CURIOS

Malawi is known as one of the best places in southern Africa for curios, in terms of both price and quality, and the cheap surface mail from Malawi makes shipping out your purchases a viable prospect. Among the more popular items are polished soapstone carvings, malachite jewellery, and a wide range of basketwork and pottery items. But Malawi is best known for its hardwood carvings, and for the carved wooden chairs which dominate the stalls in the larger cities. Just remember though: every purchase has contributed to the demise of a rare hardwood tree.

Though curios cannot be described as expensive anywhere in Malawi, they are generally cheapest away from Blantyre, Lilongwe and the more popular lakeshore resorts. You must expect to bargain over prices, and should also be aware that many curio sellers will be as happy to barter their wares against used clothing.

Three places that have been recommended as being particularly good value are the stalls at the Mangochi turn-off 3km from Liwonde town, which specialise in carvings, the long line of stalls at Salima, and the stalls 1km from Machinga towards Liwonde, which are good for chairs. There are also good curio stalls at Nkopola and Nkhata Bay and near to Mua Mission on the Monkey Bay turn-off.

Mt Mulanje in the southern region of Malawi is home to the endemic Mulanje cedar, grows naturally only on the high-altitude plateaux of Mulanje. From the wood of this tree great cedar boxes are made, renowned in the whole of Malawi for their distinct, but pleasant smell and light colour – but a bit heavy for a rucksack...

MEDIA AND COMMUNICATIONS

EMAIL Most towns and many of the hotels, lodges and backpackers' hostels now offer email. There is never any difficulty in finding a small internet service in the towns, and as they tend to open and shut with some frequency, individual cafés are not listed in this book. The price per minute varies enormously, with higher prices in the more upmarket hotels. It is definitely worth asking before you start whether it is a high-speed connection or not. Broadband arrived in Malawi in 2006, so over the next few years we can expect to see even faster change in this market. There is now a number of wireless hotspots in cafés, restaurants and lodges in the cities provided by Skyband.

POST International post in and out of Malawi is slow and unreliable: allow at least three weeks for mail to get through. Mail out of Malawi is very cheap, particularly surface mail, which makes it an excellent place from where to post curios.

For express courier and parcel services, DHL is well represented in Malawi.

TELEPHONE All telephone numbers in Malawi have eight digits and, presumably because there are so few phones in the country, there are no area codes. The international dialling code for Malawi is +265. Small it may be, but Malawi's telephone service is reasonably efficient by African standards, and lines are generally clear, though more unreliable during the rains. Phone booths, some of which actually work, can be found outside most post offices. More convenient are the many small phone booths along most roads in towns where you can pay by the minute. If you see anyone sitting on a bench with a phone in her hand, it's likely to be a phone booth.

If you are spending anything more than a week in Malawi it is definitely worth buying a local SIM card (US$5). Top-up cards can then be bought from street vendors, petrol stations and most supermarkets. The mobile phone network in Malawi is operated by two companies – Telkom carries the prefix digits 08 and Celtel uses 09. International roaming with your mobile phone from home is also possible.

Please note that telephone numbers in Blantyre city centre changed from 016 to 018 in 2006; telephone lines further out of town remain as 016.

It is also worth mentioning that mobile (cell) phone numbers are more likely to change than other numbers; these are the 08 and 09 numbers listed in this guide. If the number is correct, however, they can be more reliable than land lines.

NEWSPAPERS Malawi has a free press, and a number of newspapers and magazines are available, most of which are printed in English, and, it must be said, are fascinating for their coverage of local news, politics and local sport. The newspapers most widely available are *The Nation* and *The Chronicle*; *The Nation* is also available online (*www.nationmalawi.com*).

TELEVISION There is an erratic state television service in Malawi, MTV. The televisions found in hotels and in private homes pick up satellite broadcasts from South Africa, including Sky-TV and CNN, mostly advertised as DSTV.

ELECTRICITY

Malawi uses the British three square-pin plug and a 240 volt supply, so take adapters and transformers if necessary.

COMMUNICATING WITH MALAWIANS

As many as 40 different Bantu languages are spoken in Malawi. Of these, Chichewa has become the *lingua franca* of the southern and central regions, a role which is usurped by Chitumbuka in the northern region. Chichewa is the national language.

The official language of Malawi is English. Most education takes place in the official language, and so a high proportion of urban Malawians speak fair English. Even in rural areas, it is most unusual to hit the sort of situation you might in some other African countries where nobody speaks a word of English. For this reason, unless you plan on spending a long time in Malawi, there is very little motivation to learn local languages. That said, it is polite to know the basic greetings and to be able to respond to them, and it is always true that even the clumsiest attempt to speak a local language will go a long way to making friends in Africa. However many words you learn, the most current language is always going to be smiles and laughter.

BANTU LANGUAGES Chichewa is classified as a Bantu language, a linguistic group that had its origin in west Africa about 2,000 years ago, and which now includes practically every language spoken in sub-equatorial Africa. Bantu languages share a common pronunciation and grammar, and many have closely related vocabularies – if you speak one Bantu language, be it Swahili, Shona or Zulu, you will recognise many words that are similar or identical in Chichewa. For pronunciation and phrases, see *Appendix 1, Language*, page 237.

SPEAKING ENGLISH TO MALAWIANS The very first thing in every conversation is an exchange of polite greetings, however much of a rush you think you are in. 'Hello, how are you?' must be responded to and the question asked of the other person.

Then it's important to remember that not all Malawians are fluent in English; to many it's a difficult second language. For most non-fluent Malawians, the wish to please overrides all problems of comprehension, and your every question will be answered affirmatively, so it's important to phrase your questions well.

If you have ever attempted to speak a foreign language, you will probably have noticed that your skill at communicating is largely dependent on the imagination and empathy of the person you are speaking to. The moment some people realise you speak a few words of their language, they will speak to you as if you are fluent and make you feel thoroughly hopeless. Other people will take care to speak slowly and to stick to common words, and as a result you feel like you're making real progress. The same sort of thing applies in reverse: when you speak English to somebody who knows it only as a second language, the ease of communication will to a large extent reflect your own ability to adapt your use of English to the situation.

The standard of English spoken in Malawi is much higher than in most African countries. Many educated Malawians speak English fluently and grammatically. Nevertheless, the majority of Malawians who speak English have a relatively small vocabulary, use many words idiosyncratically, and tend to use phrasings and pronunciations which are obviously derived from Bantu grammar and will add in extra vowels for poetic effect. Because so much English is spoken in Malawi, it is arguable that adjusting your use of English to reflect Malawian norms will prove to be a more important communication skill than would picking up a few phrases of Chichewa. The first and most obvious rule when speaking English to Malawians is to talk slowly and clearly.

Listen to how Malawians pronounce words. Often, they will use Bantu vowel sounds even when speaking English (just as many English speakers use English

MY GAP YEAR AT ST THERESA PRIVATE SCHOOL

Pete Bexton

I was sent to Malawi by a gap-year organisation called Project Trust, which specialises in 12-month placements. I was working as a volunteer teacher at St Theresa Primary School in Chiwembe, a township on the outskirts of Blantyre. The school was set up by Mrs Kotokwa, a local Malawian, in 1994. Initially she rented a single room in a decrepit government building, where she had three pupils in different classes and only two teachers – herself and one other. As can be imagined, this was a task in itself; however, after much dedication, she now owns her own land and buildings. Over 300 pupils attend the school and she has 20 trained teachers working alongside her. Although incomplete due to lack of funds, St Theresa is improving greatly because of the dedication and perseverance of both Mrs Kotokwa and the teachers.

Government schools in Malawi are free, but the standard of education is very poor and classes are grossly overcrowded. Classes may consist of up to 150 pupils, with a maximum of two teachers in charge. At present the school day lasts from 07.30 to 15.00, and consists of nine lessons, a morning break and a lunch break. St Theresa is a private school, so classes range from nursery to Standard 8, equivalent to an English primary school. Children's ages range from three years up to 16 or 17; this is because children have to resit classes if they fail. Occasionally a child will miss a year's schooling to help support his or her family. As with an English school, St Theresa's pupils study English, mathematics, French, religious education, general studies, science and drawing. Although the national language is Chichewa, all subjects are taught in English. Since Malawi is such a poor country, and the school has very limited funds, the children have no bought toys. Sports equipment is non-existent and textbooks are old, incomplete and few and far between. However, the children are used to their lack of resources and are able to make games using both balls and rope made out of plastic bags. Although their games are simple, they find great enjoyment in them, and they are very innovative when they need a new pastime.

In Malawi, the next stage of education after primary school is secondary school. To get to secondary school, the children must pass the General Certificate of Education (GCE) at the end of Standard 8. Children who do not pass the GCE have either to pay fees and go to a private school, or stop their education. Because of this there is a large number of children in Malawi who do not continue their education after about the age of 13.

My role at St Theresa was the same as that of any other teacher. I had a full timetable every day of the week, and I had my roster of doing break and lunch duties. This is one of the things that made my year even more enjoyable, as I was on the same level as all the other teachers, and was able to make friends with them as an equal. I was also able to give the teachers a Western perspective on teaching methods, and help with timetabling the school day. It was a great privilege working alongside the Malawians, and I learnt more in this year than I ever could have hoped.

vowel sounds when attempting to speak a Bantu language), and they may also carry across the Bantu practice of stressing the second-last syllable. For instance, a word like 'important' may be pronounced more like 'eem-POT-int'. Another common habit is inserting vowel sounds between running consonants (for instance 'penpal' might be pronounced 'pin-EE-pel') or at the end of words (*basi* for 'bus').

Remember, too, that there is always a tendency to use the grammatical phrasing of your home tongue when you speak a second language. In most Bantu languages, the majority of enquiries are made by making a statement in an enquiring tone of voice. 'There is a room?' is more likely to be understood than 'Do you have a room?' 'This bus is going to Lilongwe?' is better than 'Do you know whether this bus is going to Lilongwe?'

Make your questions as direct as possible, as it's easy to confuse people with excess words. Bear in mind, however, that politeness is most important in African cultures, with '*zikomo*' or thank you thrown in many times.

You will find that certain common English words are readily understood by Malawians, while other equally common words draw a complete blank. For instance, practically anybody will know what you mean by a resthouse, but they may well be confused if you ask where you can find accommodation. Another example of this is the phrase 'It is possible?' which for some reason has caught on almost everywhere in Africa. 'It is possible to find a bus?' is more likely to be understood than 'Do you know if there is a bus?' Likewise, 'Is not possible' is a more commonly used phrase than 'It is impossible'. This sort of thing can occur on an individual level as well as on a general one, so listen out for words which are favoured by somebody with whom you have a lengthy conversation.

SOCIAL ETIQUETTE Most Malawian etiquette is very swift to pick up. There are many spots in Malawi that are thoroughly modernised, but the villages remain very traditional and some areas of the cities and resorts will treat you with more respect if you adhere to Malawian social etiquette. Markets and bus stations are also curiously old-fashioned. I have noted a few guidelines here to reinforce those already mentioned elsewhere in this guide, none is essential but they will help the way people accept you:

- Always use the formal greetings of 'hello, how are you?' and plenty of 'thank yous' too
- Women should wear a *chitenje* or a skirt in the villages
- People may find too much contact between men and women offensive
- If you want to camp in a village, always ask the permission of the chief
- No public smoking of drugs
- Pay for lifts if you choose to hitch
- Respect other people for the job they have been trained to do

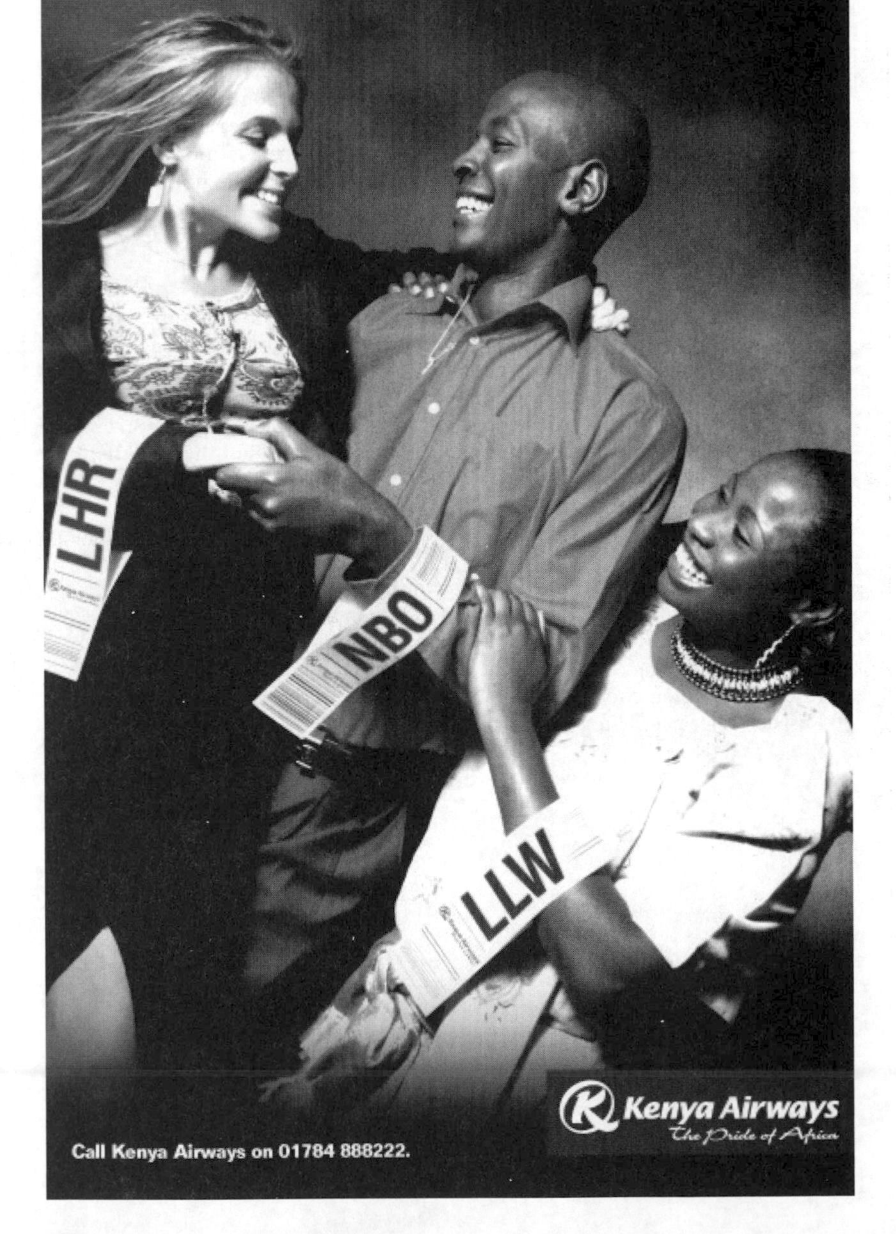
London and Lilongwe get connected in Nairobi.
London to Nairobi daily. Nairobi to Lilongwe six times a week.
Connect directly or stay in the world's most spectacular holiday destination.
www.kenya-airways.com
LHR
NBO
LLW
Kenya Airways
The Pride of Africa
Call Kenya Airways on 01784 888222.

Part Two

THE GUIDE

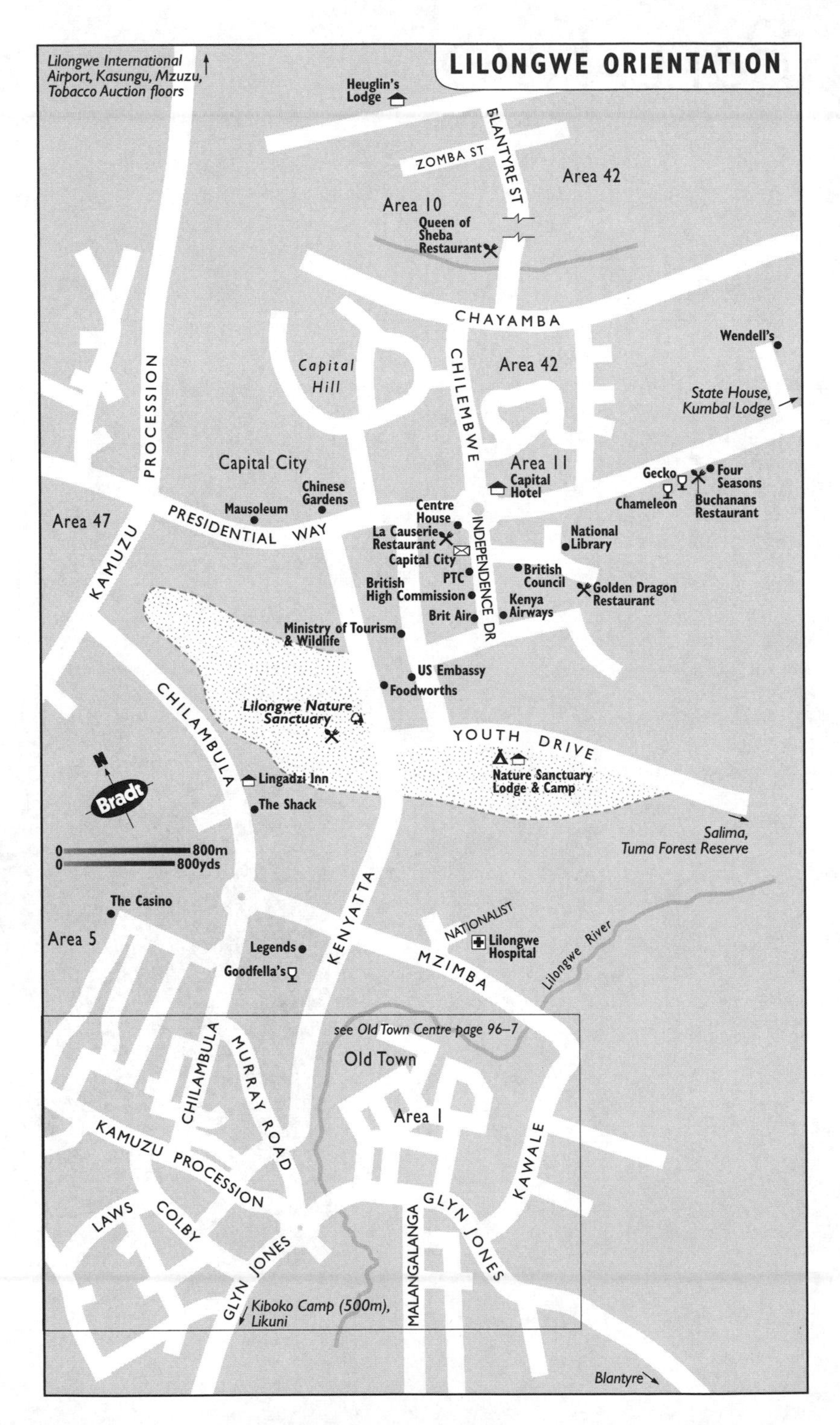
LILONGWE ORIENTATION
Lilongwe International Airport, Kasungu, Mzuzu, Tobacco Auction floors
Heuglin's Lodge
ZOMBA ST
BLANTYRE ST
Area 42
Area 10
Queen of Sheba Restaurant
CHAYAMBA
Wendell's
Capital Hill
CHILEMBWE
Area 42
State House, Kumbal Lodge
PROCESSION
Capital City
Area 11
Capital Hotel
Gecko
Four Seasons
Chameleon
Buchanans Restaurant
Chinese Gardens
Mausoleum
Area 47
PRESIDENTIAL WAY
Centre House
La Causerie Restaurant
Capital City
INDEPENDENCE DR
National Library
KAMUZU
PTC
British Council
British High Commission
Golden Dragon Restaurant
Kenya Airways
Brit Air
Ministry of Tourism & Wildlife
US Embassy
Foodworths
CHILAMBULA
Lilongwe Nature Sanctuary
YOUTH DRIVE
Nature Sanctuary Lodge & Camp
Lingadzi Inn
The Shack
Bradt
N
Salima, Tuma Forest Reserve
0 800m
0 800yds
The Casino
Area 5
KENYATTA
NATIONALIST
Lilongwe Hospital
Lilongwe River
Legends
Goodfella's
MZIMBA
see Old Town Centre page 96–7
Old Town
CHILAMBULA
MURRAY ROAD
Area 1
KAMUZU PROCESSION
KAWALE
LAWS
COLBY
GLYN JONES
MALANGALANGA
GLYN JONES
Kiboko Camp (500m), Likuni
Blantyre

6

Lilongwe

Lilongwe is the blandest of African capitals. It is split into two parts, Old Town and City Centre, and in many ways there's not much to either of them. Arriving, as most visitors do, in the so-called 'Old Town', which is the city's main focus, what you'll see is indistinguishable from any number of small southern African towns. Yet despite this, Lilongwe is one of the most equable capitals in Africa: the climate is comfortable, getting in and out of town is simplicity itself, cheap accommodation is abundant and conveniently situated, and shops and markets are well stocked.

To a large extent, Lilongwe comes across as an urban microcosm of the country it governs – small but deceptively populated, friendly and personal, dusty and colourfully chaotic, and full of contrasts. Behind the houses and offices, within eyeshot of parliament, people still grow maize in their gardens. At night, the silence is regularly broken by the eerily evocative whooping of spotted hyenas, resident in the nature sanctuary that divides Old Town from New. Villagers cycle miles from outlying areas to sell produce at the country's largest market, weaving between the buses that form jerking, hooting, belching queues in the old town centre.

HISTORY

Lilongwe was founded in 1906 on the banks of the Lilongwe River, initially as a settlement for Asian traders, though its pleasant climate rapidly attracted European business. In 1909, the fledgling township's future status was assured when it became the terminus of the first road connecting Malawi to Zambia. By the 1930s, Lilongwe boasted a hotel, a hospital, a European sports club, and a mosque and Muslim Sports Club built by the thriving Asian business community. In 1947, Lilongwe was accorded full township status. By the time of Malawi's independence, Lilongwe was, with a population of around 20,000, second only in size to Blantyre, and its central position made it the obvious choice to replace the colonial capital of Zomba. Lilongwe was formally made the capital of Malawi in 1975, since when its population has easily quadrupled.

Most visitors end up staying in Area 3 or Area 1 in Old Town (walking distance), or 10, 11 or 12 in the new City Centre (minibus or taxi distance). The system for naming different areas of the town seems quite arbitrary until you learn that it is chronological, with Area 1 being the oldest part of town, Area 2 the second-oldest etc. House numbers – where they exist – follow the same confusing logic. Navigating yourself around Lilongwe (or anywhere in Malawi) is thus more a test of spatial awareness than of remembering numbers of buildings. Fortunately, public transport is easy to master, making travel into, around and out of town very simple.

CLIMATE

Lilongwe lies on a plateau west of the Rift Valley at a medium altitude of 1,067m. Daytime temperatures are pleasantly moderate or warm, and most of the annual average rainfall of around 750mm falls between November and April.

GETTING THERE AND AWAY

Getting in and out of Lilongwe couldn't be more straightforward. All buses and minibuses to Lilongwe terminate at the large bus station in Old Town. Buses to most destinations in Malawi leave from the same bus station throughout the morning through to mid afternoon, so there is no reason for rushed early starts. The Shire bus line also has a depot opposite Shoprite and Coachline services start and end at the Capital Hotel in City Centre (they also stop at the Shire Bus depot).

Although most buses travelling north or south on the M1 will stop at the turn-off to Kamuzu International Airport, they may not drive all the way in. An airport bus service was resumed in 2005, costing MK800 each way and meeting most international flights. Taxis between the city centre and the airport cost a fixed fare of MK2,400 and take about 30 minutes.

AIRLINES

✈ **Air Malawi** NBS Bldg, Manadala Rd; ☎ 01 753181; **f** 01 701008
✈ **Air Zimbabwe** Mitco Hse, Capital City; ☎ 01 783804; **f** 01 783780
✈ **British Airways** ADL Hse, Capital City; ☎ 01 771747; **f** 01 772747
✈ **Ethiopian Airlines** Mitco Hse, Capital City; ☎ 01 772001
✈ **KLM** Capital Hotel; ☎ 01 781413; **f** 01 784293
✈ **Kenya Airways** Independence Dr; ☎ 01 774227 or 01 774 330
✈ **South African Airways** see *Chapter 16, Blantyre,* page 207

ORIENTATION

Old Town (areas 1–3) – to all intents and purposes Lilongwe as it was prior to the Capital City being built in 1975 – is the main business and shopping area, and it's where you'll find most of the hotels. The main business road through the old town is Kamuzu Procession, and the most important intersection is that with Kenyatta Avenue (the road that leads to Lilongwe Nature Sanctuary and Capital City). Along Kamuzu Procession, within 200m of this intersection, are, from north to south, the Lilongwe Hotel, the main post office, the Nico Centre, the tourist office, and the Times Bookshop. There is a minibus rank where you can pick up transport to Capital City on Kenyatta Avenue about 100m from the intersection in front of Shoprite.

About 100m south of the post office, Kamuzu Procession forms a large roundabout with Glyn Jones Road to the west and a small unnamed road straight ahead. The Golf Club lies on this corner, and the map sales office lies at the end of the unnamed road. From the roundabout, Kamuzu Procession continues across a bridge over the Lilongwe River to the west, where it climbs through the old Indian trading quarter. About 500m past the bridge, before the two mosques, traffic lights mark the intersection with Malangalanga Road, which is where you'll find the bus station, market and the majority of cheap private resthouses.

Capital City lies 5km from the old town along Kenyatta Avenue. The two parts of town are separated by the *brachystegia* woodland of Lilongwe Nature Sanctuary and blue-gum plantations planted to fuel the city. Aside from housing most of the embassies and airline offices, as well as the British Council, there are few urgent reasons why visitors might want to visit Capital City.

Lilongwe International Airport lies 26km north of the city centre on the M1 to Kasungu.

GETTING AROUND

During daylight hours, minibuses run back and forth pretty much non-stop between the old town and Capital City. The best place to pick these up in the old town is near the main bus station, opposite the Caltex Garage and also from in front of Shoprite. The fare is cheap (MK50 for any distance) and tourists are not overcharged.

There are plenty of taxi cabs in Lilongwe, and fares are cheap by international standards. Main taxi ranks in the old town are opposite the bus station, then also next to Shoprite, in front of the post office, and in the grounds of the Lilongwe Hotel. In Capital City, you will find taxis in the grounds of the Capital Hotel. Taxis are also available at the airport.

CAR HIRE **Avis** is the only international car-hire firm operating out of Lilongwe. The main office lies off Chilambula Road (*01 756105*) about 1km from the old town centre, so on foot it's more convenient to contact the branch offices in either the Lilongwe Hotel or the Capital Hotel.

There are plenty of other local car-hire companies operating out of Lilongwe, including:

SS Rent A Car 01 751478; f 01 751529

Ceciliana Car Hire 01 756055; f 01 756052

WHERE TO STAY

UPMARKET There are now extremely appealing options in the mid to luxury range of accommodation available in Lilongwe.

Kumbali Country Lodge Nature's Gift Ltd, Capital Hill Dairy Farm, Area 44; 09 963402/09 228437/09 967983; e kumbali@kumbalilodge.com; www.kumbali.com. A short drive to the south of Lilongwe, sited on a working farm up on a hill beyond State House, only 8km from City Centre, this has stunning views and 250ha of indigenous forest in which to wander before any international flights. Kumbali is renowned for its fine restaurant, serving fresh veg and meat straight from the farm. It also has superb chalets, with every detail lovingly designed and made with exceptional craftsmanship. Each room has a balcony overlooking the gardens and business travellers can log on to a fast-access web server from their own rooms. A conference centre is also available. *Great value for standard stes sgl/dbl US$70–85/100–120 and executive stes sgl/dbl US$95–115/130–160.*

Sunbird Capital Hotel Capital City; 01 773388; f 01 771273; e capitalhotel@sunbirdmalawi.com; www.sunbirdmalawi.com. This is very much geared towards the business community, and conveniently located on Capital Hill within easy walking distance of the centre. Facilities include a large swimming pool, satellite TV in all rooms, a business centre, representative offices of several airlines and a Times Bookshop in the foyer. There is a well-regarded upmarket restaurant in the hotel, as well as a good snack bar. A wide selection of rooms is available. *Standard rooms sgl/dbl US$106/126, superior sgl/dbl US$147/167, deluxe stes sgl/dbl US$220/240.*

Lilongwe Hotel Old Town; 01 756333; f 01 756580; e lilongwehotel@sunbirdmalawi.com; www.sunbirdmalawi.com. A well-known and conveniently central landmark in Old Town, a location that is probably more attractive to most tourists than the relatively bland Capital City Hotel. Built in the colonial era, this hotel is more atmospheric than its counterpart in the new city centre, with flowering gardens, an attractive swimming pool area and a popular bar. Large, comfortable rooms with satellite TV. *Sgl/dbl US$95/110, stes sgl/dbl US$107/122.*

Cresta Hotel Kamuzu Procession Rd in the Crossroads Complex near the Mchinji roundabout;

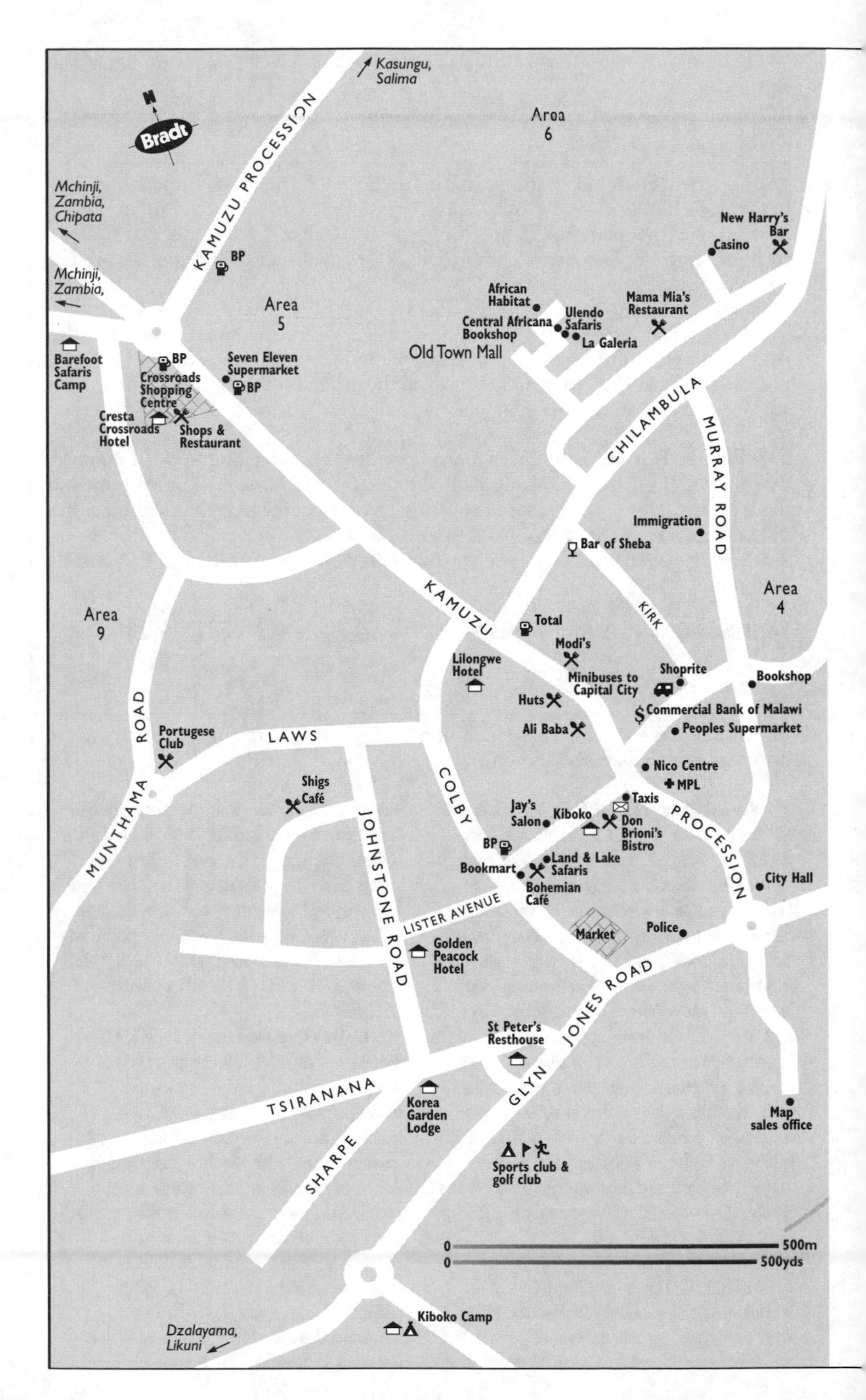
Kasungu, Salima
Area 6
Bradt
KAMUZU PROCESSION
Mchinji, Zambia, Chipata
Mchinji, Zambia,
BP
Area 5
New Harry's Bar
Casino
African Habitat
Mama Mia's Restaurant
Ulendo Safaris
Central Africana Bookshop
La Galeria
Old Town Mall
Barefoot Safaris Camp
BP
Crossroads Shopping Centre
Seven Eleven Supermarket
BP
Cresta Crossroads Hotel
Shops & Restaurant
CHILAMBULA
MURRAY ROAD
Immigration
Bar of Sheba
KIRK
Area 4
Area 9
KAMUZU
Total
Modi's
Lilongwe Hotel
Minibuses to Capital City
Shoprite
Bookshop
Huts
Commercial Bank of Malawi
Ali Baba
Peoples Supermarket
ROAD
Portugese Club
LAWS
Nico Centre
MPL
Shigs Café
COLBY
Taxis
Jay's Salon
Kiboko
Don Brioni's Bistro
PROCESSION
MUNTHAMA
JOHNSTONE ROAD
BP
Land & Lake Safaris
Bookmart
Bohemian Café
City Hall
LISTER AVENUE
Police
Market
Golden Peacock Hotel
GLYN JONES ROAD
St Peter's Resthouse
TSIRANANA
Korea Garden Lodge
Map sales office
SHARPE
Sports club & golf club
0
500m
0
500yds
Kiboko Camp
Dzalayama, Likuni

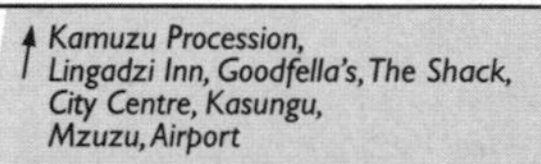

LILONGWE OLD TOWN CENTRE

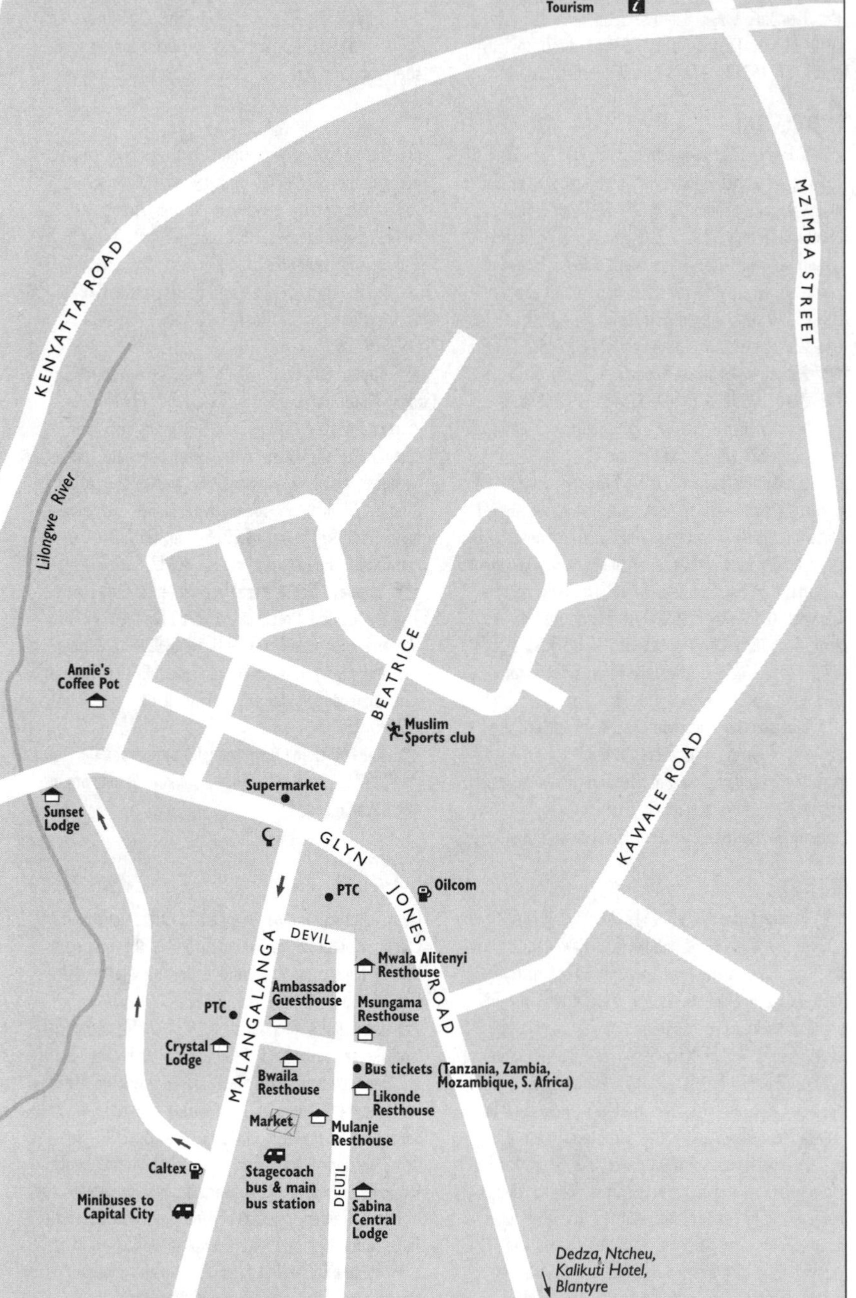

☎ 01 750333; e cresta@malawi.net; www.cresta-hospitality.com. Stepping inside is a holiday in itself (from Malawi) with soothing piped music and a large AC foyer leading to nice rooms. *Sgl/dbl/ste US$120/140/160.*

🏠 **Heuglin's Lodge** Blantyre St in Area 10 just north of City Centre; ☎ 01 793564 direct to lodge, or 01 771153/01 771393 to Wilderness Safaris; e info@wilderness.mw or heuglins@globemalawi.net; www.wilderness-safaris.com. Run by Wilderness Safaris, this is a delightful and homely place, with a large bar and dining area, a swimming pool and comfortable rooms. *US$130 FB (sgl supplement US$30) or sgl/dbl US$95/140 and US$66 pp for rooms with shared bathrooms.*

MID RANGE

🏠 **Korea Garden Lodge** Area 3; ☎ 01 753467; f 01 756612; e kgl@kglodge.net; www.kglodge.net. Set in quiet gardens behind St Peter's Resthouse, the comfortable lodge has a swimming pool next to the restaurant which serves excellent Korean food and has good security for yourself and vehicle. *Sgl/dbl US$15/20 with shared bathroom, s/c sgl/dbl US$32/39, executive rooms sgl/dbl US$45/52.*

🏠 **Kiboko Town Hotel** Mandala Rd, Area 3; ☎ 01 751226/01 754978 or 09 838485/09 848586; e kiboko@malawi.net, info@kiboko-safaris.com or reservations@kiboko-safaris.com; www.kibokohotel.com. An old 1940s-style place with attractive safari-style renovations, just above the post office in Old Town and offering smart, affordable and central b&b accommodation. A long balcony overlooks the street below, and Don Brioni's and the rest of Lilongwe Old Town is only just a step outside the door. *Standard room sgl/dbl US$40/45, luxury room sgl/dbl US$50/55 – executive room sgl/dbl/trpl US$70/75/80.*

🏠 **Lingadzi Inn** Chilambula Rd, between Old Town and City Centre; ☎ 01 720644; e lingadzi@sdnp.org.mw. An adequate and moderately priced hotel, now a training hotel for people working in tourism. The best features of this hotel are the neat, pretty grounds. Oddly enough, this is perhaps the only hotel or lodge in Malawi where you can be pretty certain of hearing hyenas at night, since it borders the Lilongwe Nature Sanctuary and as with other Le Meridien hotels, can be booked in advance through the Central Reservations Office at the Mount Soche Hotel in Blantyre. *Sgl/dbl US$90/126.*

🏠 **Capital City Motel** About 3km from Capital City along Youth Drive; ☎ 01 772561/01 774911; e mactambala@yahoo.com. Similar in style and standard to the Lingadzi Inn with adequate rooms. Facilities include a pleasant bar and restaurant, and satellite TV in every room. There is live jazz music here every Sun from 14.00. *Sgl/dbl US$30/40 using communal showers and s/c sgl/dbl US$45/65.*

🏠 **Wendel's Bed & Breakfast** Close to City Centre and the Capital Hotel; ☎ 01 770237; f 01 771771; e wendels@malawi.net; www.wendels.com. German-run and highly recommended, especially for business visitors needing a homely environment. *Sgl/dbl US$70/95.*

🏠 **Kalikuti Hotel** Biwi triangle, 3km from Old Town ☎ 01 725392/01 725570; e kalikuti@sdnp.org.mw. Also recommended.

BUDGET

🏠 **Kiboko Camp** ☎ 01 751226/01 754978/09 838485/09 848586; e kiboko@malawi.net, info@kiboko-safaris.com; www.kiboko-safaris.com. Soon to change hands, Kiboko has become the most popular backpacker haunt in Lilongwe, and also offers safaris within Malawi and to Luangwa National Park in Zambia (see page 106). Camping costs US$3 pp, with separate sites for overland trucks and for independent travellers, while dormitories cost US$5 pp and chalets and A-frames are US$15 pp. Facilities include a bar and a barbecue area. Kiboko Camp lies on Likuni roundabout, which is on Glyn Jones Road about 1km past the golf club. If you are coming from the main bus station, the best way to get to Kiboko is to pick up a minibus heading to Likuni and ask to be dropped at the roundabout. Coming out of town, Kiboko Camp is the property with a high reed fence and hedge on the far left side of the roundabout.

🏠 **Land and Lake Safaris** ☎ 01 757120; e info@landlake.net; www.landlake.net. Land and Lake Safaris are due to open a spacious lawned campsite (and lodge) on the Lingadzi River inside the Nature Sanctuary at the end of 2006 or early 2007 and with the added attraction of a rehabilitation centre for animals returning to Africa from zoos around the world. Also offers regular budget safaris to Victoria Falls, South Luangwa etc. *Camping US$5.*

🏠 **Annie's Coffee Pot** Area 1, near the mosque. More central, and also catering specifically for backpackers, this local restaurant has rooms: *4-bed dormitory US$3 pp, 2 private rooms US$6 dbl, camping US$2.*

St Peter's Resthouse, Area 3, opposite the golf club in the grounds of the eponymous church. Basic but practical, it's been popular with travellers for some years. It has 2 dbl rooms, 1 triple, and 3 4-bed dorms, all with nets. The problem with both of these places is that bed space is limited, so you may well do the walk from the bus station only to be turned away. *US$5 pp.*

Sunset Lodge Malangalanga Road near the bus station; 01 724770/01 724718. This newly opened lodge is a popular choice, with executive accommodation for MK1,500 for s/c room.

James' Joint, signposted off Mchinji Road, 10 mins' walk from the Crossroads complex; 09 493626/01 752626, e thejoint@africa-online.net, jameshansford2@hotmail.com. A new place with rooms and camping, hot showers, bar/restaurant and DSTV all on site. An average meal will set you back US$5. *US$20 per room, dorm bed US$5, camping US$3.*

Golden Peacock Hotel Area 3; *01 742638.* A simple, no-frills place which benefits from sharing its grounds with the delicious Korea Garden Restaurant. All rooms are dbl with nets and fans. *Rooms using communal showers US$9, s/c rooms with hot showers US$13.*

There are numerous cheap lodgings along the back roads around the bus station and market. Of the dozen other hotels in this part of town, the first two are similar value; the rest drop in terms of price and quality:

Sabina Central Lodge is set back from the bus station and surprisingly quiet and well kept. *S/c rooms US$10/12.*

Sunset Lodge In the same league. *S/c rooms US$10/12.*

Crystal Lodge Looks acceptable. *US$5/7 sgl/dbl or US$10 s/c dbl.*

Likonde Resthouse Similar standard, with a nice courtyard. *US$4.*

Lilongwe Golf Club The basic rooms are popular with travellers. *US$15 pp, which includes use of the club's facilities.*

WHERE TO EAT AND DRINK

CAPITAL CITY Not many travellers get to eat in Capital City, even though there are plenty of restaurants from which to choose.

Kumbali Country Lodge Nature's Gift Ltd, Capital Hill Dairy Farm, Area 44; 09 963402/09 228437/09 967983; e kumbali@kumbalilodge.com; www.kumbali.com. An 8km drive out of town, it's worth the effort; tables at its appetising restaurant must be booked in advance.

Buchanan's Just 2km out on Presidential Way from City Centre towards State House; 01 772846. A stylish restaurant and bar within the Four Season's nursery garden complex, with fine food in the US$5–15 range.

The Queen of Sheba Area 10. This Ethiopian restaurant is also recommended but extremely difficult to find.

Golden Dragon Restaurant Behind the British Council and near the National Library. The long-standing eatery retains a good reputation in the US$20–30 range.

Capital Hotel The hotel restaurant has meals in the US$10–12 range, with regular buffet-style *braais* in the evenings.

La Causerie Behind Centre House in City Centre. Excellent service and good food from US$4–8.

OLD TOWN

Don Brioni's Bistro Near the post office; 09 967482/09 933 627; e donbrionismw@hotmail.com. This one is a great favourite. A comfortable place of faded chic, it has a varied international menu with an emphasis on Italian dishes. Pizzas are something of a speciality, at around US$5–6, while most meat and fish dishes cost around US$8.

Mama Mia's Old Town Mall, off Chilambula Rd; 01 758362. An upmarket Italian trattoria serving excellent pizzas and superb Italian food. From the gleaming stainless-steel kitchen to cosy corners and shaded patio, the place exudes class and is value for money too, serving pizzas at US$3.50–5.50 and pastas at around US$7.

Modi's Restaurant Kamuzu Procession; 01 751489/01 757694/08 835592. Modi's has an eclectic menu with delicious items ranging from steaks to grilled fish and prawns, and with the emphasis on Indian dishes. Main courses are in the US$5–7 range, and the portions are large.

✂ **Huts** ☎ 01 752912 The only other Indian restaurant in Lilongwe is close to Modi's in all senses: physically, in standard, and in price.

✂ **Korean Gardens Restaurant** In the same building as the Golden Peacock Hotel. This place is highly rated for Korean food, with prices comparable to Modi's.

✂ **Ali Baba Take-Away** A cheaper option, serving a variety of Lebanese dishes (hummus, kebabs, schwarmas) as well as burgers, steaks and the like. Portions are generous and very reasonably priced.

CAFÉS AND LUNCH VENUES

✂ **Shigs Café** in Area 3 (the old Four Season's café). A good place for lunch with running water, fig trees and an all-too-perfect setting.

✂ **Annie's Coffee Pot** Serves hamburgers, piri-piri chicken, fried *chambo*, vegetable curry etc for around US$2–3 per main course. The food is good and very reasonably priced, though the portions aren't particularly generous. There's definitely no reason to get excited about the coffee.

✂ **Bohemian Café** If coffee is what you're after, head straight here. It's also a good place for breakfasts and lunches – cappuccino, scrumptious fresh fruit juice, chocolate cake, pastries, pies and toasted sandwiches. Closed evenings and Sun.

✂ **Lilongwe Hotel** The coffee and cakes here are also pretty good.

The cheapest places to eat out are the local restaurants around the market and bus station, where you can get a standard chicken and *nsima* or rice for less than US$1.

LILONGWE'S BARS AND NIGHTCLUBS Most of the bars also serve good food, with more limited menus perhaps but always good value. All except Chameleon are in Old Town.

Harry's Bar ☎ 09 923576; e umunthu@eomw.net. Harry's Bar is currently on Mandala Rd but is due to move to even better premises next to the COSOMA building on the Mchinji/Chilumbula roundabout road. It will be Lilongwe's first real arts centre with bar, restaurant, theatre, exhibition space etc. This ever-popular bar attracts a great mix of people, and is a good place for a drink and pepper steak at only US$4. Even on a lively night you'll be impressed by the swiftness of the bar staff, as well as the quality of the music – with dancing if you stay late enough. Harry's Bar also organises two major events in Lilongwe, the Mango Festival in early Nov and the Rain Dance Festival around New Year (see page 21) as well as the Lake of Stars Festival at Chintheche.

Goodfella's Off Chilambula Rd. Another good place for a drink, with a sports bar with satellite TV, a good selection of drinks, pool tables and good value pub meals.

Pirates' Casino Also off Chilumbula Rd. This tends to be more of a late-night drinking, gambling and dancing place, full of fun and quite some style.

Alexanders, Sol Farm, French Corner and **Chez Ntemba** are other good nightspots.

The Shack Next door to Lingadzi Inn on Chilambula Rd. A great pub-cum-social club started by the Round Table and supported by most of Lilongwe's younger expats. With volleyball outside on Wed evenings and Happy Hour on Fri, it's a good place to make sporting and social contacts.

The Chameleon In Four Seasons, Presidential Way. This is a club that fills up after 22.00. It has regular karaoke and live music nights and on other evenings has good music and atmosphere.

SHOPPING

There are three new shopping complexes in Lilongwe, all with security guards for shoppers and their vehicles. The Shoprite Centre on the corner of Kamuzu Procession and Kenyatta has a supermarket, where virtually anything is available, as well as some small specialist shops. Across the road is the Nico Centre, with its PTC Hyperstore as well as three pharmacies and two forex bureaux.

The **central market**, next to the bus station, is the best place to buy fresh fruit and vegetables. It is also a good place to buy cheap clothes, music most notably from Malawi, South Africa and the Congo, and practically anything else you can think of, from curtains, TVs and coal irons to chickens, pots, baskets and shoes.

BOOKS AND NEWSPAPERS **Bookmart** next to Land and Lake Safaris on Mandala Road has the widest range of books in Lilongwe, all secondhand. The main branch of the **Times Bookshop** is in Old Town in the Shoprite Centre. There are also branches in the PTC supermarket in Capital City, at the airport and in the foyers of the Lilongwe and Capital hotels. The branches in the hotels are open seven days a week. The **Central Africana Bookshop** (*01 756317;* e *centralafricana@africa-online.net; www.centralafricana.com*) in Old Town Mall is a fascinating bookstore with a fabulous selection of new and antiquarian books, including some very valuable Africana, and an exclusive wine and food emporium, video hire, an opticians and dental surgery. Its second Lilongwe shop (*01 774129*) is in Four Seasons Lifestyle Centre on Presidential Way, Area 12. Newspapers can be bought from the sellers on the street; international newspapers are hard to come by.

CRAFTS AND CURIOS In terms of things you might want to take home, the most upmarket complex is the Old Town Mall, off Chilambula Road. Not only does it house Mama Mia's, but there are also the offices of Ulendo Safaris, and **La Galeria** (the sister shop to La Caverna gallery in Blantyre) which exhibits paintings, sculpture and textiles by the top Malawian artists (*01 757742;* e *lacaverna@malawi.net*). Also here is **Central Africana** (see above) and **African Habitat** (*01 752363;* e *africanhabitat@malawi.net*), a beautiful craft and curio shop selling high-quality carvings, furniture and textiles. Old Town Mall is a treat to visit when you've had your fill of markets and poorly stocked supermarkets. Nearby is the **Mtendere Art Gallery** run by mouth-painter Chrisford Chayera.

Below the Kiboko Town Hotel is a packed new shop, **Things of Africa** (*08;* e *thingsofafrica@africa-online.net*), selling art and craft work from the whole region.

Up in the **Crossroads Complex**, near the Mchinji Roundabout, there's a mass of tempting shops (and a few cafés and restaurants to rest in), including **Wenzy's** which has craft, clothes, shoes and curios from all over east Africa.

The main cluster of curio sellers is outside the post office in Old Town. There are also quite a few curios on sale in the main car park on Independence Drive in Capital City.

MAPS The Department of Surveys' Map Sales Office sells a good range of 1:50,000 and 1:250,000 maps, covering most of Malawi. The office is in the old town near the golf club on a side road that radiates from the roundabout where Glyn Jones Road meets Kamuzu Procession. Maps cost between US$7 and US$12.

MOTOR SPARES AND REPAIRS Go to the industrial area bordered by Kamuzu, Kenyatta and Chilambula roads. Look out for Halls (*01 740677*) for Land Rover, and Toyota Malawi (*01 721566*), or phone Cranko Auto Repairs (*01 759010/09 951168;* e *cranko@malawi.net*) if you need help. Also try the Asian part of town.

SUPERMARKETS If you want to put together your own food, there's a good range of fruit and vegetables on sale at the market. Most supermarkets sell a fair range of foodstuffs – the best being the **Peoples PTC** in the Nico Centre. Across the road, in a shop-until-you-drop class of its own, is **Shoprite Supermarket**, where you can get anything – when it opened a few years ago, everyone walked around it with their mouths open in amazement. Other foody meccas are Foodworths by Wilderness Safaris on Kenyatta Avenue, Seven-Eleven and Foodzone opposite and in the Crossroads Centre. Both the PTC and Shoprite have adjoining fast-food outlets for good cheap chicken-and-chip-type meals.

OTHER PRACTICALITIES

TOURIST INFORMATION The tourist office has moved to the Ministry of Information, Tourism and Parks just off Convention Drive in City Centre (☎ *01 775499*). The Department of National Parks and Wildlife (☎ *01 752671*) has moved to Kenyatta Drive adjacent to the Petroda filling station. For good local information often your best bet is to talk to other travellers and visit the safari companies' offices.

COMMUNICATIONS

Internet There are email facilities in any number of small internet cafés in Old Town and also at the business centre in the foyer of the Capital Hotel, as well as at the ADL Building in Capital City. When finding the best value, it's worth asking what type of connection the internet café has. Many will also do copies and faxes. The best internet connection in the most pleasant surroundings, though, is in the library at the British Council in Capital City.

Post The main post office is in Old Town on Kamuzu Procession. This is where any poste restante mail addressed to Lilongwe will be kept, though poste restante is rarely used now. If you want to collect your mail at the post office in Capital City, then have it addressed to Lilongwe Capital City. The poste restante system in Lilongwe is reasonably efficient as these things go. Proof of identity is required to collect mail, and US$0.50 is charged for duration of stay.

Note that Lilongwe PO box numbers of four numerals or less are in Old Town post office, while five-numeral PO boxes are in Capital City post office.

EMBASSIES

- **China** PO Box 30221; ☎ 01 774181
- **Germany** PO Box 30046; ☎ 01 782555; f 01 780250
- **India** PO Box 30348; ☎ 01 780766; f 01 781332
- **Israel** PO Box 30319; ☎ 01 782933
- **Mozambique** PO Box 30579; ☎ 01 784100
- **South Africa** PO Box 30043; ☎ 01 783722
- **UK** PO Box 30042; ☎ 01 782400; f 01 782657
- **United States** PO Box 30016; ☎ 01 783166; f 01 780471
- **Zambia** PO Box 30138; ☎ 01 782100
- **Zimbabwe** PO Box 30187; ☎ 01 784988

Note that the German Embassy also handles visas for France, Belgium, The Netherlands, Luxembourg, Spain, Portugal and Austria.

FOREIGN EXCHANGE Foreign currency can be changed into kwacha at any of the main banks or at one of the private forex bureaux that dot the city centre. Outside normal banking hours, there is a 24-hour foreign exchange service at Lilongwe International Airport, though it's probably easier to change money at one of the tourist-class hotels or on the street. The black market is pretty non-existent beyond the border posts.

HAIR AND BEAUTY TREATMENT When in Rome, why not do as the Romans do? Hair, nail and beauty salons are all over Malawi. There are many good hairdressers and beauticians in Lilongwe, able to cut men and women's hair equally well. Several will do hair treatments and colouring at a fraction of Western prices, for example US$40 for professional cut and highlights at **Jay's** opposite the Bohemian

Café. If your budget allows you to have the occasional inexpensive treat, then, girls, it's all there, from pedicures, waxing, facials, braiding etc.

HEALTH A laboratory called Medicare in the NBS Building in the old town opposite the Bohemian Café is the best place to go for tests of any sort. A malaria test, for instance, takes ten minutes to produce and costs US$5. Likuni Hospital, a few kilometres out of town on the Likuni road, is regarded as the best in the Lilongwe area, though Lilongwe Hospital on Nationalist Road is more central for simple routine checks. Dr Martin Huber has a surgery near the Likuni roundabout where his wife assists him, doing tests. There are also three pharmacies in the Nico Centre, one next to Shoprite and one next to Land and Lake Safaris. There is a good dentist in Old Town Mall.

IMMIGRATION The immigration office is a short way off Chilambula Road – the route is signposted from the Lilongwe Hotel. Visa and visitors' pass renewals are processed here in a matter of minutes. When you know it's so easy it's really not worth the hassle of overstaying your visitors' permit.

TOUR OPERATORS AND SAFARI COMPANIES It can make your travels a lot easier if you organise your safari from one of the Lilongwe-based tour operators or travel agents. With up-to-date knowledge, their advice is valuable and their prices impressive for both internal travel and travel to neighbouring countries.

Several reliable tour operators have their main offices in Lilongwe:

Central African Wilderness Safaris Bisnowaty Bldg, Kenyatta Rd, Capital City (next door to a BP garage); ☎ 01 771153; f 01 771397; e info@wilderness.mw; www.wilderness-safaris.com. One of the country's best and most reputable operators, an affiliate of the Wilderness Safaris group that operates throughout much of southern Africa. They are also the concessionaires for Mvuu Camp in Liwonde National Park and the Chintheche Inn on the northern lakeshore, as well as running Heuglin's Lodge in Area 10. Booking agent for Kaya Mowa, Kayak Africa and other Malawi destinations.

Land & Lake Safaris Mandala Rd, Area 3; ☎ 01 757120; f 01 754560; e info@landlake.net, reservations@landlake.net;; www.landlake.net. Another very reputable company, with an office in Old Town behind the Bohemian Café. In addition to organising a wide variety of safaris in Malawi and Zambia, including weekly drive-in safaris to Zambia's South Luangwa National Park, they operate the forest lodge in Dzalanyama and are developing a lodge and campsite in Lilongwe's Nature Sanctuary. Booking agent for all lodges in Malawi and South Luangwa in Zambia.

Ulendo Safaris Old Town Mall; ☎ 01 754950; f 01 756321; info@ulendo.malawi.net. A comprehensive inbound and outbound travel service. Booking agent for Malawi hotels and safaris as well as South Luangwa in Zambia. Booking agent for all major, regional and charter air services including BA, SAA, Kenya Airways, Zambia Airways.

Barefoot Safaris Mchinji Rd; ☎/f 01 707346/09 307359; e barefoot@globemw.net; www.barefoot-safaris.com and www.projectafricanwilderness.org. A safari company concentrating on conservation and ecology, particularly Mwabve Game Reserve. Also known for bush adventures across southern Africa.

Kiboko Safaris Livingstone Rd, Area 3; ☎ 01 751226; f 01754978; e kiboko@malawi.net; www.kiboko-safaris.com They also run the Kiboko Town Hotel and the very popular Kiboko Backpackers' Camp in Lilongwe and also organise budget tours around Malawi and weekly drive-in safaris to South Luangwa National Park.

Soche Tours and Travel Capital City; ☎ 01 782377; f 01 781409; e sochetoursll@sochetoursmw.com; www.sochetourmalawi.com. For all internal travel, car hire and hotel bookings.

Other established tour operators include:

BushCamp Company ☎ 08 204838/01 794196; e info@bushcampcompany.com; www.bushcampcompany.com, www.mfuwelodge.com and www.clubmak.com. Operate safaris from Mfuwe Lodge and bush camps in South Luangwa National Park, and also Club Makokola on the southern lakeshore.

Makomo Safaris ☎/f 01 721536/01 723547/09 947475; e info@makomo.com; www.makomo.com. For travel in Malawi, Tanzania and northern Mozambique.

Rainbow Travel Crossroads Complex, Mchinji Roundabout; ☎ 01 755760/01 751556/09 941871; f 01 755763; e rainbowtvl@africa-online.net. Outbound travel from Malawi and internal hotel bookings.

Pangolin Tours ☎ 09 278903; e info@pangolin-tours.com; www.pangolin-tours.com. For 14–18-day and tailor-made safaris. Also operates Safari Cottage in Nkhata Bay.

Jakamaka Express Area 9; ☎ 01 752042/09 960398; e jakamaka@jakamaka.net; www.jakamaka.net. For charter service on twin-engined aircraft for tourism and business flights to Club Makokola, South Luangua National Park, Nyika National Park, Liwonde National Park and Likoma Island.

WILDLIFE AND NATIONAL PARKS OFFICES The Wildlife Headquarters is on Kenyatta Drive, adjacent to the Petroda filling station (*tel 01 752671*). The Lilongwe branch of the Wildlife and Environment Society of Malawi (WESM) (e *wesm@africa-online.net; www.wildlifemalawi.org*) is based in the Lilongwe Nature Sanctuary. WESM has a large national membership and organises monthly talks as well as excursions, education and activities. Each branch publishes newsletters and an annual WESM calendar is a popular present to take home.

WHAT TO SEE AND DO

Lilongwe is not the most inspiring of cities: it takes time to get to know. For short-stay visitors to Malawi, it's tempting to suggest you avoid Lilongwe altogether or, if you're forced to pass through, to hop off the bus and get straight onto one heading to your next destination.

LILONGWE NATURE SANCTUARY If you find yourself with a spare day in Lilongwe, and don't want to go shopping, get your hair done, or relax in a bar, café or a bookshop all day, then the place to head for is the Lilongwe Nature Sanctuary, which lies between the New and Old towns. Any minibus heading along this route can drop you near the entrance gate, where US$0.40 is charged for entrance and a small map and booklet is sold. Until plans are completed to improve and update it into a reintroduction sanctuary, you probably won't want to linger too long around the small zoo near the entrance (a leopard, a few monkeys, a hyena, a python and a crocodile); instead, devote a couple of hours to exploring the small network of trails that run through the reserve. These pass through pristine *brachystegia* woodland before descending to the riparian forest along the banks of the Lingadzi River.

A fair number of large mammals occur naturally in the reserve, including spotted hyena, otter, porcupine, bushpig, grey duiker and bushbuck. Of these, you'll be very lucky to see more than the rump of a fleeing bushbuck. You can be more confident of seeing a few crocodiles next to the river, and the odd troop of vervet monkeys along the footpaths. But the main point of interest is birds: over 150 species have been recorded in the reserve, and the paths along the river in particular can offer quite excellent birding, especially at dusk (my list included three types of kingfisher, Hueglin's robin, brown snake eagle, a variety of weavers and finches, and the dazzlingly colourful Schalow's turaco). The offices of the Wildlife and Environment Society of Malawi, Lilongwe branch, are based here (*www.wesm.com*).

When you've finished exploring the reserve, you might want to stop for a meal or drink at the tasty restaurant outside the gate.

MAUSOLEUM Perhaps the most striking modern addition to the city is the newly rebuilt mausoleum to HE Dr Kamuzu Hastings Banda, who did not quite remain the Life President of Malawi, despite having been held in great esteem. His recently enlarged memorial is worth visiting. It is easy to spot on Presidential Way shortly after the T-junction with Kenyatta Avenue, on the edge of the **Chinese Gardens** – which make a surprisingly pleasant visit in themselves.

TOBACCO AUCTION FLOORS An eye-opening visit is to go early morning to the Tobacco Auction Floors, out on the Salima road, where guided visits can be booked in advance from April to September through the safari companies. With three types of tobacco sold in over 10,000 bales from the floor each morning it is a mesmerising sight, as the buyers, sellers and auctioneers walk up and down the rows of carefully numbered 100kg bags. The warehouse stores over 80,000 bales of tobacco at any one time.

ACTIVITIES If you're into sport, then a trip to the golf club would soon find you playing golf, tennis, squash or swimming, with partners, caddies and ball boys all ready to take part too. A day's membership costs MK450.

SHORT TRIPS FROM LILONGWE

Several short trips are possible from Lilongwe, though most are of more interest to residents looking for a weekend break than to tourists. Useful details of places of interest around Lilongwe (including areas like Dedza, Salima and Ntchisi which are covered elsewhere in this guide) are contained in the 60-page booklet *Day Outings from Lilongwe* (Judy Carter, Wildlife Society of Malawi, 1991). This costs around US$1 and can be bought at any Times Bookshop.

TUMA FOREST RESERVE This 164km^2 forest reserve lies to the east of Lilongwe about 25km off the Salima road, and it is part of a much larger complex of protected areas which until recently has seen little scientific exploration and even less tourist development. Tuma spans the Rift Valley Escarpment from an altitude of 575m to 1,550m, and it protects a corresponding variety of habitats, including *brachystegia* woodland, bamboo forest and evergreen forest.

The reserve is bounded by the Lilongwe River to the north and the Linthipe River to the south. Management of the reserve has been taken over by the Wildlife Action Group (*www.wag-malawi.org*), who have managed to control poaching with the co-operation of local villagers, and hope to make Tuma something of a flagship reserve for their linked goals of protecting some of Malawi's lesser-known wilderness areas and opening them up to revenue-generating tourism.

In addition to having an untrammelled wilderness atmosphere, Tuma offers the opportunity to track a wide variety of large mammals on foot. Some 40-odd large mammal species have been recorded, including elephant, buffalo, leopard, baboon, vervet monkey, several antelope species (the magnificent greater kudu is particularly common) and a variety of small predators. A bird list is still in the process of being compiled, but the combination of habitats ensures that many notable birds are present, and the reserve has already thrown up one new record for Malawi in the form of the Natal francolin.

NKOMA MOUNTAIN AND NKOMA MISSION An hour southeast of Lilongwe, the mission is worth visiting for its stunning Dutch Cape architecture, and for its small craft shop but also for the incredible atmosphere of the hospital/mission/church. Nkoma Mountain is a huge dry mountain, brilliant hiking country for the intrepid.

SOUTH LUANGWA NATIONAL PARK, ZAMBIA

This low-lying park, which covers an area of 9,050km^2 in Zambia's Luangwa River Valley, is widely regarded as one of the finest wildlife reserves anywhere in Africa. The reserve harbours innumerable elephant, buffalo and hippo, as well as a wide variety of antelope and other ungulates, substantial numbers of lion, leopard and spotted hyena, and smaller numbers of cheetah and wild dog. The entrance to South Luangwa and its main cluster of lodges lies little more than 100km from Mchinji on the Malawi–Zambia border west of Lilongwe, and since Malawi itself lacks any reserve comparable in size or in game viewing, South Luangwa is visited from Malawi with increasing frequency.

Any Lilongwe-based tour operator can organise an excursion to South Luangwa, either as part of a longer tour of Malawi or else as a self-contained trip out of Lilongwe. The cost of such an excursion will depend greatly on whether you camp at one of the cheaper sites or stay at an upmarket lodge. For a budget trip, try Land and Lake Safaris or Kiboko Safaris, while for lodge-based trips, you're best off using Central African Wilderness Safaris or Ulendo Safaris (all details under Lilongwe's tour operators above). For visitors needing a Malawian visa, remember to get a double-entry one, so as to be able to return after your side trip to South Luangwa. Zambia also requires a yellow-fever certificate which may be asked for at the border and a fine imposed if it cannot be produced. The best months to visit are from June to September, though game viewing is excellent throughout the year.

For adventurous and patient backpackers, taking a bus or hitching to South Luangwa is a real possibility. The springboard for a hitching trip to South Luangwa is Chipata, a large town situated roughly 30km from the Mchinji border (see *Chapter 3, Getting there and away, From South Africa*, page 48). The best place to stick out your thumb is outside the Chipata Motel, and you are advised against accepting any lift that doesn't go all the way to Flatdogs, Thornicroft, Croc Valley, Marula Lodge or Wildlife Camp, the only four places in the park that cater for budget travellers. All of these places have accommodation for around US$20 per person and allow camping for around US$5 per person, in addition to which the daily park entrance fee of US$15 must be paid, and they can organise game drives for visitors without transport. I would strongly advise you make advance contact before heading out this way: Flatdogs (☎ *+260 62 46074*), Thornicroft (☎ *+260 62 46034*), Wildlife Camp (☎ *+260 62 21606*), Croc Valley (☎ *+260 62 46074* **f** *+ 260 62 46040*) and Marula Lodge (☎ *+260 62 46034*). If you get stuck, a taxi will take you from Chipata to the Mfuwe area for around US$70, or you could wait for a minibus to fill (it took me two days) and get there for around US$7 from Chipata. Buses from Lilongwe to the Mchinji border cost between US$3 and US$6 depending on speed, then you will need to take a taxi or hitch over the border and into Chipata. Some buses go as far as the Zambian border where there is always a rank of bright blue taxis.

More extensive details on South Luangwa and travel elsewhere in Zambia are to be found in *Zambia: The Bradt Travel Guide*, written by Chris McIntyre. Please note that telephone numbers in Mfuwe have changed their first three digits from 450 to 460.

DEDZA POTTERY This is a good day trip from Lilongwe, barely an hour south on the M1 from Lilongwe. See page 173 for more information. It's also worth noting that the Nkhotakota Pottery (see page 146), where you can create your own designs or learn about local traditional pottery methods, is just two hours from Lilongwe on the lakeshore road north of Salima (*www.dedzapottery.com*).

NYANJA ART STUDIO On the Salima road, this studio is a short drive from the Salima turn-off and is where you can buy unframed works by many Malawian artists, including all of the Chodola brothers. Gallery artists can also be seen at www.nyasaarts.com.

KAMUZU DAM Kamuzu Dam lies on the road from Likuni towards Dzalanyama, about half an hour from Lilongwe. The dam has created a huge artificial lake where it's possible to hire sailing dinghies to sail on Lilongwe's main water supply.

LAKE MALAWI The lake is just over an hour away from Lilongwe, with the Kuti Game Reserve en route (see page 169). Many people who work in Lilongwe head for Salima and Senga Bay for day trips (see page 165).

FURTHER AFIELD

DZALANYAMA FOREST RESERVE This forest reserve lies on the Mozambican border, 58km southwest of Lilongwe past Kamuzu Dam. *Dzalanyama* means 'place of animals'. The forest is rated to have the greatest diversity of *brachystegia* birds in Malawi, and also protects typical forest mammals including samango monkeys and leopards.

Where to stay

Dzalanyama Forest Lodge Is privately operated by Land and Lake Safaris (see page 43). The idyllically positioned self-catering lodge offers accommodation, with bedding, for 8 people in 4 rooms. It is staffed and contains all necessary equipment, including refrigerator and cooking facilities. Unless you organise transport through Land and Lake Safaris, you need your own transport to reach the lodge, and should be aware that the access road sometimes becomes impassable after rain. *US$15 pp sharing or US$100 for the entire house which sleeps 8 people.*

BUNDA MOUNTAIN AND DAM With your own vehicle, this would be a rewarding day trip from Lilongwe, though it's not really practical on public transport. Bunda Mountain is a large granite dome rising to 1,410m to the west of the M1. In addition to being the site of an important Chewa rain shrine (traditional rain ceremonies are still performed here twice annually), the mountain offers good views and the opportunity to see rock-nesting raptors such as the black eagle. Bunda Dam, which lies within the grounds of the Bunda College of Agriculture, is popular with birdwatchers, and the adjacent marshes can be a good place to see crowned crane, pelicans, and a variety of waterfowl, herons and waders.

To get to Bunda, follow the M1 south of Lilongwe for 10km, then turn right towards the Bunda College of Agriculture, the entrance gate of which lies about 20km from the M1. The dam lies 5km from the entrance gate; turn into the gate and ask directions from there. To get to the base of the mountain, continue past the gate for 500m, then turn left on to a track which follows the edge of a plantation forest, and then, when you reach a T-junction, turn right.

This is the fastest and most direct route between Lilongwe and Mzuzu, and offers relatively little in the way of tourist attractions. The major towns along this route are Kasungu and Mzimba; the former is the gateway to Kasungu National Park and also has a good connecting road to Nkhotakota Game Reserve and the latter is close to the forest lodges in the Viphya. Only 40km from Lilongwe is the turn-off for Ntchisi, one of the most rewarding dirt roads in the country, leading to Ntchisi Forest Reserve.

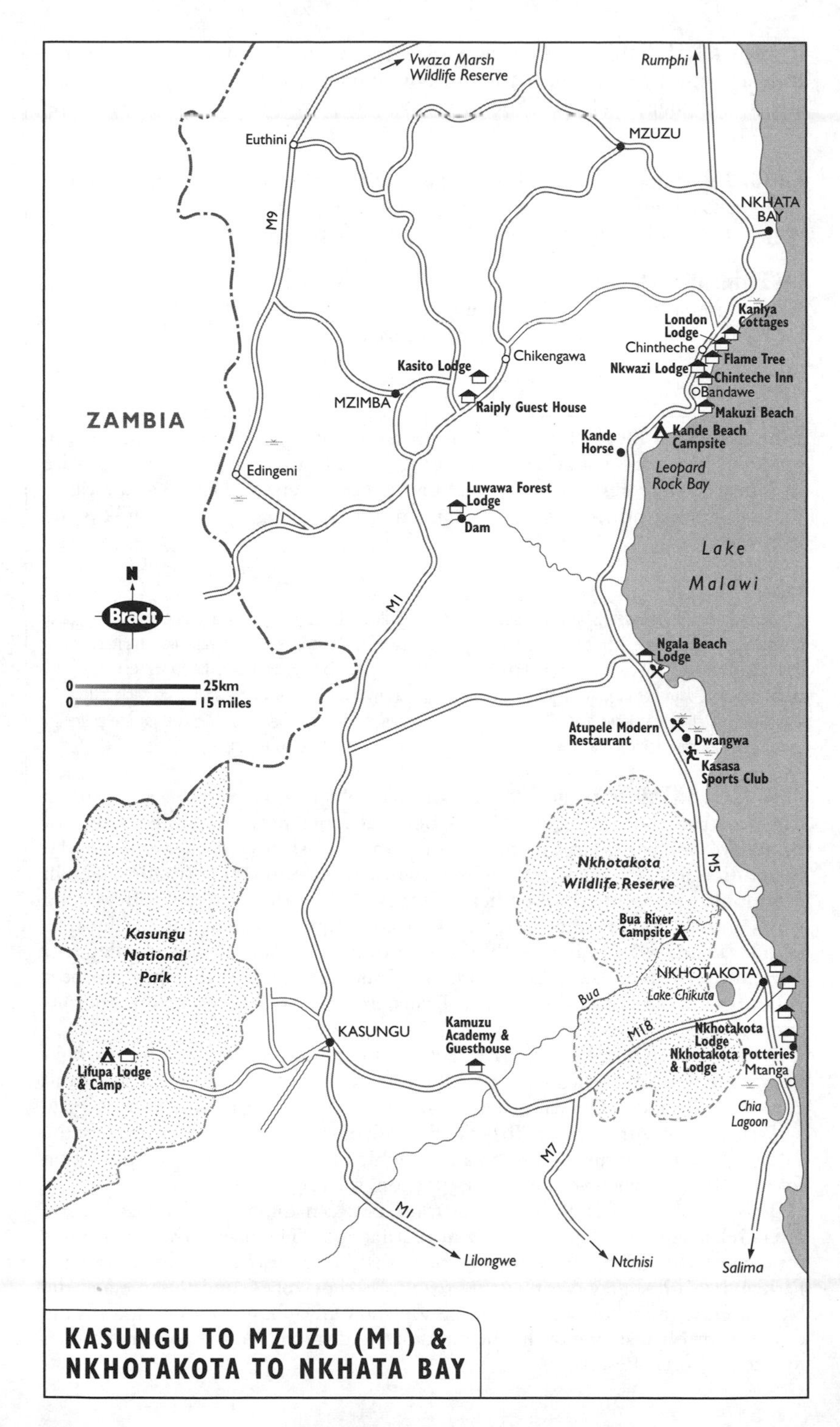
Vwaza Marsh
Wildlife Reserve
Rumphi
Euthini
MZUZU
M9
NKHATA
BAY
ZAMBIA
Kanlya
Cottages
London
Lodge
Chintheche
Flame Tree
Chikengawa
Kasito Lodge
Nkwazi Lodge
Chinteche Inn
Bandawe
MZIMBA
Raiply Guest House
Makuzi Beach
Kande
Horse
Kande Beach
Campsite
Leopard
Rock Bay
Edingeni
Luwawa Forest
Lodge
Dam
Lake
Malawi
N
Bradt
M1
Ngala Beach
Lodge
0 25km
0 15 miles
Atupele Modern
Restaurant
Dwangwa
Kasasa
Sports Club
Nkhotakota
Wildlife Reserve
M5
Kasungu
National
Park
Bua River
Campsite
NKHOTAKOTA
Lake Chikuta
Bua
KASUNGU
Kamuzu
Academy &
Guesthouse
M18
Nkhotakota
Lodge
Nkhotakota Potteries
& Lodge
Lifupa Lodge
& Camp
Mtanga
Chia
Lagoon
M7
M1
Lilongwe
Ntchisi
Salima
KASUNGU TO MZUZU (M1) &
NKHOTAKOTA TO NKHATA BAY

7

The M1 between Lilongwe and Mzuzu

CLIMATE

Kasungu and surrounding areas lie at a medium altitude and have a similar temperate climate to the capital city. Mzimba and the Viphya Plateau are high and cool. Mzuzu is also cool.

GETTING AROUND

In a private vehicle, the 367km stretch of the M1 between Lilongwe and Mzuzu is a straightforward four- or five-hour drive along a tar road. Shire express buses also do the run in around six hours, stopping at Kasungu, Mzimba, Chikengawa and a handful of other large settlements. There is also a daily Shire bus which does the lakeshore route between Lilongwe and Mzuzu. There are two buses each day from Lilongwe, though the first 07.00 bus has been known to be one and the same as the one leaving at 14.00. There are several minibuses which do the whole route at some speed.

NTCHISI FOREST RESERVE

Ntchisi Forest Reserve protects one of the most extensive patches of montane forest remaining in Malawi. There is a forest lodge at the reserve entrance, which means it is easy to explore the forest and its surrounds over a day or two. The main stand of evergreen forest covers the upper slopes of the 1,705m-high Ntchisi Mountain. It is home to a variety of large mammals including samango and vervet monkey, red and blue duiker, bushpig, porcupine and leopard. The occasional elephant used to stray into the forest from the neighbouring Nkhotakota Wildlife Reserve, though this seems unlikely now that local villages and farmland have expanded. The forest also protects a wide variety of forest birds and butterflies, while the lower slopes around the lodge protect characteristic *brachystegia* birds.

GETTING THERE AND AWAY Coming from Lilongwe, the turn-off to Ntchisi Forest Lodge is signposted about 40km along the M7, and about 12km before Ntchisi Town. The signpost isn't particularly obvious if you're coming from Lilongwe as it's posted on a tree and faces in the direction of Ntchisi Town. There is a small village at the turn-off, and a tall radio mast on a hilltop about 1km closer to town, so if you pass the radio mast you know you've gone too far. The lodge is about 16km from the turn-off along a poor dirt road. You should get through in a saloon car in the dry season, but a 4x4 is necessary after rain.

If you are using public transport, buses between Lilongwe and Ntchisi will drop you at the turn-off. The bus stage you need is called Chindembwe, which is the name of the small village about 5km along the road to the lodge. It shouldn't be

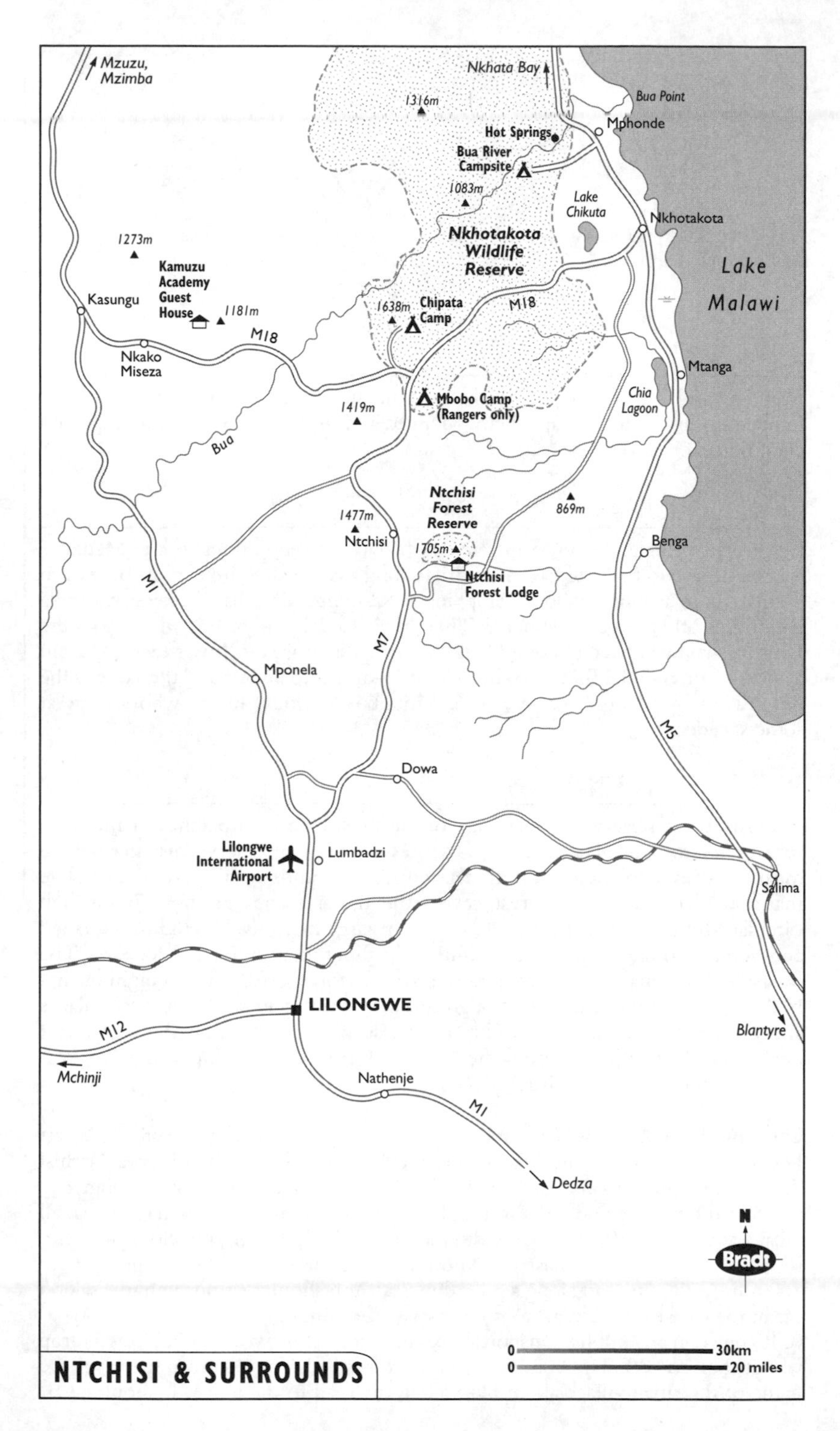
Mzuzu, Mzimba
Nkhata Bay
Bua Point
1316m
Mphonde
Hot Springs
Bua River Campsite
1083m
Lake Chikuta
Nkhotakota
Nkhotakota Wildlife Reserve
1273m
Kamuzu Academy Guest House
1181m
Kasungu
M18
Lake Malawi
1638m
Chipata Camp
M18
Nkako Miseza
Mtanga
Mbobo Camp (Rangers only)
1419m
Chia Lagoon
Bua
Ntchisi Forest Reserve
869m
1477m
Ntchisi
1705m
Benga
Ntchisi Forest Lodge
M1
M7
Mponela
M5
Dowa
Lilongwe International Airport
Lumbadzi
Salima
LILONGWE
M12
Blantyre
Mchinji
Nathenje
M1
Dedza
N
Bradt
0
30km
0
20 miles
NTCHISI & SURROUNDS

difficult to find a *matola* ride from the turn-off to Chindembwe, but you'll probably have to walk the final 11km.

This is one of the great cycling routes of Malawi, as you can follow small scenic roads all the way to the lake.

WHERE TO STAY

Ntchisi Forest Lodge Just within the forest reserve entrance with the forestry school just nearby. Built as a holiday residence by a colonial district commissioner, it has a splendid position, with views across to Lake Malawi. There are 5 s/c rooms (a total of 14 beds), all with wood-heated hot showers. There is no electricity in the lodge, but hurricane lamps are provided at night, and there is even a paraffin fridge. You should bring all the food you need with you or order meals days in advance, the cooking is very good, especially the fresh bread. *Booking through Lilongwe safari offices. US$25 pp self-catering, camping in the garden for US$7.*

WHAT TO SEE AND DO The walking possibilities from the lodge are practically unlimited, and not just restricted to the forest reserve – the surrounding countryside is also very beautiful, with good views over the lake. If you're spending a while in the area, it would be well worth buying a 1:50,000 map.

The obvious route if your time is limited is to follow the road past the resthouse uphill towards the edge of the evergreen forest. This road passes through moss-covered *brachystegia* trees, then through alternating patches of plantation forest, boulder-strewn grassland and isolated stands of indigenous forest. From the end of the road, which is about 3km from the resthouse, a clear path leads into the forest, past tortuously shaped strangler figs, lush fern-bordered watercourses and mossy rocks. The variety of habitats along this walk makes for excellent birdwatching – look out for red-throated twinspot, east African swee, starred robin, and a variety of bulbuls, canaries and sunbirds, as well as baboons and red squirrels.

NTCHISI

One Malawian described Ntchisi to me as the most remote town in the country. The town is really too nondescript to live up to this sort of mystique, but it is certainly very isolated – the kilometre-long stretch of tar road along which it sprawls seems absurdly misplaced. Nevertheless, Ntchisi is the sole piece of urban punctuation along the M7, and travellers using public transport may well end up staying there for a night. There are a few resthouses, and even a rather well-stocked PTC supermarket, and... well, that's Ntchisi.

KASUNGU

Kasungu is a chaotic one-street town offering anything and everything from the hardware stores and supermarkets to the huge dusty market which sprawls behind the main street. It seems like a town that has been by-passed, and indeed most people will drive straight past without knowing of its existence. There's not much to draw you into the town itself except the road passing Kamuzu Academy through to Nkhotakota and for a quick stop before going into Kasungu National Park.

GETTING THERE AND AWAY All buses between Lilongwe and Mzuzu stop at Kasungu. The ride takes around two to three hours, depending on whether you take an express or country bus. A few minibuses and *matolas* connect Kasungu to Nkhotakota daily.

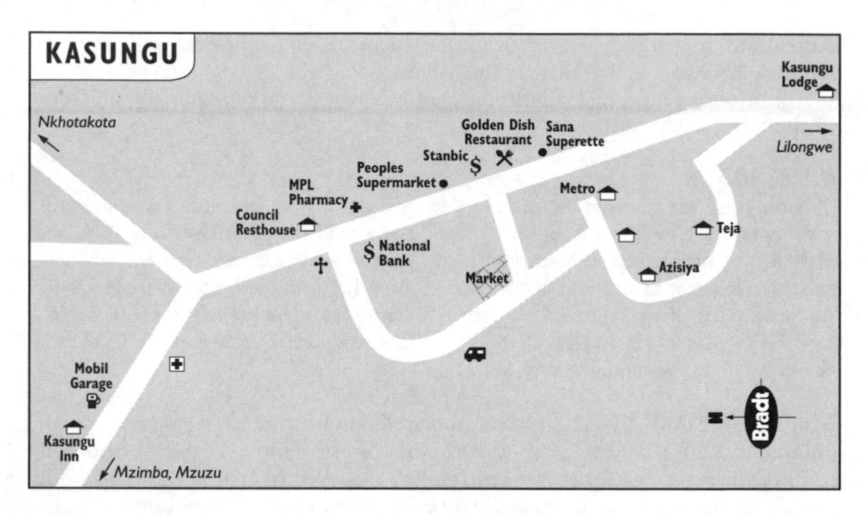

WHERE TO STAY

Kasungu Inn ☎ 01 253306/09 387009. A short walk out of town along the Mzimba road, this has large but slightly tired, s/c twin rooms with mosquito nets and hot showers. *Sgl/dbl US$35/45.*

There are several private resthouses near the bus station, though they're not all that easy to find:

Teja Resthouse (☎ *09 286097*). Bring your own loo seat. With ordinary (US$4) and s/c dbls (US$6).

The same owners have two other resthouses, the **Azisiya** which is as rough as the Teja and the more appealing **Kasungu Lodge** which is newly built just near the southern junction to the M1, with prices in the US$4–7 range (*also* ☎ *09 286097*).

WHERE TO EAT Most of the resthouses around the bus station do the standard stews with chips, rice or *nsima* for around US$1.50. More tasty meals can be found in the exceedingly drab restaurant at the Kasungu Inn for US$3–8 including the standard steak, chicken and fish.

KAMUZU ACADEMY The self-styled 'Eton of Africa' may seem like a strange tourist attraction, but this enormous sprawling public school in the middle of nowhere is of considerable interest, not only for its own merits and facilities, but also for the amount of exploring that can be done in the surrounding area. A resthouse in the grounds has three affordable en-suite bedrooms. Bookings must be made in advance (☎ *09 964010*). The sports facilities are the best in Malawi, and attract athletes from all around the country. Guided visits to nearby tobacco estates can be arranged, while Chipota Mountain (just into Nkhotakota Game Reserve) is within striking distance by car. A recent birding group found 109 species in the school grounds, thanks partly to the presence of a large artificial lake in front of the main buildings. The school estate supports 6,000–8,000 people, and it even has a working farm, with 1,000 chickens providing eggs for all the pupils' breakfasts. The academy is easy enough to reach by minibus, about 30 minutes out of Kasungu towards Nkhotakota.

KASUNGU NATIONAL PARK

This 3,727km² national park (*entrance US$5 pp per day and US$2 per car*) is the second largest in Malawi, protecting an area of *brachystegia* woodland along the

Zambian border west of Kasungu Town. Several rivers run through the park, the most significant of which are the Dwangwa and Lingadzi. Kasungu probably supports a greater number of large mammal species than any other reserve in Malawi, but populations have been devastated by poaching, which along with the dense nature of the vegetation means that general game viewing is extremely poor by comparison with Liwonde, Nyika, Vwaza or Lengwe national parks, though recent clampdowns on poaching give some cause for future optimism. Kasungu was once the best place in Malawi to see black rhinoceros, but these are now locally extinct. Common ungulates include Burchell's zebra, warthog, buffalo, puku, sable antelope, roan antelope, kudu, reedbuck and the very localised Lichtenstein's hartebeest. In addition to the wildlife, Kasungu boasts several prehistoric sites, including an iron-smelting kiln, rock paintings, and the remains of fortified villages. However, if you go to Kasungu, you must go without expectations of wildlife, but be content with the grunting and snorting of hippo, the calm sight of puku sitting in the sun and incredible flowers, including many orchids in the first months of rain.

Kasungu National Park was once the meeting place for weekenders coming from the farms and cities to relax in the bush. It is now a place to come and escape the rest of the world, be lulled to sleep by frogs and be woken by fish eagles. It's a hideaway that's not so far from anywhere, but miles from everywhere. It's accessible in terms of price for both backpackers and more comfort-loving creatures. There's a quiet simplicity about the place now that attracts people wanting to get away from commercial comforts. Having said that there is a good mobile phone signal thanks to the British Army which comes on exercise three times each year, leaving a healthy legacy of roads, bridges, culverts etc.

Kasungu National Park is, above all, a real unspoilt bush experience. The park is slowly trying to recover from severe poaching in the 1980s and 1990s. Now the low prey stock means that whilst you might hear the occasional roar of a lion you will seldom see one. Leopards, genets and civets are the most common predators. The ecosystem of the park is complete, meaning that the populations of cheetah, wild dog, black rhinoceros now locally extinct could potentially be reintroduced in the future. Once poaching is properly controlled, the populations of antelope and elephant will multiply quickly. The University of Pretoria came in 2005 and estimated the elephant population to have dropped to as low as 150, shocking when you learn that the park once had the highest population of elephant in the country. However it is still excellent terrain for elephant, with woodlands, grazing areas and Lake Lifupa in front of the lodge, where in the dry season at least half the population will come down to drink twice a day. The camp pet is a large young bull elephant called Jonathon.

There is a possibility that Peace Parks Foundation will help co-ordinate relations between Zambia National Parks and Malawi National Parks to open game corridors. Among the rare sights of Kasungu is a grey leopard, seen only four times; some ask if this is a colour morph or simply melanistic – ie: a panther, a black cat, which is quite a common phenomenon in some areas.

One of the loveliest views in Kasungu is from Black Rock, a hill to be climbed up where the whole of the park stretches endlessly before you, with hills behind hills as far as the eye can see.

GETTING THERE AND AWAY The national park entrance gate lies roughly 38km from Kasungu Town along the dirt D187, past the enormous empty palace built by Banda. From the entrance gate it's another 22km to Lifupa Lodge. The turn-off from the M1 is clearly signposted. The D187 was at the time of writing navigable in any vehicle – in fact, the main danger along this road is not getting stuck so much as skidding off it, so do drive carefully, especially when you might meet tobacco lorries, and then inside the park there's the danger of bumping into an elephant.

Without private transport, it's best to take a taxi from Kasungu Town, which is not prohibitively expensive though you will need to bargain over prices (we were initially asked US$60 but settled at US$25 with a minimum of fuss) and assuming that you got a good price on the way there, you'll be glad to have jotted down a phone number for the same driver to collect you on the way out in case there aren't any other vehicles leaving that day.

WHERE TO STAY Note that the park entrance fee is payable by all visitors in addition to lodge fees.

Lifupa Lodge Bookings 01 254079/09 925512. The lodge overlooks Kasuni Dam, a lake which supports a number of hippo as well as attracting animals coming to drink. The lodge can sleep 35 people in thatched chalets each with en suite bathrooms and private balconies, while there is plenty of space in the campsite which has hot showers and a self-catering kitchen and dining area. All guests can use the lodge's attractive communal bar and dining area, with its dramatic thatched upper deck. It has extremely tasty food, particularly famous for the delicious homemade chutneys, jams and pickles. *Sgl/dbl US$55/70 FB, camping US$5, dorm US$10.*

WHAT TO SEE AND DO Lifupa Lodge runs morning game drives and night drives, the latter – seriously chilly in winter – offering the opportunity to see a variety of nocturnal predators. Game activities range from US$5–20, including fishing, game drives and walking safaris. With a good map it is quite possible to drive around the park without a guide.

Best bet of all, the campsite on Lifupa Dam is an excellent place to chill out for a few days, waiting for the game to come to you – in addition to the certainty of sighting hippo, puku and several varieties of bird, large herds of elephant tend to visit the dam daily in the dry season. A few days in Kasungu, even including the taxi in, can therefore be extremely reasonable if you're self catering and camping and also won't break the bank if you're not.

MZIMBA

From Kasungu, the M1 runs north through the koppie-strewn central plateau before ascending gently through dense *brachystegia* woodland into the pine forests of the Viphya Hills and the leafy, breezy town of Mzimba. Lying some 15km west of the main highway to Mzuzu, Mzimba feels slightly isolated, but it's a well-equipped and pleasant little place, and very friendly. The town itself lacks any obvious points of interest, but it could be a possible stopover before catching an early-morning bus to Vwaza Marsh Wildlife Reserve (see pages 130–2).

GETTING THERE AND AWAY Some buses between Lilongwe and Mzuzu divert to Mzimba. A bus leaves Mzimba for Kazuni and Rumphi at about 14.00, stopping at Kazuni Tented Camp in Vwaza Marsh Wildlife Reserve and minibuses leave when full in the morning.

WHERE TO STAY The **Mame Motel** on the outskirts of town is a good clean place to stay, with rooms from MK800–3,000. The **Shumami Mame Resthouse** and the **Kanjinja Resthouse** in town have rooms at much lower prices, with bucket showers only. The **Mbanasi Resthouse** has self-contained rooms for MK600.

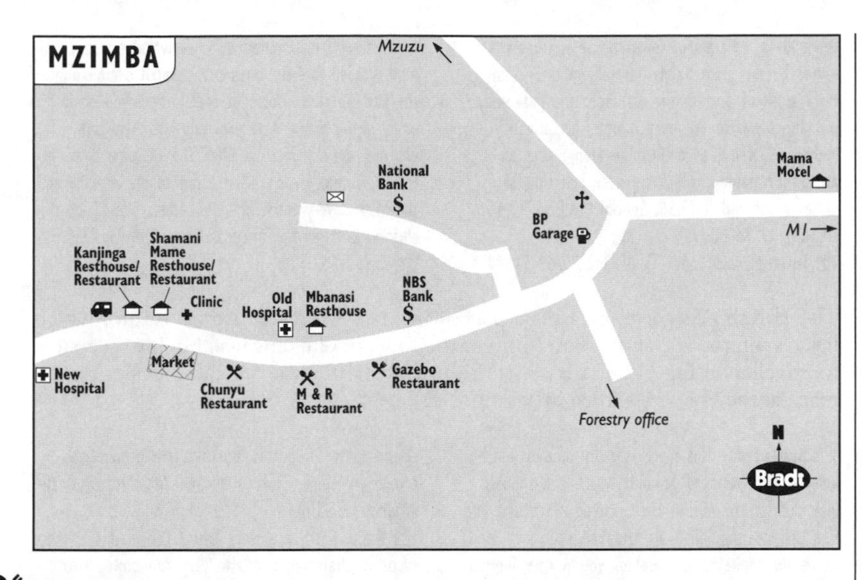

WHERE TO EAT There are plenty of restaurants scattered around town; the best place is the **M&R Restaurant**, and the **Chunyu Restaurant** a close second, both serving plates for less than US$2. If you're stocking up for a visit to one of the forestry resthouses or to Vwaza Marsh, there's a good vegetable market and supermarkets.

VIPHYA FOREST RESERVE North of Mzimba, as the M1 continues climbing on to the Viphya Plateau, thick *brachystegia* woodland gives way to the exotic pine plantations of Viphya Forest Reserve. Set at an altitude of around 2,000m, this area has a refreshingly crisp climate. Viphya is Africa's second-largest pine plantation, but there are also some significant patches of indigenous forest.

This is lovely walking country: the scenery is beautiful and there is still some game around. Duiker and vervet monkeys are likely to be seen by visitors, but bushpigs and leopards are also resident. The area offers excellent birdwatching, with several species that are otherwise restricted to the less accessible Nyika Plateau and is perhaps the best area in the country for mountain biking.

Getting there and away Any country bus running along the M1 between Mzimba and Mzuzu will drop you at the Kasito Lodge bus stage, which lies about 20km north of Mzimba and 4km south of Chikengawa. Kasito Resthouse is directly opposite the bus stage, while Kasito Lodge is about 500m further down the road towards Mzuzu.

When you're ready to leave, you may find buses are reluctant to pick up passengers at the Kasito bus stage. It's better to walk about 1km up the M1 towards Mzimba and wait at Macdonald's bus stage (named after a Scottish forestry officer who camped on the site for several years in the colonial era). To pick up an express bus, it's best to walk the 4km to Chikengawa.

Luwawa Forest Lodge lies to the east of the M1. Without transport, you might call the lodge to see if there's a lift going, or hike in the 8km on the D73. By road there are three access roads off the M1, two of them clearly signed, the third is guesswork. It depends which direction you're coming from as to which you should take.

Where to stay

Raiply Guesthouse 01 340241. An attractive overnight stop and a good base for birdwatchers and walkers, 21km past the Mzimba turn-off on the M1 and only a couple of kilometres from the road.

Originally a government forest house it is now owned by the giant Raiply sawmill, so there's an extra smell of pine in the air. From the gate they will direct you to the neat rooms with private bathrooms. It has a comfortable lounge and an attached restaurant which serves a selection of dishes at around US$3.50. *Sgl/dbl MK1,557/3,400, camping US$6 pp.*

Luwawa Forest Lodge 01 342333/09 915442; e wardlow@malawi.net; www.luwawalodgemalawi.com. An upgraded forestry resthouse situated overlooking the Luwawa Dam. This is a place where you could easily spend a few days exploring the area and enjoying the activities on offer. The welcome is warm (not only that, there's often a fire in the hearth) and the food is very tasty. *En-suite chalets US$40 pp BB sharing (children half-price, sharing), camping US$5 pp, dorm US$10 pp.*

The Forestry Department runs a pair of inexpensive resthouses at Kasito, which lies just off the M1 about 4km south of the town of Chikengawa. Highly accessible to travellers using public transport. Enquiries about either of these places can be made at the Forestry Office in Mzimba.

Kasito Lodge This place is sadly unused and unloved, with terraced grounds where you should look out for the African citril, a type of canary. This is a 'self-catering' lodge, so bring all your own food, which the cook can prepare for you. A very limited range of goods (sodas, vegetables and rice) can be bought at the market in Chikengawa. The lodge sleeps up to 20 people, but as often as not it's completely empty. *Rooms MK700 pp, camping in the grounds US$3 pp.*

Kasito Resthouse Near Kasito Lodge, this is more rustic in character, and also very run down, with similar facilities to the lodge. *Rooms MK500 pp.*

What to see and do There is plenty of good walking in the Viphya, from hikes all the way to the lake, to short walks around your lodge. Luwawa Forest Lodge is run by outdoor and environmental enthusiasts, so if you stay here you might find yourself doing anything from visiting any of the seven village projects (and taking part) or hiking, abseiling, rock climbing, mountain biking, sailing, canoeing and orienteering (there's suitable equipment for hire). The forest walks and birding are very rewarding and montane grassland is also accessible. Fishing on the dam is permitted in season. Surprisingly there's squash, table tennis, volleyball, sailing, canoeing, forest fitness courses and 4x4 challenges as well. Of all this though, Luwawa is best known for its mountain biking, and the lodge has developed a three-day mountain-bike safari to Lake Malawi (a bit longer by foot).

The annual Luwawa International Charity Mountain Bike Marathon takes place in June.

LUWAWA INTERNATIONAL CHARITY MOUNTAIN BIKE MARATHON

The annual Luwawa International Charity Mountain Bike Marathon (sponsored by Limbe Leaf Tobacco Company) takes place in June. The race starts at Kasito Lodge, Chikangawa and finishes 42km later at Luwawa Forest Lodge. Bikers hurtle from Kasito Lodge on the main M1 road (40km north of Mzimba) through the south Viphya Forest Reserve on good dirt roads, passing through pristine indigenous brachystegia woodland over the Viphya Mountain ridge road to Luwawa dam. Beautiful scenery lines the well-marked tracks up and down remote hills, taking in the biggest pine forest in Africa. Cyclists are encouraged to enter the race sponsored in aid of local charities and particularly the Luwawa Environmental Trust. Entry fees are MK600 pp (Malawi Nationals MK300), which includes course marshalling, vehicle backup and first-aid support. *For enquiries, contact Luwawa Forest Lodge;* *09 915442;* e *wardlow@malawi.net; www.luwawalodgemalawi.com.*

From the garden of Kasito Lodge, you can follow a clear path to the base of the valley and over a small stream, where, after about 200m, it connects with a disused road. Turn left into this road, and after perhaps 2km, passing through plantation forest and dense undergrowth, rich in butterflies and notable for several immense communal webs built by a type of spider with a bright purple body the size of a thumb, you should come to a five-point junction. Take the first left downhill into a thick patch of indigenous forest which can be extremely good for birds: among the more interesting species I saw here were olive-bellied mountain bulbul, Fulleborne's black boubou and golden weaver. The middle path meanders to Kasito Dam, an attractive spot set in a pine plantation, and reasonably rewarding for birds. It takes about 15 minutes to walk from the junction to the dam, and once there you can follow a track past the dam for another ten minutes or so to reach the M1, where a left turn will take you back to the lodge. Wozi Hill is also off this junction by only a couple of kilometres, from where you will have views over the whole area. Also worth a look is the riverine forest which runs along a stream about 100m west of the M1 towards Chikengawa. There are several side roads off the M1 in this area which you could explore.

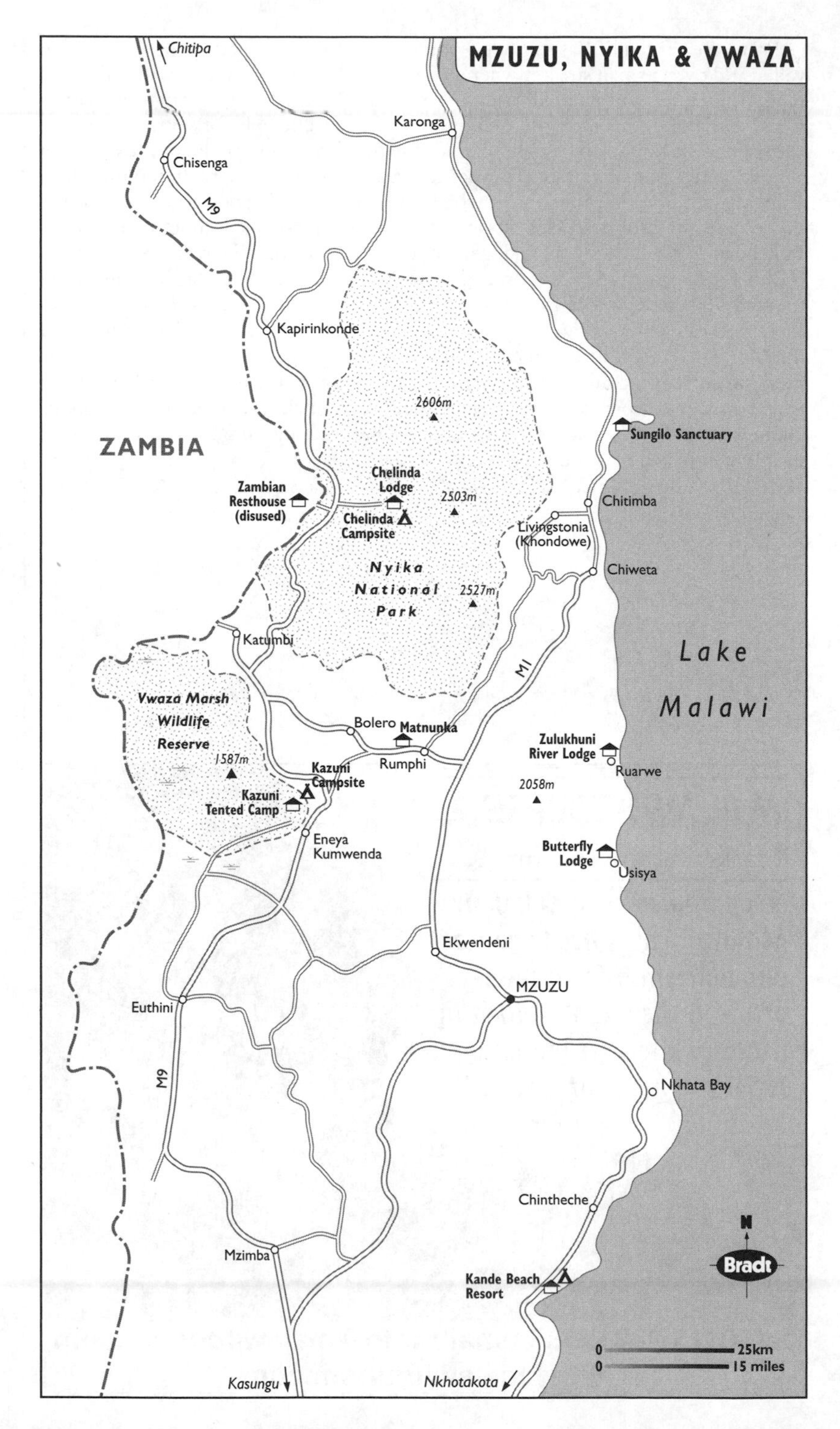
MZUZU, NYIKA & VWAZA
Chitipa
Karonga
Chisenga
M9
Kapirinkonde
ZAMBIA
2606m
Sungilo Sanctuary
Zambian Resthouse (disused)
Chelinda Lodge
Chelinda Campsite
2503m
Chitimba
Livingstonia (Khondowe)
Chiweta
Nyika National Park
2527m
Katumbi
Lake Malawi
M1
Vwaza Marsh Wildlife Reserve
Bolero
Matnunka
Rumphi
Zulukhuni River Lodge
Ruarwe
1587m
Kazuni Campsite
Kazuni Tented Camp
2058m
Eneya Kumwenda
Butterfly Lodge
Usisya
Ekwendeni
MZUZU
Euthini
M9
Nkhata Bay
Chintheche
N
Bradt
Mzimba
Kande Beach Resort
0 25km
0 15 miles
Kasungu
Nkhotakota

8

Mzuzu, Nyika National Park and Vwaza Marsh Wildlife Reserve

Mzuzu is the largest town in northern Malawi and the region's major route focus, lying on the junction of the M1 between Lilongwe and the Tanzanian border and the lakeshore road from Nkhata Bay. Mzuzu is one of Malawi's friendliest towns, there's a people culture here that means that it's a good place to sit and chat in one of the cafés or bars. The university just out of town is gathering pace and now has over 1,000 students. There is a fair choice for shopping, hotels, restaurants, markets, cafés, bars and clubs. For travellers continuing on north to Tanzania, it's a good transport hub too.

Mzuzu and the nearby town of Rumphi are springboards for visits to two of Malawi's finest conservation areas: Nyika National Park and Vwaza Marsh Wildlife Reserve. Nyika is a beautiful, rolling highland plateau where visitors can walk freely amongst a variety of big game species. Vwaza Marsh is readily accessible both to motorised travellers and to backpackers, and it offers exceptional game viewing, elephants being particularly numerous.

CLIMATE

Mzuzu has an attractive moderate climate, and it's one of the few towns in Malawi where rain can fall at almost any time of the year. The Nyika Plateau lies at an altitude of over 2,000m and is thus one of the coldest parts of Malawi, with winds that can make it searingly cold at night. Vwaza Marsh, on the other hand, is low-lying, hot and humid, and mosquitoes and tsetse flies are abundant.

GETTING AROUND

Mzuzu is a major public transport hub. There are regular buses between Mzuzu and Lilongwe, Karonga and Nkhata Bay. Between Mzuzu and Rumphi (the gateway town to Nyika and Vwaza Marsh) buses are supplemented by a steady stream of minibuses.

There is not much public transport west of Rumphi. One bus runs daily in each direction between Rumphi and Mzimba (on the Viphya Plateau), passing within 1km of Kazuni Tented Camp at Vwaza Marsh. Nyika is more difficult to reach without private transport, and even if you manage to get a lift to the Thazima Gate, you have to hitch or walk the last 16km to Chelinda Camp. It is however, very much worth the effort.

If you have private transport, it's advisable to check the current condition of the roads to Vwaza and Nyika at the Wildlife Office in Mzuzu or Rumphi, especially if your vehicle is not a 4x4 and you are travelling during the wet season. Assuming the roads are passable, it will take less than an hour to reach Vwaza from Rumphi, and perhaps four hours to reach Chelinda Camp in Nyika.

MZUZU

Mzuzu, the official capital of Malawi's northern province, has a sleepy provincial atmosphere, compared with which even Lilongwe and Blantyre seem positively cosmopolitan. This is not surprising when you discover that less than 50 years ago Mzuzu was merely the name of a stream running through rural hillside. It has a relatively small town centre, with huge residential areas in the outskirts. Even until the time of Malawi's independence, Mzuzu was practically inaccessible during the rainy season; the highlight of the expatriate social calendar was the arrival every Friday of a Beaver plane from Lilongwe.

Despite this, or perhaps because of it, Mzuzu is regarded by many to be the most likeable of Malawi's three regional capitals. In size and atmosphere, it fits somewhere between small town and city (it only officially received city status in 1991); climatically it occupies a mid-altitude (1,200m) niche between the lakeshore humidity of nearby Nkhata Bay and the breezy highland chill of the Viphya Hills, while an average annual rainfall of around 1,750mm ensures the town and the surrounding hills are green and fertile all year through.

As for tourist-related facilities, Mzuzu has several smart hotels, small resthouses, a few decent restaurants and cafés, supermarkets, a couple of internet offices and several banks. For all that, few travellers do more than pass through Mzuzu, and, pleasant as the town may be, it's difficult to think of any compelling reason to do otherwise.

Mzuzu Museum is an excellent resource for local schools and is worth a quick guided tour (*08 870809 for Aupson Tholy, the curator*) as many of the exhibits are living history (the types of baskets and spoons etc that you can see in any village). More interesting than the exhibits however is the range of activities that can be arranged though the museum; traditional music groups and dancing is often put on at the museum on request. There's Zulu-language lessons twice a week, if you're there for a long time.

GETTING THERE AND AWAY Well-surfaced roads connect Mzuzu to Lilongwe in the south, Karonga in the north, and Nkhata Bay on the lakeshore. There are regular buses along all these routes. A Shire bus connects Lilongwe and Mzuzu, leaving from the Capital Hotel in Lilongwe and the Mzuzu Hotel in Mzuzu at 07.00 daily in both directions. The Express bus takes about five hours and costs MK1,200, from the main bus stations in each city.

WHERE TO STAY

Business class

Mzuzu Hotel 01 332622; e mzuzuhotel@sunbirdmalawi.com. Set in attractive grounds on the outskirts of town. The s/c rooms are large and clean, with satellite TV and 24-hour room service. On Fri nights the Choma Bar is the place to go. Facilities include a good restaurant and bar with pool table, airport transfers, hairdressing, car hire, internet, photocopy, fax and secretarial services, and foreign exchange at a good rate for hotel residents only. Air Malawi and DHL offices are here. *Sgl/dbl US$88/101, standard rooms sgl/dbl US$76/89, stes sgl/dbl US$100/131.*

Mzuzu Lodge About 1km out of town on the Nkhata Bay road; 01 332097; e mzuzulodge@sdnp.org.mw. The large, comfortable rooms with fans are good value. *Sgl/dbl US$30–40/35–45 or US$50/55 for a sgl/dbl executive room with a panoramic view of the hills below the city.*

Chenda Hotel Town centre, near the bus station; 01 335255. High in standard, though very different in style with acceptable s/c rooms with hot showers. *Sgl/dbl/twin/trpl MK2,000/3,500/4,500/5,000.*

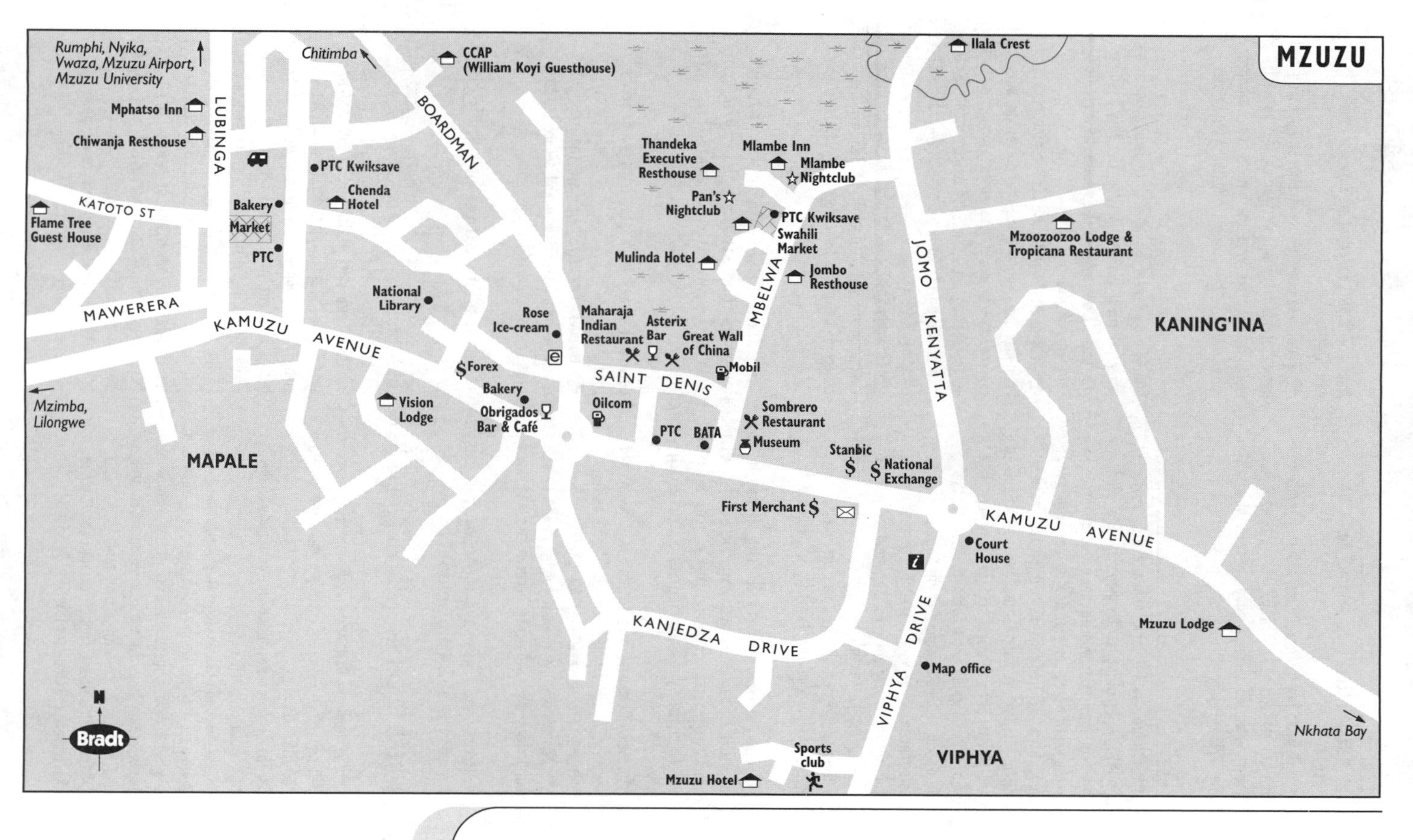
MZUZU
Rumphi, Nyika, Vwaza, Mzuzu Airport, Mzuzu University
Chitimba
CCAP (William Koyi Guesthouse)
Ilala Crest
Mphatso Inn
Chiwanja Resthouse
LUBINGA
BOARDMAN
PTC Kwiksave
Chenda Hotel
Thandeka Executive Resthouse
Mlambe Inn
Mlambe Nightclub
Pan's Nightclub
PTC Kwiksave
Swahili Market
Mzoozoozoo Lodge & Tropicana Restaurant
KATOTO ST
Flame Tree Guest House
Bakery
Market
PTC
Mulinda Hotel
Jombo Resthouse
MBELWA
JOMO KENYATTA
National Library
MAWERERA
KAMUZU AVENUE
Rose Ice-cream
Maharaja Indian Restaurant
Asterix Bar
Great Wall of China
KANING'INA
Forex
SAINT DENIS
Mobil
Mzimba, Lilongwe
Vision Lodge
Bakery
Obrigados Bar & Café
Oilcom
PTC
BATA
Sombrero Restaurant
Museum
Stanbic
National Exchange
MAPALE
First Merchant
KAMUZU AVENUE
Court House
KANJEDZA DRIVE
VIPHYA DRIVE
Mzuzu Lodge
Map office
N
Bradt
Nkhata Bay
Sports club
Mzuzu Hotel
VIPHYA

Mid range

Ilala Crest Lodge Jomo Kenyatta Rd; ☎ 01 331834.

Mphatso Inn Karonga Rd, only 5 mins' walk from the bus station; ☎ 01 334205. The restaurant at the Mphatso Inn serves a good selection of meals in the US$2–4 range. *Ordinary rooms sgl/dbl MK1,250/2,500, excellent s/c superior dbls MK3,000.*

Flame Tree Guest House Katoto St. Appealing and homely, it has a calm quiet garden feel about it and is not too far from the bus station. *Standard rooms MK1,500, s/c rooms MK2,500, inc b/fast.*

Budget

Mzoozoozoo Off Jomo Kenyatta Rd, ☎ 01 864493; e espositopilat@yahoo.com. The liveliest place in town with wooden dorm and rooms, a retro caravan and an ever-flowing bar with good food from the Tropicana Restaurant and music, often live. One of Malawi's top bands, the Souls of the Ghetto often rehearse and perform here. If you're backpacking you'll want to head to the 'Zoo'. You will find a mine of up-to-date information about what's available in terms of tourism in the region from the owner or just by reading the posters in the bathroom. Giving it its full title, unsigned on any road, the Mzoozoozoo Backpackers Lodge and Campsite is not easy to find (the sign went on holiday to Kande Beach and never returned) but ask anyone and they'll guide you there. *Dorms MK500, en-suite dbl MK1,000, camping MK500.*

William Koyi Guesthouse CCAP compound off Boardman Rd. Another good (but somewhat more conventional) option. It is often full, though it's still worth checking out as it's not too far from the bus station. *Dorm MK300 pp, 2 s/c dbls MK950 each, camping MK250.*

Chiwanja Resthouse Karonga Rd, only 5 mins' walk from the bus station; ☎ 01 333362. Offers a variety of basic but clean rooms *MK350–700.*

These three options in the budget range stand out. By comparison, the main cluster of budget accommodation, which lies in the backstreets behind the banks and supermarkets, is none too salubrious, as the same area is also dense with nightclubs, pick-up joints – and dodgy drains:

Jombo Resthouse with scruffy rooms in the old wing for around MK210/480 sgl/dbl and much better dbls in the new wing for MK600.

Mlambe Inn The cleanest rooms around here, but its position, sandwiched between two nightclubs, doesn't bode well for a peaceful night or fellow clientele.

Thandeka Executive Resthouse The more expensive rooms seem clean and secure but the cheaper rooms are shockingly grim.

Otherwise, there are close on ten resthouses in this area, most of which charge around US$2/4 single/double.

WHERE TO EAT There's a surprising choice in Mzuzu:

The **Tropicana Restaurant** at Mzoozoozoo serves a delicious range of meals, including daily specials, in the US$3–5 range.

The **Sombrero Restaurant** serves reputedly the best steak in town.

The **Obrigado Café** is a great place to hang out during the day or evening, with a shady garden and a good Malawian menu for US$2–4; the garden also has a boxing ring, a stage, a children's play area, and a music venue with a pool table.

For fresh spices straight from the coast, go to the **Maharaja Restaurant** (☎ *09 351550/01 331839*), with tasty curries for MK450, and by special order a laden pizza for MK1,000. It's worth going there if you're on your way to Tanzania by bus at midnight, as last food orders are not until 22.00 especially for travellers.

The **Great Wall of China** is an appetising Chinese just next door with similar prices. The restaurant at the **Chenda Hotel** might also be worth a try.

The restaurant at the **Mzuzu Hotel** serves decent meals in the US$5–6 range.

The **William Koyi Guesthouse** serves good wholesome cheap meals at US$1.50.

RUMPHI

This small town, attractively ringed by hills, is the springboard for visits to Nyika National Park and Vwaza Marsh Wildlife Reserve, the two prime game-viewing areas in northern Malawi.

As far as travel practicalities go, most of the essentials are to be found in Rumphi. In addition to a few resthouses and restaurants, Rumphi has supermarkets (though not nearly as well stocked as those in Mzuzu), a bank, and a decent market. There is also a wildlife office a short distance out of town, back towards the main Mzuzu–Karonga road.

GETTING THERE AND AWAY Minibuses between Mzuzu and Rumphi leave regularly in either direction on a fill-up-and-go basis. Buses between Mzuzu and Karonga generally divert to Rumphi. There is a twice-weekly *matola* service from Rumphi to Livingstonia (see page 138) along one of the most scenic routes in the country and a daily bus connecting Rumphi with Mzimba via Vwaza Marsh (see page 114). There is an option to walk from Rumphi to Vwaza on an organised walk with Matunka Safari Camp using local guides and taking only a maximum of five people per group, which also guides a two-day hike to Chelinda on the Nyika Plateau.

WHERE TO STAY Accommodation in Rumphi is mostly spotlessly clean and of a good standard. The closest thing to upmarket accommodation is the **Luninya Motel**, which has ordinary rooms with three-quarter beds and mosquito nets for around MK350 and very pleasant self-contained doubles (hot showers, fans) for MK700. The **County Accommodation** and **County Annexe** nearby have perhaps the best rooms in town for MK700. Of the more local resthouses in Rumphi, the **Chitukuko Resthouse** and the **Yangotha Hideaway Resthouse** are the best, with clean rooms for US$1/2 single/double, and communal baths. Cheaper still is the pretty basic **Fumbauzi Resthouse**, with rooms for around US$1.

Matunkha Safari Camp 3km out of town towards Nyika; 08 203424/08 202641; e ecotourism@matunkha.com; www.matunka.com. Any minibus will drop you there. This eco-tourism camp, set on the hillside and in the grounds of an impressive orphanage, has very attractive and reasonably priced chalets, guesthouses and camping to generate money for the orphanage. Whilst you will find that lodges in Malawi are often quietly supporting a raft of community projects and

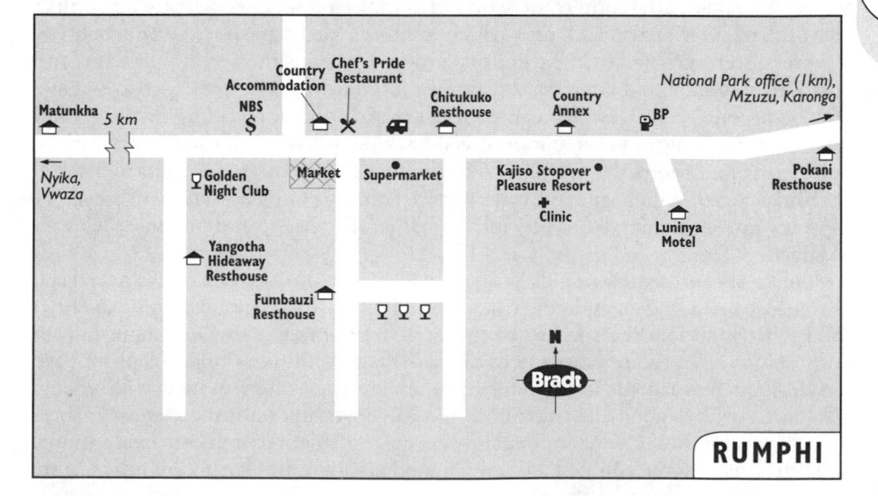

orphanages, this is nevertheless very impressive and a stay here will be very informative. There's a restaurant on site for guests (MK400 supper/lunch) and a small craft shop. *Rooms from MK400–800 pp, camping MK300.*

WHERE TO EAT

The best place to eat is the **Mbakajiso Restaurant** (part of the Kajiso Stopover Pleasure Resort), though you could also try one of the several local eateries around the bus station, of which the **County Restaurant** and the **Chef's Pride Restaurant** are recommended.

And *don't* miss out on a cold beer at the **Kajiso Stopover Pleasure Resort**, a riotous pick-up joint which, with its blaring sound system, flashing lights and myriad bar girls, wouldn't look out of place in downtown Nairobi, particularly during the tobacco season when local farmers roll into Rumphi to drink away their profits.

WHAT TO SEE AND DO Matunkha Safari Camp offers a range of activities, including guided cultural walks in nearby villages and hikes to the camps at Vwaza Marsh and Nyika National Park, of particular interest to anyone who wants to continue the trek over the other side of the Nyika Plateau to Livingstonia. The Camp has its own stables, and offers horseriding at US$5 per hour, including tours in the lower slopes of the Nyika. They will also organise day trips to Livingstonia by vehicle and have a range of further-afield safaris including three-week tours to North and South Luangwa National Park in Zambia.

NYIKA NATIONAL PARK

Malawi's largest national park, Nyika (*entrance fee US$5 pp per 24 hours; daily fee for private vehicles US$2*), was gazetted in 1965 and extended to its modern size of 3,134km² in 1978, though parts of what are now the national park have been under government protection since the 1940s. At the heart of the park, averaging over 2,000m in altitude, lies the gently undulating Nyika Plateau, where montane grassland and fern heather communities, notable for their prolific wild flowers during the rainy season, are interspersed with isolated stands of indigenous forest and exotic pine and eucalyptus plantations. Although the Nyika Plateau is very much the centrepiece of the park, and the only part of it which is readily accessible to tourists, the *brachystegia*-covered lower slopes of the Nyika range also lie within its boundaries.

Nyika's main attraction is the wonderful montane scenery, a landscape unlike any other in Malawi, and one which reminds many visitors of Europe (an impression reinforced by the extensive pine plantations in the Chelinda area and the chilly winter nights characteristic of the plateau). The park is also notable for being one of the few African national parks with horseriding facilities, and for allowing visitors the freedom to walk as they please along a vast network of dirt roads and footpaths. Of particular interest to botanists are the roughly 200 orchid species which generally flower in January and February; of these, 11 species are endemic to Nyika and a further 27 are found nowhere else in Malawi.

Nyika also protects a rich diversity of mammals: almost 100 species have been recorded, including an endemic race of Burchell's zebra (*Equus burchelli crawshayi*) and what is widely regarded to be the most concentrated leopard population in central Africa. In recent years a herd of more than 40 altitude-loving elephant have made their permanent home here, and they are now often spotted with young. Game viewing is good all year round, and the open nature of the plateau ensures excellent visibility. Owing to extensive poaching in more remote areas, animal populations are concentrated around Chelinda (sometimes spelt Chilinda) Camp,

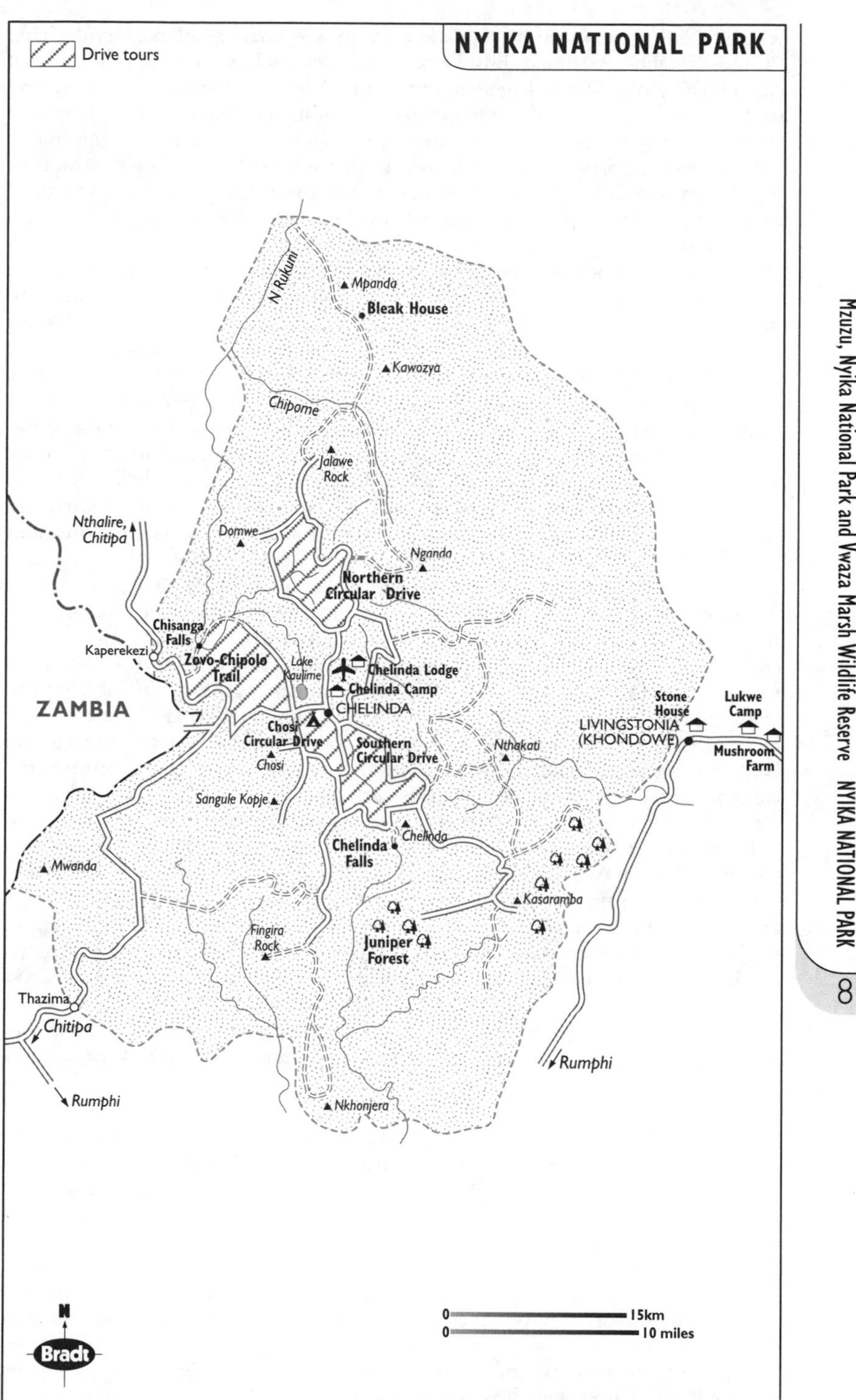
NYIKA NATIONAL PARK
Drive tours
N Rukuru
Mpanda
Bleak House
Kawozya
Chipome
Jalawe Rock
Domwe
Nthalire, Chitipa
Nganda
Northern Circular Drive
Chisanga Falls
Kaperekezi
Zovo-Chipolo Trail
Lake Kaulime
Chelinda Lodge
Chelinda Camp
CHELINDA
ZAMBIA
Chosi Circular Drive
Chosi
Southern Circular Drive
Nthakati
Stone House
Lukwe Camp
LIVINGSTONIA (KHONDOWE)
Mushroom Farm
Sangule Kopje
Chelinda
Chelinda Falls
Mwanda
Kasaramba
Fingira Rock
Juniper Forest
Thazima
Chitipa
Rumphi
Nkhonjera
Rumphi
N
Bradt
0 15km
0 10 miles

where visitors are practically guaranteed to see roan antelope, scrub hare, Burchell's zebra, reedbuck, bushbuck and eland, and stand a good chance of encountering one of the leopards that haunt Chelinda Forest. The *brachystegia* woodland of the lower slopes supports significant populations of buffalo and elephant, though – perhaps fortunately for walkers – these animals only rarely move up to the grassy plateau. Lion and cheetah are listed as infrequent visitors to the plateau, and although they haven't been seen in years, visitors do stand a good chance of encountering hyenas and smaller nocturnal predators on night drives out of Chelinda Camp.

With well over 400 species recorded, Nyika supports the greatest diversity of birds found anywhere in Malawi, though this figure is rather deceptive as many of the species included on the checklist occur only in the inaccessible *brachystegia* woodland of the lower slopes and are thus unlikely to be seen by visitors who stick to the plateau. Nevertheless, the grassland around Chelinda Camp is inhabited by several tantalising birds. Foremost among these is the wattled crane, a large, striking bird which is internationally endangered; nowhere in its wide range is this very localised species as likely to be seen as it is in the marshes around Chelinda. The dam in front of Chelinda is a good place to pick up the yellow and black mountain marsh widow, a species restricted to a handful of montane areas in central Africa. Other grassland birds of note include the localised Denham's bustard and the exquisite scarlet-tufted malachite sunbird. More rewarding than the grassland for general birding are the forests, particularly the large Chowo Forest near the Zambian Resthouse, where localised species such as Sharpe's akalat, bar-tailed trogon, olive-flanked robin, white-breasted alethe and a variety of other robins and bulbuls may be seen. Four birds found at Nyika have been recorded nowhere else in Malawi (yellow mountain warbler, chirring cisticola, crackling cloud cisticola and mountain marsh widow), while the Nyika races of red-winged francolin, rufous-naped lark, greater double-collared sunbird and Baglafecht weaver are endemic to the plateau. There are also three butterfly species endemic to the plateau, and one species each of chameleon, frog and toad which are found nowhere else.

From a practical point of view, 1997 was a time of great change at Nyika. Chelinda Camp was leased by the government to the private Nyika Safari Company, which also has the sole concession for organising activities such as night drives, horseriding, overnight wilderness trails and the granting of fishing permits. Access to the reserve has also improved, and the roads are generally in good condition. In addition, the German KFW bank has provided funding of US$8 million towards the improvement of tourist facilities and an anti-poaching service, in the hope that Nyika might yet generate enough profit through tourism and timber production to satisfy the requirements of the government, the private sector and local communities.

FURTHER INFORMATION A highly recommended purchase is Sigrid Anna Johnson's 150-page *A Visitor's Guide to Nyika National Park, Malawi* (Mbabazi Book Trust, Blantyre), which is available at most good bookshops in Blantyre and Lilongwe as well as at Chelinda Camp for around US$4. This book provides a detailed historical and ecological background to Nyika, 20 pages of special-interest sites and recommended walks and hikes, as well as complete checklists of all mammals, birds, butterflies and orchids which are known to occur in the park. A range of other books, pamphlets and maps relating to Nyika is sold at the shop in Chelinda Camp.

The best source of current practical information is the Nyika Safari Company (*01 330180*; e *reservations@nyika.com; www.nyika.com*).

GETTING THERE AND AWAY By road, Chelinda Camp lies roughly 100km from Rumphi, and is reached along recently regraded dirt roads which shouldn't present any problem in the dry season but which may require a 4x4 vehicle after heavy rain. The route is clearly signposted: from Rumphi you need to follow the S85 westwards for around 50km, then turn right into the S10 to Chitipa. Thazima Entrance Gate is 8km along the S10. About 30km past the entrance gate, a signposted turn-off to the right leads to Chelinda, a further 16km away. If you are driving yourself, take note that the last place where you can buy fuel before reaching Chelinda is at Rumphi. During the rains it might be worth stopping overnight in Mzuzu or Rumphi on the way.

Without private transport, getting to Chelinda cheaply by road can be problematic (the Nyika Safari Company does offer road transfers from Mzuzu, but at US$100 per person this isn't an option for budget travellers). There is no public transport all the way through. In the dry season, a twice-weekly bus between Rumphi and Chitipa can drop you at the last turn-off, from where you'll either have to walk the last 30km to Chelinda (it's reasonably flat!) or else hope to hitch a lift. In the rainy season, there is no bus but you can easily get a *matola* lift from Rumphi along the S85 (ask for a vehicle heading to Katumbi), and then walk the 8km from where you will be dropped at the entrance gate. Provided you have a tent, it is permitted to camp at the entrance gate, though facilities are basic.

It is now possible to do a two-day hike up to Chelinda from Rumphi (see *Rumphi*, *What to see and do* above) and then to traverse the Nyika across to Livingstonia over two or three days (see *What to see and do* below). It would doubtless be possible to leave excess baggage at Matunka.

If you happen to have your own plane, there is an airstrip at Chelinda and Nyika Safari Company also have a charter flight option linking Chelinda with Mzuzu (US$300 per plane, max five people) and Likoma Island (US$555) as the most popular routes.

WHERE TO STAY AND EAT There is only one area to stay on the Nyika unless you are on a guided safari with overnight stops:

Chelinda Lodge is an upmarket stone lodge on the edge of the forest at Chelinda, where 8 luxurious en-suite log cabins command stunning views across the montane grasslands of the plateau. Rates are US$310 pp inclusive of all meals and game drives.

Chelinda Camp is a picturesque cluster of old colonial forestry accommodation a little lower down, overlooking an attractive small dam and encircled by an extensive plantation of exotic pines. The camp consists of 6 recently renovated s/c dbl rooms, each of which costs US$150 pp FB. In addition to the rooms, there are 4 private self-catering chalets costing US$120 per unit. Each chalet has 2 dbl bedrooms, a large lounge, an en-suite shower and toilet, and a fully equipped kitchen.

Chelinda Campsite is about 2km from the main camp and is one of the loveliest places to stay due to the sweeping views over the undulating grasslands. It has welcome hot showers in a large ablution block and you can pitch your own tent for US$5 pp. The walk back from the bar at night is a bit intrepid, given that hyena and leopard are around. There's a sign all campers should heed in the campsite, to tidy all belongings away as 'hyenas eat everything', and have even been known to gnaw on car tyres.

Visitors staying in the chalets or campsite have the option of preparing their own food, but you must bring all your provisions with you or risk being very hungry. The nearest shops are four hours back in Rumphi. Should you want to eat in the camp dining room, you must book well in advance – continental breakfast US$5, full breakfast and lunch US$10 per person, dinner US$15. There is also a snack menu. Any bookings and enquiries can be addressed to the Nyika Safari Company (see page 126).

WHAT TO SEE AND DO Nyika National Park is rich in scenic spots, archaeological sites, mammals and birds, and the extensive network of roads and trails within the park gives visitors a practically unlimited number of hiking and driving options. The following synopsis of major attractions serves as a taster only; visitors to Nyika are strongly urged to supplement it with the more detailed information included in the book *A Visitor's Guide to Nyika National Park*.

Note that while visitors are free to walk where they please by day (and to explore the park by road if they have private transport), all guided activities and night drives *must* be organised through Nyika Safari Company.

Unguided walks around Chelinda Plenty of roads radiate from Chelinda Camp, and it would be quite possible to spend four or five days in the area without repeating a walk. The marshy area immediately downstream of Chelinda Dam (which lies right in front of the camp) is a good place to see bushbuck and a variety of birds, and the dam itself attracts nocturnal predators such as hyena and leopard. A good short walk for visitors with limited time is to the **two dams** near Chelinda. The road here follows a *dambo* (a seasonal or perennial marsh) and the area offers good game viewing, as well as frequent sightings of wattled crane. The round trip covers 8km and takes two hours.

Another good short walk (about an hour) is from behind Chalet Four to the Kasaramba turn-off and then left along Forest Drive through the pine plantation back to Chalet Four. At dusk, there is a fair chance of seeing leopards along this walk, and daytime sightings are not uncommon.

A longer walk takes you to **Lake Kaulime**, which lies 8km west of Chelinda. This is the only natural lake on the plateau and is traditionally said to be the home of a serpent which acts as the guardian to Nyika's animals. More certain attractions than legendary serpents are migratory waterfowl (in summer) and large mammals, particularly roan antelope and zebra, coming to drink. It is also a very attractive spot, circled by indigenous trees.

Horse safaris A stable of around 30 horses is kept at Chelinda, with animals suitable both for novices and experienced riders. Visitors can do anything from a short morning ride to a ten-night luxury riding trail with superb guiding and grooms. Shorter rides can be arranged at a moment's notice, and are an excellent way of getting around, as well as getting in amongst the game – eland in particular allow horses to approach far more closely than they would a vehicle or pedestrian, as do the wary Nyika elephants. Horse rides cost US$20 per hour or US$100 for a full day or US$320 overnight. Longer riding safaris should be booked well in advance. Contact the Nyika Safari Company for details (see page 43). The lower slopes above Rumphi also have riding possibilities (through Matunka Safari Company, above).

Night drives Spotlit night drives out of Chelinda are highly recommended as they offer the best opportunity to see nocturnal predators. Leopard and serval are often seen on the fringes of Chelinda Forest, while spotted hyena and side-striped jackal are common in grassy areas. When we last visited, we were lucky enough to see a pair of honey badgers crossing the road – a first for both of us. Especially in winter, the plateau gets really cold at night, and you should take all your warm clothing with you in the vehicle.

Angling The rivers and dams on the Nyika Plateau are stocked with rainbow trout, and are thus popular with anglers. The dams are closed to anglers from April through to September, but the rivers are open throughout the year. Fishing permits must be arranged through the Nyika Safari Company at Chelinda. Licences cost US$4 per day and rods can be hired for US$5 per half day.

FURTHER AFIELD Many of the more interesting points in Nyika are too far from Chelinda to be reached on a day walk, though they are accessible to visitors with vehicles. Perhaps the most memorable viewpoint anywhere in Malawi, **Jalawe Rock**, lies about 1km (to be done on foot) from a car park 34km north of Chelinda. The views here are spectacular, stretching over a close range of mountains to Lake Malawi's mountainous Tanzanian shore. With binoculars, it is often possible to see buffaloes and elephants in the *brachystegia* woodland of the Mpanda Ridge below. A variety of raptors, as well as klipspringer, are frequently seen around the rock, and the surrounding vegetation includes many proteas and aloes.

At 2,606m, **Nganda Peak** is the highest point in northern Malawi. It lies about 30km northeast of Chelinda, and can be reached by following the Jalawe Rock road for about 25km, then turning left on to a 4km-long motorable track. It's a steep 1.5km walk from the end of the track to the peak.

Kasaramba Viewpoint lies 43km southeast of Chelinda. You can motor to within 1.5km of the viewpoint and then walk the final stretch. When it isn't covered in mist, the views to the lake are excellent, and you can also see remnants of the terraced slopes built by the early Livingstonia missionaries. The most extensive rainforest in Nyika lies on the slopes below Kasaramba, and visitors frequently see the localised crowned eagle and mountain buzzard in flight. From Kasaramba, a 3km road leads to the top of the pretty, 30m-high **Nchenachena Falls**.

Further along the road to Kasaramba, also 43km from Chelinda, is a large juniper forest, the most southerly stand of *Juniperus procera* in Africa, and the first part of the Nyika Plateau to be afforded official protection back in the 1940s. A short trail through the junipers offers the opportunity of sighting forest animals such as leopard, elephant shrew, red duiker, bushpig and a variety of forest birds. The forest can also be explored from the firebreaks which surround it.

The **Zovo Chipolo Forest** lies on the Chitipa road near to where the Zambian Resthouse used to be. It is of special interest to birdwatchers, and harbours several mammal species, the most commonly seen of which are bushbuck, blue monkey and elephant shrew. An unmarked trail runs through the forest, which is best visited with a local guide, at least if you hope to pick up the calls of such elusive forest birds as the bar-tailed trogon. The larger **Chowo Forest**, which lies in the Zambian part of the park, used to be popular with people staying at the Zambian Resthouse, but it is now somewhat off the beaten track.

Fingira Rock is a large, granite dome lying 22km south of Chelinda. On the eastern side of the rock, an 11m-deep and 18m-long cave was used as a shelter by humans around 3,000 years ago – excavations in 1965 unearthed a complete human skeleton and a large number of stone tools. Several schematic rock paintings can be seen on the walls of the cave. A motorable track runs to the base of the rock, 500m from the cave.

The *brachystegia* woodland around Thazima Entrance Gate is the most accessible in the park. The area is rich in birds, and noted for harbouring unusual species. Walking here, you are also likely to see mammal species which are rare at higher altitudes.

Guided wilderness trails Six wilderness trails have been designated within Nyika National Park, ranging from one to five nights in duration. Visitors wishing to use these trails must supply their own camping equipment and food, and are required to make an advance booking through the Nyika Safari Company, page 126.

The most popular of Nyika's wilderness trails is the **Livingstonia Trail**, which leads from Chelinda all the way to Livingstonia on the Rift Valley Escarpment east of the national park. This three-day, two-night guided hike is recommended only in the dry season, and it costs US$80 for one or two people and another US$10 for every additional person. It is not permitted to hike this route in reverse, as a guide and park fees cannot be organised at Livingstonia, though this may become possible.

Of particular interest for wildlife viewing is the four-night **Jalawe and Chipome River Trail**, passing through the *brachystegia* woodland in the northern part of the park and offering the opportunity to see elephant, buffalo, greater kudu and a variety of other mammals which are generally absent from the plateau. This and all other trails cost US$30 per person for the first night for the first two people and an additional US$20 per night thereafter for the first two people. Additional people are charged at a rate of US$5 per person per night. In other words, one person would pay US$50 for a two-night trail, two people would each pay US$70 for a three-night trail, and four people would each pay US$55 for a four-night trail.

Porters are available for all trails at a small extra charge.

VWAZA MARSH WILDLIFE RESERVE

Vwaza Marsh Wildlife Reserve covers an area of 1,000km^2 along the Zambian border west of Rumphi (Zambia's Nyika National Park) and south of Malawi's Nyika National Park, and there are plans to link all three game areas through a project with the Peace Parks Foundation. It is, without doubt, Malawi's best-kept game viewing secret, a highly attractive and surprisingly accessible and affordable target to anybody with an interest in natural history. Rich in wetland habitats, Vwaza may be named after a rather inaccessible marsh in the northeastern corner of the reserve, but the main focus for tourism is Lake Kazuni in the southeast, which lies on a public transport route and offers inexpensive hutted accommodation and camping.

Aside from the wetlands, Vwaza Marsh primarily consists of flat terrain supporting mixed *brachystegia* and mopane woodland. The large mammal populations have suffered badly at the hands of poachers in the past, and they are to some extent seasonal, but the reserve remains reasonably well stocked because animals can move freely between it and the neighbouring Luangwa ecosystem in Zambia. Some 2,000 buffalo and 300 elephant are thought to be resident in Vwaza Marsh, and a variety of antelope are present, including roan, greater kudu, Liechtenstein's hartebeest, eland, puku and impala. Lion and leopard are around, but they are not often seen by tourists, while a few recent sightings of African wild dog suggest this endangered creature may be in the process of re-colonising the reserve from Zambia.

Because the camp looks over Lake Kazuni, you can see plenty of game just by sitting on the veranda of your hut. It is, in any case, an atmospheric and sumptuously African setting: an expanse of flat water surrounded by low hills and *brachystegia* woodland, with hippo splashing, crocodiles basking and a steady stream of mammals coming down to the shore to drink. It is emphatically worth paying the small charge to take a guided game walk out on to the floodplain, where it's reasonably easy to approach animals on foot. The 1998 animal census estimated there to be 545 hippo living in the lake in 17 pods, and they are generally very approachable on foot (provided that they are already in the water). A couple of substantial elephant herds visit the lake on most days. Other large mammals that currently visit the lake include baboon, impala, puku and greater kudu, while three herds of buffalo are resident in the area. It should be stressed that walking out towards the lake without an armed ranger is forbidden, not to say foolhardy, as there is a real risk of being charged by buffalo or hippo.

The Kazuni area also offers some good birdwatching. The lake itself supports a great many waterfowl, waders and storks, and I've seen osprey, fish eagle and palmnut vulture there on different occasions. The thick woodland around the camp is rattling with birds, especially in the morning – you might easily tick 50 species in a few hours, notably trumpeter hornbill, Carp's black tit, Hueglin's robin and a number of attractive small warblers. According to *Newman's Birds of Malawi*, this should be a good place to see the extremely localised babbler-like, white-winged babbling starling. If you feel like taking an unguided stroll, you stand a good chance of seeing some animals by walking along the 1km stretch of public road between Kazuni gate and the village (there's an electric fence, so it's safe to walk here unescorted). Even if you don't see much, it's quite interesting to look at the mudfish traps along the South Rukuru River as it flows out of the park near the gate.

Visitors with private vehicles can explore the network of internal roads within the reserve, though they are advised to check conditions with the warden at Kazuni before doing so.

GETTING THERE AND AWAY Kazuni Camp at the reserve's entrance gate lies approximately 25km from Rumphi along the 'old' dirt road that connects Rumphi to Mzimba. To get there, follow the S85 out of Rumphi towards Nyika for about 10km, then turn left on to the S49, which is signposted for the reserve. You can normally reach the gate in a saloon car, though a 4x4 may be necessary after rain. Internal roads are generally closed during the rainy season.

Access to Vwaza Marsh on public transport is surprisingly easy. In the dry season, there is at least one bus daily between Mzimba and Rumphi, apparently leaving Mzimba at 14.00. This bus doesn't stop right at the gate, but at Kazuni village, which is about 1km from the gate in the direction of Mzimba. A better option coming from Rumphi is to look for a *matola* lift to Kazuni. There seems to be a steady stream of pick-up trucks travelling between Rumphi and the tobacco farms in the Kazuni area, and you shouldn't have to wait longer than an hour for a lift. Private vehicles will generally drop you right at the gate, from where it is a five-minute walk to the camp. The best place to wait for a lift out of Rumphi is under the trees directly opposite the PTC supermarket.

WHERE TO STAY

Kazuni Safari Camp lies 500m inside the entrance gate, where it sprawls attractively in a grove of evergreen woodland overlooking Lake Kazuni. Leased by the Nyika Safari Company, and given a thorough overhaul, the camp now accommodates 8 guests in 4 luxury en-suite reed huts at US$190 pp, on a FB basis. Nearby are 5 smaller self-catering huts, each of which lies on a raised concrete block with a thatched roof, and has 2 beds with mosquito netting, 2 chairs, a table, and a small veranda. The huts cost US$10 pp, which is excellent value. Alternatively, you can pitch your own tent for US$5 pp. An additional park entrance fee of US$5 pp per 24 hours is levied. Facilities at the camp include clean long-drop toilets, showers, and a fireplace with grid, firewood and cooking utensils provided. You must bring your own food; the nearest place to stock up is at the supermarket in Rumphi, though there is a better selection of goods on sale in Mzuzu. The staff will cook for you on request. Beer and sodas are normally available at a kiosk just outside the reserve entrance, while a limited range of goods can be bought at Kazuni village 1km back towards Mzimba. The night-time atmosphere at Kazuni is utterly compelling: just you, the trumpeting of elephants if you're lucky, snorting hippo, fluttering fruit bats and swooping owls. And, it must be said, rather a lot of mosquitoes – so cover up! Not far from Kazuni is Chigwere Cultural Village, where you can try your hand at maize pounding or just join in with whatever is going on at the time. Visits can be arranged from the camp.

Camping is permitted at three other sites in the game reserve. None of these sites has any facilities worth speaking of, and they are accessible only in a private vehicle.

Zaro Pool In the southwestern corner of the reserve

Turner Camp On Vwaza Marsh

Khaya Camp On the Luwewe River

As with Nyika National Park, the best source of reliable up-to-the-minute information about all practicalities surrounding a visit to Vwaza Marsh is Nyika Safari Company.

9

Livingstonia and the Northern Lakeshore

This chapter covers the far north of Malawi. The main town in this region, Karonga, is the gateway to and from northern Zambia and southern Tanzania, and as such, it is many backpackers' introduction to Malawi. Any visitor to the north should make the trip to the turn-of-the-century Scottish mission of Livingstonia, perched on top of the western Rift Valley Escarpment overlooking the lake and the far Tanzanian shore. Karonga, with its recent hominid and dinosaur finds and its interesting World War I history, is just waiting to be discovered, especially now that there is the impressive 'Malawisaurus' Cultural and Museum Centre. The Lake Malawi shore north of Livingstonia is arguably the most dramatic stretch of the lake, with immense mountains rising to either side, and a burgeoning number of low-key resorts have recently been built around the beautiful Chombe Bay, many of which make you want to stay for ever. This is an area ideal for low-spend visitors with lots of time to relax by the beaches and take vigorous exercise in the mountains.

CLIMATE

The Karonga area has a typical lakeshore climate – hot, sunny and humid. Of the other places mentioned in this chapter, only Livingstonia and Chitipa have moderate climates, as they are both at higher altitudes.

GETTING AROUND

Most of the places described in this chapter lie along the surfaced M1 which connects the regional capital of Mzuzu to Songwe on the Tanzanian border. There are plenty of buses along this road as far north as Karonga, and minibuses and *matola* pick-up trucks daily between Karonga and Songwe. Livingstonia lies 16km west of the M1 by road: many travellers walk there, but you can generally get a *matola* ride if you prefer or take the more scenic open-truck *matola* route from Rumphi which runs twice a week on Tuesdays and Thursdays.

BETWEEN RUMPHI AND CHITIMBA

There is a couple of attractions along the road between Rumphi and Chitimba, of particular interest to those travelling in their own vehicle.

Sadly, the legendary Mr Ngoma, once described as 'the greatest and most depressing raconteur of the North', recently fulfilled the morbid fixation with his own death that had led him to prepare his own grave, coffin and tombstone decades before the event – ironically, he was not buried where he had planned to be. Mr Ngoma's peculiar two-storey house can still be seen from the road, and his role has swiftly been superseded by Mr Abel Nuasulu, whose entrepreneurial spirit

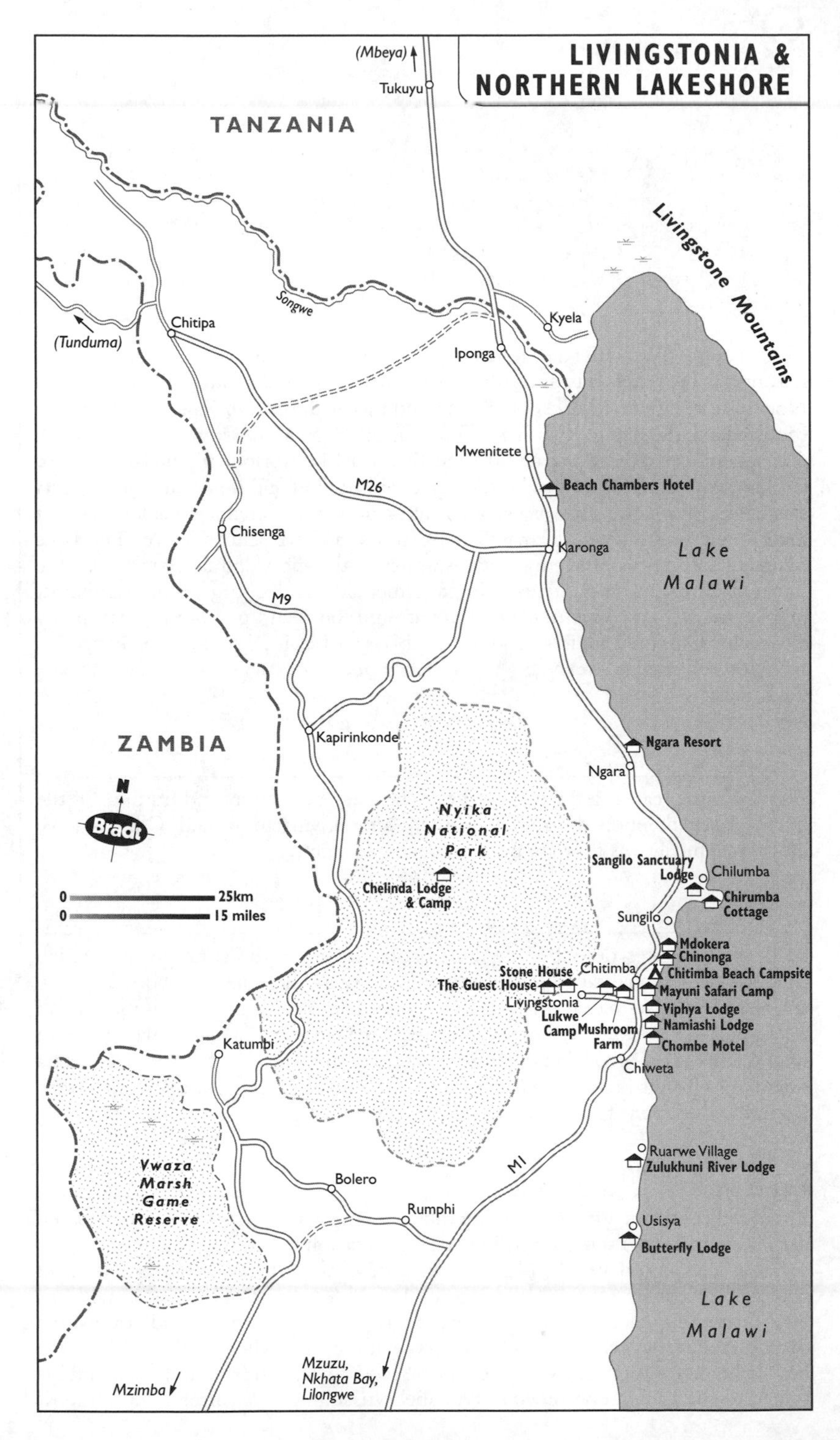
LIVINGSTONIA &
NORTHERN LAKESHORE
(Mbeya)
Tukuyu
TANZANIA
Livingstone Mountains
Songwe
Kyela
Chitipa
(Tunduma)
Iponga
Mwenitete
Beach Chambers Hotel
M26
Chisenga
Karonga
Lake
Malawi
M9
Kapirinkonde
ZAMBIA
Ngara Resort
Ngara
N
Bradt
Nyika
National
Park
Sangilo Sanctuary
Lodge
Chilumba
Chelinda Lodge
& Camp
Chirumba
Cottage
0
25km
0
15 miles
Sungilo
Mdokera
Chinonga
Stone House
Chitimba
Chitimba Beach Campsite
The Guest House
Mayuni Safari Camp
Livingstonia
Viphya Lodge
Lukwe
Camp
Mushroom
Farm
Namiashi Lodge
Chombe Motel
Katumbi
Chiweta
Ruarwe Village
Zulukhuni River Lodge
Vwaza
Marsh
Game
Reserve
M1
Bolero
Rumphi
Usisya
Butterfly Lodge
Lake
Malawi
Mzuzu,
Nkhata Bay,
Lilongwe
Mzimba

is as fascinating as his tourist attraction – a grotto where he regales you with stories of the ancestors, takes you into a sacred hut and calls the ancestors to find out where they are and receive messages that his visitors should give a donation. Don't miss it! He will also take you on a walk to the waterfalls and to Zuwurufu Hanging Bridge, a basket suspension bridge just across the road, initially constructed in 1904 and maintained by the villagers who still use it every day. Going across it is not for the faint-hearted. Mr Nuasulu and the Zuwurufu Bridge dwell 32km north of the Rumphi turn-off, and the site is clearly signed 'Tourist Attraction'.

There is enough traffic along this road that backpackers could ask to be dropped at either of these places and then catch the next vehicle when they've finished looking around.

THE LAKESHORE AROUND CHITIMBA

North of Rumphi, the M1 follows the course of the North Rukuru River in a breathtaking descent of the Rift Valley Escarpment which brings you out at Chiweta on the northern shore of Lake Malawi. There is a drama to the northern lakeshore that is lacking further south with both the Malawian and Tanzanian shores flanked by the precipitous and thickly wooded mountains of the Rift Valley Escarpment. Until recently, this area was largely undeveloped for tourism, but the last couple of years have seen a rapid development of inexpensive low-key campsites and more commodious chalets and motels along Chombe Bay, which lies between the villages of Chiweta and Sungilo. Several more are spaced out along the shore towards Karonga.

The most serious boating accident ever recorded on Lake Malawi occurred in Chombe Bay in 1946, when a passenger ship, the *Vipya*, sank in storm-related circumstances which have never been satisfactorily explained. The tragedy resulted in the death of all but 49 of the 200 or more passengers and crew. The hulk of the *Vipya* reputedly still lies submerged in the bay.

The largest settlement along Chombe Bay is Chitimba, which consists of little more than a few resthouses and homesteads concentrated between the beach and the M1 (where it forms a T-junction with the road to Livingstonia). Chitimba is often and inaccurately marked on maps as Khondowe. Khondowe is actually the traditional and official name for the village which is more often referred to as Livingstonia (after the Livingstonia Mission that lies within it).

Uranium is found in the mountains in this area, and Australian speculators are currently planning to start mining operations in the near future, hopefully with stringent enough controls on sulphuric acid pollution.

GETTING THERE AND AWAY All express and country buses between Mzuzu and Karonga stop at Chiweta and Chitimba. If you want to be dropped elsewhere along Chombe Bay, you need to use a country bus or minibus. Several other *matola* vehicles also operate between police checks.

WHERE TO STAY Chombe Bay is a beautiful place to spend a few days, with a marvellous beach and fabulous scenery. In general, accommodation is less crowded than it is further south along the lake and it's difficult to imagine that there would ever be a problem finding a bed for the night in the ongoing proliferation of resorts.

In and around Chitimba Chitimba itself is rather dull, despite its proximity to the lake, and there's little reason to stay there unless you happen to be heading up to Livingstonia. If you need a room, there are several cheap resthouses:

Brothers-in-Arms Resthouse A short way up the hill towards Livingstonia. This is the only one that can be recommended.

Florence Resthouse Right on the junction. This place also has cheap rooms and it allows camping for US$1per tent. It does, however, serve reasonable meals, and is one of the few places where I've been offered cassava chips.

Chitimba Beach Campsite Clearly signposted only 1km from Chitimba. A far more attractive option and ever popular, nonchalantly and efficiently run by ex-overland truck drivers. This is the main backpacker focus on this part of the lakeshore. Set on a huge white beach looking down the lake many hours, days, even weeks could be spent here. Meals and drinks are available at an attractive beach bar and trips can be arranged up to Livingstonia Mission. *Inexpensive camping facilities US$3, dorm beds US$4, accommodation for 2 in reed huts US$10, s/c dbl rooms US$12.*

Namiashi Lodge A wonderful setting. Large, comfortable dbl rooms (using communal showers) with mosquito nets. *Sgl/twin/dbl MK1,000/2,000/2,250, camping US$2 pp.*

Between Chitimba and Ngara Towards Chitimba from Chiweta are many beach site lodges and campsites:

Mayuni Safari Camp This camp has recently been set up by Brown Mayuni, who used to run safaris from Lilongwe. The campsite is reached via a pleasant trek through a village and it has a bar and restaurant; meals MK200. *Camping US$3.*

Mdokera Lodge This characterful place offers good Malawian simplicity with scattered furniture in the 5 reed and bamboo rondavels, each of which has a bucket shower to one side and an intriguing eco-flush toilet to the other. There is also a shop here selling everything but the kitchen sink, though not much fresh produce.

Chinongo Lodge This place appears to be under never-never construction, though it's possible to camp, perhaps an option to consider as it has a nice beach.

Sangilo Lodge 09 395203/08 392611; www.sangilo.net. Undoubtedly the most stylish place to stay on the northern lakeshore, with a far-reaching reputation for the quality of its food, much of which is grown in the lodge's own garden. Meals typically cost US$3–5. Sangilo is next to Sungilo village, and the rooms with carved beds are perched on a private beach. Also from the lodge boat trips can be organised for US$40 per hour (includes sunset cruises, water skiing, and fishing trips). *Family cottages US$40 en-suite, sgl/dbl rooms US$15/30, camping US$4.*

Ngara Resort (5 chalets, 9 rooms) 08 830033. Further north, and attractively located high on the beach, this is a great place for families or groups. When last visited, though, the reeds needed clearing from the beach and there was talk of bringing in extra sand. It's a beautiful place, with a great bar (meals MK350), but lacking in atmosphere. *Camping MK300, chalets MK1,500, VIP rooms MK3,000.*

LIVINGSTONIA (KHONDOWE)

The Livingstonia Mission was founded in 1875 at Cape Maclear by Dr Robert Laws. It was named in honour of Dr Livingstone, and its original purpose was to further the famous explorer's goal of using Christianity and commerce to end the slave trade which had caused so much suffering in the Lake Malawi region. In 1881, the mission moved to Bandawe. Finally, due to the high incidence of malaria around the lake, Laws decided to move the mission to a higher altitude. He settled on the small village of Khondowe, 900m above the lakeshore, for its healthy climate, fertile land and abundant supply of water. The modern mission was built in 1894, and many of its stone buildings are still in use today, one of which houses a very interesting museum.

The Scottish missionaries of Livingstonia have been highly influential on modern Malawi. In the early days, under Laws, they played an important role in stopping the slave trade and the Ngoni raids on neighbouring tribes. More recently, they provided education to many influential members of the African nationalist movement, so much so that Banda himself once referred to Livingstonia as the 'seed-bed' of the Malawi Congress Party.

Livingstonia is without doubt one of the most scenic places in all of central Africa. The vertiginous views from the edge of this historical town plummet down the escarpment and lake to the Livingstone Mountains in Tanzania. It is quite breathtaking. With imagination and on a clear day you can see distances far enough to see the curvature of the earth.

Livingstonia Town is curiously unfocused, though extremely atmospheric: the resthouses, a school, a technical college and turn-of-the-20th-century hospital are dotted along the escarpment. Also in the vicinity are a couple of poorly stocked grocery shops, a few scattered patches of plantation forest and a rather bizarre stone circle and clocktower surrounded by blooming flower beds. The overall effect may give the impression that somebody started transporting a Victorian English village onto the edge of the Rift Valley Escarpment, but got bored before they finished the job. However, when you arrive at the vast mission church, and the Stone House nearby, Livingstonia's focus suddenly becomes apparent. As with so many of Malawi's mission churches, it is a feat of architecture and building skill, and is used by many hundreds each Sunday. The person showing me round was not sure how many church choirs there were, 'something over 12' he told me. On such an exposed mountain the buildings of Livingstonia are strikingly powerful.

Not far from the Livingstonia Mission is the magnificent 125m-high **Manchewe Waterfall** which crashes down the Rift Valley Escarpment about 2km outside of town. Surrounded by lush rainforest, this waterfall is truly spectacular, and crawling to its edge is a vertigo-inducing experience. To get to the falls from Livingstonia Town, walk back towards Chitimba for about 2km until you see the Manchewe Falls Grocery. A short path directly opposite the grocery leads to the edge of the waterfall. People hiding from slavers used to flee to the caves behind the waterfall; these can be visited following a steep walk. The truly brave at heart can abseil down the side of the falls, this is sheer terror exhilaration but you're in the capable hands of Mick from the Mushroom Farm.

GETTING THERE AND AWAY The main road connecting Livingstonia to the M1 was closed for roadworks in early 2006 (it is so steep that concrete was being put down over the most serious bends) but it should reopen long before you read this. This 16km road climbs over 700m in altitude along a series of hairpin bends (20 if you're counting), passing through dense *brachystegia* woodland, with spectacular views back to the lake, and is often described as one of the most exciting roads in Africa – particularly if the vehicle you are in has dubious brakes!

There is no public transport between Chitimba and Livingstonia, but a few vehicles switchback up and down every day, and with an early start you can be reasonably confident of finding a *matola* lift. Alternatively, Chitimba Beach Campsite offers regular Land Rover trips to Livingstonia, and motorised excursions to the mission can be organised at Nkhata Bay. It might also be worth calling the Mushroom Farm in case they could collect you. Do not attempt this road in your own vehicle, unless it is tough and has high ground clearance. Preferably it should be a 4x4, as the road is steep, rough and often wet or washed away.

The walk to Livingstonia is popular with fit travellers. You'll enjoy the walk a lot more if you leave as much luggage as possible at the base (Chitimba Beach Campsite would be your safest bet). I would also resist the temptation to make use of the steep short cuts that plunge between the switchbacks, not so much because of the environmental degradation caused by using short cuts (over 99% of the pedestrian traffic on this route is local people, so a couple of tourists is neither here nor there), but because they are impossibly steep. And don't get overexcited when you pass bend 20 – you still have around five (admittedly relatively flat) kilometres to cover before you reach Livingstonia.

There are two other routes to Livingstonia, each of them long and extremely scenic. The one of key interest to visitors is the dirt road from Rumphi, unadvisable in anything but a 4x4 and impassable in the rainy season. Mr Four Kwacha from Livingstonia runs a twice-weekly service between Rumphi and Livingstonia, and for no more than US$2 each way this is an experience not to be missed. The truck leaves Livingstonia on Tuesdays and Thursdays at 06.00 reaching Rumphi at about midday, where the driver reloads ready to leave Rumphi at 14.00 from outside the PTC.

Another walking route to Livingstonia often forgotten about is the path down from the Nyika Plateau. It takes two days to walk it, so you will need camping equipment. The most popular trek is between the Mushroom Farm and Chelinda (Nyika Safaris) and then on down to the lakeshore. Both will organise a guide and a game scout for you. It is one of Malawi's most wonderful walks.

WHERE TO STAY There are two resthouses in Livingstonia, both run by the CCAP Church, both with verandas offering amazing views down to the lake, communal showers, and kitchens that can provide basic meals if you order before 15.00 or thereabouts. There are also two well-run alternatives a short distance outside that are very reasonably priced and share those phenomenal views of the lake.

Stone House This is the original house built by Robert Laws and is by far the more atmospheric, and not prohibitively expensive. *MK850 pp.*

Resthouse The other resthouse, known simply as the Resthouse, is also very pleasant, and cheaper. The village headman opposite the path to the Manchewe Falls will let you camp next to his hut for a couple of dollars and can often provide food too. *MK350 pp.*

The Mushroom Farm 08 591564/09 652485; e mickmitchell2001@yahoo.com. The Mushroom Farm is the place to go for adventure; the owner is the type of experienced rock climber and outdoor enthusiast who would inspire you to jump (or simply walk) off mountains. Not only that, but the place is friendly and informal, and a good place to dream. A family chalet for 4 will soon be operational. The toilet and shower were built by permaculture enthusiasts, meaning that at night you have plants and a staggering ceiling of stars to gaze at. *Dbl or twin rooms (with views) MK2,000, MK1,350 sgl, MK400 camping – or you can hire a tent, mattress, sheets and blanket for MK600.*

Lukwe Camp 08 204648/09 434985; e lukwecamp@africa-online.net; www.lukwe.com. Permaculture first came to Livingstonia at the highly regarded Lukwe Camp, which lies 2km from Livingstonia close to the Manchewe Falls. There is also a family cabin which sleeps 6, and spaces for vehicles with roof tents. The best view of the Manchewe Falls is from here too. *4 chalets with spectacular views US$12/18 sgl/dbl inc b/fast (subsequent nights discounted), camping US$3. Meals MK250–500.*

WHAT TO SEE AND DO Livingstonia Mission is a place where you could spend many hours as you wander through the town and up to the mission house. The museum in the Stone House is marvellous, not really because of what is in it, but because it's there at all. The most interesting exhibits for me included a letter from David Livingstone to his son, telling him of Mary's Livingstone's death from malaria, Dr Robert Laws's amazingly antiquated anaesthetic machine (the first in central Africa) and then the various bits of early 20th-century entertainment equipment, an early cine camera and a collection of glass plates for slide shows.

The Lukwe Permaculture Garden next to Lukwe Camp makes for an interesting visit; here all manner of fruit and vegetables are grown on terraces with streams and ponds flowing between them. The otters apparently love it, though I wondered at how great the production rate really was. In terms of irrigation, there are many people in Malawi who could learn from this place.

Qualified climbing instruction is offered by the Mushroom Farm, as well as abseiling and hiking. Any adrenalin freak would be in bliss here. The steep mountain watercourses are exciting places for rapid jumping and there is even a Free Fall Gorge, where you can do a 30m bungee jump/swing and abseiling excursions to Chombe Plateau. All activities include lunch and cost US$65. The abseil down Manchewe Waterfall is perhaps the most popular adrenalin rush at US$30 per person. All enquiries to the Mushroom Farm (see page 138 for contact details).

Livingstonia may seem an unlikely springboard for trekking, but there are some exceptional routes, linking Nyika Plateau to Livingstonia and Lake Malawi (again contact the Mushroom Farm). Hiking from or up to Nyika Plateau is usually a two-day hike. A three-day (US$75) hike from Livingstonia to the lake takes you along the top of the escarpment under Chombwe Plateau, then down the escarpment past thermal springs and a river so hot you can scarcely get in it, to the Maize Mill at Mlowe. The second day is a relaxing walk along the lakeshore footpath through countless villages and a second night's camping on the lakeshore. The last day continues along untouched shoreline to Rurawe village and the gorgeous Zinlancuni Lodge, a small place accessible only by boat or by foot. Most people then catch the MV *Ilala* from here or take a boat taxi further south.

CHILUMBA

This small harbour village is situated on a peninsula several kilometres from the M1 towards Karonga. Chilumba is not without natural charm, though, rather surprisingly, there is nothing in the way of tourist development. True, there's no obvious reason to stop over in Chilumba – but neither is there any obvious reason not to, especially as all buses between Mzuzu and Karonga divert to Chilumba, and it's also the northern terminus of the ferry service on Lake Malawi. There are several dollar-a-night resthouses to choose from.

KARONGA

Karonga is the largest town on the northern lakeshore and the springboard for overland crossings into northern Zambia and southern Tanzania. The fertile hills around Karonga are home to the Nkonde, an agricultural people who were considered by early visitors to be the most peaceful and hospitable in central Africa. Consul Elton described Nkondeland as the 'finest tract of Africa [he] had yet seen', comparing its climate and fertility favourably to Natal in South Africa; while the explorer Joseph Thomson, who passed through the area in 1878, described it as 'an enchanted place' and 'a perfect Arcadia'.

The favourable impression made by the Nkonde is perhaps because this was one of the few parts of central Africa not to have been devastated by the slave traders or the Ngoni. All this was to change, however, when a Swahili trader called Mlozi arrived in the area from the Luangwa Valley in Zambia. In 1886, Mlozi set up base about 10km from Karonga and proceeded to raid Nkondeland for human booty. Monteith Fotheringham, the manager of the African Lakes Company (ALC) store at Karonga, attempted to negotiate with Mlozi in order to stop the slave raids, but to no avail. From 1887 onwards, the Karonga area became the setting of a largely forgotten war between Fotheringham and Mlozi.

This war was initiated in October 1887, when Mlozi ordered the massacre of hundreds of defenceless Nkonde who had been lured by his spies to congregate at the marshy mouth of the Rukuru River (a few kilometres north of Karonga). A distraught Fotheringham watched the massacre helplessly, and he was further enraged when, a month later, Mlozi declared himself the Sultan of Nkondeland

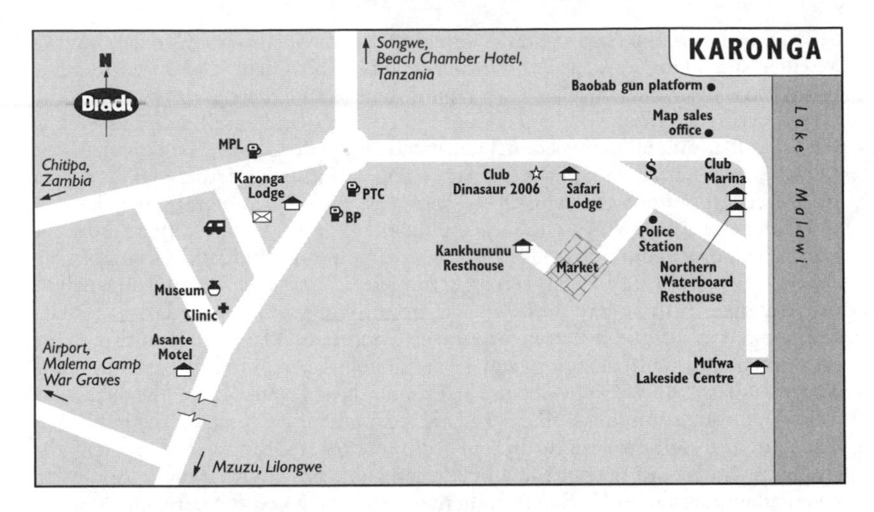

and then tried to capture the ALC fort in Karonga. In June 1888, a British raid on Mlozi's stockade was repulsed and almost resulted in the death of its leader, Captain Lugard (who 30 months later was to be instrumental in Britain's capture of Kampala in Uganda, for which effort he was made Lord Lugard). In 1889, Harry Johnston restored temporary peace to the region by signing a treaty with Mlozi. But, over the next six years, even as Johnston managed to conquer or negotiate with every other slave trader in the land, Nkondeland remained in the terrible grip of its self-styled sultan, who became more prosperous and powerful than ever in the first half of the 1890s.

In 1895, Johnston returned to Karonga, and on 3 December he led a successful attack on Mlozi's fort. When Johnston's troops entered the fort, they found it littered with Nkonde bodies, victims of Mlozi's most recent raid. Over 500 people were found alive but imprisoned in the slave stockade, awaiting shipment towards the coast. The next day, Mlozi was tried by a group of Nkonde elders, and Johnston had him hanged from a tree in Karonga. With the capture of Mlozi, Johnston effected the last blow to organised slavery in Malawi.

During World War I, Karonga was the focus of hostilities between the adjoining German East African Colony (later Tanganyika) and British Nyasaland. War in the region commenced with a 'naval victory' that was almost certainly the first of the war, and without doubt the most comic. When the British Commissioner in Zomba received news of declaration of war, he decided the first priority must be to sink the *Hermann Von Wessman*, Germany's only ship on Lake Malawi. HMS *Gwendolyn* was dispatched into German waters under Captain Rhoades, its only gun manned by a Scotsman who hadn't seen battle in over a decade. Rhoades found the *Wessman* docked in Liuli harbour and, when finally the rusty aim of the Scottish gunner and a live shell coincided, the German boat was sunk. Rhoades was then startled to see his enraged German counterpart and old drinking partner, Captain Berndt, leap into a dinghy and climb aboard the *Gwendolyn* screaming curses and questioning Rhoades's sanity. It transpired that news of the war had not reached Liuli. Rhoades sat Berndt down with a whisky, explained the situation, then led away his angry prisoner of war – who was by now loudly berating the German officials at Songea for not having informed him of developments in Europe.

The Germans at Songea did indeed know of the war. Immediately after securing his naval victory, Rhoades was dispatched to Karonga to repulse the German troops gathered at Nieu Langenberg (now Tukuyu). The Battle of Karonga of 8–9

September 1914 proved to be almost as farcical as the naval battle – the opposing troops marched straight past each other on the Nkonde Plateau and when they finally met the next day they were facing each other in the wrong direction. However, the skirmish resulted in tragic loss of life, mostly on the German side, with 19 out of 22 German officers being killed in the most bloody battle, and even heavier losses among the African conscripts. That Britain won was more a matter of luck than judgement (it so happened that the British troops accidentally stumbled on the Germans from behind, forcing them to flee into an ambush which would otherwise have been ineffective) but win they did, and after the Battle of Karonga, Nyasaland was never again seriously threatened by the neighbouring German territory. The war cemetery is on the way to the airport.

Few relics of Karonga's history remain. In the mission cemetery lies the grave of James Stewart, who was commissioned by the ALC to build the Stevenson Road between lakes Malawi and Tanganyika (the road was abandoned after Stewart's death). The Armstrong gun in front of the District Commissioner's Office is the one used by Captain Lugard in his abortive raid on Mlozi's fort. British and German war graves from the Battle of Karonga lie in the small cemetery behind the District Council Office. Another World War I relic is a large baobab tree (outside the old post office) which was used as a gun platform and which now has a mango tree growing out of it.

To add to all this fascinating history is the recent local discovery of a virtually intact 12m skeleton of a *malawisaurus* dinosaur that roamed the area 100 million years ago. Under the enthusiastic leadership of Professor Friedemann Shrenk, a team of archaeologists has also unearthed a 2.5-million-year-old jawbone, one of the oldest remains found of genus *Homo*.

GETTING THERE AND AWAY There are several express and country buses daily between Lilongwe and Karonga, passing through Mzuzu. There are also several buses daily between Mzuzu and Karonga.

Matola pick-up trucks and minibuses ply back and forth all day between Karonga and the Tanzanian border post at Songwe. After crossing into Tanzania, it is easy to get a lift on a bicycle-taxi through to the main Mbeya–Kyela road, where you can pick up a bus in the direction of your choice.

If you're heading towards Zambia, you need first to get to the remote highland town of Chitipa on one of the worst roads in Malawi (though work has commenced on tarring it). No buses run this route, only pick-ups and trucks, which cost US$4. The best accommodation is at the Chitipa Inn, which has rooms and camping, a bar and restaurant and safe parking.

WHERE TO STAY

Assante Annexe 01 362254. On the road on the outskirts of town to the south this small lodge offers the cleanest rooms I saw in town and with DSTV in each room. *Sgl/dbl MK1,850/2,550 BB.*

Club Marina PO Box 16, Karonga; 01 362391. Dirty and uninspiring, though in a pleasant enclosed setting, situated on the lakeshore about 10 mins' walk from the town centre.The restaurant serves reasonable meals, certainly the best in town (which isn't saying a great deal) and not at all expensive. S/c rooms with fans, nets and hot water. *US$10/15 sgl/dbl.*

Northern Waterboard Guesthouse (3 rooms) 08 582772. Practically next door to Club Marina this small guesthouse is a whole lot nicer, with a manager who's mad about football. *Sgl/dbl MK2,500/3,500 BB.*

Safari Lodge Town centre; 01 362340. Offers good rooms, parking and a relaxed atmosphere. *Sgl/dbl MK1,125/1,375 inc b/fast.*

Kankhununnu Resthouse Opposite the Gondwe Bottlestore & Bar. This place is cheaper and a lot sleazier. I liked it a lot as it had great character and lovely lady owner – until I went into the toilets and nearly retched. S/c VIP rooms with acceptable plumbing were better. *MK250.*

Out of town

🏠 **Malema Camp** Signed 3km off the M1 south of Karonga; ☎ 01 362579/08 870345; e uraha@malawi.net; www.paleo.net/cmck. A smart casual place, not expensive, currently used only by archaeologists and groups visiting or working on the sites.

🏠 **Beach Chamber Hotel** About 5km north out of town towards the Tanzanian border; ☎ 01 362534. A pleasantly isolated place. Camping is permitted, though the reedy beach site is nothing to write home about, but there's a good bar and restaurant serving meals for around MK350. Any pick-up truck heading between Karonga and Songwe can drop you at the hotel, which lies right on the main road. S/c rooms or slightly more expensive and very good VIP suites with satellite TV. *S/c sgl/dbl MK1,750/2,500, VIP suites MK2,800–3,500.*

SHOPPING Beautiful clay pots are brought across the lake by dugout canoe from the renowned pottery community at **Matema Beach** in Tanzania and sold on the beach opposite Club Marina. They are not 'tourist junk', but well crafted and wonderfully decorated pots for cooking and carrying water and used by the local people in their everyday lives. They cost very little (US$1–2) and make a great gift or memento of Malawi.

Of more practical interest to travellers is the good PTC supermarket near the main roundabout. There is also a well-stocked map sales office on the road to the Club Marina, which you should definitely visit if you've just arrived in Malawi from Zambia or Tanzania.

WHAT TO SEE AND DO

Cultural Museum Centre (*Private Bag 16, Karonga; ☎/f 01 362579/08 870345; e uraha@malawi.net; www.palaeo.net/cmck; open Mon–Sat 08.00–17.00, Sun 14.00–17.00*). The main attraction in Karonga and definitely worth a visit, the Cultural Museum Centre is home of the famous 'Malawisaurus'. For an entrance fee of MK500 you will find yourself in modern exhibition hall architecture (situated opposite the town assembly) and a thoroughly absorbing display of exhibits, including the astonishing mounted skeleton of the 12m dinosaur found in the nearby hills and plenty of information about the tribes and history of the northern region. This is an essential visit for anyone coming through town. There is also a traditional café and it is linked with Malema Camp, 3km south of Karonga. Don't miss it.

10

The Lakeshore from Nkhotakota to Nkhata Bay

This chapter follows the Lake Malawi shore, starting in the south at the old slaving centre of Nkhotakota, then passing a string of isolated lakeshore resorts to the very popular resort town of Nkhata Bay in the north (see map page 108). In recent years this part of the northern lakeshore has overtaken Cape Maclear in popularity for independent budget and party-conscious travellers. It is an area of white beaches with the occasional rocky cove, the best known of these being Nkhata Bay, a small port whose population can double in season. Inland from the coast, the Nkhotakota Game Reserve stretches over the tsetse forests, before the Dwambazi River delta at Dwangwa with its sugar and tobacco estates, and then smallholder farms stretching through the hills to the gum forests of Nkhata Bay.

CLIMATE

Hot and sticky.

GETTING AROUND

The lakeshore road between Salima and Mzuzu is generally in excellent condition. If you have a private vehicle, getting around is straightforward, though some of the side roads between the main road and the various lakeshore resorts should be taken with care, particularly if you don't have a 4x4.

There is plenty of public transport, including a daily return Lakeshore Express bus between Mzuzu and Lilongwe. Alternatively express buses and minibuses run between Lilongwe and Salima, and at Salima you can pick up the express buses which travel between Blantyre and Mzuzu via Nkhotakota and Nkhata Bay. These stop at all large towns but not at more obscure bus stages, so you'll be dependent on slower country buses if you plan on stopping at some of the more isolated resorts along the lake.

The lake steamer MV *Ilala* provides a popular way of travelling along this stretch of the lake, connecting Monkey Bay in the south to Nkhotakota, Nkhata Bay and Likoma Island, among other places. For full details, see *Chapter 11, The Lake Ferry and the Islands*, pages 157–9.

NKHOTAKOTA

Nkhotakota is a town of considerable historical note. For much of the 19th century it was the largest slave market on Lake Malawi: the terminus from which as many as 20,000 slaves were shipped every year across the lake to Kilwa Kivinje on the Tanzanian coast. The slave trade at Nkhotakota was founded in the early 19th century by an Arab half-caste called Jumbe. The Jumbe dynasty ruled Nkhotakota for several generations, and a descendant of Jumbe was still the local chief at the end of World War II.

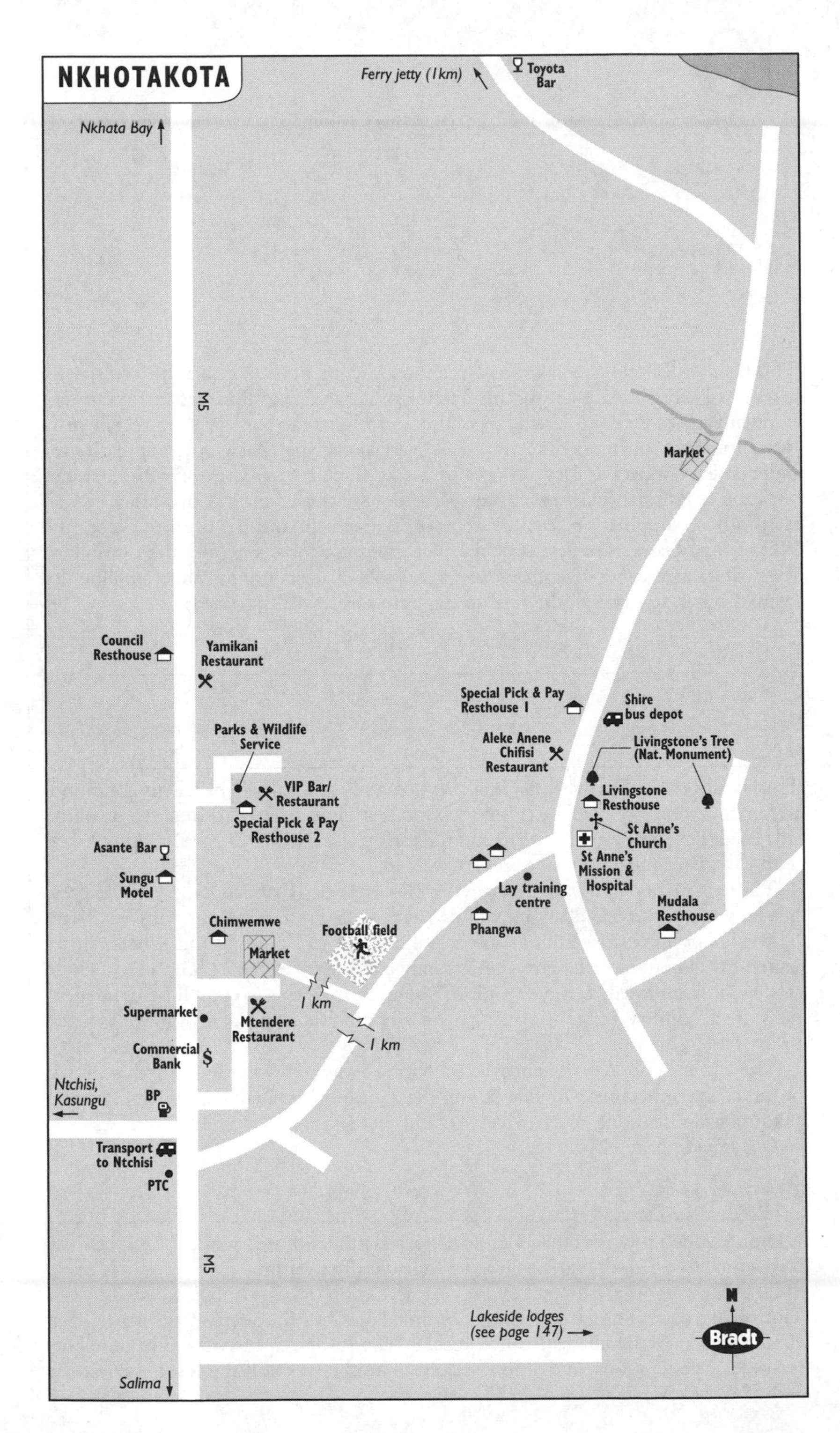
NKHOTAKOTA
Ferry jetty (1km)
Toyota Bar
Nkhata Bay
M5
Market
Council Resthouse
Yamikani Restaurant
Special Pick & Pay Resthouse 1
Shire bus depot
Aleke Anene Chifisi Restaurant
Livingstone's Tree (Nat. Monument)
Parks & Wildlife Service
VIP Bar/ Restaurant
Special Pick & Pay Resthouse 2
Livingstone Resthouse
St Anne's Church
St Anne's Mission & Hospital
Asante Bar
Sungu Motel
Lay training centre
Mudala Resthouse
Chimwemwe
Football field
Phangwa
Market
1 km
Supermarket
Mtendere Restaurant
1 km
Commercial Bank
Ntchisi, Kasungu
BP
Transport to Ntchisi
PTC
M5
Lakeside lodges (see page 147)
N
Bradt
Salima

When, in late 1861, Livingstone led the first European expedition on Lake Malawi, he described the area around Nkhotakota as an 'abode of lawlessness and bloodshed ... literally strewed with human bones and putrid bodies'. On 10 September 1863, Livingstone returned to Nkhotakota in a futile attempt to convince the incumbent Jumbe ruler to abandon the trade in slavery. The 'magnificent fig tree' under which Jumbe and Livingstone met is still standing in the mission compound. The slave trade out of Nkhotakota was only stopped in the 1890s, when Commissioner Harry Johnston persuaded the ageing Jumbe to sign a treaty in exchange for British protection.

Historical claims aside, it is only the attractive stone mission (the church here, built in 1894, is the burial place of the first bishop of Likoma, Chauncey Maples) and a strong Muslim influence that distinguishes Nkhotakota from any other similarly sized Malawian town.

Although the town has recovered from its history, several writers have noted a brooding sense of evil, a century after the last slaves were shipped out of its port, and certainly it is difficult not to see Nkhotakota's present in the light of its cruel history. More obtusely, Nkhotakota is often referred to as the largest traditional market village in east and central Africa, a label which is thoroughly meaningless as the modern market is, thankfully, quite unexceptional.

Like many others in Malawi, the town is divided into two sections, with the main centre of activity now centring on the main road, rather than its once-famous large market or its fishery station port. The modern town, with a PTC supermarket, bank and post office, sprawls along the main lakeshore road, about 1km inland of the lake. A shady avenue, planted in the slaving era, connects the lakeshore road to the older part of town, where you'll find the ferry jetty, the mission, the bus station and a cluster of cheap resthouses.

About 10km south of town is a cluster of lodges, including the Nkhotakota Potteries from where it is easy to organise trips into Nkhotakota Wildlife Reserve (see page 147)

GETTING THERE AND AWAY All buses between Nkhata Bay and Salima stop at Nkhotakota. The town can also be approached via Ntchisi (see also page 109) and Kasungu on the new M18 road. Nkhotakota is the last port of call for northbound lake steamers before they cross to Likoma Island. The MV *Ilala* stops at Nkhotakota in the early hours of Saturday on its northbound leg.

WHERE TO STAY

In town Most of the accommodation along the main road through the 'new' town consists of grotty resthouses, with two exceptions and one good option in the 'old' town.

Sungu Motel On the main road; ☎ 01 292233. Has a bar and restaurant and good rooms. *Sgl/dbl MK2,000/3,500.*

Pick and Pay 2 Off the main road. Possibly a more lively place to stay with a popular bar. *Dbl or twin room MK350–500, camping MK200.*

Council Resthouse ☎ 0 1292422/09 331134. A good value resthouse. *Standard dbl US$2, large s/c dbl US$4 with net and fan.*

Special Pick and Pay Resthouse In the old town, next to the Aleke Anene Chifisi Restaurant. Popular with travellers for years; it is certainly one of the better options in town, though none of the rooms appears to have nets or fans. *Dbl or twin room MK350–500, camping MK200.*

On the beach There are several options along the beach some 10km south of Nkhotakota Town and about another five down to the lake, all within walking distance of each other from the beach and signed from the road, including the rather smart-looking **Stone Terrace**, the as-yet-unfinished **Kumvana's Cottages**, **Mlambe Beach Lodge** and the small **Kasa Jinsi.**

Sani Beach Resort Set under a grove of fig trees high on the beach. *MK1,000 with shared facilities, s/c rooms MK1,500, camping MK250.*

Nkhotakota Safari Lodge Bookings should be made through Nkhotakota Pottery (see below). The old Njobvu Safari Camp has thankfully recently been taken under the excellent management of Nkhotakota Potteries. Now renamed Nkhotakota Safari Lodge it is soon to have a superb and much-needed facelift and change of style, with luxury outdoor bathrooms for some chalets. Boat rides and sailing are also now on offer on this beautiful stretch of beach. Guided safaris into the nearby Nkhotakota Game Reserve include a packed meal, drinks and park entry fees. Walks are conducted by experienced armed game scouts (US$26/35pp half day/full day; minimum charge US$52/69, less if you have your own vehicle). Discounts for groups and children. *About US$25 pp with camping for US$3.*

Nkhotakota Pottery and Lodge t 01 223069/01 292444; f 01 262391; e nkhotakotapottery@africa-online.net; www.dedzapottery.com. In case of difficulty contact Dedza Pottery; t 01 223069; f 01 223131; e dedzapottery@africa-online.net or Mzuzu Pottery Shop; t 01 332622. Another 4km takes you down to this lakeside branch of Dedza Potteries just around the next cove or at 15km south of Nkhotakota and 90km north of Salima. Most guests want to learn how to make traditional pots, but it's also a good springboard for Nkhotakota Game Reserve and it has a good beach. You can also use the pottery workshop, which is fully equipped with electric and foot-driven potters wheels and offers raku and electric-kiln firing, for an hourly fee of US$2. The coffee shop serves delicious lunches and dinners. Better still, if you're keen on learning more about pottery, sign up for an all-inclusive weekend. You'll get accommodation, 3 meals a day, tuition and use of the workshop as well as a session with local village potters making traditional pots – all for US$72 weekend or US$104 3-day midweek. *En-suite rooms US$14 pp.*

BETWEEN THE M1 AND NKHOTAKOTA

The dirt road connecting Lilongwe to Nkhotakota via Dowa and Ntchisi is one of the most obscure routes in Malawi, but it is also one of the most rewarding, giving access to the excellent Ntchisi Forest Reserve, as well as the old road to the western side of Nkhotakota Wildlife Reserve where it joins the new tar road through the reserve for around 30km. The area is dominated by the vast tract of dense forest, the tsetse area of Nkhotakota Wildlife Reserve. It is pristine bush: *miombo* woodland on rugged hills and is totally undeveloped for game viewing and accommodation. There is plenty of game here, but the temptation to get out and walk for miles is madness (and illegal) without a game ranger as lions, elephant and buffalo pose a serious threat. Hitching or cycling along the road is also inadvisable; one roadside epitaph tells of the death of a lady taken from her bicycle by lion. Nkhotakota Wildlife Reserve can be accessed from the lakeshore road from Nkhotakota Town where you can also pick up game rangers and guides at the Wildlife Office.

GETTING THERE AND AWAY The access to Nkhotakota has been much improved since the main road from Kasungu to the lake was completed. It goes through the Nkhotakota Wildlife Reserve, and is a good route for own-vehicle travellers and public-transporters alike. It also makes a good loop from Lilongwe, through the Kasungu National Park, the Nkhotakota Wildlife Reserve, down to the lake at Nkhotakota and back along the lake via Salima. Note that transport to Ntchisi and Nkhotakota leaves Kasungu not from the main bus station but from the junction of the M1 and the Nkhotakota road. All transport leaving Nkhotakota town for Ntchisi or Kasungu waits for passengers in front of the Peoples supermarket. On the way between Kasungu and the junction with the Ntchisi–Nkhotakota road, you may want to stop at Kamuzu Academy (see page 112). Founded by Banda as the self-styled 'Eton of Africa', the students (all Malawian, including scholarship

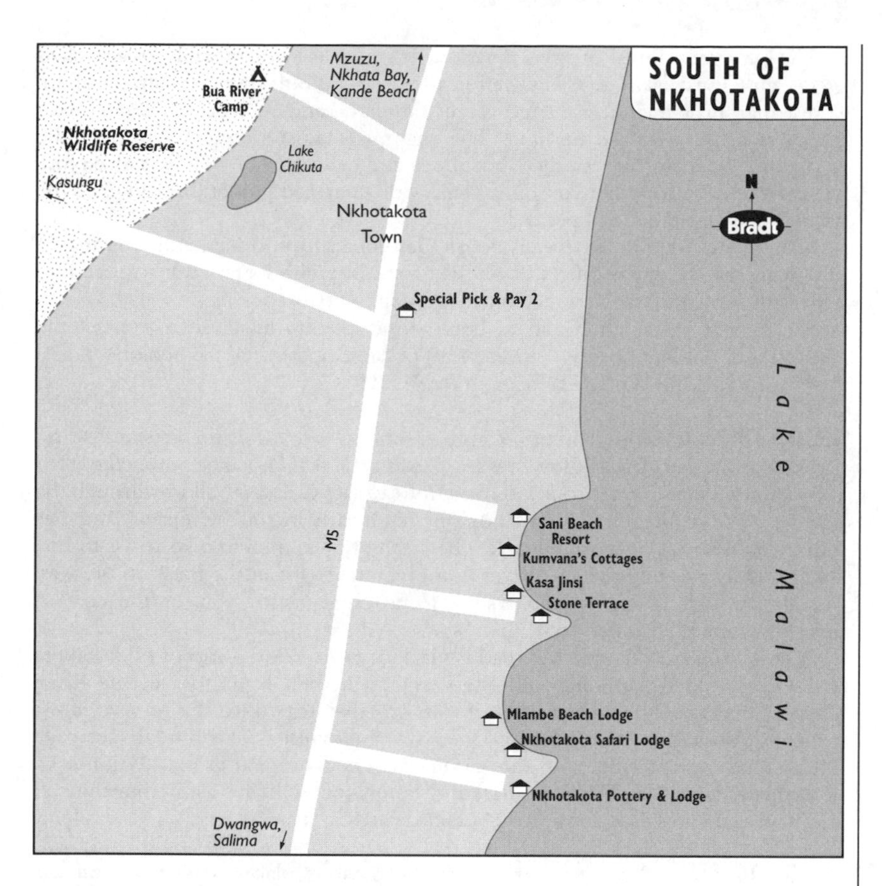

students from remote villages) once wore a bizarre colonial uniform of shorts and a boater, and still learn Latin and Greek.

NKHOTAKOTA WILDLIFE RESERVE

The oldest wildlife reserve in Malawi protects the scenic, well-watered Rift Valley hills west of Nkhotakota Town. The *brachystegia* woodland of Nkhotakota Wildlife Reserve supports a rich diversity of mammals including elephant, buffalo, sable antelope, warthog, lion and leopard, but the undulating terrain and thick vegetation make animal spotting difficult. The most recent game count suggests that there are 45 lions resident. The elephants here are said to be the largest in Malawi, a recent game count estimates that numbers may have dropped to between 1,000 and 1,500 from an estimated 1,700 in 1998, though even helicopter surveys would be difficult in this hilly and wooded terrain. As in every reserve in Africa surrounded by villages, the rangers are most likely greatly outnumbered by poachers, especially as here there are only 20 rangers. The upland woodland is dominated by *julbenadia* species, and close to the top of Chipata Mountain are huge 80m-tall trees, which ten people with their arms outstretched can scarcely reach around. Below there is woodland, going down to riverine forests, including the impressive raffia palms and the large adina microsofala and fruiting trees. Rare tree orchids can be found in the reserve. Hot springs are also found near to the Bua River.

The evergreen forest protects a variety of unusual birds, notably moustached green tinkerbird, starred robin, yellow-streaked bulbul and grey-olive bulbul. Forest mammals include blue and vervet monkeys, and such secretive nocturnal creatures as leopard and bushpig. The mammals most frequently seen in the *brachystegia* woodland are warthog, bushbuck and baboon. The best way to explore the reserve is on foot, but you must walk with an armed guide; this can easily be arranged for around US$4 per walk.

Nkhotakota Wildlife Reserve is poorly developed for tourism, and long may it last – this may be one of Malawi's finest secrets, but with its proximity to the lake added to its own merits, it is a gem just waiting to be discovered.

For further information and to book game rangers in advance, contact the Nkhotakota Wildlife Office (*01 292464*) or call Robert Bita, the Senior Wildlife Assistant Parks and Wildlife Officer (*09 915799*).

GETTING THERE AND AWAY Chipata Camp, in the southwest of the reserve, is best accessed from the M18 halfway between Kasungu and Nkhotakota – watch out for the memorial marking the spot where an unfortunate woman, walking through the reserve, was caught and eaten by a lion one night early in 2002. Chipata Camp lies 7km from the road on a rough track. The best option is then to hike across to Bua River Campsite along the Bua River, camping one night in the bush on the way. For this trek it is essential to take a game ranger with you, at the cost of approximately US$10 per day.

Access from the lakeside M5 road is via a turn-off 12km north of Nkhotakota at a village called Mphonde. A rough 4x4 track then leads to the Bua River Camp. Several of the lakeside lodges can organise trips into the reserve, most reliably Nkhotakota Pottery and Lodge, and Nkhotakota Safari Lodge (see page 146). They will arrange for the game rangers from Parks and Wildlife to accompany you. The Wildlife Office in Nkhotakota will also assist, but they do not have transport (see above for contact details).

WHERE TO STAY If you have transport the obvious places to stay are on the lakeshore (see below). Locally, there are two options:

Bua River Camp An attractive site on the riverbank. This place is for camping only and one must be completely self-sufficient though there is a temporary ablution block. *US$5 pp.*

Chipata Camp This camp has a toilet and shower block but again no other facilities. It is refreshing to be somewhere so completely undeveloped and to be completely on your own in the bush with no other visitors and no-one looking after you. *US$5 pp.*

FROM DWANGWA TO KANDE BEACH

From the northernmost part of the Nkhotaktota Wildlife Reserve there is a fairly empty stretch of lakeshore, where the beaches are punctuated by three lodges before reaching Chintheche.

Starting in the south, the first place of interest along this stretch of the lake is Dwangwa, a fair-sized town sprawling around the large Kasasa Sugar Estate. Dwangwa is an odd little place, notable as much as anything for the odour of molasses that clings to the air, and it is rather short on aesthetic appeal.

WHERE TO STAY It would take a perverse nature to actually want to spend a night in one of the identikit resthouses clustered along Dwangwa's main road.

Kasasa Club 01 295266; e essdwangwa@africa-online.net. The one relatively upmarket option in the area. The sports club has a golf course, swimming pool, and attractive clubhouse with TV, bar and restaurant. Although the club is aimed primarily at estate workers, visitors are welcome to stay in one of the pleasant s/c chalets in the grounds. In theory, accommodation here should be booked in advance, but the chalets are rarely full. To get to the club, take the left turn next to the filling station about 1km south of the town centre, and follow it for 3km. *MK5,170 pp.*

Ngala Beach Lodge 01 295359/09 340369; e ngala@malawi.net; www.ngalabeachlodge.co.za. Halfway between Dwangwa and Dwambazi river mouth a highly attractive lodge on a promontory between two secluded private beaches and with gardens full of birds. The individually decorated en-suite chalets and bungalows are delightful. There's also a beautiful beach and good bar, and many people are attracted by the gourmet restaurant. There's a huge campsite by the beach. Excursions include walks, waterfall village US$10–15 including lunch, mountain bikes US$5 per day and day trips up to Kande Beach for horseriding and diving at Kande Beach Resort. Dwangwa has a golf course, tennis courts and a volleyball court at the Sports Club. If you are using public transport, ask for Ngala bus stage. *Rooms US$38 BB pp, US$55 dinner, BB or US$60 FB. Camping MK350.*

Kande Beach Resort 01 357376; e kandebeach@hotmail.com; www.kandebeach.com. The favoured backpackers' haunt along this stretch of lake, and famed throughout Africa. Kande lies about 20km south of Chintheche, 3km from the main road; the turn-off is signposted from Kande village (the bus stage here is used by both express buses and country buses). Kande Beach Resort encompasses not only Kande Beach camp, but also Kande Horse Trails, Aqua Nuts PADI Resort, Soft Sand Café, the Kande Internet Café and Co'cnut Shop. Positioned on a beautiful stretch of beach, and run with the permission and co-operation of the local chief, Kande has the sort of atmosphere which tempts travellers into staying on for weeks; busy and sociable when a few overland trucks pull in, peaceful and intimate when the trucks are absent, and plenty to do or not do whatever mood takes you. There is a large open Africa-shaped bar and a restaurant serves deliciously filling meals. A nice alternative to the rooms are attractive stone and thatch double-storey cottages sleeping 5 people, ideal if you want to cook too. Kande is the hub of activities in the area, not only for nightlife but notably for horseriding and scuba diving. A games room has table tennis, a pool table and dartboard. Every 3 months or so there is what has become known as a 'Kande Classic' when local bands and DJs draw in the crowds for a weekend of partying, usually coinciding with polocrosse matches at the stables. *Camping MK450 pp, dorm bed MK700, twin-bedded beachfront chalet MK2,000; standard room MK2,500, en-suite with 3 beds MK3,600, 4 beds MK4,000; 5-bed cottage MK6,000.*

KANDE ACTIVITIES At the top end of the site, the highly regarded **Aquanuts Dive School**, a PADI Resort (e *aquanuts@africa-online.net; www.aquanuts.info*), offers four-day courses for US$265 per person, day dives for ticketed divers at US$30 per person, and day 'resort courses' for non-qualified divers at US$55 per person. There's also an internet café.

Also available for hire at Kande Beach Resort are catamarans, canoes, pedal-boats, windsurfers and snorkelling equipment.

Kande Horse Trails (*08 500416;* e *kandehorse@africa-online.net; www.kandehorse.com*) has the most impressive stable I have seen in Africa, with 25 sleek horses, a floodlit gymkhana, and the beginnings of a huge wine cellar. The bareback swim in the lake at the end of a ride through the bush and villages makes this thoroughly enjoyable, suitable for novices or experts. Two hours US$35, three hours US$50, half-day rides US$65. Riding lessons US$20 per hour and a two-hour polocrosse introduction course US$40. Kids' forest rides (45mins)US$10. Longer rides and treks can be arranged in advance.

CHINTHECHE

This small trading centre lies just west of the main lakeshore road about 40km south of Nkhata Bay. The town (if you can call it that) was fairly important in the colonial era, and several old buildings from this time remain, notably the post

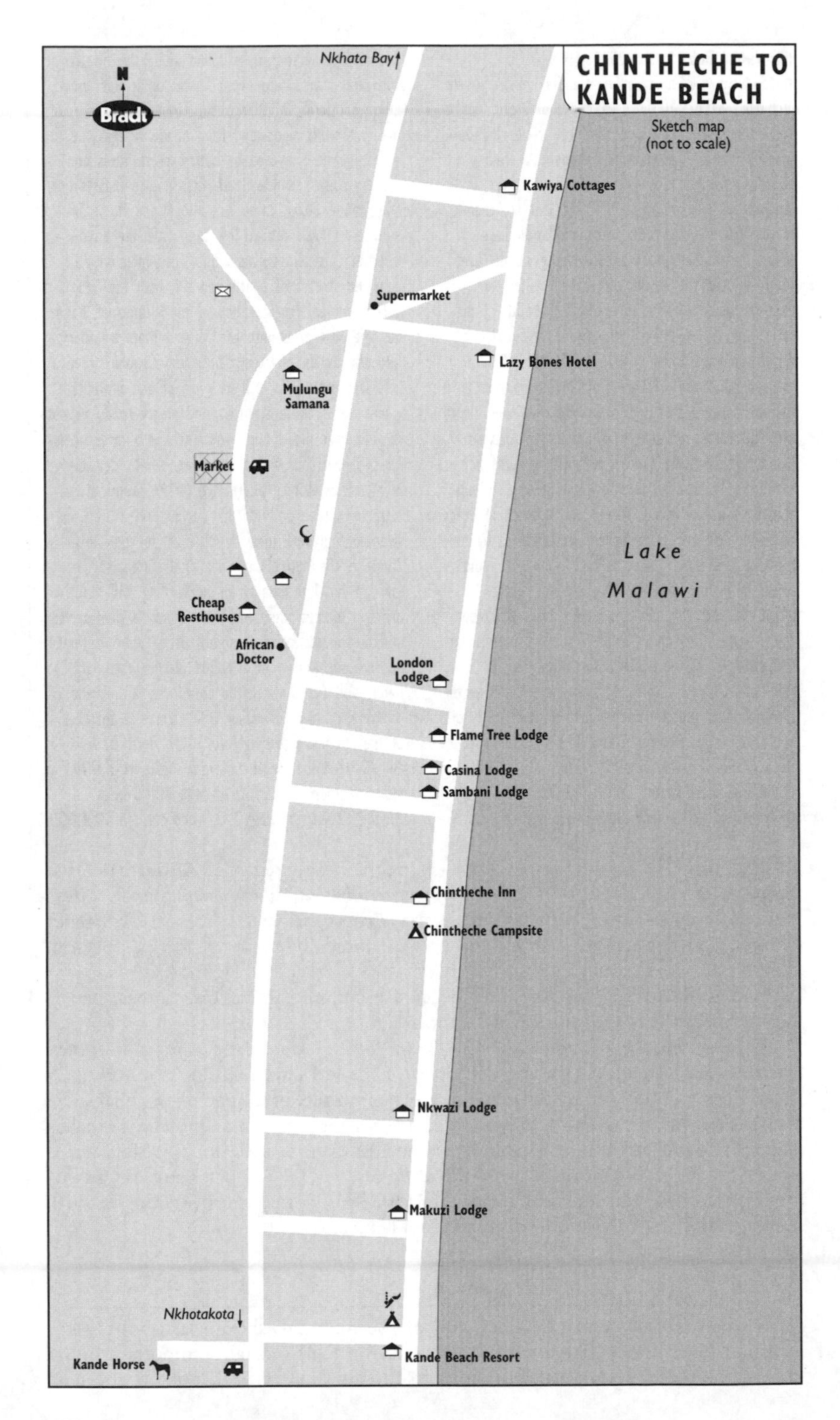
CHINTHECHE TO KANDE BEACH
Sketch map (not to scale)
Bradt
N
Nkhata Bay
Kawiya Cottages
Supermarket
Lazy Bones Hotel
Mulungu Samana
Market
Lake Malawi
Cheap Resthouses
African Doctor
London Lodge
Flame Tree Lodge
Casina Lodge
Sambani Lodge
Chintheche Inn
Chintheche Campsite
Nkwazi Lodge
Makuzi Lodge
Nkhotakota
Kande Beach Resort
Kande Horse

office. But today Chintheche isn't anything to shout about, especially as it lies a kilometre or so inland of the lake. The surrounding beaches, on the other hand, are paradise: perfect white sand rescued from picture-postcard anonymity by jagged rocky outcrops, patches of *brachystegia* woodland, and even some remnant forest. Chintheche lies on the widest part of the lake, with the Mozambican shore an indistinct blur on the horizon; here more than anywhere on Lake Malawi it is easy to be lulled into the feeling you are at the ocean.

In 1880, Dr Robert Laws moved the Livingstonia Mission from its temporary site at Cape Maclear to Bandawe, on the lakeshore about 10km south of Chintheche. At this time the Tonga people of the lakeshore lived in terror of the murderous annual raids of the Mombero's Ngoni clan, which generally resulted in village after village being razed to the ground and hundreds of Tonga people being killed. Dr Laws at first had an uneasy relationship with Mombero, but when one of the missionaries was asked to pray for rain during a severe drought and a thunderstorm ensued, Mombero became more friendly and allowed Laws to persuade him to cease harassing the Tonga. The other major achievement made by Laws at Bandawe was in the field of education; one of the most influential products of the mission school was Edward Kamwama, who in 1908 founded the Ethiopianist Watch Tower Church in Bandawe.

In the end, the mission site at Bandawe proved to be as unhealthy as the one at Cape Maclear, despite Laws's practice of facing all buildings inland (he believed that malaria was caused by 'miasma' rising from the lake). In 1894, Bandawe was abandoned for Khondowe on the Rift Valley Escarpment, where the Livingstonia Mission still operates today. The Bandawe Mission can be reached via a 2.5km sand road, clearly signposted from the main lakeshore road about 2km south of the Chintheche Inn. The original church, a somewhat warehouse-like brick construction built between 1886 and 1900, is still standing, and the priest welcomes visitors – he has in fact compiled a short history of the mission, illustrated with period photographs. There is no entrance fee but a small donation will be appreciated. Roughly 500m from the main mission building lies a small cemetery, a literal 'White Man's Graveyard', where several of the early Scottish missionaries are buried, most of them victims of malaria, many of them in their early twenties. A more recent grave is that of 'Mama' Jane Jackson, the owner of a nearby lodge who died tragically in a paragliding accident in Zimbabwe in 1997. Close by is the grave of an unidentified mazungu who drowned on the nearby lakeshore in 1986.

GETTING THERE AND AWAY All express and country buses between Nkhotakota and Nkhata Bay stop at Chintheche, and it's worth asking a country bus or a minibus to drop you at the appropriate stop.

WHERE TO STAY There are a few basic resthouses in Chintheche Town, though it's rather difficult to think of a convincing reason why any traveller would want to stay at one of them.

Lazy Bones Hotel 08 583392. Still open. *Rooms sgl/dbl MK1,200/2,400.*

London Lodge 01 357291/09 360911. A better option for those on a budget. On the beach about 500m from town. Meals are available for MK350, b/fast is MK200–300. *Sgl/dbl s/c rooms with nets MK550/750, camping US$2.50 per tent.*

Kaniya Cottage 01 357298. A charming 3-bedroom cottage and campsite under thick trees by the beach just out of town. *Whole cottage MK1,200.*

There are several resorts a bit further out of town:

Flame Tree Lodge 01 357276. An attractive, easy-going place set on a shady wooded peninsula. The lodge is overpriced but the restaurant is very good. To reach Flame Tree Lodge, you can either walk for 15 mins south along the beach from London Lodge, or else follow the main lakeshore road south of Chintheche for about 2km, then take a signposted 3km turn-off to the lodge. *Rooms are s/c at MK2,500 pp, camping MK400 pp.*

Casina Lodge. Right next door to Flame Tree and the best budget option, it's a small relaxed place. *Rooms only MK500pp.*

Sambani Lodge 08 358260. Signposted about 5km south of Chintheche and another 2km over rough road to a pretty beach surrounded by trees. Sambani Lodge is much better than Flame Tree Lodge, and the rooms are larger. *MK1,500 pp, camping MK400 pp.*

Chintheche Inn 01 357211/01 357246/08 202717. One of the most tranquil spots on the lakeshore, managed by Central African Wilderness Safaris (*all bookings and enquiries can be addressed to Central African Wilderness Safaris;* *01 771153;* e *info@wilderness.mw; www.wildernesssafaris.com*). The huge gardens include one of the best campsites in Malawi. It's there that the Lake of Stars Festival happens each year, when international singers, bands and DJs swoop into Malawi to perform alongside local talent (see page 21). Chintheche also has extremely attractive rooms. The campsite is in trees on a grassed area near the beach; it has its own ablution block and a separate beach bar. With a swimming pool, tennis court and warm welcome for kids, Chintheche is also an ideal family resort. Facilities include snorkel hire for US$3 per day (there is good snorkelling in the nearby rocks) as well as boat hire, a book exchange service, and a good range of literature about Malawi. Organised excursions include a trip to the Bandawe Mission (US$40), bird walks (US$5 pp) and a trip to a fishing village (US$5 pp). The restaurant serves substantial à la carte meals in the US$5–10 range as well as a 3-course set dinner for US$15.

There are two lovely lodges just south of Chintheche:

Nkhwazi Lodge 09 283708, Nkhwazi is 10km south of the village and then another 2km down to the shady, grassed site above two little coves. 'Nkhwazi' means fish eagle, and there are certainly some of those around. The stand of trees as you go down to Nkhwazi is a reminder of how thick the forests once were around the lakeshore, and it is fiercely protected by the lodge owner. A ski-boat is available for diving, fishing and snorkelling, and there's a small reef just offshore. The 2 rooms are astonishing, attractively decorated and the campsite is very neat and comfortable with clean ablutions and is great value. *Split-level rooms US$40 per room. Camping US$4 pp.*

Makuzi Beach 09 273287/09 283980/01 357296; e makuzibeach@sdnp.org.mw; www.makuzilodgemalawi.com. About 2km past Nkhwazi. A little piece of paradise. The rondavels and campsite overlook a private bay and the service is friendly and attentive. This is the only lakeshore lodge to offer yoga retreats. The other special-interest tour organised by Makuzi is a fly-fishing safari, taking in angling challenges of three rivers in Nkhotakota, Nyika and Nkwichi over in Mozambique. The owners are involved in the local community and have built a new school at the old Bandawe Mission Station, next door. Email and internet access is available for guests. *En-suite chalets US$58/73 BB: dinner, BB US$74/89; US$80/95 FB. Camping US$4 pp.*

NKHATA BAY

Nkhata Bay's attractions are manifold. The lakeshore is gloriously lush and scenic: a twin pair of bays spilling into the wooded mainland and separated by a long, narrow peninsula. Just as alluring to many is the strong sense of traveller community that has developed in the village. The place is addictively laid back, to the extent that it seems to paralyse the will of many travellers, but Nkhata Bay's fortunes have fluctuated. From being one of the best-kept secrets on Malawi's backpackers' trail, this small port now vies with Cape Maclear as the most popular travellers' congregation point on the lakeshore, if not anywhere between Zanzibar and Victoria Falls.

A more mundane point is that many travellers are caught out by the absence of

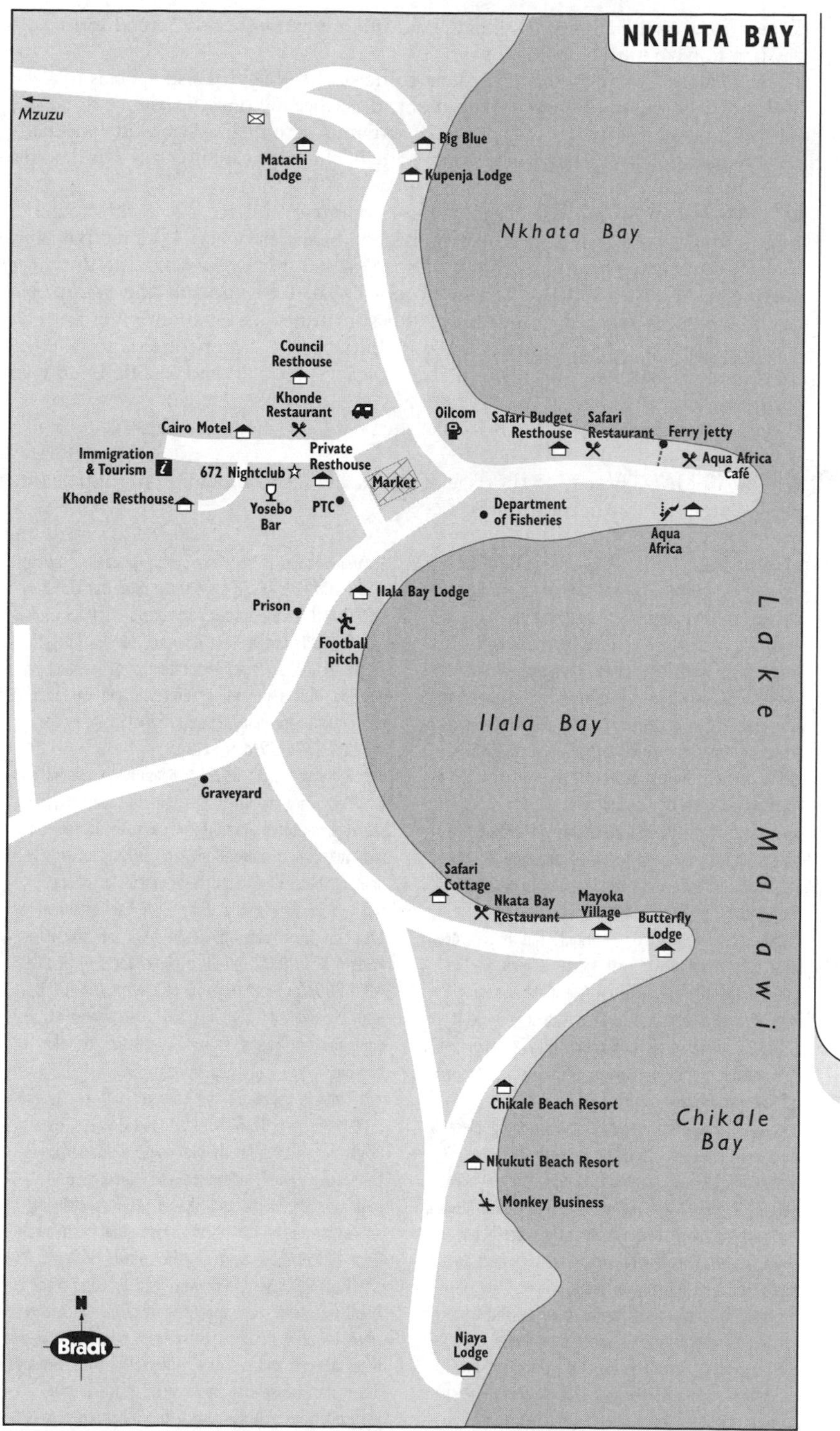
NKHATA BAY
Mzuzu
Matachi Lodge
Big Blue
Kupenja Lodge
Nkhata Bay
Council Resthouse
Khonde Restaurant
Cairo Motel
Immigration & Tourism
672 Nightclub
Khonde Resthouse
Yosebo Bar
Private Resthouse
PTC
Market
Oilcom
Safari Budget Resthouse
Safari Restaurant
Ferry jetty
Aqua Africa Café
Department of Fisheries
Aqua Africa
Ilala Bay Lodge
Prison
Football pitch
Ilala Bay
Lake Malawi
Graveyard
Safari Cottage
Nkata Bay Restaurant
Mayoka Village
Butterfly Lodge
Chikale Beach Resort
Chikale Bay
Nkukuti Beach Resort
Monkey Business
Njaya Lodge
N
Bradt

foreign exchange facilities in Nkhata Bay, and are consequently forced to make a day trip to Mzuzu to change money.

The waters around Nkhata Bay host some of the 600-plus fish species in Lake Malawi. It's a unique diving environment, described by one experienced diver as 'fresh water with sea equivalents'. Other activities here include kayaking and fish-eagle feeding, or there's anything from football, chess or watching the world go by.

GETTING THERE AND AWAY Regular buses connect Nkhata Bay to Nkhotakota and points south. There are also plenty of buses between Nkhata Bay and Mzuzu: a spectacular 50km stretch of road, which sees you whizzing down or puffing up the Rift Valley Escarpment past expansive grassland and *brachystegia* woodland, with the lake glittering in the sun hundreds of metres below. The lakeshore bus arrives at about 21.00 from Lilongwe. A faster route is to take the Sacremento Bus from Lilongwe (daily). It leaves at 06.00 and 18.00. Then take a minibus from Mzuzu.

The other appealing option is to take the MV *Ilala* (see pages 157–9).

WHERE TO STAY There is no shortage of affordable accommodation in Nkhata Bay, with something to suit most tastes.

Aqua Africa 01 352284/09 921418; f 01 352308; e aquaafrica@sdnp.org.mw or info@aqua-africa.co.uk, www.aqua-africa.co.uk. The most upmarket in town, mostly used by dive school guests. Aqua Africa also offers PADI and NAUI courses. The diving here is all-weather, as the coast is a crenellation of different coves offering protection from the occasional wind with deep dives, and cichlid heaven. The Harbour Café is also operated by Aqua Africa, with cappuccinos and all sorts of breakfasts at MK50–300, Western-style cuisine, tea and fabulous cakes, lunch for MK200–500 and supper for MK400–600. Satellite has come to Nkhata Bay, and so email is now possible at Aqua Africa assuming the electricity is working. This is regarded as a very good dive school, safety is high on the agenda and there's no better place for spending 3 weeks on a dive master course. Casual dives cost US$20 inclusive of all equipment, with a maximum of 6 people per tutor. *Rooms US$20 pp.*

Mayoka Village 09 268595; e mayokavillage@yahoo.co.uk. An inspiring place built on the steep hill that falls into the lake. Started in 1998 as a group building project between people of the village and an energetic South African, the party scene is here. Small chalets perch on the slope, while camping sites are tucked in next to the paths. It's a multi-national place, where Chief Nyirenda installs himself in his chair in the bar with his mobile chocolate and sweet shop every night and will regale anyone with stories. Also on the premises is a woodcarving workshop. They have a pick-up service from the ferry (a relief at 02.00). Accommodation is very reasonably priced. *Camping US$3 and huts US$8 sgl, shared mud hut US$5, or US$16/18 for the totally gorgeous s/c sgl/dbl chalets.*

Butterfly Lodge Next door to Mayoka Village; 09 265065. A good reputation and beautiful position with a promising reception and bar area, but quite unappealing chalets. *Sgl US$9, en suite sgl/dbl US$15/30, dorm US$5.*

Big Blue 01 352316. Beautifully situated on a rocky beach about 500m from the market (you'll see it sign-posted from the main road as you come into town). Accommodation here consists of rickety bamboo huts. Good food is available for about US$3–5 in the slightly dishevelled bar/restaurant area. The pool table should be back any day now. *Huts MK500/900 sgl/dbl, a chalet for 3–4 people MK1,200, camping MK450 pp, dorms MK400 pp.* Both Mayoka and Big Blue offer free snorkelling equipment to guests, as well as all the fun of a dug-out if you can keep upright.

Matachi Lodge On the opposite side of the road to Big Blue; 09 522899/01 352355. The Matachi is getting away from its old name of 'Backpackers Connection', now modernised and carpeted with business-style rooms and shared facilities including an extraordinary bath, and a restaurant with meals from MK250–550. *Sgl/twin MK1,600/1,800.*

Kupenja Lodge A fun-loving and practical place. There was some very appetising cake on the counter when I visited, the local chess team meet there several times a week and welcome visitors for MK50. Although the rooms are spartan, it's a great place to stay, particularly as you can watch the fishermen come in with their catch in the morning. There's a restaurant too, and Mon night is curry night. Just watch out for the steep paths. *Sgl/dbl MK450/600 with nets.*

Safari Budget Lodge and Restaurant. Near to the ferry jetty with uncared-for rooms and ablutions.

Cairo Motel Very centrally located, a somewhat dingy and atmospherically challenged triple-storey monolith offering acceptable rooms. *Sgl/dbl US$1.60/2.40.*

Ilala Bay Lodge 01 352362. Built as an upmarket hotel next to the Department of Fisheries it has slightly stale but serviceable rooms. Its restaurant on the beach looks much more promising. *Sgl/dbl MK2,200/2,850.*

Safari Cottage All enquiries to Budget Safari and Pangolin Tours; 09 278903. A very nice private cottage just before Mayoka Village – it sleeps 5 people and has DSTV. The owner also runs safaris to Nyika, Vwaza and Livingstonia as well as longer tours to Zambia and the south of Malawi. *MK3,500 for the whole cottage.*

Chikale Beach

Njaya Lodge About 20–30 mins' walk from the town centre; 01 352342; e Info@njayalodge.com; www.njayalodge.com. Njaya is slightly past its heyday, or awaiting a new one – with a huge bar just waiting to be filled with the party people again. Camping space is also available. *From US$7 pp per night for budget beach bandas to US$25 pp per night for family cottages. Credit cards accepted.*

Chikale Beach Resort 01 352338/09 329776. Chikale offers a number of comfortable but dingy chalets. The best thing about it is the bar on the beach. *Sgl/dbl MK1,800/2,800.*

Nkhukuti Resort and Conference Centre 01 352286/08 572469; e ada@globemw.net or info@cbrtoursandtravel.co.mw. Originally one half of Chikale, with the same rooms but with much better maintenance and furnishing. The campsite in the shade of the mango trees could belong to either of them. Further information from CBR Tours and Travel; tel 265774937; fax 265773192; e info@cbrtoursandtravel.co.mw, who can arrange transfers as well. *Rooms US$50 pp, camping US$3 pp.*

WHERE TO EAT Aside from the backpacker lodges and resthouses, most of which serve food, there are a few decent restaurants in Nkhata Bay though it's evident that many open and close with the seasons. For European food, the Ilala Bay, Mayoka, Aqua Africa and Big Blue are the best.

The **Nkhata Bay Local Restaurant** is definitely worth the walk for good Malawian meals from MK180–280. It's at the top of the hill towards Njaya and Mayoka with stunning views of the town.

WHAT TO SEE AND DO For most travellers, activity in Nkhata Bay comprises mainly eating, drinking, sitting on the beach, recovering from hangovers, and generally just hanging out. For the more active, **Aqua Africa's** highly regarded residential diving courses are US$200 or US$260 including the PADI book. I heard only praise from several people who'd done the course. If a week's diving isn't enough, a high proportion of people sign on for a second week's advanced course. If those are too much, you can take a single US$20 dive.

Operating from the boat shed on Chikale Beach, the guys at **Monkey Business** (*08 583490/08 572157*) offer highly popular kayak trips from deep water fishing (including all equipment and breakfast) at US$12, to a full day of activities around Nkhata Bay (bushwalk, kayak ride, diving and lots of fun) for US$40. **Chimango Tours** organise canoeing trips and mountain biking; you will find them at Mayoka Village if you ask.

11

The Lake Ferry and the Islands

This chapter covers ferry transport on Lake Malawi, as well as Likoma and Chizumulu islands, both of which lie within Mozambican waters on the eastern side of the lake. They are destinations that have long held something of a special fascination for travellers, largely because they can only realistically be reached by using the ferry. For local people, the ferry forms the only connection between the mainland and the islands, and the crowded lower deck is testament to its importance to the islanders. For travellers, who mostly can afford to use the spacious first-class deck, the attraction of the ferry is primarily aesthetic. This is one of Africa's great public transport rides, a leisurely cruise on one of the continent's largest and most scenic lakes, offering fantastic sunsets and night skies, as well as a welcome break from the grind of bus travel. Although many travellers do use the ferry as a means of visiting one of the islands, a far greater number travel on it for its own sake, as an alternative means of transport between the popular lake resorts of Cape Maclear (near the southern ferry terminus at Monkey Bay) and Nkhata Bay further north. A few intrepid travellers even cross into Mozambique.

Owing to the unusual nature of the subject matter covered in this chapter, the format deviates somewhat from that used elsewhere in the guide.

THE LAKE FERRY

Malawi Lake Services has recently been privatised and will hopefully now be more reliable. This is not to say that the flagship, the MV *Ilala*, is not under constant threat of being taken out of service for unseaworthiness. The *Ilala* still continues to run a weekly service up and down the lakeshore, from Friday through to the next Wednesday. It also calls at Cobue and Metangula on the Mozambique side of the lake, making it possible for travellers to enter that country via this adventurous route.

Since 1957, the MV *Ilala* has run up and down the lake once a week. Its present route is as follows: Starting at Monkey Bay in the south, it runs up the lake's western shore to Nkhotakota, across to the Mozambican ports of Metangula and Cobue, then to the Malawian islands of Likoma and Chizumulu, back across to Nkhata Bay, right up the west coast to Chilumba, returning to Monkey Bay using the same route in reverse. Sometimes stops are also made at the smaller ports of Makanjila and Chipoka in the south and Mangwina, Usisya, Ruarwe, Tcharo and Mlowe in the north.

Four types of ticket are available for the *Ilala* (prices have risen in recent years). By far the cheapest is lower deck class, with ticket prices comparable to bus transport (around US$15 from Monkey Bay to Nkhata Bay), but the lower deck is very crowded and sweaty, and there's a real risk of theft. Many travellers do use deck class, but, to quote one reader: 'vomiting children, chickens on your lap, cockroaches on your backpack and spiders on your legs without any space to move for 15 hours might sound very romantic, but it can cause frustration in the long run.' There is also lower deck second class which is very comfortable for short trips to places like Ruware from Nkhata Bay as it is not crowded; you normally get a big padded chair with table. The second-class option is not recommended for the journey between the islands and Nkhata Bay, even if you can sleep on your chair and there is access to the outside at the front of the boat, as it becomes very crowded. For many travellers, the compromise between cost and comfort is the first-class deck ticket which works out at around US$50 from Monkey Bay to Nkhata Bay. It costs US$20 to travel directly between Likoma or Chizumulu and either Nkhata Bay or Nkhotakota. First-class passengers sleep on the breezy, uncrowded upper deck, where there is a shaded bar, as well as a restaurant below. There is no need to book tickets for deck or first class, and if you embark anywhere but Monkey Bay or Nkhata Bay, tickets can only be bought once you are on the boat.

If you can afford it, the most comfortable way to travel on the *Ilala* is cabin class. A first-class cabin is US$70. The Captain's Cabin with private bathroom is US$100 per person. Cabin space is limited, so it's essential to book in advance. Cabin bookings can be made at the Malawi Lake Services office in Monkey Bay (☎ *01 587311*) or through a tour operator such as Soche Tours in Blantyre or Central African Wilderness Safaris in Lilongwe (see relevant chapters for further details). The latter company tells me that they are increasingly reluctant to make ferry bookings, because many customers have blamed them for delays which are totally out of their control. Perhaps it's worth pointing out the obvious, which is that

THE MV ILALA TIMETABLE (2006)

	day	*arrives*	*departs*
Monkey Bay	Friday		10.00
Chilinda	Friday	12.10	13.40
Nkhotakota	Saturday	05.30	07.00
Metangula (Mozambique)	Saturday	10.30	12.00
Cobue (Mozambique)	Saturday	15.45	17.00
Likoma Island	Saturday	17.25	19.30
Chizumulu Island	Saturday	20.45	22.45
Nkhata Bay	Sunday	05.00	07.00
Chilumba	Sunday	18.30	02.00 (Monday)
Nkhata Bay	Monday	14.45	20.00
Chizumulu Island	Monday	23.30	02.00 (Tuesday)
Likoma Island	Tuesday	03.15	06.15
Cobue (Mozambique)	Tuesday	06.40	08.30
Metangula (Mozambique)	Tuesday	12.15	14.15
Nkhotakota	Tuesday	17.25	19.20
Chilinda	Wednesday	10.15	12.00
Monkey Bay	Wednesday	14.00	

This timetable has not changed significantly for several years, except for the dropping of Tanzanian ports in favour of Mozambican ones, but is flexible and subject to delays. For simplicity's sake, it includes only the larger ports. For details of minor ports visited (these include Makanjila and Chipoka in the south and Mangwina, Usisya, Ruarwe, Tcharo and Mlowe in the north), or to confirm that the times given here still hold good, you are advised to contact the Malawi Lake Services' office in Monkey Bay (*PO Box 15, Monkey Bay;* ☎ *01 587311;* **f** *01 587203;* **e** *ilala@malawi.net*).

booking through the most reliable tour operator won't affect the ferry's punctuality (or lack thereof), and you probably shouldn't be using the ferry if you aren't prepared for the delays which are almost inevitable. Vehicles can be taken on the ferry at surprisingly reasonable prices (around US$60 from Monkey Bay to Nkhata Bay, less for shorter journeys).

So far as facilities go, there is a well-stocked bar on the upper deck, normally selling biscuits and other packaged snacks. The restaurant serves good three-course meals for around US$4, and it is advisable to reserve lunch and dinner a few hours in advance. The first-class toilets are reasonable, and the communal showers have hot water. At ports other than Monkey Bay and Nkhata Bay, there are no jetties, and the bays are too shallow for the ferry to come in close, so passengers and goods are transported to and from the ferry on a smaller boat. If you are embarking at a port where the ferry docks at some distance from the town (for instance Nkhotakota) you might well want to bring along something to nibble and drink while you wait.

Aside from the *Ilala*, the only reasonably reliable ferry on the lake at the time of writing was the Tanzanian MV *Songea*. It connects two ports in Tanzania, Mbamba Bay (on the eastern shore) and Itungi Port (near Kyela on the lake's northwestern tip). The ferry leaves Itungi at 07.00 on Mondays and Thursdays and arrives at Mbamba Bay at around midnight the same day, after stopping at Lupinga, Manda, Lundu and Liuli. After arriving at Mbamba Bay, the ferry turns around almost immediately, to arrive back at Itungi at 17.00 the next day. The *Songea* does come to Nkhata Bay but not on a regular schedule, only once or twice a month, arriving at Nkhata Bay on a Friday and leaving early on Saturday, though it is not so easy to find out in advance when exactly it will do this.

LIKOMA ISLAND

The island of Likoma, 8km long and 3km wide, lies within Mozambican waters but is territorially part of Malawi, mainly as a result of its long association with Scottish missionaries. In 1886, Likoma became the site of an Anglican mission, established by Bishop Chauncey Maples with the help of his close friend and fellow Oxford graduate, the Rev William Johnson. Maples was consecrated as the first bishop of Likoma in London in 1895, but he never actively assumed this post as he drowned in a boating accident near Salima, caused by his enthusiasm to return to Likoma despite stormy weather. Maples was buried in the church at Nkhotakota. Johnson went on to become one of the most fondly remembered of all the missionaries who worked in Malawi. He arrived at the lake in 1882 and for 46 years he preached from a boat all around the lakeshore, despite being practically blind and well into his seventies when he died in 1928. Johnson's grave at Liuli (on the Tanzanian part of the lakeshore) remained for several decades a popular site of pilgrimage for Malawian Christians.

The Likoma Mission founded by Maples and Johnson remained the headquarters of the Anglican Church in Malawi until after World War II. During this period, the educational zeal of the missionaries ensured that Likoma was probably the only settlement in Africa with a 100% literacy rate. The most obvious physical legacy of the missionaries work is the large and very beautiful St Peter's Cathedral (similar in size to Westminster Cathedral) designed by Frank George and built between 1903 and 1905 in a cruciform shape using local granite. The site of the church, chosen by Maples before his death, is where in 1889 he witnessed and was unable to prevent three witches being burnt to death. Notable features of the church include carved soapstone choir stalls, some fine stained-glass windows and a crucifix carved from a tree which grew near Chitambo (the village in Zambia where David Livingstone died in 1873).

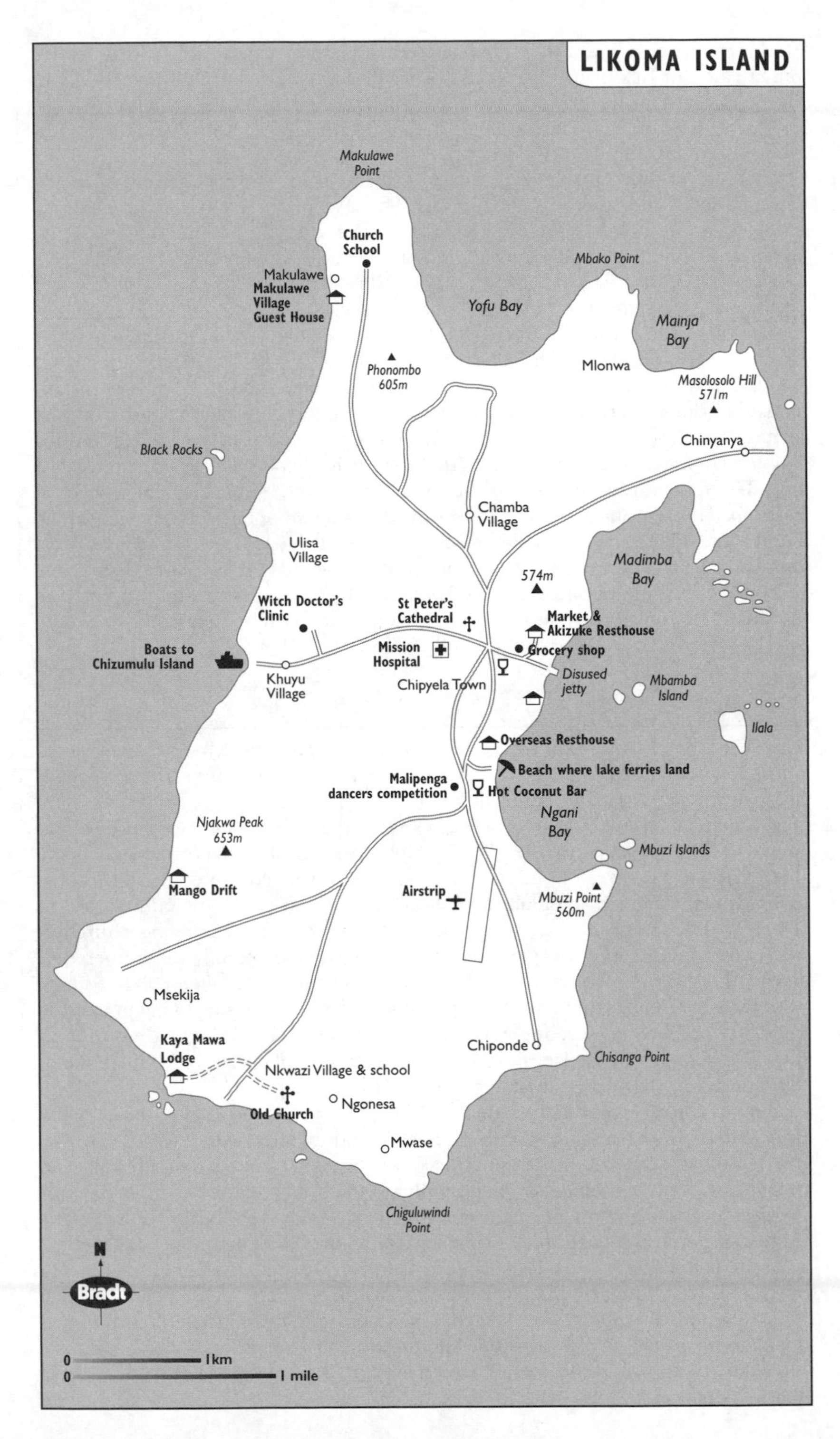
LIKOMA ISLAND
Makulawe Point
Church School
Makulawe
Makulawe Village Guest House
Mbako Point
Yofu Bay
Mainja Bay
Phonombo 605m
Mlonwa
Masolosolo Hill 571m
Black Rocks
Chinyanya
Chamba Village
Ulisa Village
Madimba Bay
574m
Witch Doctor's Clinic
St Peter's Cathedral
Market & Akizuke Resthouse
Boats to Chizumulu Island
Mission Hospital
Grocery shop
Khuyu Village
Chipyela Town
Disused jetty
Mbamba Island
Ilala
Overseas Resthouse
Beach where lake ferries land
Malipenga dancers competition
Hot Coconut Bar
Ngani Bay
Njakwa Peak 653m
Mbuzi Islands
Mango Drift
Airstrip
Mbuzi Point 560m
Msekija
Kaya Mawa Lodge
Chiponde
Chisanga Point
Nkwazi Village & school
Old Church
Ngonesa
Mwase
Chiguluwindi Point
N
Bradt
0
1km
0
1 mile

Historical interest aside, Likoma's main attraction for travellers is its isolation and mellow atmosphere. This is no conventional tropical island paradise, though the beaches really are splendid with the mountainous Mozambican shore rising above them, while the interior has a certain austere charm, particularly the southern plains which are covered in massive baobabs, shady mango trees and studded with impressive granite outcrops. Likoma has always generated a great deal of interest among travellers, but it remains surprisingly little visited. Above all, perhaps, Likoma has an overwhelmingly friendly mood, making it a good place to get to know ordinary Malawians.

Most visitors to the island are content to while away their time on the beaches or to explore Chipyela, the island's largest town. Chipyela lies between the cathedral and the jetty, and is named after the spot where witches used to be burnt (Chipyela translates as 'the place of burning'). It is an unusual town: the neat, cobbled roads and stone houses have, according to one resident, led to it being nicknamed 'Half London', a strange epithet for a metropolis that not only lacks an underground but until recently boasted a grand total of only one car, the ambulance belonging to the mission hospital. The central market is dominated by a massive strangler fig with a hollow base large enough to stand in. Worth asking about are the regular *malipenga* dancing competitions held on most weekends about 500m out of town opposite the Hot Coconut Bar – these are generally held in the afternoon, and are rather boozy affairs, notable both for the interesting traditional instruments that are used and for the bizarre colonially influenced costumes the men wear.

Further afield, a half-hour walk eastwards from Chipyela takes you to the village of Khuyu, where visitors are normally welcome at the witch doctor's clinic. Reputedly one of the most important 'witch doctors' in Malawi, he is regularly visited by people from as far away as Tanzania and South Africa, and his influence over the islanders is immense, despite the superficial trappings of Christianity associated with Likoma. Another good excursion is a boat trip to Cobue on the Mozambican shore of the lake, where there is a large ruined church – this is best organised through the management of Kaya Mawa, and visas aren't a problem for day trips.

GETTING THERE AND AWAY Unless you can afford to charter a plane or boat to Likoma, there is only one way of reaching the island from the Malawian mainland. This is with the MV *Ilala*, which is scheduled to stop at Likoma on Saturday evening on its northbound trip and on Tuesday morning on the southbound trip. Allowing for delays, this means that you need to allocate at least five days to the round trip, spending three or four nights on the island. The *Ilala* docks a few hundred metres offshore at a beach about five minutes' walk from Chipyela. It is usually docked here for about two hours, which means, in theory, that ferry passengers who are travelling on could still hop off the boat and take a quick look around the cathedral. In practice, however, the complexities of transporting passengers between the *Ilala* and the beach make this inadvisable, unless you're prepared to risk the boat sailing away without you.

Other than the MV *Ilala*, it is possible to travel between Likoma and Chizumulu islands and Cobue on the Mozambican mainland using a local fishing boat.

WHERE TO STAY AND EAT

Akizuke Resthouse This fairly run-down place is in Chipyela, facing the central market, about 5–10 mins' walk from the beach where the ferry docks. There are basic but clean rooms with mosquito nets, and facilities include a flush toilet, running showers and a spasmodically functional generator. The bar attached to the resthouse serves cold beers and soft drinks when the generator is running, and the restaurant prepares basic meals by advance order, generally fish, beans and rice, though you can also ask them to buy you a chicken. *Sgl/dbl US$3/5.*

Overseas Resthouse So far as we could establish, the only other accommodation close to Chipyela is this even more run-down resthouse next to the beach where the ferry lands. There is nowhere else to eat in town, but a couple of stores on the road between the mission and the Akizuke Resthouse sell tinned provisions and cold soft drinks and mineral water. Opposite the entrance to the Likoma Mission (next to a volleyball court) is a building housing a bar with a fridge, but nowhere to sit.

The closest thing to a nightspot in this neck of the woods is the **Hot Coconut Bar**, an open-air bar with a fridge and shaded tables, about 10 mins' walk from town, not far from the beach where the ferry lands.

Kaya Mawa Satellite 00871 761 684 670; e kaya01@bushmail.net; www.kayamowa.com. A wonderfully laid-back spot, the name of which translates somewhat appropriately as 'maybe tomorrow', set on an idyllic beach, book-ended by large rocky outcrops and stands of baobab, near Nkwazi village on the southwestern end of the island facing the Mozambican shore. This popular old backpackers' place has been completely changed and rebuilt as the spectacular and exclusive Kaya Mawa Lodge, and offers luxury accommodation, including a tiny honeymoon island just offshore, accessible only by boat. Boat transfers to and from the island can also be arranged at US$200 pp, one way. For more information and bookings contact Central African Wilderness Safaris. *US$250 pp FB and includes government taxes and all non-motorised watersports (kayaking, sailing and snorkelling).*

Mango Drift The place for backpackers to head for – even if it's in a bit of a slump period at the moment. It's about 1km north of Kaya Mawa, an idyllic spot with a bar under a mango tree and grass huts on the beach. They also run a PADI dive school which offers the 4-day Open Water course for only US$150, including free camping. Dinner is about US$3. *Camping US$2 pp, dorm bed US$3 pp, huts US$4 pp. Bookings through Kaya Mawa (see above).*

A small 2-roomed resthouse is at the northern point of the island in Makulawe village (*www.lakemalawiprojects.com*).

CHIZUMULU ISLAND

Smaller than Likoma, and even more remote, the island of Chizumulu is noted for excellent diving and snorkelling in the surrounding waters, and for attractive beaches lined by large, ancient baobabs. Like Likoma, this is essentially a place to chill out, free of roads, cars and hassle, and widely regarded to offer the most beautiful sunsets in Malawi. Few travellers make it to Chizumulu, but those who do invariably regard it as a highlight of their time in Malawi.

GETTING THERE AND AWAY Most people travel to Chizumulu on the MV *Ilala*, which stops there between Likoma and Nkhata Bay on both the northbound and southbound parts of its weekly circuit. If the timing works, travellers who want to visit both islands can use the *Ilala* to get between them. Alternatively, a fishing boat ferries passengers between Likoma and Chizumulu daily for around MK100 per person. This boat leaves Khuyu Beach on Likoma at 10.00 and it arrives at Same Beach on Chizumulu roughly at 14.00, though timings are pretty vague, as it is wind dependent and it doesn't run at all in rough weather. A more romantic option is to charter a sailing dhow between the two islands for MK1,500.

WHERE TO STAY

Wakwenda Retreat 01 357286/01 357272; e nickchisi2000@yahoo.co.uk; www.wakwenda.com. The only place to stay on the island, this excellent backpacker-friendly lodge is set on the beach a few hundred metres from where the *Ilala* stops and about 1km from Same Beach, where dhows and fishing boats from Likoma set anchor. Wakwenda offers simple but comfortable accommodation and camping, as well as drinks and meals. Scuba diving can be arranged (for experienced divers only), and snorkelling equipment is free. There is a focus on food here, generally rated as big and delicious, and a good range for vegetarians too for MK500–600. *Camping MK200, dorm bed MK300, grass huts MK800–1,000/500–600 dbl/sgl, all pp per day.*

WHAT TO SEE AND DO Like Likoma this is a place to chill out, play boa (a board game involving competitive bean snatching), swim and watch the sunset with a Green in your hand. For the more active though there are plenty of options. A walk up the mountain takes about an hour and a half, or you can walk around it in just one hour. The walk around the whole island takes four to six hours and is rewarding for the contact you have with local people more than for any other reason. Swimming, snorkelling and diving are endlessly interesting, especially if you can find a fish expert, as there are many cichlid species here not found elsewhere. Wakwenda Retreat organise boat excursions and scuba-diving trips, costing between US$20 and US$35, depending on how far you go.

OVER TO MOZAMBIQUE

The Mozambique coast near to Likoma is a rugged pile of rocks tumbling into the lake, with far fewer fishing villages than on the Malawi side. This area of coast is described here because it is really only accessed from Likoma and Malawi, being cut off from the rest of Mozambique by vast tracts of emptiness.

GETTING THERE AND AWAY Fishing boats to Cobue and to Manda Wilderness are probably best organised through the staff of Kaya Mawa (see above), who can also advise you on the current situation with Mozambican visas. Should you be crossing into Mozambique rather than just paying a day visit, you might also want to ask them about the current transport situation on the road connecting Cobue to Lichinga.

MANDA WILDERNESS RESERVE A small reserve comes right down to the lakeshore. Zebra, monkeys and otters are the most frequently seen mammals, though others are present, including lion and wild dog. Bookings can be made through any Malawi-based tour operator, or e mdw01@bushmail.net.

Where to stay

Mchenga Nkwichi Lodge This is the only accommodation in the reserve, where tracking animals may well give way to activities on the lake such as canoeing, snorkelling or sailing. There again, you can just sit in a hammock. The rooms are luxurious and, like Kaya Mawa on Likoma, simply ingeniously thought out to be natural and harmonious. Sgl/dbl *US$210–270/160–220 FB, price depending on season.*

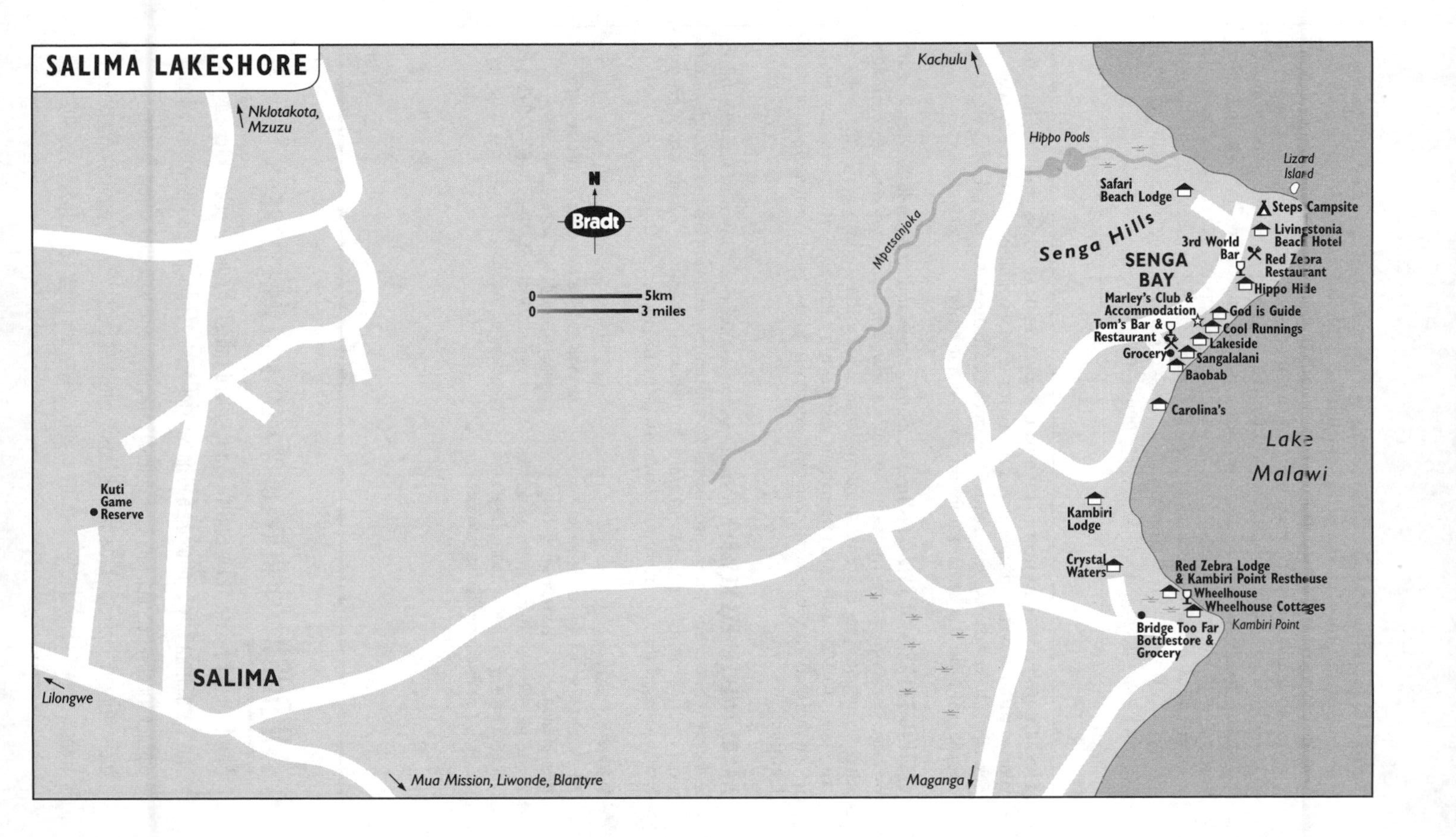
SALIMA LAKESHORE
Nklotakota, Mzuzu
Kachulu
Hippo Pools
Mpatsanjoka
Lizard Island
Safari Beach Lodge
Steps Campsite
Livingstonia Beach Hotel
Senga Hills
SENGA BAY
3rd World Bar
Red Zebra Restaurant
Hippo Hide
Marley's Club & Accommodation
God is Guide
Tom's Bar & Restaurant
Cool Runnings
Lakeside
Grocery
Sangalalani
Baobab
Carolina's
Lake Malawi
Kambiri Lodge
Crystal Waters
Red Zebra Lodge & Kambiri Point Resthouse
Wheelhouse
Wheelhouse Cottages
Kambiri Point
Bridge Too Far Bottlestore & Grocery
N
Bradt
0 5km
0 3 miles
Kuti Game Reserve
SALIMA
Lilongwe
Mua Mission, Liwonde, Blantyre
Maganga

12

The Lakeshore around Salima

The Lake Malawi shore around Salima has become a popular weekend getaway for people from Lilongwe and it also forms a useful last stop for visitors before going to the airport. As a result, the 5km stretch of beach between Senga Bay and Kambiri Point is as well developed for tourism as any part of the lake, with a friendly atmosphere. The Salima area, it must be said, has neither the natural beauty of Nkhata Bay or Cape Maclear, nor the sense of isolation of some of the resorts on the northern lakeshore. It is popular simply because it is closer to Lilongwe than any other part of the lake. Nevertheless, it is an attractive enough spot, relatively rich in birds and mammals, and a very comfortable place to settle into for a few days.

Salima itself lies 15km from the lake; it is a thoroughly dull small town, and purely of interest as a route focus and as the gateway to Senga Bay on Lake Malawi. The only motivations for exploring Salima beyond its bus station are practical: it has a bank, a post office, a bustling market and a couple of well-stocked supermarkets. Most visitors simply head straight on to Senga Bay. The main points of interest around Senga Bay are the Mpatsanjoka River (excellent birding and resident hippo), Lizard Island, the tropical fish farm near Kambiri Point and the private Kuti Game Reserve.

For anyone travelling southward from Salima, the Mua Mission is a not-to-be-missed stopping point – its museum gives a fascinating insight into the cultures and tribes of the central region and into the modern Malawian psyche as a whole.

CLIMATE

Salima has the hot, sticky climate typical of the Lake Malawi shore.

GETTING AROUND

Salima is a major route focus, connected to Lilongwe by the recently tarred M14. The M14 intersects with the southern lakeshore road (to Cape Maclear, Mangochi, Zomba and Blantyre) about 2km west of Salima, and with the northern lakeshore road (to Nkhotakota, Nkhata Bay and Mzuzu) about 4km west of Salima.

Minibuses travel regularly between Salima and Lilongwe. All buses which follow the lakeshore road between points north and south of Salima stop there to pick up passengers. A steady stream of *matola* pick-up trucks run between Salima's bus station and the market in Senga Bay. From the market, it's about 4km along the tar road to the Livingstonia Beach Hotel and Steps Campsite. South of the Livingstonia Beach Hotel, several resorts, hotels and campsites stretch along the beach towards Kambiri Point. These resorts can be accessed from the tarred Salima–Senga Bay road by a series of signposted side roads. On foot, they can also be reached along the beach.

The best way to reach any of the resorts towards Kambiri Point is to take transport towards Senga Bay; ask to be dropped at the appropriate turn-off (the resorts are all signposted from the Salima–Senga Bay road), and then walk or hitch to the lakeshore (between 30 minutes and an hour on foot, depending on the resort). The alternative is go right through to Senga Bay, continue along the tar road to the Livingstonia Beach Hotel, and then turn left onto the beach and follow it southwards. In terms of distance, there's not much in it, but walking along the beach will be tiring and slower, especially if you have a heavy pack.

WHERE TO STAY

SALIMA With Senga Bay only 15km away, it's difficult to think of a convincing reason why any traveller would actually choose to stay in Salima. On the other hand, its strategic position does mean that you might just end up there for a night at some point. Accommodation in town is limited to a few very ordinary resthouses dotted around the bus station.

THE NORTHERN TIP OF SENGA BAY

Livingstonia Beach Hotel t 01 263222; f 01 263452; e tdic@sdnp.org.mw. The oldest hotel on Lake Malawi was built in the 1930s, when it was known as the Grand Beach Hotel, with an overall shape and design instantly recognisable from the many old photos that line the walls of the public areas. The compact flower-filled grounds, beautiful private beach, comfortable rooms, and whitewash and creosote exterior, vaguely reminiscent of the Cape Dutch style, could easily combine to make the Livingstonia the finest hotel in Malawi. However, it seems to rely on reputation and exclusivity too much, and currently has a somewhat slack attitude with mediocre and overpriced food, though hopefully things will improve. These are things that can change. Facilities include watersports and snorkelling equipment hire, a swimming pool and tennis court, an atmospheric residents' lounge, a library, and an excellent first-floor restaurant. The management can arrange walking trips to the nearby hippo pool and viewpoints, as well as boat trips to several islands and car trips to Mua Mission, the Stuart Grant Fish Farm and other local points of interest. The checklist of birds recorded in the grounds, available from reception, includes several interesting species. *Sgl/dbl US$80/95, chalet US$115/130, suite US$139/154, family room US$154.*

Steps Campsite The spacious site has a great position next to the Livingstonia Beach Hotel and is under the same management. Its facilities include a bar, laundry, hot showers and credit card and money exchange facilities and electricity is available for a small extra fee. Campers are welcome to eat at the neighbouring hotel, but they should be prepared to abide by the relatively formal dress code (no shorts or flip-flops). *Camping US$5 pp.*

Hippo Hide Resthouse In Senga Bay village, close to where the *matola* vehicles stop, this resthouse offers basic but adequate rooms, and you can pitch a tent in the compound. Facilities include a communal shower and toilet, a fridge with cold beers and sodas and meals can be ordered a few hours in advance. *Rooms US$15 pp, camping slightly less.*

There are also a few rooms at similar prices at the **Top Hill Restaurant**, which has a great position, about 500m from the entrance to the Livingstonia Beach Hotel, and at the nearby **God is Guide Resthouse** – both of these places are similar in quality to Hippo Hide, but they're likely to be more peaceful because of the absence of touts.

Safari Beach Lodge t 01 263143; e safwag@africa-online.net; www.dawisafaris.co. To reach this upmarket lodge, turn left just before the gates of the Livingstonia Beach Hotel and travel about 1km up the hill. Situated in a forestry reserve, the lodge has 2 dbl en-suite rooms and 5 large tents with decks overlooking the lake. There is also a private beach, 10ha of forest to ramble through and the owners can organise safaris into the Tuma Forest Reserve. *Sgl/dbl US$44/65 including b/fast.*

CENTRE OF SENGA BAY A separate cluster of chalet-type accommodation lies in the centre of Senga Bay and can be reached from the main Salima–Senga Bay road via a 3km-long turn-off signposted 'Carolina's'.

Carolina's 01 263220; e anydemel@yahoo.com. The most appealing of the options in the first cluster, as well as inexpensive camping and excellent 'huge' meals. Canoeing, kayaking and volleyball are all free. *Sgl/dbl MK2,000/3,500, chalet MK5,500, dorm MK550.*

Baobab Next door to Carolina's with more basic chalets. *Sgl/dbl MK2,300/3,000 inc b/fast, camping MK250.*

Sangalalani 01 263350. Beyond Baobab but no restaurant facilities at all. *Chalets MK1,500, camping MK200.*

Cool Runnings 01 263398/09 915173; e coolrunnings@malawi.net. There are not very many rooms here, but worth staying here so that you can enjoy the best food in the bay and enjoy the relaxed atmosphere. The garden is worth mentioning as it is overhung with impressive trees, attracting at least 43 bird species and a resident family of genet. There's a catamaran that you can take out for US$30 or a 6-man boat for US$10 per 2 hours. Surfing and water skiing are also possible. *Room with 2 beds US$20, 2-bedded dorm in garden US$5, camping US$2.*

Tom's Bar The Cool Runnings management is also setting up a small place attached to Tom's Bar. *Dorm room MK500 pp, camping MK150.*

KAMBIRI POINT ON SENGA BAY The southernmost cluster of accommodation lies about 5km from the Livingstonia Beach Hotel as the crow flies. By road, the turn-off to these places is about 8km towards Salima, and clearly signposted. From the turn-off, it's a further 4–5km, depending on where you're heading, and there is no public transport.

Wheelhouse 01 261485. The first place from Kambiri Point, best known for its raised wooden wheel-shaped bar overlooking a reed-lined (ie: high risk of bilharzia) beach. It's an ideal place for campers and there are also several self-catering cottages. Simply furnished with few frills, the cottages are often booked up, so advance booking is necessary. *The Bottom House can be rented for US$60 and sleeps 7 people, the Big House sleeps 10–12 people for US$50, and the Small Cottage sleeps 2–3 people for US$30. Camping US$2.50 pp.*

Red Zebra Lodge Tel 01 263165 or 09 233428/09 913630; Tel/Fax 01 263407; e stuart@lakemalawi.com; www.lakemalawi.com. Often referred to as Stuart Grant's Fish Farm, with comfortable, s/c rooms. The owner will, if you're lucky, regale you with stories and engage you in discussion, and, as the lake's most renowned cichlid specialist, could tell you a lot about fish too. Red Zebra offers guests and day visitors a variety of different boat trips, including sundowner cruises (US$20) or day trips ranging from US$82–271 depending on destination. You can also take a tour of the tropical fish farm (US$0.50). *Sgl/dbl US$38/56 or US$60 FB*

Crystal Waters 01 263033. This is an incongruously large and smart hotel, with classy tiling everywhere giving a fresh cool clean appearance. The rooms are large and there is a pleasant stretch of beach as well as a swimming pool. *Sgl/dbl MK5,900/8,700 and MK7,900/9,100 for executive stes.*

Kambiri Lodge 01 263052. A large hotel with conference facilities, with decent rooms and a very pleasant setting a little back from the lake, with beach frontage too. *Sgl/dbl MK5,550/7,800 family room MK9,800.*

WHERE TO EAT

Livingstonia Beach Hotel The restaurant may be the most upmarket in the area, though currently not good value at US$20, available to non-residents of the hotel provided that they dress reasonably smartly.

Top Hill Restaurant On the main tar road about 500m from the Livingstonia Beach Hotel. An idiosyncratic little place with walls plastered with raves from passing travellers. The banana pancakes here have acquired something close to legendary status. Main meals such as fish or chicken with mashed potatoes, chips or rice must be ordered in advance, at US$2.50 per plate.

Red Zebra Café Next door to Top Hill. The Red Zebra is much more pleasant, with a garden and good food, excellently served. Most meals cost about US$4.

Third World Bar Restaurant In Senga Bay village, 100m from the market. Local food for around US$1.

Carolina's and **Crystal Waters**, further afield,

have varied menus with most dishes in the US$3–6 range – tempting lunchtime goals if you're looking for an incentive to stroll down the beach.

Red Zebra Lodge At Stuart Grant's Fish Farm. This place also does a good lunch on the beach, and supper if reserved in advance, with meals around US$3–6 and excellent Malawian specials by request.

If you're cooking for yourself, the market in Senga Bay is pretty basic. It would be better to stock up in Salima, where there are supermarkets. The market has a fair range of vegetables, fruit and fresh meat.

WHAT TO SEE AND DO

Lazing around on the beach, or perhaps hiring some watersports equipment, will be enough to occupy many people's time at Salima. There are, however, a couple of options for those who want to explore.

LIZARD ISLAND This small rocky island, which lies just off the beach in front of the Livingstonia Beach Hotel, is known for its dense population of monitor lizards, and also as the breeding ground for large numbers of white-breasted cormorants. It's easy enough to organise a day trip to the island (inclusive of a fish barbecue) with guides in Senga Bay village – expect to pay around US$10 per person, depending on group size and to a lesser extent your negotiating skills. Several of the lodges will organise cruises there. Stuart Grant at Red Zebra Lodge operates the best and most comfortable boats in the area.

Mpatsanjoka Dambo The lush and seasonally marshy Mpatsanjoka River runs in an arc north of Senga Hill, before emptying into Lake Malawi about 2km north of Senga Bay. The river is home to a small resident population of hippos, crocodiles and water monitors, and is also noted for its prolific birdlife. The simplest way to reach the hippo pools is to adopt a local child as your guide (ask around in the village), and you may find beach touts who will offer to escort you, though it's not too difficult to find your own way there. Take the path crossing the hill from the road to Safari Beach Lodge, then descend to the beach and follow it through the reed fishing village northwards for a good 30 minutes to the river mouth. From here, it's about 3km upriver to the area where you're most likely to see hippos (you know you have gone far enough when you connect with a dirt road that bridges the river).

Seeing the hippos requires a little luck: we could hear them and approached them within metres, but they remained submerged beneath thick overhanging vegetation. Especially in the morning, it would be wise to be very cautious (at least two people have been killed by hippos in this area in the last ten years). If you don't see the hippos, you can be certain of seeing plenty of birds – they are everywhere, even when the water is low. I saw a good variety of hornbills, kingfishers, weavers and finches, and it's a good pace to see the localised and very colourful Boehm's bee-eater, as well as the secretive rufous-bellied heron.

In the wet season, you could cross the bridge and continue north along the road for about 2km to an area of rice cultivation, where several unusual birds (including crowned crane and common pratincole) are regulars.

Enthusiastic birders may want to explore the several other seasonal marshes in the Senga area; good directions and a map are included in the booklet *Day Outings from Lilongwe*.

Tropical fish farm This farm (*01 263165; e redzebra@lakemalawi.com; cost US$0.50*) near Kambiri Point was established by Stuart Grant to breed various cichlid species for the European tropical fish market and as a holding point for fish being exported from the lake. A huge variety of cichlids can be seen in the tanks, many of them rare species, and visitors are welcome.

Kuti Game Ranch Kuti Game Ranch (☎ *09 913525; admission MK200 for a vehicle, MK100 pp. Horseriding MK800 per hour, camping MK250, tent rent MK250*) is an area of grassy *brachystegia* woodland which is being restocked with game after having been decommissioned as a cattle ranch several years ago. The most striking area in Kuti is a large swamp-like lake covered in water lilies and papyrus. Local fishermen use small balsa wood coracles to punt through the marshland and the area is teeming with birds. Further into Kuti Game Ranch you can visit fenced areas where two non-indigenous species can be found – giraffe and ostrich. How Kuti will continue as a tourist destination is under discussion, as there are plans afoot to convert it into a hunting concession. However, until that happens, it is still worth the visit, with riding and walking a possibility.

SOUTHWARDS TO LIWONDE FROM SALIMA

MUA MISSION Less than an hour from Senga Bay, and about 35mins south of Salima, is Mua Mission (*for all enquiries,* ☎ *01 262706*). This Catholic Mission is one of the oldest in Malawi, established at the base of the Rift Valley Escarpment by the so-called 'White Fathers' in 1902. Mua is now one of the key points on the tourist map of Malawi, as its compact ethnographic museum is undoubtedly the best in Malawi. It is a source of endless information about the three main tribes of the central region, and the main religious practices, and is very much about living culture rather than the past. A two- to three-hour tour of the **KuNgoni Museum** (*closed Sat afternoons and Sun*) costs US$5 per person, though it would be easy to spend a day here. The historical murals on its outside walls are worth being guided around as they give a pictorial history of Malawi. The museum also gives the history of the impressive seminary and church at Mua, and if you have time it is worth going into the church to look at the carvings and enjoy the stillness.

The mission is a main training centre for woodcarving, and it's possible to visit the workshop where you will see the carvers holding down the wood they are working on with their feet while they carve intricately. The **KuNgoni Arts Centre** at the mission sells the work from two sites.

The museum offers courses, seminars and retreats for interested individuals or groups wishing to explore more detailed aspects of the local culture and its interaction with Christianity (these should be booked in advance).

Getting there and away Mua lies about 45km south of Salima along the main tar road to Balaka. The roughly 1km-long dirt turn-off to the mission is clearly signposted 'Mua Parish'. Note that Mua lies at the base of the scenic road through the Mua-Livulezi Forest Reserve, making it the terminus of a route that already has much to offer keen hikers and cyclists coming from Dedza.

Where to stay

KuNgoni Mua Mission; ☎ 09 511884/09 294320/01 262706; e admin@kungoni.org; www.kungoni.org. Mua Mission has dreamy simple accommodation and a dining area, set high on a rock opposite Mua village, with a river clefting its way in between. There are 5 well-appointed authentically African rondavels built in the grounds of KuNgoni, with further rooms at the seminary accommodating up to 20 guests. Each en-suite chalet sleeps 2 guests. Discounts are available for groups or individuals participating in other cultural programmes. *US$20 pp.*

If you get stuck and need accommodation between Salima and Mua, or if you are taking the *Ilala* lake ferry, then the little lakeside town of **Chipoka** is your best bet.

Chipoka Lake View Lodge ☎ 09 292523/09 394763. Situated right on a lovely beach, the fairly crummy rooms, despite having fans and TVs, looked pretty bad, dark and without sheets or much in the way of cleaning but the restaurant was evidently extremely popular, with meals costing US$2.50. *Sgl/dbl MK600–1,400/1,500–3,100.*

Modern Tourism Lodge Another option in Chipoka is this much smaller place, which is more rustic and better quality. *Sgl/trpl MK1,000/1,500.*

BALAKA Balaka is a large market town on the M1, just south of the intersection with the Blantyre road and only 30mins' drive from Liwonde and on all the bus routes between the north and the south. There are several small resthouses and restaurants. Though Balaka is now bypassed, the huge Catholic church is on the edge of the town and is clearly visible from the road. Balaka Mission is also important for the Montfort Press which publishes a range of books and magazines. An interesting by-product of the printing press is Chifundo Artisans Network (☎ *08 365 960 or 01 545 760, www.ChifundoArtisansNetwork.com*) where you can see paper being made by hand and textiles being dyed and made into clothing. This was originally a Peace Corps programme which has developed into a sound business and a welcome tourist attraction, complete with a café serving cold drinks and Italian coffee. The paper-making, tie-dyeing and finishing workshops can be visited on weekdays, signposted behind the mission church towards the Montfort Press and about 3km on dirt roads. Another attraction in Balaka, attached to the Mission, is the Chapel of Reconciliation, which was built so that people leaving Malawi's prisons could go to church without community disapproval, a first step to re-integration. The chapel has carvings and murals from KuNgoni (*www.kungoni.org*).

WHERE TO STAY

Mlambe Motel (18 rooms) On the main road, near the bus station; ☎ 08 315888/09 440344. The best bet if you get stuck in town, with a calm and friendly environment and residents' car park. Standard and executive rooms, the latter with DSTV. *Standard sgl/dbl MK1,300/1,600 pp, executive sgl/dbl MK1,550/1,750.*

Zembani Lodge, Bar and Restaurant ☎ 08 343830/08 393094. *Standard sgl MK800*

13

Dedza and Surrounds

This chapter covers Dedza, a sizeable town lying along the M1 south of Lilongwe, as well as some of the forest reserves that surround it. Dedza is known primarily for its pottery, but the surrounding area is not often visited by tourists, and it lacks the obvious attractions of somewhere like Cape Maclear. Nevertheless, its mountains and forests have much to offer keen walkers and birdwatchers, and it will be attractive to people who have the urge to explore a part of Malawi that is both accessible and beautiful, yet which might go weeks on end without seeing a tourist.

There are several forest reserves around Dedza. The three covered in this chapter – Dedza Mountain, Chongoni and Mua-Livulezi – are selected on the basis of accessibility. Dedza Mountain can be explored on foot as a day trip from Dedza Town. Chongoni requires a little more exertion to reach on foot, but once you are there, you can take several days to look around, staying at the forestry resthouse that lies within the reserve. It would be possible to hike between Dedza and Mua, finding a camping spot in between. If you want to visit some of the less accessible reserves, the booklet *Day Outings from Lilongwe* is your best source of printed information. It may also be worth speaking to the Forestry Office in Dedza: my experience is that they are very willing to offer advice to visitors, and they may well agree to let you camp in some forest reserves. The Forestry Office is on the outskirts of Dedza Town (*01 220275*).

Before you head to this area, you'd do well to get hold of the 1:50,000 map of Dedza (sheet 1434A4) for Dedza Mountain and Chongoni Forest Reserve, supplemented by the 1:50,000 map of Golomoti (sheet 1434B3) for Mua-Livulezi. These can be bought at the map sales offices in either Lilongwe or Blantyre. If they're not available, the Monkey Bay map (sheet 7) in the Malawi 1:250,000 series is also very useful.

Nkoma Mission lies east of the M1 between Lilongwe and Dedza, 16km from the road. Nkoma Mountain is the large massif that can be seen south of Lilongwe and makes excellent walking. The mission and hospital is interesting architecturally as it is in the Cape Dutch style.

CLIMATE

The Dedza area has a pleasant highland climate, warm by day and cool by night. Temperatures are higher in Mua-Livulezi than in the other reserves, as it is at a much lower altitude.

GETTING AROUND

Dedza lies on the M1 between Lilongwe and Blantyre. This road is the quickest route between Malawi's two largest cities, and thus carries a relatively heavy volume

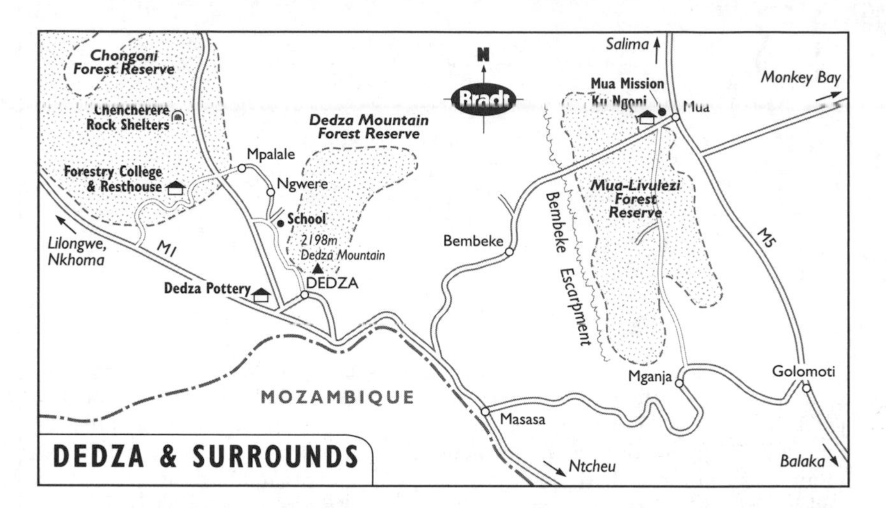

DEDZA & SURROUNDS

of traffic. In a private vehicle, the drive from Lilongwe to Dedza shouldn't take much more than an hour. All buses that travel between Lilongwe and Blantyre on the M1 stop at Dedza, express buses included. The bus journey from Lilongwe to Dedza takes less than two hours. Minibuses leave regularly from in front of the bus station in Lilongwe. If you're heading between Dedza and Blantyre, the main town you'll pass through on the M1 is the vegetable growers' market town of Ntcheu. All you need to know about Ntcheu is that it is on the Mozambican border, it's thoroughly dull and scruffy, and it has several resthouses, a good supermarket and a bank. You're unlikely to get stuck in Ntcheu unless you want to.

If you are travelling between Dedza and Lilongwe, look out for the Diampwe Bridge, the oldest bridge in Malawi, restored in 1991 for use as a footbridge and as a tribute to a new public awareness of heritage in Malawi. The arched brick structure was built in 1923 and it was once a vital link for the growing 'outpost' of Lilongwe. Just north of Dedza, it crosses the second of the Lilongwe river tributaries.

NKOMA MOUNTAIN

Reaching a height of 1,784m, this *brachystegia*-covered mountain lies to the east of the main road between Lilongwe and Dedza, and it offers some rewarding walking as well as great views over the surrounding plains. The mission near the base of the mountain offers accommodation, and access is straightforward whether you are driving, cycling or dependent on public transport, making this yet another excellent off-the-beaten-track excursion in the Dedza area.

The turn-off to Nkoma lies on the M1, 35km south of Lilongwe, and from there it is 16km to the mission grounds. On Saturday, which is market day in Nkoma Town, there is direct transport between Nkoma and Dedza. On other days, there is a least one bus daily between Lilongwe and Nkoma. There is an inexpensive and clean resthouse in the mission grounds, and more basic local accommodation can be found in town, near to the market. You could also ask at the mission about the rustic hut that lies halfway up the mountain. The ascent from the mission to the rocky summit is quite steep (550m over 2km), and the staff will be able to point you along the right path. It's worth spending some time in Nkoma Mission, not only for the architecture and atmosphere, but also to browse in the impressive craft shop, which is open on weekdays – and serves good coffee and snacks!

DEDZA

Dedza lies 84km south of Lilongwe at the southern foot of the 2,198m-high Dedza Mountain, and in the centre of an area noted for its striking granite outcrops and plentiful forests. Dedza is an unremarkable town, but it is very agreeable, with a comfortable highland climate and attractive setting. It's also the base of Dedza Pottery, which is famous not only for its pots, tableware and ornamental garden ceramics, but also for serving delicious food, including its famous cheesecake and coffee. Dedza is also of interest to travellers as the base from which to visit Dedza Mountain and the little-visited Chongoni and Mua-Livulezi forest reserves.

GETTING THERE AND AWAY All buses between Lilongwe and Blantyre stop at Dedza.

WHERE TO STAY AND EAT

Rainbow Resthouse 01 223403. This is not bad, and it serves Malawian food in the restaurant for MK150–600. *Rooms MK600/800 sgl/dbl.*

CTC Mini-Motel Not a great place, though the rooms are cheaper. *Dbl US$2.*

Golden Dish Catering and Winners Lodge has been taken over by the Golf Club, and is much better value. It also does the best meals in town for around US$2.50. *S/c dbl around US$2.50.*

Dedza Pottery Coffee Shop 01 223069. It's well worth walking the 2km out of town for a lazy afternoon tea under a thatched gazebo at the pottery, which will soon be offering accommodation in the mid-price range. This excellent and rather unexpected place serves filter coffee, lemonade, lasagne, quiches, scones, fresh bread with jam, and a variety of other

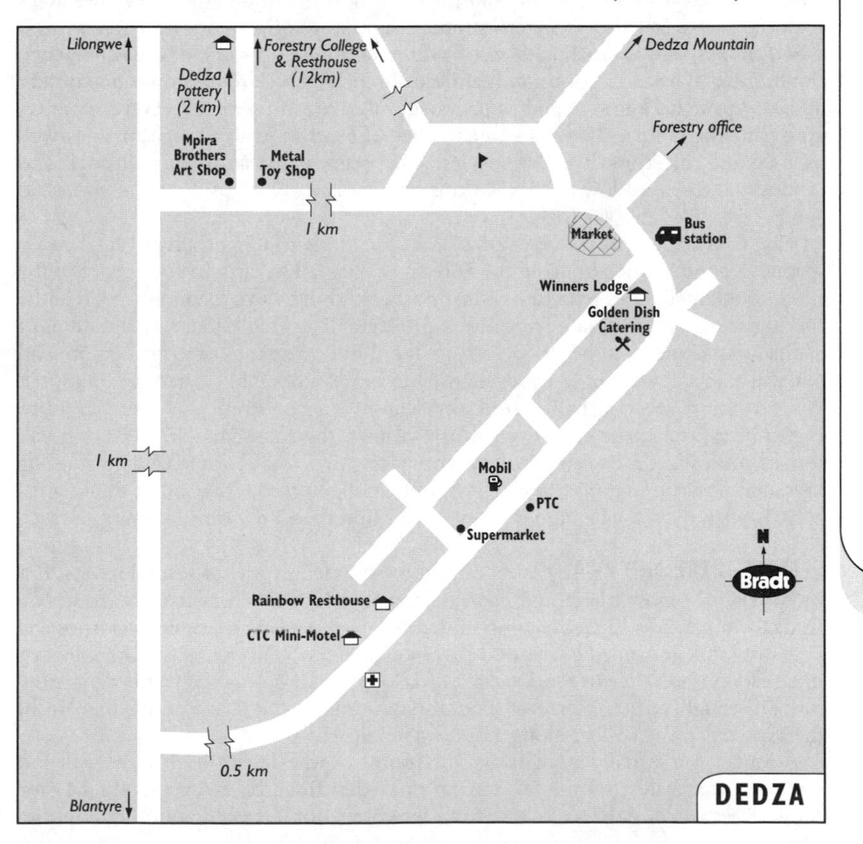

homemade goodies you won't come across too often in Malawi. The cheesecake is famous. The coffee shop is not, by Malawian standards, cheap, but nor is it so expensive you'll regret the treat. You may also want to look in at the adjacent pottery shop for a useful and colourful memento of Malawi.

There is a reasonably well-stocked supermarket in Dedza and a good market.

DEDZA MOUNTAIN FOREST RESERVE

Dedza Mountain lies immediately north of Dedza Town. The mountain is largely covered in plantation forest, but there are still remnant patches of evergreen and riverine forest on the upper slopes, supporting typical forest animals such as samango monkey, bushpig, baboon and even leopard. The indigenous forest is also notable for birds and epiphytic orchids, while more open areas are rich in wild flowers after the rains.

The mountain can be climbed as a day trip from behind the Golf Club Resthouse using any of several converging and diverging routes. You first need to climb for about 2km towards the post office transmission tower (clearly visible from town), from where it's about 3km to the peak. With the 1:50,000 map, you shouldn't get lost, but if you're uncertain ask at the Forestry Office in Dedza for directions.

CHONGONI FOREST RESERVE

This large forest reserve, about 10km northwest of Dedza, is the site of Malawi's main Forestry College. Chongoni supports a mixture of plantation and *brachystegia* woodland, as well as small patches of evergreen forest on some of the hills which dot the area. The most common mammals in the reserve are baboons, grey duiker and klipspringer. Leopard and samango monkey are present in evergreen forest. Birdwatching is varied, with a similar range of *brachystegia* to Dzalanyama, as well as a limited selection of forest species. The many paths and roads through and around the reserve allow for days of unstructured rambling using the resthouse at the Forestry College as a base.

One of the more interesting walks in Chongoni is to Chencherere Hill, a steep granite outcrop about 5km from the Forestry College. The simplest way to reach the hill is to follow the dirt road to Linthipe north for about 4km, then to turn left at the fork signposted for **Chencherere Rock Shelters**. Reportedly, there are hundreds of unmarked paintings to be discovered in these hills, but they are not easy to find without a guide, and those in several of the more accessible shelters are obscured beneath more recent half-witted scrawling of the 'Fred was here' variety. Nevertheless, Chencherere is well worth visiting: the stiff scramble to the top will reward you with some wonderful panoramic views over the forest to the surrounding hills, and possible sightings of rock hyrax and baboon. From the top of the hill, it's apparent that there are enough potential walks in this area to keep you busy for days.

GETTING THERE AND AWAY Chongoni can be reached by any of several routes. For motorists, the most direct approach is from the M1. For walkers, the route via Dedza Mountain is highly recommended. From the M1 the simplest route to the Forestry College, and the one that involves the least walking, is to take a bus or hitch along the M1 between Dedza and Lilongwe until you reach the signposted turn-off roughly 10km north of Dedza. According to the signpost, it's 6km from the turn-off to the college along a motorable dirt road.

A longer but equally straightforward route, again open to both motorists and walkers, is to head from the bus station in Dedza Town back towards the M1 for about 1.5km until you see a turn-off signposted for Dedza Pottery. Follow the turn-off, past Dedza Pottery and a large sawmill. After about 10km, you will see the turn-off to the Forestry College signposted to your left. The resthouse is about 1.5km along this turn-off.

If you're walking out to the college, you may prefer to use the more interesting and scenic cross-country route via Dedza Mountain Forest Reserve. This route starts behind the golf course: follow the road in front of the Golf Club's Resthouse (see Dedza Town map, page 173) northeast for about 1km, where you must take a right fork, then, after another 500m or so, a left fork. There are some striking granite outcrops to your left along this stretch of road, and the vegetation immediately around you is quite open. After the second fork, you pass through plantation forest for about 2km before skirting a group of buildings to the left. Keep to the road for another 1km, then take a left fork downhill, across a small wooden bridge, and into Dedza Secondary School. Shortly after you enter the school compound, a fork to the right takes you across a concrete bridge and then through the main school buildings, from where it's about 1km along a rough road to a T-junction and a cluster of buildings including a Chibuku bar. Anybody at the bar will be able to show you the footpath that leads north to Ngwere village (about 1km) then eastward to Mpalale village (a further 2km). From Mpalale, it's about 500m to the dirt road between Dedza Pottery and Chongoni. Turn left into the main road and you'll reach the signposted turn-off to the Forestry College after about 200m. If you use this route, it will help if you have a map, though you can't really go wrong by asking for directions (ask for the secondary school, then Ngwere, then Mpalale). The total distance using this route is about 12km.

WHERE TO STAY

Chongoni Forestry Resthouse lies in the college grounds, in a patch of *brachystegia* woodland at the base of the impressive granite dome of Chiwawa Hill. The rooms at the resthouse are excellent value for money. Standard and s/c dbls, the latter complete with hot bath, heater, dressing table and mirror. You can also camp in the resthouse compound. Facilities include a well-equipped kitchen, a communal dining room and lounge, and a bar serving cold beers and sodas. You must bring all the food you need with you. The resthouse often goes for weeks without visitors, but it does occasionally fill up with forestry people, so before you head all the way out it's advisable to check availability with the Forestry Office in Dedza Town (*01 220275*). *Standard dbl US$3, s/c dbl US$4, camping US$1.50, all pp.*

MUA-LIVULEZI FOREST RESERVE

This sizeable forest reserve, which lies at an altitude of around 800m below the Bembeke Escarpment, protects medium-altitude *brachystegia* and bamboo woodland rather than the plantation and evergreen forest more typically found at higher altitudes. Little information about the fauna of the reserve is available, but my own observations suggest it offers good birding, and the predominantly indigenous vegetation may still support a few mammals, most probably vervet monkey, duiker, leopard and hyena.

A combination of lovely scenery, pristine woodland, and the sense of being well off any beaten tourist track makes the Mua-Livulezi a highly attractive and relaxing area to explore over a couple of days, and the reserve is of particular interest if you want to cross between the M1 near Dedza and the southern shore of Lake Malawi.

GETTING THERE AND AWAY Even if you have no intention of exploring the forest reserve, it's worth taking the winding road that descends from Masasa (on the M1, 10km south of Dedza Town) to Golomoti near Lake Malawi, as it is one of the most scenic roads in the country. There have been roadworks here for some years so if you are driving it is worth finding out if the road is fully open all the way.

There is no public transport as such along this road, but it's easy enough to pick up a *matola* ride in Masasa, particularly if you arrive before midday.

To get to Mua-Livelezi, you want to stop at Mganja, a sizeable village about halfway between Masasa and Golomoti. Any *matola* heading between Masasa and Golomoti will drop you here. There is nowhere to stay in Mganja – a shame, as it's a pleasant and attractively situated place – but it's difficult to imagine you'd have any problems finding somewhere to pitch a tent, or any reason to worry greatly about security if you did camp.

Unless you have your own transport, the odds are you'll have to walk the 10–15km between Mganja and Sosola – no great hardship as the scenery is lovely and the road surprisingly flat given the hilly surrounds. From Mganja, you need to head out on the road signposted for Mua. This is an attractive walk, with the Bembeke Escarpment rising to the west, and small rural homesteads every few hundred metres. Ask permission, and you could almost certainly camp at one of these homesteads for a small sum. After about 5km, you enter the forest reserve (you'll be in no doubt when you cross the boundary as cultivation immediately gives way to thick *brachystegia* woodland) and a further 500m or so down the road, you veer sharply to the left to cross a concrete bridge over the clear, babbling Namkokwe River. This is a nice place for a dip, and (although I can give no guarantees) it is probably too rocky and fast flowing for bilharzia to be a realistic cause for concern.

From Sosola, instead of returning to Mganja, you could continue on to Mua on the M5 where there is superb accommodation. The Mua Mission is a fascinating place, with a good museum (see page 169). To do this, retrace your steps for the 3km back to the turn-off, but then instead of turning left towards Mganja, turn right. The distance to Mua is similar to that to Mganja, and with an early start, omitting the path to the abandoned resthouse, you could hike between Mganja and Mua in a day. This is an excellent route for cyclists, with stunning scenery the whole way.

WHERE TO STAY

The only official place to stay is down at **Mua Mission** (see page 169) and you would be wise to make a reservation in advance. The rustic and isolated Sosola Forestry Resthouse within the reserve was officially closed in 1997 and unfortunately has not yet reopened.

14

The Lakeshore from Mangochi to Cape Maclear

The southern shore of Lake Malawi is an area of fishing villages, rocky outcrops and sandy coves. Between Cape Maclear and the town of Mangochi a plethora of lodges are tucked away along the lakeshore, while Cape Maclear itself hosts Malawi's most famous travellers' haunt, as well as a range of lodges, restaurants and activity centres that belie the fact that it is still really a big fishing village surrounded on all sides by a National Park.

Lake Malawi National Park encompasses both land and lake, protecting the trees from deforestation and the fish from over-fishing, and allowing the traveller to enjoy all the wonders of one of the most lovely areas of the lake.

The largest town in the region, Mangochi, lies on the west bank of the Shire River a short way south of Lake Malawi and north of Lake Malombe. Nevertheless, Mangochi is best grouped with the southern lakeshore – not least because its main source of tourist traffic comes from travellers who have arrived at Cape Maclear to discover that Mangochi is the nearest place where you can change foreign currency into local money.

CLIMATE

Hot and sticky.

GETTING AROUND

There is plenty of public transport along the surfaced road connecting Monkey Bay to Mangochi and to Liwonde, Zomba and Blantyre. This road is also good for hitching.

Most of the resorts along the southern lakeshore are within 2km of the tarred road, and so they are easy to walk to. The exception is Cape Maclear itself. There is no public transport along the 18km road between Monkey Bay and Cape Maclear, so you will either have to hitch or else wait for a *matola* ride: you'd be unlucky to wait more than an hour or two.

If you are heading to this part of the lakeshore from somewhere further north, be aware that road transport is not quite so straightforward due to the poor state of the Golomoti–Mtakataka road that connects the main Salima–Balaka road and main Monkey Bay–Blantyre road. If you are approaching from Mua, the road is usually called the Golomoti Road, if you are approaching from Monkey Bay side, then it is called the Mtakataka Road. In fact there were once two roads, but they have been merged by one enormous and incomplete road project. If the money ever comes back in to complete the road then the journey will be bliss and make Cape Maclear only a three-hour journey from Lilongwe.

There are a few buses and minibuses that connect through from Salima daily. There's usually a choice of routes on direct minibuses from Lilongwe (some go via

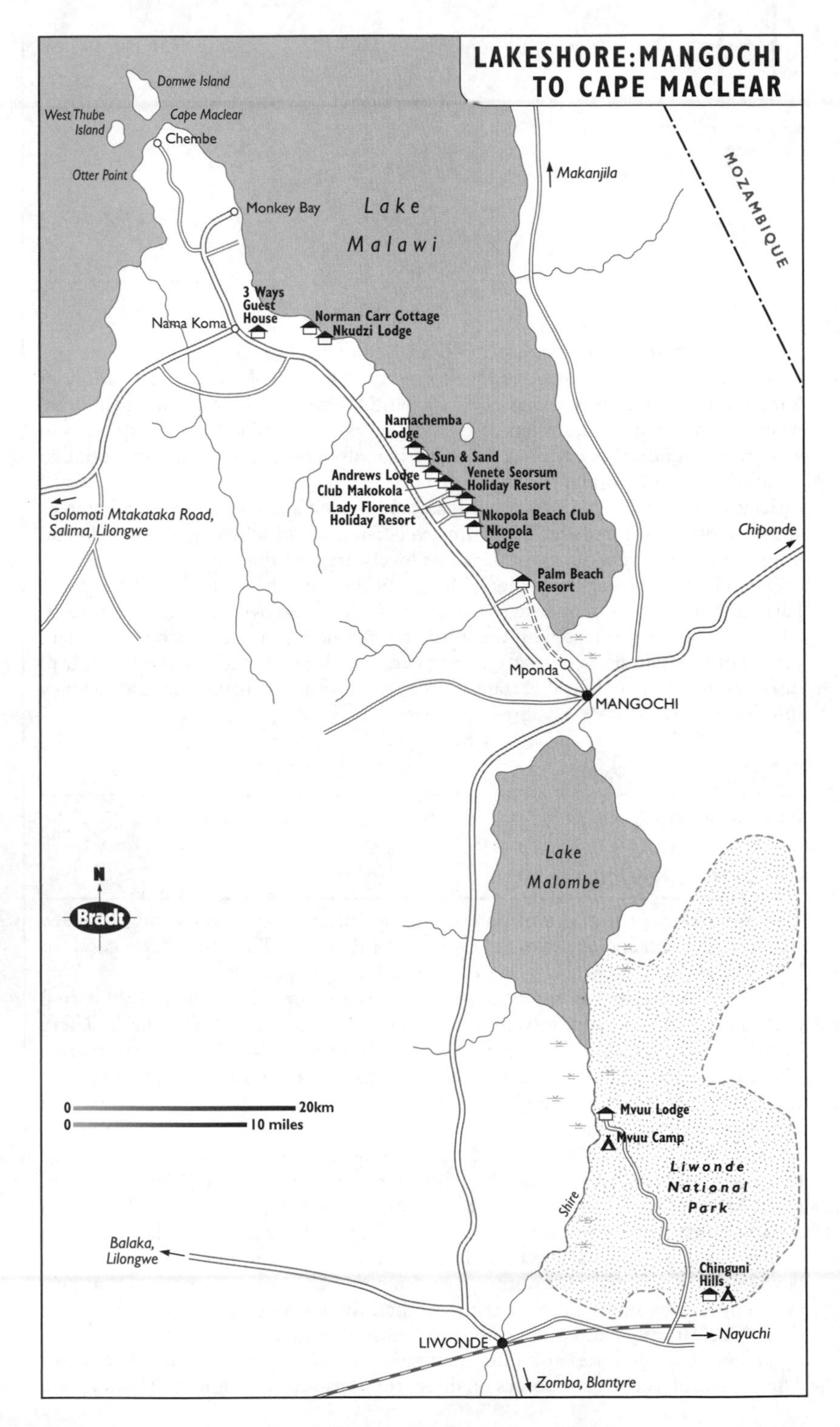
LAKESHORE: MANGOCHI TO CAPE MACLEAR
Domwe Island
West Thube Island
Cape Maclear
Chembe
Otter Point
Monkey Bay
Lake Malawi
Makanjila
MOZAMBIQUE
3 Ways Guest House
Nama Koma
Norman Carr Cottage
Nkudzi Lodge
Namachemba Lodge
Sun & Sand
Andrews Lodge
Venete Seorsum Holiday Resort
Club Makokola
Lady Florence Holiday Resort
Nkopola Beach Club
Nkopola Lodge
Golomoti Mtakataka Road, Salima, Lilongwe
Chiponde
Palm Beach Resort
Mponda
MANGOCHI
Lake Malombe
N
Bradt
0 20km
0 10 miles
Mvuu Lodge
Mvuu Camp
Liwonde National Park
Shire
Balaka, Lilongwe
Chinguni Hills
LIWONDE
Nayuchi
Zomba, Blantyre

Balaka and then up from Liwonde). To catch one of these coming from Salima, ask to be dropped off at the (unsigned) Golomoti road rather than at the turn-off that is signposted for Monkey Bay about 1km south of Mua – the latter might look to be the main road on some maps, (and is still signed) but has been impassable for a long time due to a washed-out bridge. You shouldn't wait more than an hour for a vehicle to leave, and should expect the trip to the junction with the Monkey Bay road to take about two hours.

There are two other ways of travelling between this area and points further north. The first is by one of the lake steamers which connect Monkey Bay to Nkhotakota, Likoma or Nkhata Bay (see page 157 for itinerary details). The other is to organise a private boat between Cape Maclear and Salima, a trip which takes about three hours (compared with the full day you'll be required to travel between these places by road) and costs around US$12 per person for a minimum of ten people.

LAKE MALAWI INTERNATIONAL YACHTING MARATHON Every year, around mid July, the Lake Malawi International Yachting Marathon (e *murray_kj@hotmail.com or zina@africa-online.net, or any Malawi-based tour operator*) takes place – an eight-day 560km race which has traditionally been operated as a benefit event, raising funds for lakeshore communities and wildlife projects. All classes of boat are eligible. A challenging and sometimes dangerous race, it starts at Club Makokola or Nkopola Lodge and then runs in stages, with a slightly different route each year, usually overnighting at Livingstonia Beach Resort, Sani Beach Resort, Dwanga, Likoma Island, Chintheche Inn and finishing up at Nkata Bay. Entry fees are US$200 per person and US$100 per yacht and includes accommodation, catering and transport. They tell me it's one long party!

MANGOCHI

Mangochi was previously known as Fort Johnston, after Sir Harry Johnston, the first Consul General of Nyasaland. Fort Johnston was one of the earliest colonial settlements in Malawi, established on the east bank of the Shire River in 1891 to help restrict the Yao slave trade. In 1897, the fort was relocated to the site of the modern town, on the west bank of the river. Fort Johnston was declared a township in 1899, and throughout the colonial era it remained a river port and naval centre of some importance. Shortly after Malawi's independence, it was renamed Mangochi.

The wide avenues, lined with jacarandas, borassus palms and thick fruit trees, are a vague reminder of Fort Johnston's former importance, while the crumbling buildings that line the Shire waterfront testify to a recent decline in fortunes. Walking around the old part of Mangochi, with its tangible Muslim influences (dating to the slaving era), faded whitewashed buildings, and sticky tropical atmosphere, I was reminded of some of the more run-down towns on the Swahili coast of east Africa.

Sightseeing is limited to a few less-than-riveting national monuments: a war cemetery; a waterfront clocktower, built in 1903 in memory of Queen Victoria and since dedicated to the 143 people who drowned when the MV *Viphya* sank on Lake Malawi in 1946; and, nearby, the cannon from HMS *Gwendolyn* which sank the German *Hermann Von Wessman* at Liuli in 1914. Possibly of more interest is the Lake Malawi Museum depicting the lake's history (*admission US$1*).

On a more practical note, Mangochi is a reasonable place to stock up on goods if you're heading on to camp at Liwonde or along the Lake Malawi shore. There is a good selection of shops including supermarkets. Mangochi is the closest place to Cape Maclear where you can change money at a bank.

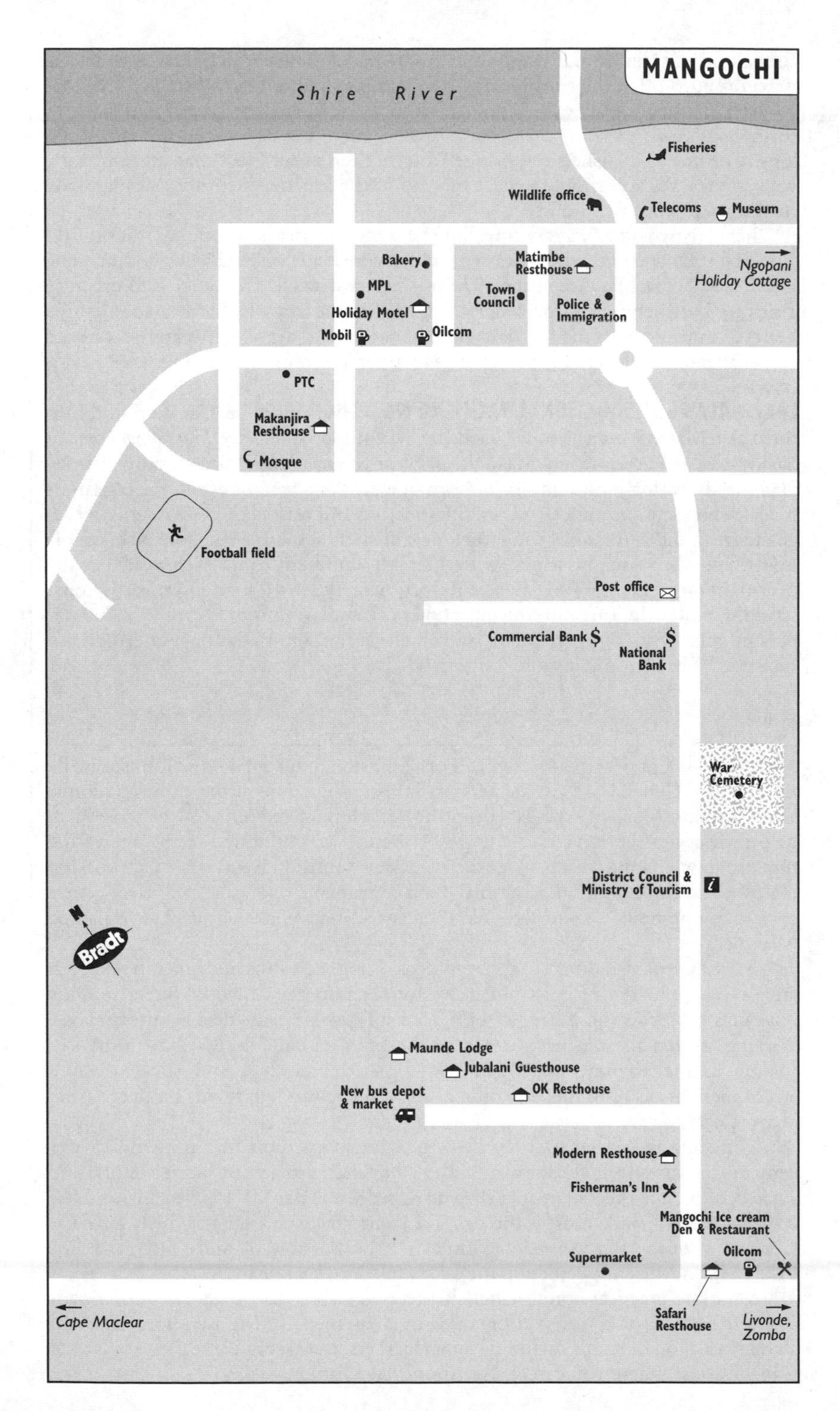
MANGOCHI
Shire River
Fisheries
Wildlife office
Telecoms
Museum
Ngopani Holiday Cottage
Bakery
Matimbe Resthouse
MPL
Town Council
Police & Immigration
Holiday Motel
Mobil
Oilcom
PTC
Makanjira Resthouse
Mosque
Football field
Post office
Commercial Bank
National Bank
War Cemetery
District Council & Ministry of Tourism
Bradt
N
Maunde Lodge
Jubalani Guesthouse
New bus depot & market
OK Resthouse
Modern Resthouse
Fisherman's Inn
Mangochi Ice cream Den & Restaurant
Supermarket
Oilcom
Safari Resthouse
Cape Maclear
Livonde, Zomba

GETTING THERE AND AWAY All buses between Blantyre and Monkey Bay stop at Mangochi, usually at the main Monkey Bay junction.

WHERE TO STAY

Near the new bus depot and market there are two new resthouses, the **Maunde Lodge** and the **OK Resthouse**.

Another new resthouse has been set up further in town, the **Matimbe Resthouse**.

The **Holiday Motel** is a pleasant enough hotel, though due for some maintenance. Ordinary rooms cost US$4/5 sgl/dbl, and s/c sgl/dbl rooms cost US$6/8. The attached restaurant is pretty good.

Quite a few cheaper resthouses are dotted around town. Probably the best bet is the **Makanjira Resthouse** behind the Peoples supermarket, where s/c dbls cost US$5.

The nearby **Jabalani Resthouse** also looks worth a try.

A few relatively scruffy resthouses are clustered at the junction with the main Monkey Bay road, 15 mins' walk from the town centre. The best of this bunch is probably the **Safari Resthouse**, a bit run-down, but clean, comfortable and friendly.

Travellers with private transport might be interested in contacting **Ngopani Holiday Cottage** (*for bookings, directions and further details;* ☎ *01 651799 (day) or 01 584567 (after hours)*), which lies on a private farm close to a couple of forest reserves about 80km by road to the northeast of Mangochi. This is a very isolated spot, and great value. *Rooms US$3 pp.*

WHERE TO EAT

The restaurant in the **Holiday Motel** does reasonable food for around US$2 per plate – the standard chicken stew, chips and the like, but much tastier than normal.

A far more interesting place to eat is the **Mangochi Ice cream Den & Restaurant** near the junction with the main Monkey Bay road. This place serves everything from curries and steaks to burgers and fish, with most dishes falling in the US$2–3 price bracket, as well as good ice cream sundaes.

FROM MANGOCHI TO MONKEY BAY

About 10km north of Mangochi, the Shire River flows from the southern heel of Lake Malawi. This far southern part of the lake consists of a roughly 15km-wide sliver of water which extends for about 50km up to Monkey Bay and the Cape Maclear peninsula.

WHERE TO STAY

Southern Lakeshore The Southern Lakeshore, as this stretch of shore is often called, caters primarily for upmarket visitors, boasting two of the lake's smartest hotels, Club Makokola and Nkopola Lodge, as well as a variety of smaller and cheaper resorts. Working from south to north:

Palm Beach Resort ☎ 01 584564; f 01 584798; e palmbeach@africa-online.net; www.palmbeach-mw.com. The resort lies about 1km from the main road and can be reached via a signposted turn-off, 12km from Mangochi and about 2km north of the Shire River outlet. The large grounds are very attractive and dotted with tall palm trees, but the resort as a whole seems slightly lacking in character. Accommodation is in s/c chalets. There is also a bar and a good restaurant where meals cost around US$4. *Normal chalet sgl/dbl MK2,400/3,200, superior chalet sgl/dbl MK3,000/4,000, camping MK100 pp.*

Nkopola In the small fishing village of Nkopola, which is situated on an attractive baobab-studded stretch of lakeshore about 10km north of Palm Beach Resort and 1km from the main Mangochi road, are several smaller lodges, after the Planet Island Restaurant.

Nkopola Lodge 01 5984444; e nkopola@sdnp.org.mw. This is the most well-patronised of the bunch, a most attractively laid-out upmarket hotel with a wonderful position at the base of a rocky and thickly wooded hill. The birdlife here is fantastic (though I wouldn't get overexcited about the walk-in aviary), and vervet monkeys inhabit the grounds. Other attractions are the large swimming pool, excellent watersports facilities, and the string of good curio stalls lining the road outside the lodge grounds. The food here is also very good, in particular the lunchtime buffet barbecue held at the swimming pool, and there is satellite TV in the bar. *Standard rooms sgl/dbl US$66/79, superior rooms sgl/dbl US$89/102, inc good b/fast.*

Nkopola Beach Club Adjacent to Nkopola Lodge, and with a similarly attractive position, this is a more family-orientated place. *Chalets US$60 for up to 3 people, caravan sites US$12, standing tents US$30 dbl.*

North of Nkopola

Club Makokola 01 594244; e clubmak@malawi.net. About 2km north of Nkopola, 'Club Mak' as it's known locally is without doubt the best known of Malawi's lakeshore hotels, and extensive renovations and refurbishments have maintained its reputation as the most exclusive lodge on the lakeshore. The rooms are beautiful and the gardens with large baobab trees are quite immaculately maintained. A neatly kept 9-hole golf course, a good selection of watersports and a huge 30m swimming pool make this a favourite holiday destination, especially as Air Malawi flies into the airstrip there. It is also the most affordable of Malawi's top lakeshore hotels. Club Mak can organise tours to local textile projects. *Prices pp including dinner, BB: superior sgl/dbl US$130/170, ste sgl/dbl US$150/195, executive ste sgl/dbl US$195/270.*

Sun 'n' Sand Holiday Resort 01 594545; e sunnsand@malawi.net; www.sunnsand.malawi.net. Offers a conference centre, large swimming pool, selection of sports and even a small supermarket, and there are ostriches in the grounds (fun if you're camping). *S/c stes sgl/dbl US$70/80, chalets sleeping 4 US$250.*

Nanachemba Lodge 09 274696/09 486243. Just reopened with chalets and rooms, very relaxed attitude, friendly dogs and fabulous cooking with home produce from their own farm at MK400–900. *US$25 pp.*

From Nkudzi Bay to Monkey Bay Nkudzi Bay is a secluded bay in the southernmost part of Lake Malawi National Park.

Nkudzi Lodge 08 515189/09 386669; e nkudzilodge@webmail.co.za; www.nkudzilodge.com. A comfortable lodge with soft lawns stretching under trees on the bank above the beach offering watersports (US$10 per hour) as well as badminton, table tennis, and volleyball; there are also inner tyres for mucking around in the water. There's a restaurant serving meals for MK300–1,200. *Rooms US$15 pp; families welcome.*

Norman Carr Cottage 01 587316/09 207506/08 355357; e taffy@africa-online.net; www.normancarrcottage.com. In the next bay north, this is a welcoming place, with an honesty bar. It's extremely comfortable, with luxury outdoor showers attached to each of the 5 rooms. The manager is a boat historian, who is doing up Alfred Bight's 1950s' wooden lake boat. *US$60 pp FB, including boats and snorkelling equipment.*

MONKEY BAY

Monkey Bay is mostly of interest to travellers as the southern terminus of the lake ferry and as the springboard for visits to the ever-popular Cape Maclear, which has had a significant revival in the past few years. Unfortunately, most of the lakeshore immediately around Monkey Bay is government property. Many travellers end up in Monkey Bay, as it is the end of the road as far as buses are concerned, but very few do anything more than head straight on to Cape Maclear. Quite a few travellers are caught by the fact there is no bank in Monkey Bay, nor is there a black market. If you don't have enough local currency, the nearest place where you can change money is Mangochi.

GETTING THERE AND AWAY Perhaps the best way to arrive in Monkey Bay is by the MV *Ilala* (see page 157). Buses from all directions terminate at Monkey Bay. Note that pick-up trucks connecting Monkey Bay and the village of Chembe on Cape Maclear habitually try to overcharge travellers – MK130 is the going rate, though it's more likely you will be charged the return price of MK170.

WHERE TO STAY AND EAT If you arrive in Monkey Bay late in the day, there are a few basic resthouses, of which the **Zawadi Guesthouse** is the best, with rooms at MK500 and lively music. Just over 1km out of town is **Centre Point** (*09 437623/01 587441*) with the Pink Panther Bar, which also has rooms for MK500 and a restaurant serving meals for MK380. They will also organise transport to Cape Maclear for MK1,500. There is also a reasonably well-stocked supermarket in town. Fuel is available at a Mobil station.

CAPE MACLEAR

Once only a sprawling 'backpackers' Mecca' beach village, attracting travellers from all over the continent, Cape Maclear is still one of the most important travellers' congregation points in Malawi. It is a place where anything goes, from the chilled-out and funky to the swish and, in a Malawian kind of way, swanky. At its peak in the early 1990s, it was described as Africa's answer to Kathmandu or Marrakech, a place to which travellers would flock in their hundreds to enjoy a *chamba* and Carlsberg-enhanced atmosphere that for most people was thoroughly irresistible. Now it has the added bonuses of providing the greatest range of water-based activities on the lake and having a wide range of accommodation, bars and restaurants. However small or large your pocket, Cape Maclear has plenty to offer.

The only drawback to the village of **Chembe** is the particularly assertive beach-boy touts, who will constantly try to persuade you that you want to go on a boat trip, buy *chamba*, talk English, look at curios, feed fish eagles, drink beers etc. Sometimes their persistence is enough to stop you wanting to do anything but stay in your own lodge bar. But there is nothing like laughter to dispel the insistence, and to say you are not in a hurry to make decisions, or just go with a quick decision to avoid any more hassle!

It is worth mentioning that this is still a spot to look after yourself and your belongings with particular care. Crime is not rife any more, but theft and attacks have happened here in the past and opportunities might well be seized if you are negligent. Women are advised not to walk alone in out-of-the-way areas.

Cape Maclear was the first site of Dr Robert Laws's Livingstonia Mission, established on 17 October 1875 and abandoned a few years later on account of the high incidence of malaria in the area. Several of the missionaries at Cape Maclear died of malaria; their graves can be seen near the entrance to the Golden Sands Rest Camp. While based at Cape Maclear, Laws became the first European to circumnavigate the lake, which he discovered to be 100km longer than Livingstone had estimated.

LAKE MALAWI NATIONAL PARK

Lake Malawi National Park, proclaimed in 1980, encompasses most of Cape Maclear and the surrounding lake waters as well as nine offshore islands. This national park is the most important freshwater fish sanctuary in Africa, if not in the world, protecting a diversity of species second to none. Scuba diving and snorkelling are popular activities in the park, offering the opportunity to see a diversity of colourful *mbuna* cichlids, an experience the equal of anything Malawi

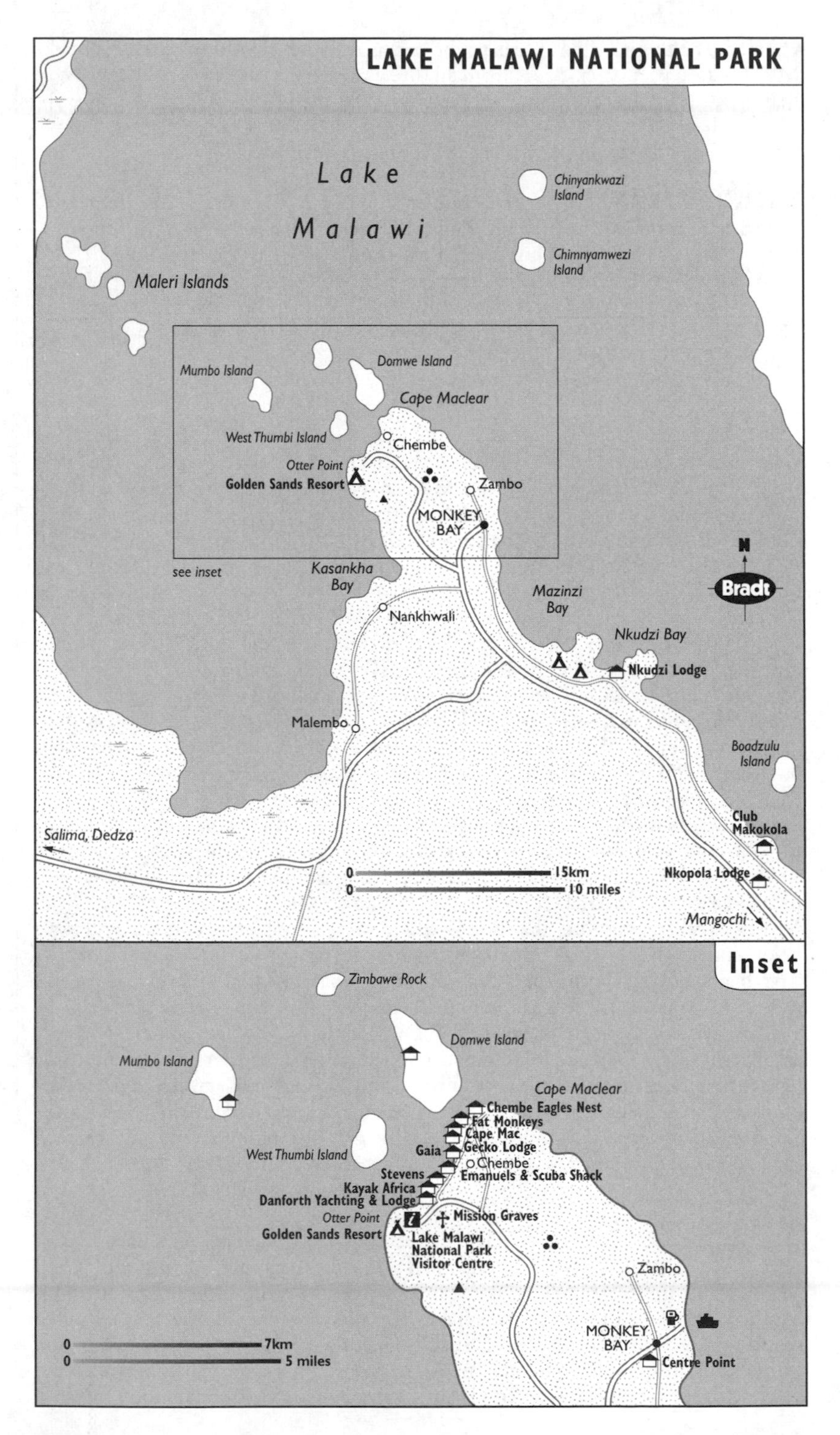
LAKE MALAWI NATIONAL PARK
Lake Malawi
Chinyankwazi Island
Chimnyamwezi Island
Maleri Islands
Mumbo Island
Domwe Island
Cape Maclear
West Thumbi Island
Chembe
Otter Point
Golden Sands Resort
Zambo
MONKEY BAY
see inset
Kasankha Bay
Mazinzi Bay
Nankhwali
Nkudzi Bay
Nkudzi Lodge
Malembo
Boadzulu Island
Club Makokola
Salima, Dedza
0 15km
0 10 miles
Nkopola Lodge
Mangochi
Bradt
N
Inset
Zimbawe Rock
Domwe Island
Mumbo Island
Cape Maclear
Chembe Eagles Nest
Fat Monkeys
Cape Mac
Gaia
Gecko Lodge
West Thumbi Island
Chembe
Stevens
Emanuels & Scuba Shack
Kayak Africa
Danforth Yachting & Lodge
Otter Point
Mission Graves
Golden Sands Resort
Lake Malawi National Park Visitor Centre
Zambo
MONKEY BAY
Centre Point
0 7km
0 5 miles

has to offer on land. Several fishing villages remain unprotected enclaves within the park; the largest, Chembe, has a population of approximately 14,000, and is the main focus of tourism in the area, with many lodges, resthouses, bars and restaurants, two scuba-diving centres, a yacht charter company, a kayaking operation and a variety of watersports and snorkelling equipment for hire.

GETTING THERE AND AWAY The turn-off to Cape Maclear is signposted from the main road to Mangochi about 4km south of Monkey Bay. The road is only obvious because of the petrol station and the array of signs to the lodges. There is no public transport along the 18km stretch of road that connects the turn-off to Cape Maclear, but it's easy enough to find a lift, and a vehicle does the run to Monkey Bay two or three times most days – listen out for the hoot of the horn. For hitching purposes, the best place to wait is at the turn-off, though *matola* vehicles generally depart from Monkey Bay itself, so they may be full when they pass the turn-off. Kayak Africa and Danforth Yachting will organise transfers for you from as far away as Blantyre and Llilongwe, with Danforth often dropping guests at Salima before an afternoon flight.

WHERE TO STAY The world is your oyster in Cape Maclear. Having survived a major slump in fortunes in the late 1990s, Cape Maclear has now picked itself up from being a sad reminder of a hazy memory to being a busy village resort, where there are plenty of vibrant places to stay. Also as a retreat from the world, there are spots in Cape Maclear which are still as appealing as ever. Chembe village is the focus of all tourism.

Luxury

Danforth Yachting ☎ 09 960077/09 960770; e info@danforthyachting.com; www.danforthyachting.com. Danforth has a lodge with 4 spacious en-suite family rooms, ranking with the best in Malawi for comfort and luxury. It makes a great base for yachting and watersports, including scuba diving in this PADI resort (see below). The restaurant is for guests only and is probably the tastiest food in the Cape. *Stay and Sail US$150; dinner, BB US$99 pp.*

Cape Mac Lodge ☎ 09 966520; e rogerl@africa-online.net. An impressive new lodge within the village, with private gardens, a plunge pool and a fine restaurant serving some of the best fresh fish you will find anywhere in Malawi as well as excellent steaks and meat dishes. The lodge buildings are architect-designed, with high thatched roofs coming down almost to the ground. If you are booking in advance, be sure to ask for a room with a view. *2-storey family room US$90, dbl US$85, sgl US$65.*

Kayak Africa Bookings through Wilderness Safaris in Lilongwe (see page 103) or direct; ☎ 09 942661 or +27 21 689 8123; e letsgo@kayakafrica.co.za; www.kayakfafrica.co.za. Only two of the tropical islands in Lake Malawi National Park have accommodation, both run by **Kayak Africa** (base camp is on Chembe beach between Steven's and Emanuel's). The islands of **Mumbo** and (to a slightly lesser extent) **Domwe** are two of the most romantic spots in the country, far away from anything and yet with lovely tented rooms each with their own balcony, good simple cooking and an honesty bar system. Most people choose to paddle their kayak across to the islands, which takes slightly less than 1hr, allowing the main boat to take the luggage. A variety of watersports, including scuba diving, is available should you be able to tear yourself away from your tent, your hammock or the beach. *Mumbo Island US$175 and Domwe Island US$150, inc all meals, kayak and snorkelling gear.*

Mid-budget **Emmanuel's** and **Steven's** used to be the only places to stay, and have always been relaxed hang-outs with a good mix of clientele, and amazingly they're still going, popular because they are situated right in the village. Doubtless during the main season, other basic resthouses will spring up in the village, ensuring that there is never a problem finding a place to stay.

Gecko Lodge ☎ 09 833856; e kite@africa-online.net. A bright and colourful place with a matching attitude. The bar has DSTV for those who want to catch up on their sport, and the lodge has a good sized garden and beachfront. *Cottage for 4 US$80, dbl US$40, dorm bed US$10 pp.*

Gaia A small but extremely busy lodge which if it had no cars parked jammed up to the bar would also be very attractive inside. Meals here are evidently also popular, with a menu from MK300–400 and specials at MK600. *Chalets sgl/dbl MK700/1,300, dorm bed MK450 and MK500, camping MK$350.*

Emmanuel's Restaurant on site. *Basic dbls MK1,000, dorms MK400, camping MK300; all exc b/fast.*

Steven's Resthouse Now also home to Scuba Shack and internet facilities. Steven's restaurant and a fairly rowdy bar still operate opposite. *Basic dbls MK1,000, dorms MK400, camping MK200; all exc b/fast.*

Fat Monkeys ☎ 09 948501. The most likely place for backpackers to wind up. Set away from the main village, it has a private beach and good security offering fairly average but comfortable rooms with shared facilities. A lively bar and restaurant serves meals for around MK480–900. *Rooms MK1,000, camping US$2 pp.*

Chembe Eagles Nest Lodge ☎ 09 216328; e chembeeaglesnest@mw.celtelplus.com or ajpumpelec@mw.celtelplus.com. On the southernmost point of the bay about 2km from the main village. It is being transformed into a pretty smart place to stay; the thatched chalets on an attractive beach are all en suite and there's some massive rocks to go and watch the sunset from. It's also possible to access straight from the main road. Day visitors can use the restaurant and bar. There is no longer any camping. *US$60 pp inc dinner; day visitors must pay MK250.*

Golden Sands Rest Camp In Lake Malawi National Park, about 2km past Steven's. Though there are no facilities whatsoever, and plenty of falling-down buildings, Golden Sands is by far the most peaceful place to stay at Cape Maclear, and it has a great position on the beach below Otter Point with monkeys and birds in abundance. Completely run-down chalets and bungalows and a campsite. *MK200 pp, camping US$0.60 pp (to which must be added an entrance fee of US$5 pp per 24hrs).*

WHERE TO EAT During the main season various small restaurants start up, under different names each year. The old favourite is always Steven's Restaurant, serving good Malawian food for under US$4.

All of the lodges have restaurants, all will provide meals for less than US$6, the new French-run Cape Mac is particularly recommended.

A popular way of eating out in Cape Maclear is to organise a **beach barbecue** through one of the children who hang around Steven's and the other resthouses. This will generally cost around US$3 per person, for which you get a generous portion of fish (normally *kampanga*), rice and tomato sauce. The atmosphere on the beach at night is great and there is little danger of going to bed hungry. It is customary to pay half the fee upfront, so that food can be bought, and while I have heard of children vanishing with the money, the system normally seems to work well.

WHAT TO SEE AND DO For many people, activity at Cape Maclear consists of spending the days hanging out on the beach, interspersed with the occasional aimless wander around the village. Armed with a cold Carlsberg, doing nothing is certainly an attractive enough prospect in the beautiful surrounds.

One of the most popular activities is a day trip to nearby **West Thumbi Island**; these can be arranged through any of the beach touts for a very reasonable US$10 per head, inclusive of a fish barbecue, snorkelling equipment and transport by boat (you may have to bargain). The cichlid community around Mitande Point on West Thumbi is regarded as one of the most diverse in the lake.

There is also excellent snorkelling at **Otter Point**, in Lake Malawi National Park, about 2km from Steven's. The clear water here is teeming with cichlids of all colours: blue, orange and yellow. On land you should see rock hyrax, baboons, a variety of lizards, and if you're lucky even a klipspringer or grysbok. Spotted-necked otters are common in the area. Entrance to the national park costs US$5 per person. You can hire snorkelling equipment in the village.

From the village, a practically limitless selection of beach and watersports is available. Unfortunately, these now include beach buggies at Chembe Lodge which can spoil the atmosphere for everybody else, and are also rather unsympathetic to the environment. Another activity that is overdue regulation is motorboats, which are often driven at speed too close to the beach. Responsible motorboat owners tend to take care and take skiers far out into the bay away from swimmers. Big toys like these sit uneasily with the thatched mud huts in the village, even if some of the owners may live in them!

Scuba Shack Next to Steven's Resthouse; 09 934220; e scubashack@mw.celtelplus.com; www.scubashackmalawi.com. Offers excellent diving courses with good modern equipment. A 2-day advance course costs US$250 excluding accommodation, or US$275 for a 4-day beginners course. Casual dives centre around an interesting old wreck and cost US$30, including equipment and national park fees.

Danforth Yachting Between Steven's and Otter Point; 09 960077/09 960770; e danforth@malawi.net/ danforth@mw.celtelplus.com; www.danforthyachting.com. Charters *Mfasa*, a fully equipped and crewed 38ft ocean-going catamaran, which sleeps 8 guests. Daysails are US$75 pp, sundowner cruises are US$25 and overnighters cost US$150. Longer yachting safaris up the lake to Mozambique and even as far as Likoma Island and beyond are also what has made *Mfasa* a runaway success, while at base dinghy sailing, diving and other watersports are also offered as part of your accommodation price. Mountain bikes are also available. Danforth offers scuba-diving tuition and PADI courses, eg: casual dives at US$25 per session and anything from Open Water Diver at US$400 to Dive Master at US$600 including HB accommodation.

Kayak Africa 09 942661; e letsgo@kayakafrica.co.za; www.kayakafrica.net. Organises popular outings to their tented camps on the islands off Cape Maclear, from where excellent kayaking, snorkelling and diving are possible. They also have scuba equipment. Prices (not including accommodation): kayak day trip US$40; boat and kayak day trip US$50; PADI open water diver (qualifying course) US$205; PADI discover scuba (introduction) US$70; casual scuba dive (qualified divers) US$30; island dive day US$80.

FURTHER INFORMATION *A Guide to the Fishes of Lake Malawi National Park* by Lewis, Reinthall and Trendall (Worldwide Fund for Nature) includes excellent background information on the cichlids and other fish of Lake Malawi. Fish that are likely to be seen within the national park are illustrated and their distribution and status is given. The book also gives details of the birds and mammals of the park, and it includes a pull-out waterproof map with notes to underwater trails in the more popular diving areas.

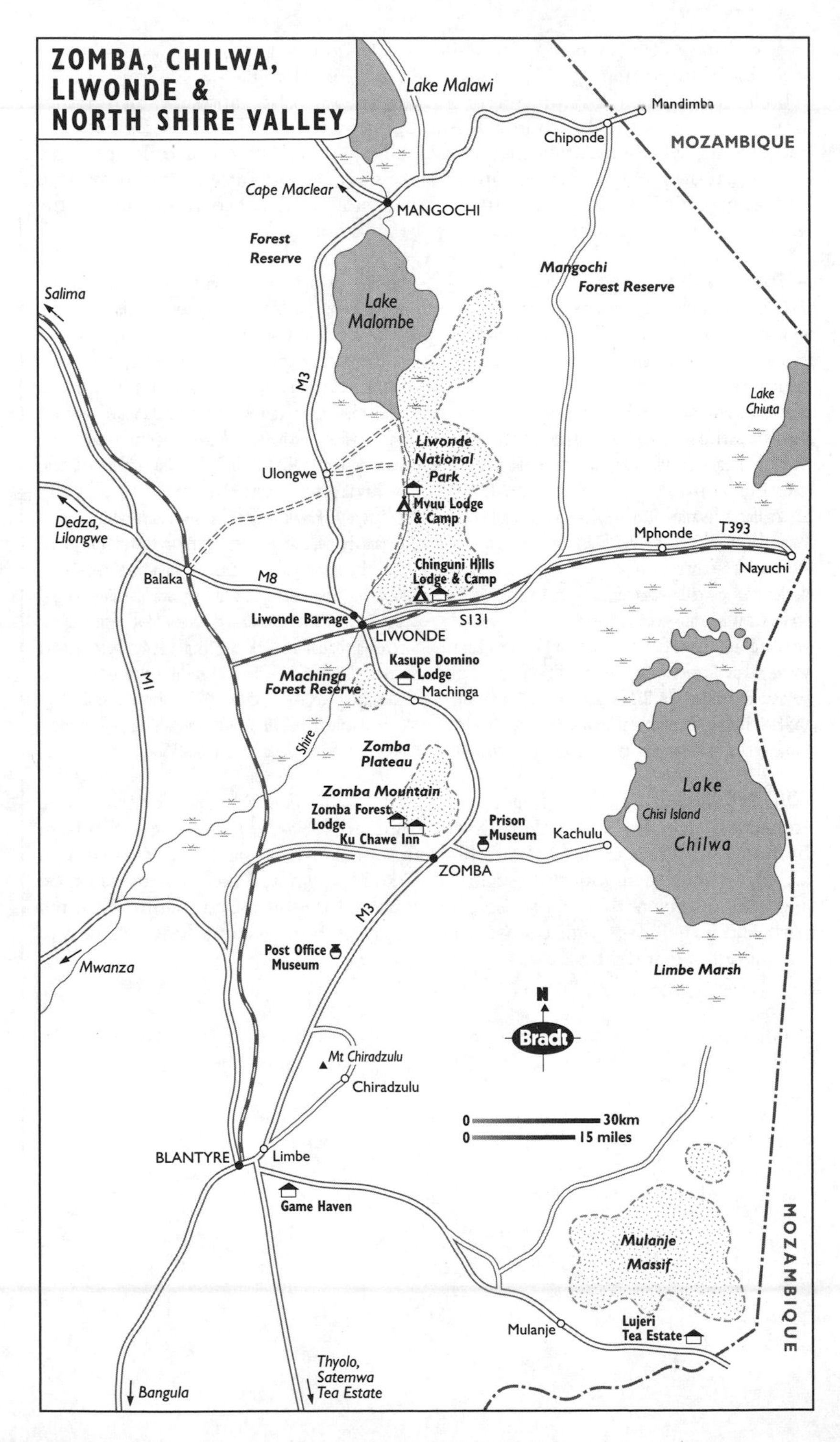
ZOMBA, CHILWA, LIWONDE & NORTH SHIRE VALLEY
Lake Malawi
Mandimba
Chiponde
MOZAMBIQUE
Cape Maclear
MANGOCHI
Forest Reserve
Mangochi Forest Reserve
Salima
Lake Malombe
M3
Lake Chiuta
Liwonde National Park
Ulongwe
Mvuu Lodge & Camp
Dedza, Lilongwe
Mphonde
T393
Nayuchi
Chinguni Hills Lodge & Camp
Balaka
M8
S131
Liwonde Barrage
LIWONDE
Kasupe Domino Lodge
Machinga Forest Reserve
Machinga
M1
Shire
Zomba Plateau
Zomba Mountain
Zomba Forest Lodge
Ku Chawe Inn
Prison Museum
Kachulu
Lake Chilwa
Chisi Island
ZOMBA
M3
Mwanza
Post Office Museum
Limbe Marsh
Bradt
N
Mt Chiradzulu
Chiradzulu
0 30km
0 15 miles
BLANTYRE
Limbe
Game Haven
Mulanje Massif
MOZAMBIQUE
Mulanje
Lujeri Tea Estate
Thyolo, Satemwa Tea Estate
Bangula

15

Liwonde, Zomba and Surrounds

This is a lovely part of Malawi, a relatively low-lying plateau interrupted by a number of large mountains, most notably the vast Zomba Mountain above the town of the same name. Liwonde National Park, only an hour distant from Zomba Mountain, is a must for any visitor to Malawi; it's a gem of a park, a microcosm of Africa and one of the prettiest parks in central Africa. Straddling both sides of the winding Shire River, flanked by the Mangochi Escarpment to the north and the Zomba Plateau to the south and with a surprising range of different river and woodland habitats, Liwonde National Park is Malawi's prime spot for game and birding alike.

Zomba Mountain is a hikers' paradise with plentiful birds and small mammals, as well as wonderful views across to Mulanje and Mozambique. The university town of Zomba has a rather special feeling about it, where old and new cultures have merged and amble onward. Zomba also has at least one excellent off-the-beaten-track option, the little-known but thoroughly worthwhile Lake Chilwa.

CLIMATE

Liwonde and the Shire River are hot and humid. Zomba and Lake Chilwa have relatively temperate climates, though the open nature of the lakeshore means it is very exposed in the midday heat. If you are staying in a lodge on Zomba Mountain, fires will be lit at night throughout most of the year – it can be cool at night.

GETTING AROUND

Zomba and Liwonde lie on the scenic route between Blantyre and Lilongwe. There are plenty of buses connecting both towns to Lilongwe, Blantyre and points in between.

Liwonde National Park has three main access points, the river by boat transfer from Liwonde Town, via Ulongwe on the Mangochi road and then by boat across to Mvuu, or by road through the southern end of the park. The boat transfer to Mvuu costs US$30 per person and is a magical journey, worth every cent, but it usually runs only during the heavy rains (*contact Wilderness Safaris; ☎ 01 771153 to check*). The usual option for backpackers is to take the bus up to Ulongwe and then hire a bicycle-taxi to take you 15km through strings of villages to the jetty opposite Mvuu Camp where a boat will then come and fetch you. Those with vehicles have the option of driving in or leaving the car at the jetty. Visitors to Chinguni (only a 15-minute drive from Liwonde) should ring Chinguni Hills (☎ *01 838159*) to see if there's a possibility of a lift or simply take a taxi from Liwonde Town.

The Zomba Plateau is within walking distance of Zomba Town, but it's a steep hike, and most people either take a taxi to the top or hitch. Lake Chilwa, the least visited of the region's attractions, is straightforward to reach on public transport – there's a couple of *matolas* daily between Zomba Town and Kachulu on the shore of Lake Chilwa.

LIWONDE

The town of Liwonde lies on the Shire River, about 50km south of its outlet from Lake Malombe. Like many Malawian towns, Liwonde is divided into two parts either side of the Shire River. The nominal town centre, which lies just off the main tar road between Zomba and Mangochi, about 1km from the river, has a selection of shops – including a PTC supermarket – a hospital and a large and well-organised market.

More scruffy, but of interest to tourists, is the lively satellite town (referred to as Liwonde Barrage) which straddles the main road on the west side of the bridge across the river. It's worth stopping at Liwonde Barrage for the vision of tropical Africa you get of the Shire River: low-wooded hills in the background, fishermen punting past in traditional dugouts, hippos grunting and snorting, and thick reed beds rustling with birdlife, all to the background of market and street noises.

GETTING THERE AND AWAY Liwonde lies on the M8 near the M3 turn-off to Mangochi, 30 minutes south of Balaka, with regular buses in every direction stopping to pick up passengers. Most buses don't actually go into town, but stop at Liwonde Barrage and (country buses only) at the turn-off to the town centre. Check how far your bus is going, and get off at Mangochi turn-off if you're on your way up to Ulongwe and Mvuu Camp, or be dropped off at the BP petrol station if you're on the way into Chinguni Hills and the southern entrance of the park. Liwonde is also the best place to board the train to Nayuchi on the Mozambican border. When in service, it departs at 06.00, Mondays to Fridays, and costs US$1.

WHERE TO STAY

Warthog's Wallow 01 542426. This lies in attractive grounds on the south bank of the river. The once-busy facilities are in neglected disrepair despite the frills and satin, but include a swimming pool. There's an antique of a boat moored in the reeds there, but apparently a different boat can be sometimes hired for visits into the park. *S/c room with fan, net and hot water sgl/dbl MK2,200/3,700 inclusive of b/fast and a 3-course dinner. Self-catering accommodation sgl/dbl MK1,250/1700.*

Manpower Shireside Lodge 01 542380. Next door to Warthog's Wallow. Aside from having a cracking name, this is a bit of a dump. Meals are good value though at MK275 per plate. *Functional s/c sgl/dbl MK500/1,000.*

Sun Village Lodge Liwonde Barrage. A decent place. *S/c executive rooms for sgl/dbl MK2950/5330.*

There are more places along the riverbank track up from the barrage:

Liwonde Holiday Resthouse (and Bottle Store) A reasonable value resthouse. *Sgl/dblMK180/270.*

Shire Camp Soon after the Liwonde Resthouse; 08 535909. Shire Camp is being built by an ex-game ranger from Nyika National Park. It looks like this will be the place to head for, as it's on the riverbank with good meals for MK200–450 and a bar area. Chalets and camping will be ready by mid 2006, with prices in the mid-range.

Hippo View Lodge 01 542822/255/221. Immaculate rose gardens and lawns overlooking the Shire. This is a huge business-class hotel, complete with conference facilities. Before you reach the swimming pool there are crocodile warnings against swimming in the river. Owned by a transport magnate, coaches can also be arranged from the cities. Once there, boat trips for 4 cost MK2,000 per hour. *Most rooms sgl/dbl MK5,000/7,000, presidential suite sgl/dbl MK8,500/10,500.*

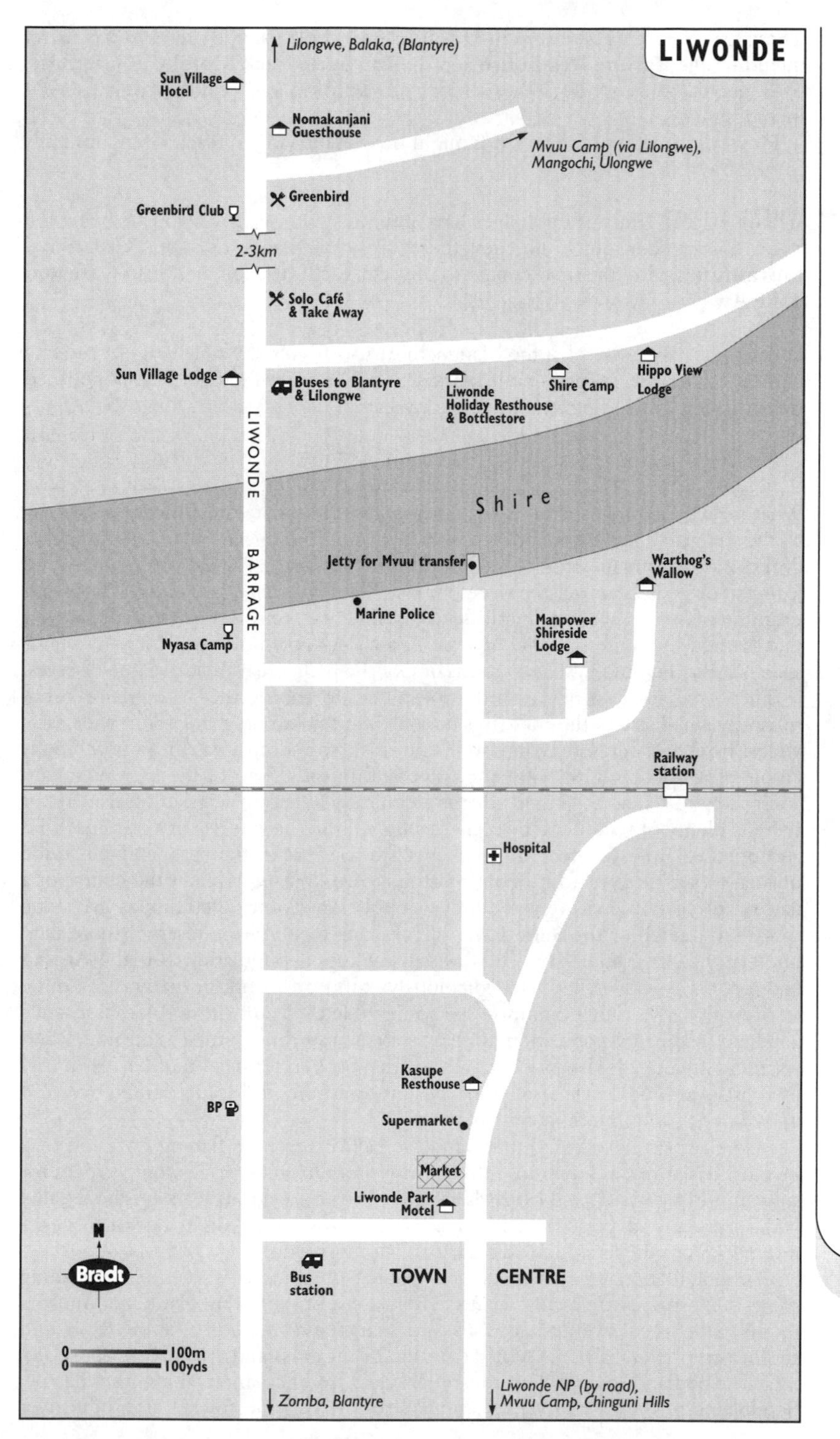
LIWONDE
Lilongwe, Balaka, (Blantyre)
Sun Village Hotel
Nomakanjani Guesthouse
Mvuu Camp (via Lilongwe), Mangochi, Ulongwe
Greenbird
Greenbird Club
2-3km
Solo Café & Take Away
Sun Village Lodge
Buses to Blantyre & Lilongwe
Liwonde Holiday Resthouse & Bottlestore
Shire Camp
Hippo View Lodge
LIWONDE BARRAGE
Shire
Jetty for Mvuu transfer
Warthog's Wallow
Marine Police
Nyasa Camp
Manpower Shireside Lodge
Railway station
Hospital
Kasupe Resthouse
BP
Supermarket
Market
Liwonde Park Motel
N
Bradt
Bus station
TOWN CENTRE
0 100m
0 100yds
Zomba, Blantyre
Liwonde NP (by road), Mvuu Camp, Chinguni Hills

There are also a few resthouses in Liwonde town centre, if you prefer to stay there, including the **Kasupe Resthouse** and the **Liwonde Park Motel** (☎ *01 542338*), with good rooms (MK1,500 with shared facilities, or sgl/dbl MK2,600/2,900 including b/fast).

However if you've got this far, it might be worth trying to reach Chinguni Hills for the night (see below).

WHERE TO EAT Most of the lodges have good restaurants, my favourite being the Shire Camp. For quick lunches there are two places of note, **Greenbird Restaurant** before the market near to the Mangochi turn-off and **Solo Café and Take Away** in Liwonde Barrage itself.

CURIOS The large market at the Mangochi turn-off is also an excellent place to buy curios. Under the purpose-built market area is a wide range of highly polished woodcarvings, including an army of straw-hatted fishermen carrying fish.

LIWONDE NATIONAL PARK

What makes Liwonde special is the atmosphere: dominated in almost every sense by the sluggish Shire River and its wildly lush fringing vegetation, it is a setting that evokes every romantic notion of untrammelled Africa. When we sat at Mvuu Camp at dusk, gazing over the river, our ears filled with the chirruping of frogs and grunting of hippos, we found it difficult to think of a scene anywhere in our travels that seemed so quintessentially African. Taken on its own merits, which in essence are aesthetic, I would rate Liwonde as one of the truly great African game reserves.

The game viewing at Liwonde doesn't quite match the atmosphere – the relatively small size of the park (it is only 548km^2; 50km long and 15km wide at its widest part) and dense human population in surrounding areas mean poaching is an ongoing concern (100,000 people live within only 5km of the park boundary attempting to scrape a living in what is technically a marginal agricultural area) but there is plenty of wildlife to be seen. Seeing wildlife here feels very genuine, wild and pristine. An estimated 900 elephants are resident in the park, and it is quite normal to see three or four herds coming to drink at the river in the course of a day. Even more impressive is the hippo population. Some 2,000 hippos live along the 40km stretch of the Shire River which runs through the reserve (more than one every 20m!), surely one of the densest hippo populations on the African continent. Crocodiles, too, are ridiculously common – and, in many cases, quite terrifyingly large. Other common species include the exquisite and localised sable antelope (estimated population 600), as well as waterbuck, impala, bushbuck and warthog. Liwonde is also excellent for birding, both in terms of numbers seen (my own list is around 150 species, and a recent ornithological tour counted over 250 in two days!) and in terms of rarities.

Above the grunts of the hippos and the call of the Pel's fishing owl, you may hear hyenas at night. Lions are infrequent visitors (a small pride were resident for some months in 2002) and leopards are there but very seldom seen. It is hoped that if the numbers of prey can be increased, then predators might return in larger numbers from the less populated parts of Mozambique.

Liwonde National Park has a range of habitats that belies its small size, including some 1,029 species of vascular plants. There are seven different plant communities in the park: reed swamps, lagoons and marshland along the Shire River and southeastern shore of Lake Malombe; floodplain grasslands mainly in the south; mixed woodland on all the hills; tall grass tree savanna along the narrow floodplains of the east to west seasonal streams; riverine thicket along the river

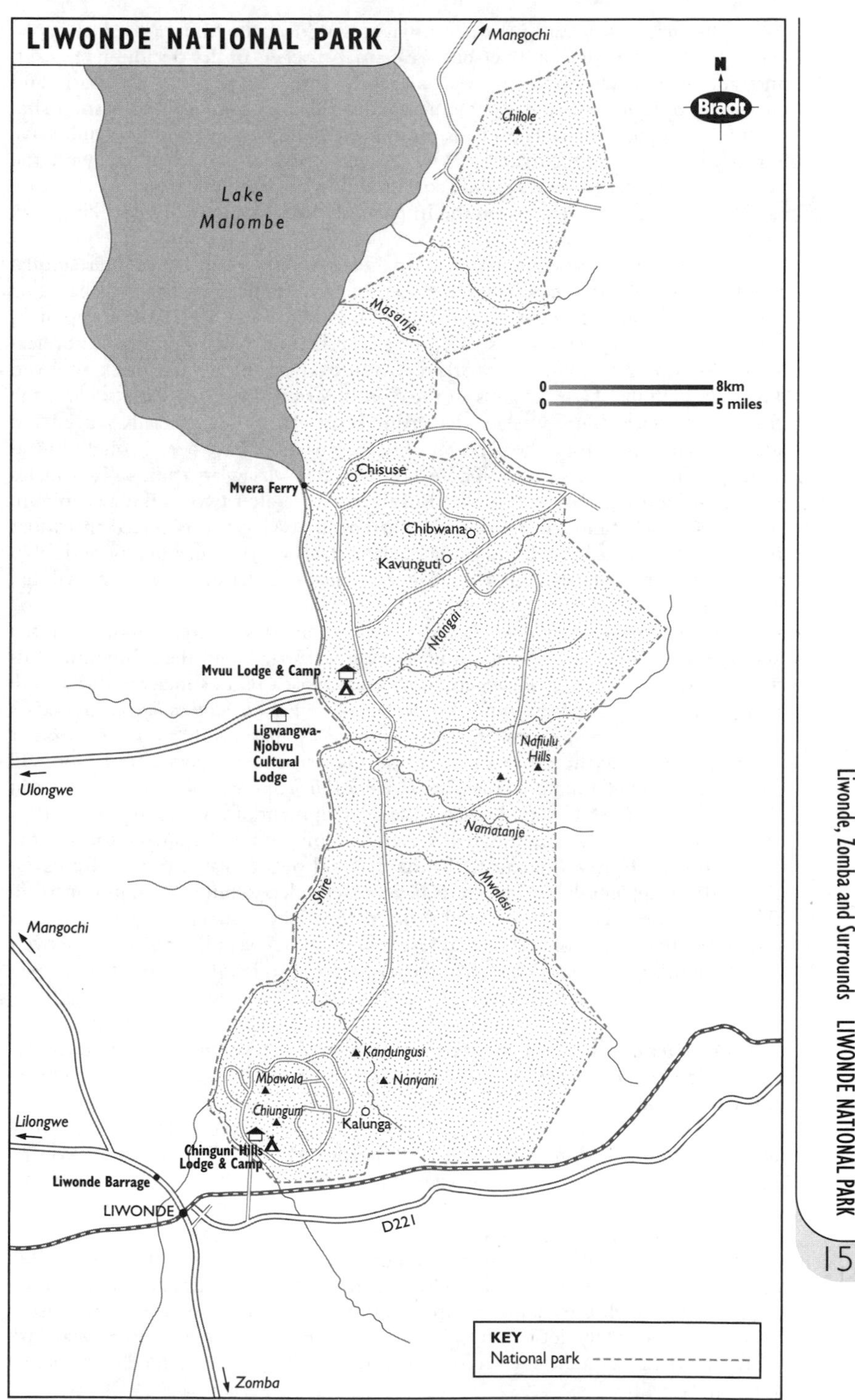
LIWONDE NATIONAL PARK
Mangochi
Chilole
Bradt
N
Lake Malombe
Masanje
0 8km
0 5 miles
Chisuse
Mvera Ferry
Chibwana
Kavunguti
Ntangai
Mvuu Lodge & Camp
Ligwangwa-Njobvu Cultural Lodge
Ulongwe
Nafiulu Hills
Namatanje
Mwalasi
Shire
Mangochi
Kandungusi
Nanyani
Mbawala
Chiunguni
Kalunga
Lilongwe
Chinguni Hills Lodge & Camp
Liwonde Barrage
LIWONDE
D221
Zomba
KEY
National park

banks and terraces of east–west perennial rivers (near the Shire a total of 50–60 woody species can be found per hectare); small pockets of dry deciduous thicket; mopane woodlands covering approximately three-quarters of the park and providing a 12m canopy and supporting the *Candelabra euphorbia*, mesmerising python vines and countless baobabs often bearing the scars of where people have removed bark for cloth making. Wild flowers are limitless, changing with the seasons, though in the rains brightly coloured flowers, lilies and ground orchids are abundant. During the dry season the Impala Lily is in bloom with its striking pink flowers.

Over the past 15 years Liwonde National Park has had a number of international wildlife and conservation agencies help to protect it and neighbouring villages. The lynchpin of them all is the Malawi-based J&B Circle. Since 1992, this group of 12 wildlife enthusiasts, with sponsorship from the famous whisky group and tireless fundraising of their own, has worked to reintroduce the extinct black rhino to Liwonde National Park. Thanks to the South African National Parks Board, the first pair of black rhinos was airlifted from South Africa to a specially fenced and guarded sanctuary within the park. Since then, two more have been brought in and numbers have grown steadily. There are now ten Malawian rhinos. Two males were translocated to Majete Wildlife Reserve in 2004 after two rival males fought. A visit into the Rhino Sanctuary can be arranged at Mvuu. It is hoped that more females will soon be brought in. Buffalo, eland, hartebeest, roan antelope and zebra have also been established. It's great to be able to report on an African wildlife success story.

Two other projects which should be mentioned here are Children in the Wilderness (a Wilderness Safaris initiative across Africa) and the Chinguni Hills Trust. Both work to bring local people around Liwonde into contact with the park in a positive way. Children in the Wilderness (*www.childreninthewilderness.com*) is a life-skills programme for orphans living around the park. Kids come on summer camp to learn everything from first aid, human rights, democracy, nutrition and about HIV/AIDS.Chinguni Hills Trust (*www.chingunitrust.co.uk*) aims to assist in the conservation, research and sustainable development of Liwonde National Park and adjacent conservation areas. Each June Chinguni Hills also organises the annual **Hippy Festival**, featuring bands from all over Malawi, to raise funds for the project – apparently the elephants have never failed to put in an appearance. To find out more about the whole project (or to volunteer in primary level environmental education, ecological research or crafts) wisit their website (above).

A national park entrance fee of US$5 per person per day is levied at the entrance gate plus US$2 per car per day (even if left parked opposite Mvuu Camp).

GETTING THERE AND AWAY Most people who take their own vehicle to Liwonde use a side road connecting the M3 between Liwonde Barrage and Mangochi to the west bank of the river opposite Mvuu Camp. This turn-off is signposted from the village of Ulongwe. After 14km, it reaches the entrance gate from where it's another 1km to the river. Staff from Mvuu will then collect you by boat. This is the easiest way to drive to Mvuu, but it has one major disadvantage in that you'll effectively be without a vehicle at Mvuu, and so will need to do all your drives in camp vehicles. If you prefer to have your own vehicle, you should use the main entrance to the national park, which is signposted from the D221 about 3km from Liwonde Town. The distance from the entrance gate to Mvuu is 30km. Although internal roads are sometimes closed during the rainy season, you should normally get through to the camp in a 4x4 at any time of year (ask Central African Wilderness Safaris for current advice; see Mvuu Lodge below for details).

A more attractive way of entering Liwonde National Park is to take a boat along the Shire River from Liwonde Barrage. If you plan on staying at Mvuu, a boat transfer can be organised in advance through the management at a cost of US$30 per person. For day trips from Liwonde Barrage, Hippo View Lodge takes boat tours along the river at a cost of MK2,000 per person (minimum four people) per hour (*bookings* ☎ *01 542822*).

For backpackers, the cheapest way to get to Mvuu is to use a bicycle-taxi from Ulongwe to the west bank of the river, and then be fetched by a boat from Mvuu. The cost of these bicycle-taxis is negotiable, but expect to pay around US$5 each way. If you like, you can normally arrange for the person who cycles you there to come back to meet you when you plan to leave.

Central African Wilderness Safaris can arrange road transfers to Mvuu from anywhere in Malawi. There is also an airstrip in the reserve, should you be in a position to charter a flight.

WHERE TO STAY

Mvuu Lodge and Camp Central African Wilderness Safaris, PO Box 489, Lilongwe; ☎ 01 771153/08 822398; f 01 771397; e info@wilderness.mw; www.wilderness-safaris.com. An outstanding set-up that caters to everybody from self-catering backpackers to upmarket tourists.

Mvuu Camp Perfectly sited on the east bank of the Shire about 25km north of the barrage, the camp lies in a group of immense baobab trees, facing a dense reed bed and a borassus palm forest. Warthogs graze the lawns by day, hippos by night, while elephants regularly come to drink on the bank opposite and are discouraged from visiting camp at night. Both the river and surrounding bush are alive with birds. Accommodation is very comfortable, and the food is excellent. Campers can eat in the restaurant, which charges US$8 for breakfast, US$10 for lunch and US$15 for dinner, but a self-catering kitchen is available for those bringing their own food. A freezer and cooking utensils are supplied, and a cook can be arranged by request. Accommodation at the main camp is in luxurious standing tents or s/c chalets, and there is also an attached campsite, making the camp reasonably affordable to budget travellers with their own tent. *Standing tents US$170 (green season US$150) FB, inc 2 game activities daily; camping US$8 pp.*

Mvuu Lodge About 200m from the camp, and run as a separate entity, Mvuu Lodge is a wonderful exclusive bush camp consisting of 5 dbl tents with private balconies overlooking a small, marshy pool on the bank of the river. Mvuu Lodge holds its own with the best luxury tented camps in southern Africa, blending a high level of comfort and tasteful décor with a wonderful bush atmosphere, and – even allowing for taste – we rate it to be comfortably the best lodge or hotel in Malawi. The raised communal deck offers excellent mammal and birdwatching (hippos sometimes graze metres away at night, a blessing if you happen to be a noisy eater!) and there is a telescope and a library of field guides with which to amuse yourself. There is also a swimming pool reserved for the use of lodge guests. *US$295 (US$230 in green season) pp FB, inc all activities, and with private rangers allocated to the lodge.*

Ligwangwa-Njobvu Cultural Lodge Book through Central African Wilderness Safaris – all proceeds go to the villagers. In an admirable attempt to help the local community in benefiting directly from tourism, Central African Wildlife Safaris have assisted them in developing this lodge. 2 new and neatly furnished huts have been constructed 6km from Mvuu where you can overnight in an African village. Food and drinks served are local specialities, as is the singing and dancing. *Accommodation US$6, bicycle-taxi US$5, dancing US$7, guided walk US$5, b/fast US$2, lunch US$3, dinner US$4 – or US$30 all inclusive.*

Chinguni Hills Lodge ☎ 01 838159; e chinguni@africa-online.net. In a beautiful setting nestled in the saddle of Chinguni Mountain and Mbawala Hill, only a short distance from the main gate in the south of the park. The lodge has 5 attractive and affordable rooms and 2 family chalets and excellent home cooking. Originally built as a park warden's residence it's now a relaxed place of rustic sophistication where you're encouraged to put your feet up and let your hair down. Lanterns and candles make the whole place even more atmospheric. *US$50 FB.*

Chinguni Hills Campsite ☎ 01 838159; e chinguni@africa-online.net. Ideal for the budget and mid-range traveller, it's a stunning campsite with thatched tents and open ground if you've brought your own, as well as bar, catering facilities and hot showers. There's also space for 30 in the dormitories, In classic meat-eating style each of the thatched tents has its own private *braai*. The restaurant option is to spend US$5 on b/fast or lunch, US$10 on dinner. *Camping US$15 for thatched tent, US$5 with your own; dorm bed US$10.*

WHAT TO SEE AND DO The areas immediately around Mvuu and Chinguni are rewarding to explore, both in areas popular with wildlife and with interesting changes in habitat.

Hippos and crocodiles are a permanent presence on the river only metres from your tents at Mvuu, as is a large variety of waterbirds, while elephants come down to drink most days and gigantic monitor lizards can be seen basking on the riverbank. The woodland around the camp offers some great birding, with a good chance of picking up several Liwonde specials, including brown-breasted barbet, Lilian's lovebird, Livingstone's flycatcher, collared palm thrush, eastern bearded scrub robin, fish eagle and Boehm's bee-eater. The localised bat hawk can be seen near the river on most evenings. People staying at the lodge are likely to see a greater variety of animals coming to drink at the pool: bushbuck and impala are regular visitors, leopards are seen on occasion, and the birdlife is outstanding.

Mvuu Camp offers a variety of game-viewing activities, including boat safaris and game drives at US$25 per person and walking safaris at US$15 per person. All activities are led by trained guides, whom we found to be very knowledgeable and sharp at identification without ever adopting a lecturing style. The cost of activities is included in full-board packages, but must be paid for by campers and those who take bed-only accommodation.

Visitors with private transport have a fair number of dirt roads to explore. Of particular interest are the road following the Shire River north from Mvuu to where it exits Lake Malombe, and the circuit of roads around Chinguni Hill, which offers excellent views as well as good game viewing. **Chinguni Hill** is the most prominent landmark in the park, a *brachystegia*-covered hill that offers exceptional panoramic views of the Shire lagoons beyond the Chikalogwe Plain and is interesting for its localised wildlife as well as being popular with elephant, kudu, sable and buffalo. At the foot of Chinguni Hill is a hollow baobab tree, containing human skeletons thrown there, thought to be leprosy sufferers. Another baobab tree along the Riverside Drive is thought to be over 4,000 years old, over 21m high and almost 18m in girth. Guided walks and canoe trips into the marsh can be arranged through Chinguni Hill Lodge and Campsite. **Chikalogwe Plain** – an open area of swamp and reeds, much loved by the elephants which often disappear altogether, belied only by the egrets taking off from their backs. In the reeds are clusters of palm trees and the occasional termite mound. Waterbuck and impala usually laze on the sands in front of the reeds. **The Rhino Sanctuary** is a fenced area of 49km^2 where the J&B Circle have successfully reintroduced breeding pairs of black rhinoceros as well as providing a safe haven for other species such as sable, buffalo, eland, hartebeest, roan antelope and zebra, all now numerous there. Rhino spotting is never easy as these guys are very shy. Elephants crash through the electric fences occasionally, but mostly this is an elephant-free zone, which is noticeable in the dense vegetation. It is a beautiful area. The ultimate aim is to drop the fences and release game into greater Liwonde Park. It will be a pleasure to see rhino at the river's edge again, but I guess this will only happen if poaching is completely stamped out. **Mvuu** is on a wide stretch of the river in the centre of the park, with access over the river from Makanga Gate via Ulongwe. Mvuu means hippo, and you are never far from one here. For idyllic retreats Mvuu Lodge and Mvuu Camp offer not only superb accommodation and food but also fully guided game drives, walking and boat safaris. A relatively recent change at Mvuu is the arrival of a colony of white-breasted cormorants which have extended their range from Lake Malawi to the Shire, opposite Mvuu. Several kilometres out of the park from the Makanga Gate is the **Njobvu Cultural Village**, set up and managed by villagers so that visitors can experience village life and local food and traditions, with two rooms for those who want to stay overnight. A large hollow baobab at **Mvera Ferry** in the north of the park is used as a shelter during the rains when people wait for the ferry; it has room for at least 20 people inside. It also has two types of strangler fig growing on it. The tree is mentioned by Livingstone in his journals as one of their campsites.

Mangochi Forest Reserve lies to the north of the park and is connected to Liwonde by a 7–8km 'corridor' at the base of the steep escarpment of the Mangochi Massif (its highest peak being 1,724m) used by all game including elephant. Below the forested slopes is the abandoned Fort Mangochi, built in 1896.

Early-morning game walks offer the wonderful experience of exploring the African bush on foot. You're not likely to see a great number of mammals on these walks (warthog, impala and hippo are most likely to be encountered near the camp and feel relieved if you haven't met a herd of elephant), but this is compensated for by the prolific birds. Mvuu Camp and Lodge organise walks around Mvuu, while a walk from Chinguni will give you a different view of the park.

Launch trips along the Shire River leave Mvuu every morning after breakfast and from Chinguni by arrangement. Close encounters with hippos are guaranteed, you can be confident of seeing elephants, waterbuck, impala, crocodile and vervet monkeys, and there is a fair chance of seeing sable antelope from the boat. Birds are everywhere: among the more common species are fish eagle, jacana, white-breasted cormorant (these breed along the river profusely in the dry season), darter, long-toed plover, African skimmer, and a variety of kingfishers and herons. The vegetation, too, is splendid: thick stands of borassus and wild date palms, ghostly baobab trees, yellow fever trees and dense beds of papyrus.

The night boat safaris from Mvuu Lodge were a first for us, and are a must for serious birders as they offer an excellent chance of spotting Pel's fishing owl in action, as well as the nocturnal white-backed night heron. We were amazed at how closely the boat was able to approach roosting birds: we crept up on several giant and malachite kingfishers (the latter nothing short of dazzling in the spotlight), as well as huddled flocks of colourful little Boehm's bee-eaters.

Morning game drives can be arranged from Mvuu on request, but it is more usual to do a drive which starts at dusk, extending into the first hours of night so that you might see elusive predators such as leopard, spotted hyena, civet and genet. Other animals which are commonly observed on night drives are bushbaby, scrub hares, sable antelope and, of course, hippos.

Chinguni Hills organises game drives (day/night) and walking safaris for US$15 per person, canoe trips for US$22.50 or a whole boat for a minimum of 3 people for US$20. Birding around Chinguni is very rewarding, with species such as the racket-tailed roller and the Narina trogan being found here. Canoeing through this marshland out on to the river is an unforgettable experience, stomach-lurching when you're near to a large animal and totally serene when you're not.

ZOMBA

The capital of Malawi until 1975, and seat of parliament until 1994, Zomba is probably the most immediately appealing of Malawi's larger towns. Admittedly, this isn't saying much, but Zomba does have in its favour a wonderful setting at the base of Zomba Mountain, and a distinct atmosphere, determined by its leafy

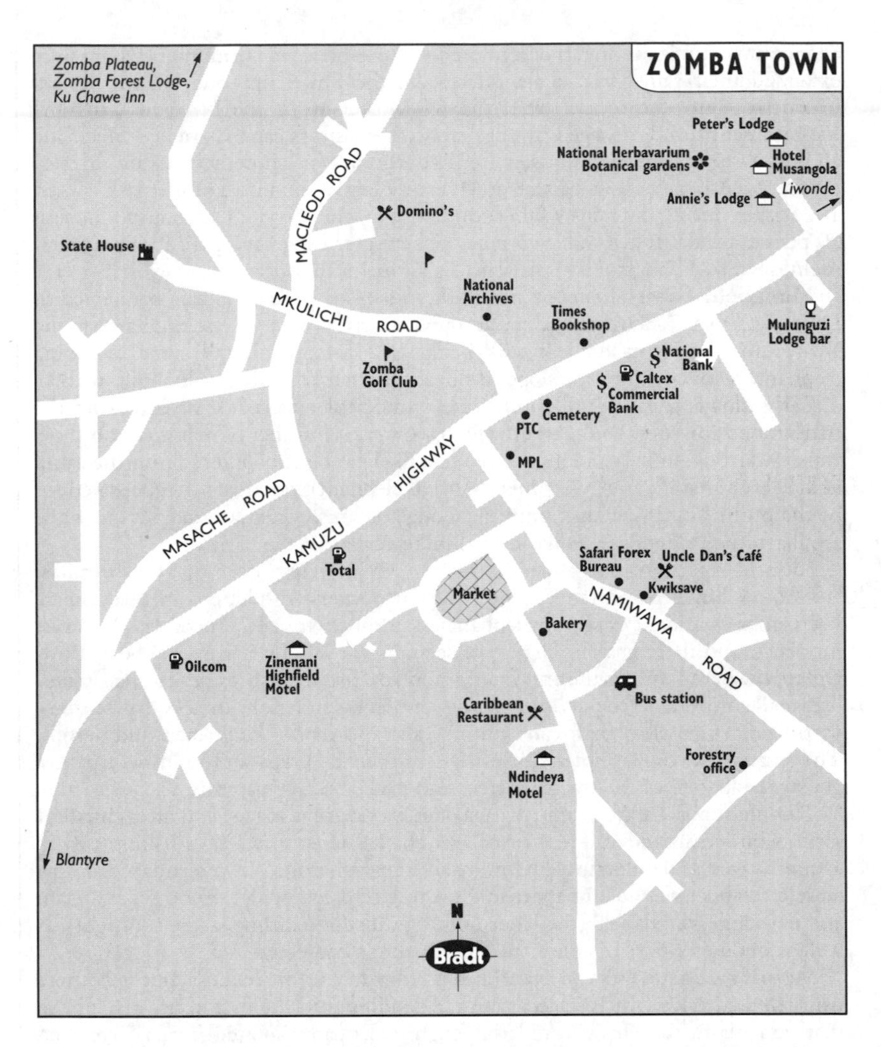

avenues and the cluster of fading colonial buildings between the main road and the wooded footslopes of the mountain. One of the most interesting old buildings in Zomba is the State House, which dates from 1901.

The Zomba area was explored in early 1859 by Livingstone's Zambezi Expedition. Livingstone and John Kirk climbed Zomba Mountain, reaching its summit near the site of the modern Ku Chawe Inn. Livingstone is also credited as the first European to reach Lake Chilwa (in fact, the lake, like many of Livingstone's 'discoveries' in Malawi, was probably already known to Portuguese traders).

In 1859, the Manganja agriculturists of Zomba were suffering greatly at the hands of Yao slave raiders. The Zambezi Expedition became indirectly involved in the Yao–Maganja war when, in August 1861, Bishop Mackenzie, together with a handful of British soldiers and over 1,000 Manganja warriors, marched from Magomero Mission onto the slopes of Zomba Mountain and razed several Yao slaving villages.

Livingstone had been impressed by the fertility of the Zomba area, and so it was the obvious choice of the Church of Scotland as the site of their first mission in the

Shire Highlands. However, the ferocity of the local slave trade and the large number of wild animals living in the area forced them instead to start the mission further south, at what is now Blantyre. The modern town of Zomba was founded in the 1890s by Sir Harry Johnston as the capital of the British Central African Protectorate.

Zomba today exudes a rustic peacefulness belying its sometimes bloody past. A small town in comparison with Lilongwe or Blantyre, Zomba nevertheless boasts a vegetable market as good as any in the country, a lovely golf course and botanical gardens, a major university, the national herbarium and several interesting buildings of Indian and British design. For all that, you can exhaust Zomba's charms in a few hours, and few travellers would bother to stop there at all were it not the gateway to Zomba Mountain, one of the most popular rambling and hiking areas in Malawi.

The Safari Forex Bureau near the bus station offers very good rates for US dollars cash and travellers' cheques. There's a National Bank with a cash machine on Kamuzu Highway.

GETTING THERE AND AWAY All express and country buses between Blantyre and points north (Monkey Bay, Lilongwe and Mzuzu) stop at Zomba. There are also regular minibuses between Zomba to Limbe and to Liwonde.

WHERE TO STAY Most upmarket tourists prefer to stay at the Ku Chawe Inn on Zomba Plateau, which is within easy reach of town, assuming that you have a vehicle.

Hotel Masongola Alongside the Botanical Gardens; 01 524688; e hotelmasongola@clcom.net. The old government resthouse is perhaps the most splendid setting in town; it's the former residence of Sir Harry Johnston and is an impressive building. *Good s/c rooms around US$60.*

Dominos (3 rooms) 01 525305; e cfg@africa-online.net. An up-and-coming place is this stylish Malawian restaurant and bar which is currently building chalets and a camping site on land adjoining the golf course.

Annie's Lodge 01 527002/09 957608; e annies@globemalawi.net. This is mainly a business hotel, but the main building is of typical colonial painted brick and green tin roof, and the bar and restaurant are attractive.

Ndindeya Motel There are only a few cheap and uncheerful small resthouses in Zomba, but the most popular of these places is the Ndindeya, which offers considerably more appealing rooms than the others. *Ordinary sgl/dbl MK600/800, executive room US$950.*

Mulunguzi Lodge This is more of a bar (a lively one and the best place for live music in town), but not a great place to sleep and it's not always open.

WHERE TO EAT

Most people head for **Uncle Dan's Café**, off Namiwawa Road, just behind the Kwiksave – it takes a bit of faith to find it, but follow the signs through the alleyways and you'll find good food for less than MK400. Open 07.00–17.00.

The restaurant at the **Ndindeya Motel** serves good meals (tasty chicken or beef stew with rice or chips) for around US$1.50.

Dominos is probably Zomba's best eatery: the delicious simple meals are popular with everyone, and it has a large bar area and tables outside (meals MK300–600).

The slightly more expensive restaurant at the **Hotel Masangola** also has good food, slightly more varied on the menu than in the kitchen (meals MK400–800) but the plates are nicely laden when they come.

The rather empty clubhouse at the **Golf Course** serves excellent meals at surprisingly reasonable prices (nothing much over US$3).

Annie's Lodge serves a good menu, though standards reportedly vary.

The supermarkets are well stocked by Malawian standards The market in Zomba is not, as is sometimes claimed, one of the largest in Africa, but it is one of the friendliest and does stock a better-than-average selection of fresh fruit and vegetables.

WHAT TO SEE AND DO It's definitely worth lounging around in Zomba's **Botanical Gardens** for a few hours, and close inspection of the labels on the trees will give you more botanical information than you are likely to remember. It's a thoroughly peaceful park where students sit on the grass reading or discussing their subjects, and church groups gather to act out Bible scenes and sing gospel songs on Sundays.

By contrast, **Mikuyu Prison**, which lies along the road towards Lake Chilwa, is the site of one of the darker moments in Malawi's recent history. During the Banda years, this is where hundreds of people were incarcerated (usually without trial) in crammed and appalling conditions. It is now the darkly interesting Prison Museum, a fairly depressing but eye-opening experience, especially if you ask yourself how much better Malawian prisons are today, less than 15 years after this one closed. The poetry of Jack Mapanje, a Malawian now based in the UK, evokes the futility of his incarceration at Mikuyu with an eloquence that the bare cells of the museum might lack, see *The Chattering Wagtails of Mikuyu Prison* Heinemann, 1993 and *Skipping without Ropes* (1998). It is also worth reading Mapanje's more recent works in *The Last of the Sweet Bananas: New & Selected Poems* (2004).

ZOMBA PLATEAU

Zomba Mountain rises immediately to the northeast of Zomba Town. It is one of the most popular areas in Malawi for walking and hiking. The extensive plateau, protected in Malawi's oldest forest reserve (gazetted in 1913), is covered largely in pine plantations, but it still contains significant patches of indigenous riverine and montane forest, as well as areas of tangled scrub and *brachystegia* woodland. A large dam was constructed in 1999 in the bowl of the mountain, but this does little to interrupt the nature of the mountain. The plateau is crossed and ringed by innumerable footpaths.

Although Zomba is noted mostly for its scenery and birds, a good variety of mammals is present, albeit in small numbers. Leopards are still seen from time to time. Antelope species include bushbuck, klipspringer and red duiker. Startled mongooses rush into the bushes. Vervet monkeys and baboons are reasonably common, and samango monkeys are seen in indigenous forests, particularly around Chingwe's Hole and Zomba Forest Lodge.

GETTING THERE AND AWAY The 13km road from Zomba Town to the top of the plateau used to split about halfway up into a separate up-road and down-road but is now two-way traffic to the top. The Ku Chawe Inn, forestry campsite and other private cottages are all clustered near the edge of the escarpment at the end of the road. To get to them, follow the road signposted for Ku Chawe Inn from the centre of Zomba Town opposite the supermarket. The road is tarred the whole way.

There is no public transport to the top of the mountain. If you are in a hurry, the best thing to do is organise a private taxi at Zomba bus station. This will cost around US$8, possibly a little less if you bargain. If you're lucky (and start early enough) you might catch a lift. The alternative is to walk, which is perfectly feasible, though steep going towards the end. If you want to walk down the mountain, then take the 'Potato Path', which is signposted from near the Ku Chawe Inn and takes about an hour to walk when dry – but is dangerously slippery and steep in wet conditions.

If you want to stay at Zomba Forest Lodge, you need to go straight at the barrier up the old up-road, then take the second left turning. It's about 4km from the turn-off on a well-maintained road along the contour of the mountain.

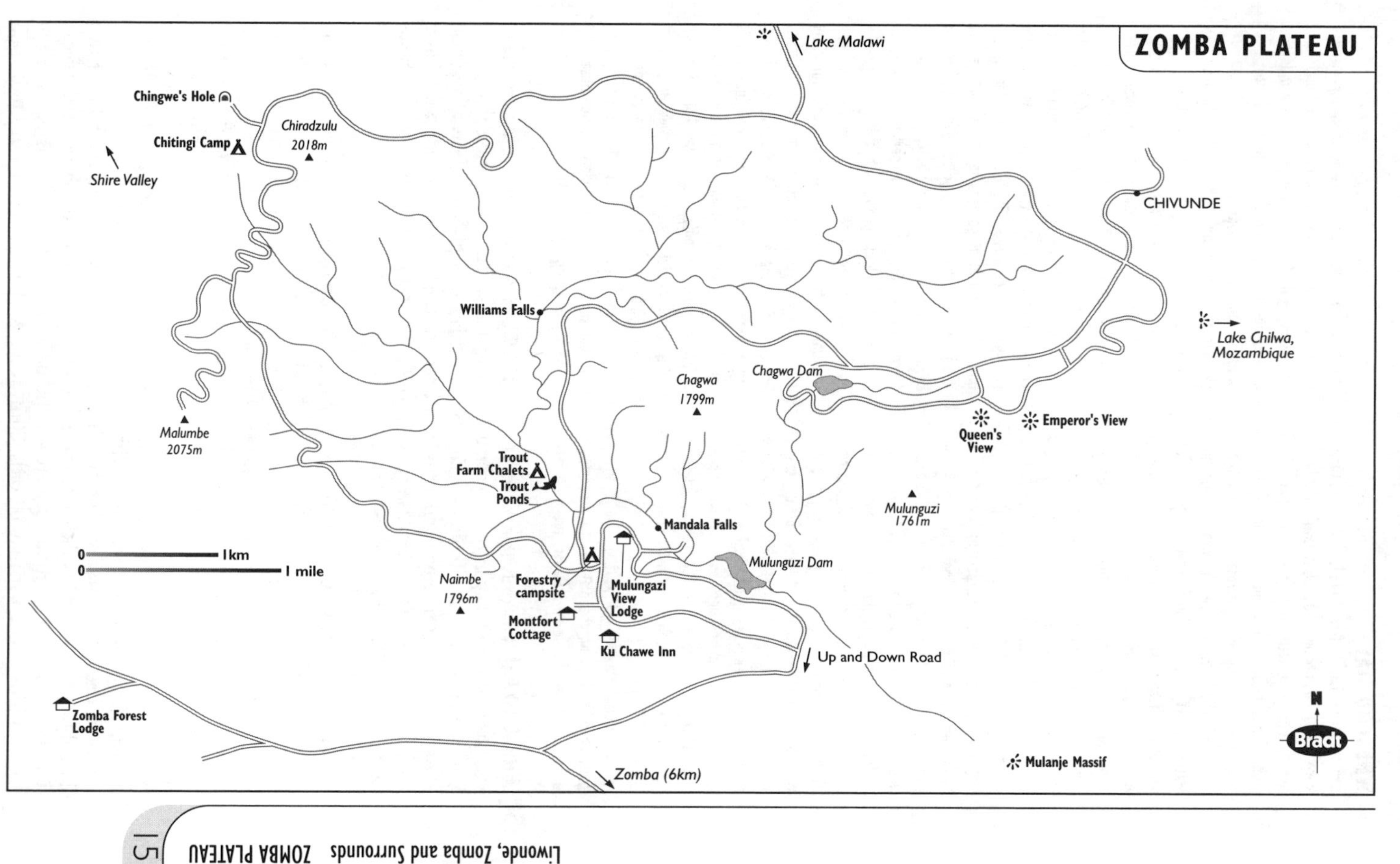
ZOMBA PLATEAU
Lake Malawi
Chingwe's Hole
Chiradzulu
2018m
Chitingi Camp
Shire Valley
CHIVUNDE
Williams Falls
Lake Chilwa,
Mozambique
Chagwa Dam
Chagwa
1799m
Emperor's View
Queen's
View
Malumbe
2075m
Trout
Farm Chalets
Trout
Ponds
Mulunguzi
1761m
Mandala Falls
Mulunguzi Dam
0
1km
0
1 mile
Naimbe
1796m
Forestry
campsite
Mulungazi
View
Lodge
Montfort
Cottage
Ku Chawe Inn
Up and Down Road
Zomba Forest
Lodge
Zomba (6km)
Mulanje Massif
N
Bradt

WHERE TO STAY

Ku Chawe Inn 01 514211; f 01 514230; e kuchawa@sdnp.org.mw. One of Malawi's flagship hotels. It is set in attractive grounds with a commanding position right on the edge of the escarpment, and the views across to Lake Chilwa are wonderful. All rooms are s/c with running hot water and TV; standard rooms have 2 sgl beds and an electric heater, while the more expensive rooms have dbl beds and log fires. The restaurant is excellent, with most dishes costing around US$8. Bookings can be made by contacting the hotel. *Superior rooms US$105/123, deluxe rooms sgl/dbl US$134/152, all inc of a full English b/fast but not taxes.*

There are several **private cottages** behind the Ku Chawe Inn. Most of these are booked out as a unit and though you'd be taking a bit of a chance if you arrived without a booking, the odds are probably in favour of you finding a vacant cottage, except at weekends and on public holidays. Rates are variable, though if you just pitch up you can probably negotiate with the caretaker of any empty cottage. All the cottages have electricity, hot water, fridges and fully equipped kitchens. The CCAP cottage is cheap and one of the best, and you can check availability beforehand at the CCAP headquarters opposite the police station in Zomba Town. *Generally around US$5 pp.*

Montfort Cottage 01 522565. One of the most beautiful huts on the plateau, the property of a nunnery in Zomba Town. Travellers are welcome to stay there, but they must make prior arrangements to collect the keys from the nunnery.

Department of Forestry Campsite This run-down place is about 1km from Ku Chawe Inn. It's a beautiful spot, surrounded by trees.

Kuchawe Trout Farm 08 860567. Another pleasant alternative. The guesthouse sleeps 4 in 2 bedrooms, sharing a lounge and kitchen. Sport fishing is offered in the nearby stream. *Guesthouse US$7 pp, camping with hot showers US$3.*

Zomba Forest Lodge *09 200369/09 926122*; intermittent e z.f.lodge@mw.celtelplus.com. Situated in the forest reserve about halfway up the mountain (see directions on page 200). With views from its bird- and flower-filled gardens to Mount Mulanje and down into the Shire Valley it is an idyllic and restful spot. It consists of 4 comfortable s/c rooms and lunches can be provided. This is perhaps the best food you will find in Malawi, with a huge range of local and European dishes laid out on the table in traditional pots. The owner also runs Look Out Tours Ltd (*09 200369*), organising safaris and treks for walkers and nature lovers. *US$95 per room HB.*

Chitinji Camp Only about 6km from Ku Chawe Inn (follow the signs), straight up the mountain via a forestry road and only suitable for 4x4s or hikers. It's a very beautiful area, near Chingwe's Hole. At 1,830m, you'd be pretty chilly up there camping, and would be warmer in the solid little stone house with hot showers and flush toilets. *Stone house US$5.50 pp, camping US$2.50 pp.*

WHERE TO EAT The only restaurant is at the **Ku Chawe Inn**, where à la carte meals cost around US$8. If you're not prepared to pay that sort of price, bring all the food you need from Zomba Town. Remarkably, Himalayan raspberries grow all over on the plateau; you can buy a generous portion from the vendors outside Ku Chawe for around US$1. There are also strawberries at most times of year, grown in fields around the villages lower down.

WHAT TO SEE AND DO The Zomba Plateau is mostly of interest to ramblers and hikers, though its major points of interest can be seen from a vehicle by following the road that encircles the plateau. There are trout in most of the streams and in the dam, but it's not easy to get a permit outside of the Trout Farm.

A short nature trail runs from the campsite past **Mulunguzi Dam** and along the forested banks of the Mulunguzi River and the **Mandala Falls**. This is a good area to see mammals (most commonly bushbuck and vervet monkey). Birds which are likely to be seen include black saw-wing swallow, mountain wagtail, Bertram's weaver, Livingstone's turaco and white-tailed crested flycatcher.

Many day visitors to the plateau will visit **Chingwe's Hole**, a natural hole that lies about two hours' walk from the Ku Chawe Inn and can be reached by car. Chingwe's Hole is rumoured to reach the base of the Rift Valley, though recent explorations suggest it may be only 20m deep. A 3km circular nature trail leads from the hole past some excellent viewpoints (views to Lake Malombe) and into a patch of montane forest where blue monkeys are seen with regularity, and a variety of forest birds (starred robin, Schalow's turaco, a variety of bulbuls and warblers, as well as the very localised Thyolo alethe) are present. There is a tradition that chiefs in the old days threw their enemies into 'bottomless' Chingwe's Hole, and a persistent rumour that Banda's regime revived this tradition.

FURTHER INFORMATION An extensive network of signposted roads and footpaths means that the walking opportunities on the Zomba Plateau are practically limitless. The relief model of the plateau in the forestry compound is useful for getting your bearings. Dedicated walkers are pointed to the excellent 36-page booklet *Zomba Mountain: A Walker's Guide* by Martyn and Kittie Cundy, which can be bought at most bookshops in Blantyre for around US$2. The book covers 15 walking routes, and includes several maps.

LAKE CHILWA

Chilwa, the southernmost of Malawi's major lakes, couldn't contrast more in atmosphere with Lake Malawi. Surrounded by flat plains and isolated hills, Chilwa's shallow, slimy, reed-lined waters extend over 650km², though they are subject to great fluctuations in water level. Only a century ago, Chilwa extended close to the bases of Mulanje and Zomba (both of which are now around 30km from the lake's shore), while in 1968, a severe local drought caused the lake to dry up altogether. There is no outlet to Lake Chilwa, and its size is almost totally dependent on the run-off from Zomba and Mulanje. Lake Chilwa has been designated a Ramsar Wetland of international importance and is receiving funding for its preservation. Water levels are up again and the lake now produces 20% of Malawi's fish requirements. With a number of fishing boats and ferries offering transport and the best aquatic-bird viewing in Malawi, Lake Chilwa is well worth a visit.

There is a definite atmosphere about Chilwa, remote and other-worldly, though at dusk, with only Mulanje and Zomba mountains punctuating the open horizon, the pink- and orange-tinged sky is the picture of serenity. The well-vegetated and in parts rather marshy shore is a birdwatchers' paradise, supporting a great variety of herons, waders and other shorebirds (glossy ibis are often common), while the baobabs on Chisi Island host the likes of trumpeter hornbill and various snake eagles. Offbeat local beliefs flourish in this environment: one oft-related legend concerns a small python-infested island that mysteriously disappeared all at once.

The best access to the lake is at a fishing village called **Kachulu**, which lies on the western shore, roughly 30km by road from Zomba Town. It's a lovely spot, and Kachulu is the sort of small, friendly workaday African village that too few visitors to Africa ever get to experience.

GETTING THERE AND AWAY Buses no longer run to Kachulu, but minibuses and *matolas* leave when full from Zomba or the turn-off just north of Zomba – cost about US$1.

An interesting and challenging travel route would be to hop aboard one of the large motorised boats that service the villages on and around the lake from Kachulu and get off on the Mozambique side at Sombe. I was told it would cost only US$2.

WHERE TO STAY There are two basic resthouses in Kachulu, both of which have single rooms for around US$1. The **Private Resthouse** seems better than the **Council Resthouse**; the long-drop toilets are reasonably clean, and the obliging staff will boil up hot water for an open-air shower. If you have thoughts of exploring the lake beyond Kachulu, you'll probably need a tent.

WHERE TO EAT There are a few restaurants in Kachulu, but you would be well advised to bring your own food from Zomba. If you're stuck, you'll probably be able to find some bread and tomatoes or bananas at one of the kiosks in the distinctly underwhelming market (which sells mostly fish). If you want to explore beyond Kachulu, you should definitely aim to be self-sufficient in food.

WHAT TO SEE AND DO Kachulu and the nearby lakeshore are certainly worth a couple of hours' investigation, particularly if you're interested in birds. You can also organise a boat to punt you across to Chisi Island, which consists of a couple of semi-submerged hills. There are some huge flocks of birds on Chisi's shore, while the baobab-studded hills are home to monkeys and hyenas. There are several small villages on Chisi and it could well be a rewarding place for self-sufficient campers to pitch a tent for a day or two. It's easy to organise a boat across to Chisi: the ride takes about 30 minutes each way and will cost about US$8. Bear in mind that dense reed beds pose a navigational hazard to inexperienced rowers, so don't hire a boat without a local fisherman to take you around.

More ambitiously, boat taxis connect Kachulu to several other points on the lake. They leave when full and charge US$0.50 to cross to the main island.

During the dry season there are mobile stilted fishing villages that are set up on Lake Chilwa; these would certainly be worth visiting – ask at Kachulu Fishery Station of their whereabouts, and be prepared for a long journey to visit them.

The northern part of Lake Chilwa is very marshy, particularly during the rains, and it is rated as one of the best birdwatching areas in Malawi, with large flocks everywhere, notably greater and lesser flamingos, pelicans and the localised black egret. With your own 4x4 vehicle, you could explore the area by driving along the D221 east of Liwonde Town, then (at Nsarama) turning left on to the dirt road T393 to Mphonde village, 8km from the Mozambican border. The best time to visit Mphonde is between September and December. As far as I am aware there is no public transport to Mphonde, but you could check it out in Liwonde.

If you do explore Lake Chilwa beyond Kachulu, it would be useful to have the appropriate 1:50,000 or 1:250,000 maps (the detail on the latter is pretty good) – and do write to tell me about it for the next edition of this book.

Wilfred J Plumbe has written to recommend the University of Malawi's *Lake Chilwa Co-ordinated Research Project: decline and recovery of a lake*, edited by Margaret Kalk, to interested readers – though it was published in 1970 and is probably now out of print. A new publication that will be of interest to some readers is the annotated bird checklist for Lake Chilwa sold (among other places) at the Wildlife Society Office in Blantyre and the Ku Chawe Inn on the Zomba Plateau. The Danish Hunters Association is currently involved in conservation projects around Lake Chilwa.

16

Blantyre

Blantyre is the oldest European settlement in Malawi. It's a bustling city, full of people, traffic and commerce. With its large buildings and compact layout, it is more obviously a city than Lilongwe, and is still more important commercially than the capital. There appears to be much more going on, too, although less so in the evenings.

The Blantyre Mission was founded in October 1876 by the Established Church of Scotland, and named after the small village in which David Livingstone was born. Under its first leader, Rev Duff Macdonald, the Blantyre Mission ruled over the surrounding hills with a despotic cruelty, flogging and killing suspected thieves and murderers without even the pretence of a trial. The behaviour of the early Blantyre missionaries caused a scandal in the British press, forcing many of them to retire, and Macdonald to be replaced by Rev Clement Scott in 1881.

The healthy, fertile climate around Blantyre proved attractive to European settlers, and the mission's strategic position served as an excellent communication centre for the traders who operated between Lake Malawi and the Zambezi Valley. The most important of these was the African Lakes Corporation which built Mandala House as its first trading post. Blantyre rapidly became the most important settlement in Malawi, and Mandala House, the oldest building in Malawi, can now be visited (see page 213). Today, the city has a population of around 550,000.

Blantyre is more intrinsically attractive than Lilongwe, lying at an altitude of 1,038m in a valley ringed by low hills, the largest of which are Michuru (1,473m), Soche (1,533m) and Ndirande (1,612m). Whilst not a tourist attraction in itself, there is plenty to keep you busy for a day or two, even if Malawi's attractions are not principally its cities. Blantyre remains the focal point of travel in southern Malawi, as well as the springboard for bus transport to Harare and Johannesburg via Mozambique's Tete Corridor.

CLIMATE

Blantyre has a pleasant, healthy climate. During the rainy season, which generally starts some time between October and December and ends in late April, temperatures are warm, the air tends to be rather humid, and rain can be expected most days, often in the form of short thunderstorms. From May to August, rain is unusual, the air is dry, and temperatures tend to be cool to moderate. The period from September to the start of the rains is the hottest season, with temperatures regularly soaring above 30°C. Humidity levels are low during this season, and the weather is frequently interrupted by heavy mists which can last for days.

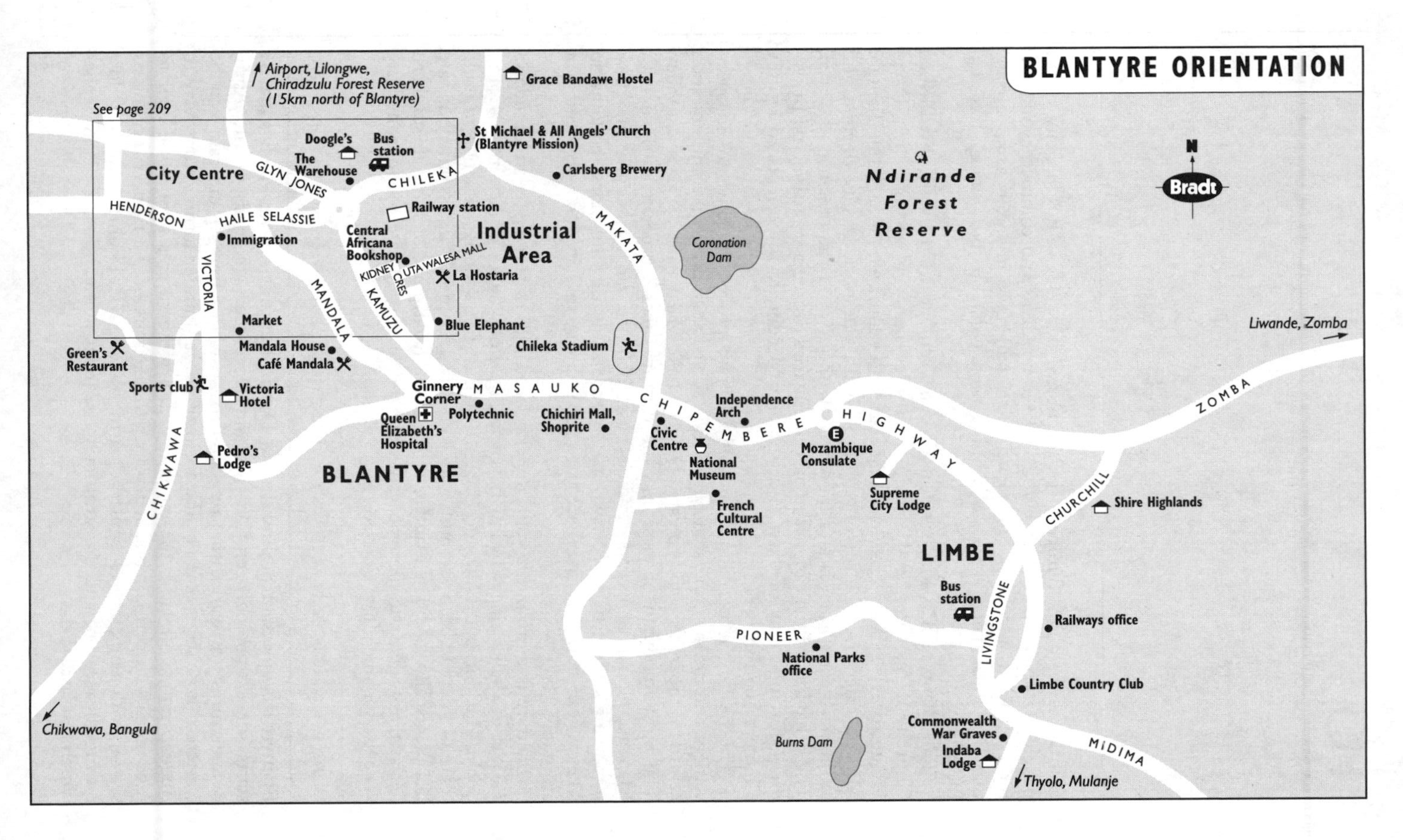
BLANTYRE ORIENTATION
Bradt
N
Airport, Lilongwe, Chiradzulu Forest Reserve (15km north of Blantyre)
Grace Bandawe Hostel
See page 209
St Michael & All Angels' Church (Blantyre Mission)
Doogle's
Bus station
The Warehouse
City Centre
GLYN JONES
CHILEKA
Carlsberg Brewery
Ndirande Forest Reserve
HENDERSON
HAILE SELASSIE
Railway station
Industrial Area
MAKATA
Coronation Dam
Immigration
Central Africana Bookshop
KIDNEY CRES
UTA WALESA MALL
La Hostaria
VICTORIA
MANDALA
KAMUZU
Market
Blue Elephant
Liwande, Zomba
Chileka Stadium
Green's Restaurant
Mandala House
Café Mandala
Sports club
Victoria Hotel
Ginnery Corner
MASAUKO
Independence Arch
Polytechnic
Queen Elizabeth's Hospital
Chichiri Mall, Shoprite
CHIPEMBERE HIGHWAY
Civic Centre
Mozambique Consulate
ZOMBA
Pedro's Lodge
National Museum
BLANTYRE
CHIKWAWA
Supreme City Lodge
CHURCHILL
Shire Highlands
French Cultural Centre
LIMBE
Bus station
LIVINGSTONE
Railways office
PIONEER
National Parks office
Limbe Country Club
Chikwawa, Bangula
Commonwealth War Graves
Burns Dam
Indaba Lodge
MIDIMA
Thyolo, Mulanje

GETTING THERE AND AWAY

Blantyre is the major transport hub in southern Malawi. **Buses** come and go regularly in every direction from the bus station on Chileka Road. Buses coming to Blantyre from the direction of Zomba or Mulanje stop in Limbe bus station before proceeding to Blantyre itself.

Travellers heading directly between Lilongwe and Blantyre will probably want to take advantage of the non-stop Coachline service between the cities run by Shire Bus Lines Limited (*01 671388*; e *fcshirebus@africa-online.net*). These coaches leave three-times daily in either direction, at 07.00, 12.00 and 17.00. The trip takes three to four hours, and tickets cost roughly US$18 per person one way.

The Shire Bus Company also goes to Johannesburg on Wednesdays and Sundays, departing at 08.00; fare MK11,500 one way (approx US$85).

City To City (*01 621346 or 09 958499*) goes to Johannesburg every day, departing at 09.00; fare MK8,500 one way. Linking Africa (*01 667045*) have changed their name to Ingwe; they leave for Johannesburg on Tuesdays, Thursdays and Saturdays at 09.00; fare MK11,500 one way. Vaal Africa (*01 821265*) leave for Johannesburg on Tuesdays and Sundays at 09.00; fare MK11,000 one way.

Munorama leaves on Wednesdays and Saturdays at 07.30; fare MK8,300 one way.

Blantyre is also the centre of Malawi's limited, intermittent and little-used **rail** network. The only route of interest for adventurous travellers is from Blantyre to Nayuchi on the eastern border, where it connects with the Mozambique rail service. It is supposed to run Mondays to Fridays, though often only runs once a week (if that), costs all of US$2.50 and entails a change at Nkaya, but it would probably be better starting in Liwonde. Not for the faint-hearted.

AIRPORT Chileka International Airport (*01 892274*) lies 19km from the city centre. It is the oldest airport in Malawi, though these days it receives few international flights as compared with Lilongwe's Kamuzu Airport. Taxis to the airport cost MK2,400.

Airlines Major airlines represented in Blantyre include:

- **Air Malawi** Robin's Rd; 01 820811
- **British Airways** Chilembwe Rd; 01 824333
- **Ethiopian Airlines** Victoria Av; 01 834676/01 833048
- **Kenya Airways** Mount Soche Hotel, 01-824524/ 01 820877/ 01 820107
- **South African Airways** Chilembwe Rd; 01 820627/9

ORIENTATION AND GETTING AROUND

Blantyre's compact city centre is roughly triangular in shape, bounded by Glyn Jones Road to the north, Haile Selassie Road to the south, and Hanover Avenue to the west. The most important road is Victoria Avenue, which runs from north to south a block east of Hanover Avenue. Among the many institutions on Victoria Avenue are the tourist office, map sales office, two major supermarkets, the main branches of the Commercial and National banks, Avis Car Hire and the Times Bookshop. The Mount Soche Hotel, which lies opposite the junction of Victoria Avenue and Glyn Jones Road, is perhaps the best-known landmark in the city centre.

Immediately east of the city centre, Glyn Jones Road and Haile Selassie Road converge at a roundabout to become the Kamuzu Highway. About 200m east of this roundabout is the clocktower where Chileka Road branches from Kamuzu

Highway to the northeast. The main bus station is 500m up Chileka Road; around it lies most of Blantyre's budget accommodation.

Kamuzu Highway connects Blantyre to the satellite town of Limbe, which lies 5km away from Blantyre and is administered by the same municipality. Although Limbe was originally a residential area and Blantyre a commercial and industrial area, Limbe now functions in most respects as a separate town, with its own main road, market and bus station. Regular minibuses connect Blantyre and Limbe via the Kamuzu Highway. The main supermarket for the city, Shoprite, lies along Kamuzu Highway towards Limbe.

CAR HIRE

SS Rent A Car 20 Glyn Jones Rd; ☎ 01 822882/01 822836 or 08 829322; e ssreantacar@malawi.net; www.ssrentacar.malawi.net. Just below the Mount Soche Hotel.

Avis Car Hire Main office: Victoria Av; ☎ 01 823792. The only internationally recognised car rental firm operating out of Blantyre.

Soche Tours and Travel (see *Travel agencies and tour operators*, page 213).

WHERE TO STAY

TOURIST CLASS There is now a number of places of high international standards.

Mount Soche Hotel PO Box 284, Blantyre; ☎ 01 820588; f 01 820154; e mountsochehotel@sunbirdmalawi.com. Centrally situated and part of the government-run Sunbird Group, the Mount Soche is the most upmarket hotel in Blantyre, with several types of accommodation, from standard rooms to superior suites. Facilities include satellite TV in every room, a business centre, gardens, a large swimming pool, and 24-hour room service. Two excellent restaurants are attached to the hotel: the very swanky and highly regarded fifth-floor Michuru Restaurant, and the mid-range Gypsy Restaurant on the ground floor (see below). *Standard sgl/dbl US$150/165, superior suite sgl/dbl US$174/189.*

Ryall's Hotel Hanover Av; ☎ 01 820955; f 01 827000; e ryalls@proteamalawi.com; www.proteahotels.com. Near to the Mount Soche Hotel, the Ryall's is more modern and just as comfortable, and boasts the most up-to-date facilities including a full business centre, and Blantyre's most exclusive Club 21 Restaurant and bar. *Sgl/dbl US$160–208/193–241.*

Victoria Hotel Bottom of Victoria Av by Mahatma Gandhi Rd; ☎ 01 823500; e reservations@hotelvictoriamw.com; www.hotelvictoriamw.com. Stylish rooms. *Sgl/dbl US$125/145.*

Eclipse Lodge Glyn Jones Rd; ☎ 0 1822969/01 821795; e eclipse@globemw.net. Offers luxurious safari-style rooms though prices might change as the hotel expands. *Sgl/dbl US$76/88.*

Supreme City Lodge ☎ 01 839406; e moda@sdnp.org. Executive rooms with panoramic views of the Naperi Valley and Soche Mountain.

Shire Highlands Hotel Churchill Rd, Limbe; ☎ 01 640055. Now a bit run down, but has gained a brilliant reputation for its cultural evenings. *Sgl/dbl US$90/100.*

Tumbuka Lodge Corner of Sharpe and Chilembwe rds; ☎/f 01 620487. In suburban Blantyre, the Tumbuka is also an attractive option. *Sgl/dbl US$95/140.*

Alendo Hotel and Kachere Restaurant 15 Chilembwe Rd. Operated by The Malawi Institute of Tourism where it trains staff to a high standard for the hospitality industry in Malawi. *S/c sgl/dbl US$55/80.*

Pedro's Lodge Close to the Sports Club; ☎ 01 833430/08 842670; e pedros@globemw.net; www.pedrosmw.com. Also recommended. *Sgl/dbl/twin US$60/70/80.*

MID RANGE AND BUDGET

Doogle's Backpacker Lodge ☎ 08 837615; e doogles@africa-online.net. Situated about 100m from Blantyre's main bus station, this large and highly popular hostel offers budget accommodation and a bar, swimming pool, a good notice board, TV lounge with video, hot showers, luggage storage and a large garden, and there's internet on site. Doogle's does good meals for around US$3–4. *Camping*

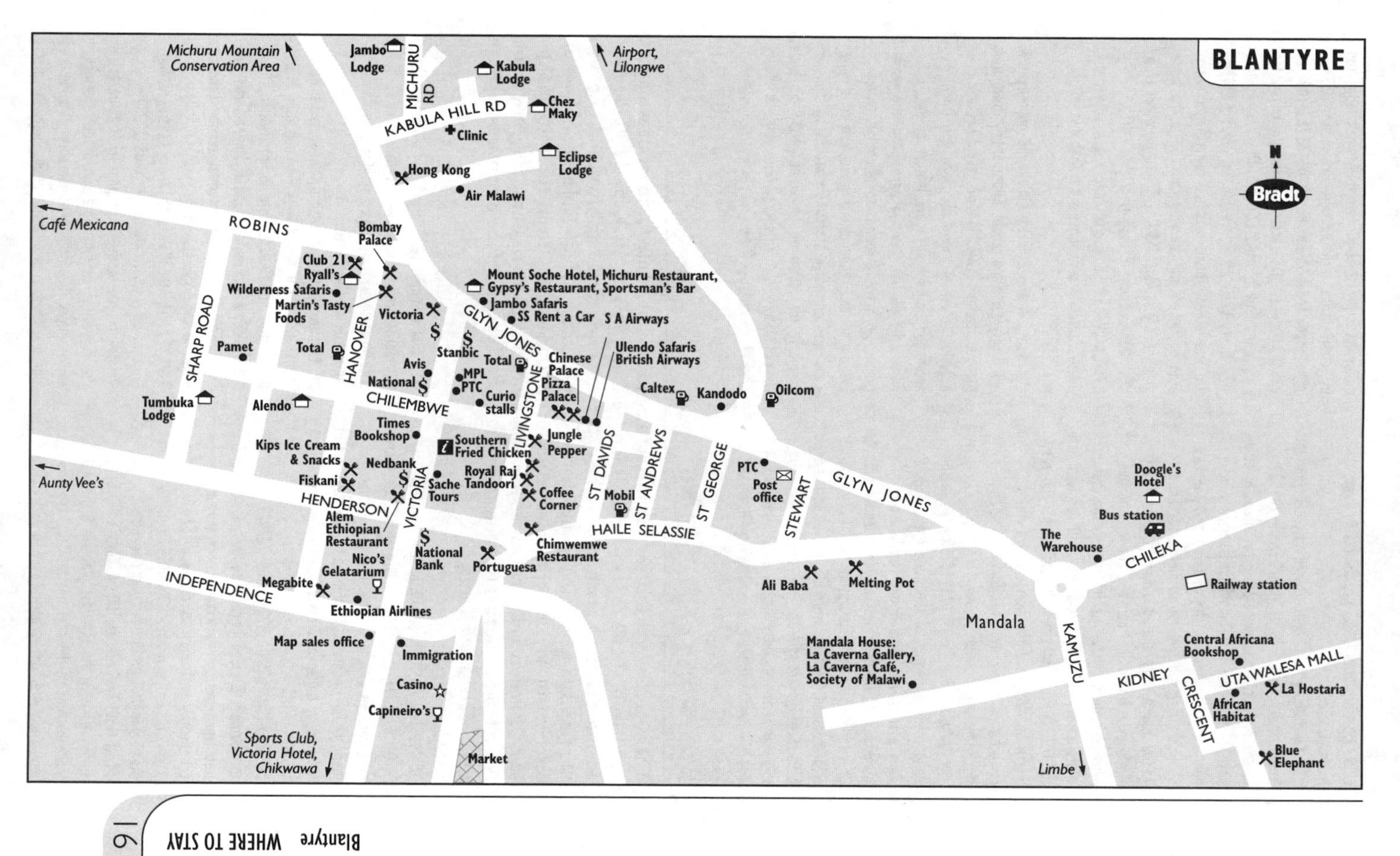
BLANTYRE
Bradt
N
Michuru Mountain Conservation Area
Airport, Lilongwe
Café Mexicana
Aunty Vee's
Sports Club, Victoria Hotel, Chikwawa
Limbe
Jambo Lodge
MICHURU RD
Kabula Lodge
KABULA HILL RD
Chez Maky
Clinic
Eclipse Lodge
Hong Kong
Air Malawi
ROBINS
Bombay Palace
Club 21
Ryall's
Wilderness Safaris
Martin's Tasty Foods
Victoria
Mount Soche Hotel, Michuru Restaurant, Gypsy's Restaurant, Sportsman's Bar
Jambo Safaris
SS Rent a Car
S A Airways
GLYN JONES
SHARP ROAD
Pamet
Total
HANOVER
Stanbic
Total
Chinese Palace
Ulendo Safaris
British Airways
Avis
MPL
PTC
National
Pizza Palace
Caltex
Kandodo
Oilcom
Tumbuka Lodge
Alendo
CHILEMBWE
Curio stalls
LIVINGSTONE
Times Bookshop
Southern Fried Chicken
Jungle Pepper
Kips Ice Cream & Snacks
Nedbank
Fiskani
Sache Tours
Royal Raj Tandoori
Coffee Corner
ST DAVIDS
ST ANDREWS
ST GEORGE
PTC
Post office
STEWART
GLYN JONES
Mobil
HENDERSON
Alem Ethiopian Restaurant
VICTORIA
HAILE SELASSIE
Chimwemwe Restaurant
National Bank
Portuguesa
Nico's Gelatarium
INDEPENDENCE
Megabite
Ethiopian Airlines
Map sales office
Immigration
Casino
Capineiro's
Market
Ali Baba
Melting Pot
Doogle's Hotel
Bus station
The Warehouse
CHILEKA
Railway station
Mandala
KAMUZU
Mandala House: La Caverna Gallery, La Caverna Café, Society of Malawi
Central Africana Bookshop
KIDNEY
CRESCENT
UTA WALESA MALL
La Hostaria
African Habitat
Blue Elephant

US$3 pp, dormitory US$5 pp, chalets $15 and dbl rooms US$21.

Chez Maky first right, signed just up from the Mount Soche Hotel; 01 822124//09 203029; e chezmaky@globemw.net. A great place to stay, possibly the only place in Malawi where you will hear classical music in the morning and the best of local music on live music nights. It's an old 1930s' house, very chilled out, with incredible views over Ndirande Mountain, and great value. Wireless internet is available from the restaurant which caters for every taste; you will eat well here for US$10. Wed night is volleyball night, and it's worth checking out the notice board for forthcoming music events. *US$50 FB, special packages for families.*

Kabula Lodge 01 821216. Situated in the quiet Blantyre suburb of the same name (follow signs past Mount Soche Hotel). Family run and popular with volunteer workers on extended stays, it offers a range of accommodation and use of the well-equipped kitchens. *From US$10 for basic sgls to US$35/45 for s/c sgl/dbls.*

Jambo Lodge Sunnyside; 01 835356/01 623709 or 09 960294; e jamboafrica@africa-online.net; www.jambo-africa.com. A small lodge run by Jambo Africa, with pleasant airy rooms. *US$45.*

Indaba Lodge Thyolo Rd; 01 657656/09 211403. A neat place with a restaurant known for its prawns. *Sgl/dbl MK2,200/3,500.*

Aunty Vee's 19 Henderson St; 01 623474. S/c and budget rooms, and the jovial Agnes can even be talked into allowing camping in the large grounds. *S/c sgl/dbl US$27/33; budget rooms US$7.*

Wenela Lodge Behind Doogle's; 01 836754/09 558058. A quiet and neatly converted house. *Standard s/c rooms MK1,750; s/c sgl/dbl MK2,500/3,250.*

Grace Bandawe Hostel Chileka Rd opposite the old Blantyre Mission, about 500m out of town from the bus station; 01 834267. Very quiet and peaceful. Variety of rooms inc clean dormitory accommodation. An attractive feature of the dormitories is that they are partitioned into semi-private sgl and dbl rooms. No alcohol is served because it is a religious institution, and it is quite a way from any other bars and restaurants. Meals are served in the restaurant for around US$3 per plate. *Sgl/dbl US$20/25 with shared bathroom, s/c dbl US$32, dorm US$10 pp*

WHERE TO EAT AND DRINK

There are several relatively upmarket restaurants in Blantyre, most of which are open from 12.00 to 14.00 and around either 18.00 or 19.00 to 22.30. You can assume that most restaurants at the upper end of the price scale will add 17.5% tax to prices quoted on the menu; service charge not included. Tables are only rarely reserved in advance. Being so close to the trade routes from the Mozambique coast, Blantyre is known for its prawns, as well as a range of European, African and Asian foods. The first two entries are undoubtedly some of the best places to escape the city for a few hours.

Mandala Old Manager's Hse, Top Mandala; 01 871932/09 917181; e lacaverna@malawi.net. La Caverna Art Gallery's café is the top choice for lunch – for under US$10 you can enjoy tasty dishes followed by coffee and cake. *Open Mon–Sat 09.00–17.00.*

Chez Maky 01 822124/09 203029; e chezmaky@globemw.net. Another popular daytime restaurant, this laid-back venue serves light continental meals such as crêpes (US$1.50), quiches (US$4.50) and moussaka. *Open 09.00–17.00 or in the evening for groups by prior booking.*

21 Grill Ryalls Hotel, Hanover Av; 01 820955. This is possibly the smartest place in Blantyre for lunch or dinner; the chef has built up a phenomenal reputation with dishes between US$8 and US$20.

Green's Sunnyside; 01 836375/08 833518; e greens@malawi.net; www.greens.sapo.no.pt. Always packed and very swish, with similar prices and reputation to the 21 Grill.

Michuru Restaurant Fifth fl, Mount Soche Hotel; 01 820588. It has a wide selection of à la carte dishes from US$12–15, more for prawns.

Gypsy's Restaurant Ground fl, Mount Soche Hotel; 01 820588. Relatively informal, serving à la carte meals in the US$8–12 range.

L'Hostaria Uta Waleza Shopping Centre, Kidney Crescent off Kamuzu Highway; 08 282828. Deservedly one of the most popular restaurants in the city centre at lunchtime and in the evenings, and it offers the winning combination of great meals and a relaxed, individualistic atmosphere. The pizzas here are really good, and reasonably priced at around US$7–10, while pasta and meat dishes fall into the US$10–15 range.

✕ **Jungle Pepper** Livingstone Av. Good pizzas at a similar price but are geared more to the walk-in take-away market.

✕ **Bombay Palace** Hanover Av opposite Ryalls Hotel; ☎ 08 950989. Delicious Indian cuisine.

✕ **Raj Tandoori Restaurant** Livingstone Av. Temporarily closed but hopefully due to reopen soon as it's always been very good. Most meals around US$10 with rice and bread.

✕ **Hong Kong Restaurant** Intersection of Glyn Jones and Robins rds. A massive plate of tasty Chinese food shouldn't set you back more than US$5 per head.

✕ **Pizza Palace** and the **Chinese Palace** Livingstone Towers, Chilembwe Rd. Both offer tempting and affordable national dishes.

✕ **Melting Pot Restaurant** (Greek) and **Ali Baba** (Indian) on Haile Selassie Rd. Both have a varied menu, with most dishes costing around US$7–8.

✕ **Blue Elephant** Just up the road from L'Hostaria on Kidney Crescent: ☎ 09 965850. A lively venue for good steak and chips, sport on the TV by day and live music on Sun.

✕ **Alem Ethiopian Restaurant** Victoria Av. This is a welcome surprise to those travellers who've already visited Ethiopia, while to others it will serve as an excellent place to try out one of Africa's most unusual cuisines. Run by a Tigrean woman, it serves a selection of Ethiopian dishes, at around US$6.

✕ **Portuguesa** (was Nando's) Corner of Henderson St and Haile Selassie Rd. Excellent Portuguese-style piri-piri chicken. A quarter chicken with chips here costs around US$3.

✕ **Martin's Tasty Foods Ltd** Top of Hanover Av. A superb fast-food restaurant with big meals under US$5.

✕ **Megabite Restaurant** Further down on the corner of Haile Selassie Rd.

✕ **Kips Ice Cream & Snacks** Hanover Av. Serves ice cream and a variety of inexpensive meals.

ENTERTAINMENT AND NIGHTLIFE

Listings for Malawi's entertainment scene can be found at www.go2malawi.com which will also send out a weekly email from The Friday Team; subscribe at www.fridayteam.co.uk or www.go2malawi.com.

French Cultural Centre, Corner Moi Rd and Kasungu Crescent; ☎ 01 671250; f 01 671259; e ccfr@malawi.net or ccf.malawi@africa-online.net. Look out for posters or leaflets advertising evening events. The quality of music, theatre and poetry performed here is staggering. *Open Sun–Fri 08.00–12.00 and 14.00–17.30; Sat 08.00–12.00.*

St Michael All Angels Chileka Rd. Also has occasional concerts.

The Warehouse ☎ 08 203622/08 203611; e masikamalawi2000@yahoo.com; www.thewarehouse-malawi.net. Located in a former railway station, The Warehouse is the liveliest place in Blantyre for regular live music, dance, film, literature, media art, photography and theatre. The Warehouse focuses on the development and promotion of Malawian culture in its existing forms, first and foremost music, performing arts (dance and drama) and written and oral literature. In addition to this, The Warehouse, in conjunction with the international NGO (Medienausbildungsprojekt Afrika/media training project Africa) promotes less developed forms of visual arts such as film and photography.

Cappinero Victoria Av; ☎ 08 843892/08 824022; e mozagua@globemw.net. A hot new pub in an old colonial house, a place where you can get decent bar food, chat to everyone, watch sport on the large screen by the outdoor bar, play pool and dance the night through.

☆ **The Casino** Next door. Another popular evening haunt.

SHOPPING

BOOKS AND MAPS The best general bookshop in Blantyre city centre is the **Central Bookshop** at Chichiri Shoprite Centre. This stocks a fair range of novels, as well as many books published in Malawi and a variety of imported field guides and travel guides.

Situated opposite L'Hostaria in the Uta Waleza Shopping Centre on Kidney Crescent off Kamuzu Highway is the **Central Africana Bookshop** which stocks the best selection of current books about Malawi, as well as a good range of obscure and out-of-print African titles. If you're looking for something specific in this line, you can contact them in advance (☎ *01 823227;* **f** *01 822236;* ✉ *africana@iafrica.com; www.centralafricana.com*).

There is a well-stocked **Map Sales Office** in the Department of Surveys' office on the southern end of Victoria Avenue (☎ *01 623722*). A 1:16,000 map of Blantyre and Limbe can be bought at any map sales office in the country.

CRAFTS AND CURIOS Meccas include **La Caverna** (*Old Manager's Hse, Mandala Rd*) (see opposite) and **African Habitat** (*Uta Waleza Shopping Centre next to L'Hostaria on Kidney Crescent;* ☎ *01 873642*). Both stock an eye-opening range of high-quality African art, sculpture and handicraft. The main area for curio street-shopping is on Victoria Avenue, though it is likely that the traders will be re-located to a covered area soon. The **Wildlife and Environmental Society of Malawi** (☎ *01 643428/643*) has a small shop with books, art and craft work at their office in Limbe near to the Shire Highlands Hotel.

Supermarkets The new Chichiri Mall at the traffic circle on Kamuzu Highway between Blantyre and Limbe has revolutionised shopping in this part of Malawi. With a huge, well-stocked Shoprite supermarket as its main tenant, the mall also boasts fashion shops, banks, a pharmacy, take-aways, a branch of Soche Tours and a Postnet agency for phone, internet, copying and DHL. Open until late and over weekends, this makes a welcome change from the smaller supermarkets dotted around the city.

OTHER PRACTICALITIES

TOURIST INFORMATION The **tourist office** (☎ *01 820300*) on Victoria Avenue is reasonably helpful and stocks a good range of free pamphlets and books about Malawi.

FOREIGN EXCHANGE You can exchange money at any branch of the Stanbic, Nedbank or National banks, or at one of the private forex bureaux in the city centre. Outside banking hours, most of the upmarket hotels will exchange money for hotel residents. The National Bank branches have Visa/MasterCard cash machines.

IMMIGRATION Visitors' passes and visas can be renewed at the immigration office on Victoria Avenue (☎ *01 823777*).

MOZAMBIQUE VISAS Travellers heading to Mozambique or using the Tete Corridor to get to Zimbabwe can buy the appropriate visa at the Mozambique Consulate on Kamuzu Highway – it's not always possible to buy them at the border. Transit visas are issued on the same day at the kwacha equivalent of around US$40. In order to take advantage of the same-day service, you must hand in your passport at the

BLANTYRE TELEPHONE NUMBERS

In 2006 Blantyre's city centre phone numbers are changing to 018 instead of 016. However some 016 numbers will stay the same. There is bound to be some confusion, so if you find that any of our 016 numbers don't work, please redial using 018 and vice versa. Please also note that you may not get through first time.

consulate before 08.30 for collection at 15.00. Any minibus between the city centre and Limbe can drop you near the consulate; ask for Masalima post office. It is also possible to arrange your transit visa through Doogle's, assuming that this is where you are staying. It may be worth noting that transit visas technically allow you to stay in Mozambique for *up to seven days from the date of issue* – proper tourist visas are considerably more expensive than transit visas and take three working days to be processed.

TOUR OPERATORS AND SAFARI COMPANIES Many of Malawi's tour operators have offices in Blantyre, making it easy to organise travel and accommodation around the country and into neighbouring countries.

Soche Tours and Travel Hardelec House, Victoria Rd, PO Box 2225, Blantyre; ☎ 01 820777; f 01 820440; e sochetoursbt@sochetoursmw.com

Jambo Africa Mount Soche Hotel; ☎ 01 835356; f 01 633489; e jamboafrica@africa-online.net; www.jamboafricatoursmalawi.com. They are linked to Nyala Lodge in Lengwe National Park and can organise trips to any destination in Malawi.

Central African Wilderness Safaris Ryalls Hotel; ☎ 01 836961/01 821219; e janice@wilderness.mw.

Ulendo Safaris 3rd fl, Livingstone Towers, Glyn Jones Rd; ☎ 01 820752; e Blantyre@ulendo.net. Ulendo are the booking agents for BA, Kenya Airways, Air Malawi, SAA, Ethiopian Airlines, Jet Airways and Zambian Airways.

INTERNET A great number of internet offices and cafés are advertised in and around Blantyre, but some are pretty dodgy and I can only recommend the services at Doogle's, and Postnet at the Chichiri Mall. A great new development is Skyband, which at the time of writing has 80 Skyband hotspots rolled out across Blantyre and Lilongwe. Anyone can obtain access using a prepaid Access Card (voucher). For more info contact Skyband (☎ *01 820200/01 757757; www.skybandhotspots.com*).

HOSPITAL The Mwaiwathu Hospital in Chileka Road, just above the bus station and Doogle's, offers a comprehensive medical service and is open all hours (☎ *01822999;* f *01 621190*). The best place currently for malaria tests is the new Seventh Day Adventist Hospital on the road towards Maky's above the Mount Soche Hotel. Queen's Hospital is the huge hospital on Ginnery Corner and is the best place for accident and emergency.

INDUSTRIAL AREA Situated to the northeast of Kumuzu Highway, the Ginnery Corner industrial area is the place to go looking for motor spares and repairs as well as having your gas cylinders filled at BOC Gases (☎ *01 871260*).

WHAT TO SEE AND DO

LA CAVERNA ART GALLERY Old Manager's House, Top Mandala on Mackie Road. If you have a day free in Blantyre, you should certainly pop into La Caverna. The oldest building in Malawi, erected in 1882 by the African Lakes Corporation, it is now home to an unbelievable reading library of Africana books on every subject, collected by The Historical Society of Malawi (☎ *01 872617; www.societyofmalawi.org*). It is also a good café. The library is opened by volunteers every morning, with late-night opening on Thursdays 18.00–19.30, and the gallery can also give you access to the library on special request.

NATIONAL MUSEUM Just off the Kamuzu Highway towards Limbe. The museum houses a range of traditional Malawian artefacts and musical instruments, as well as displays on Livingstone, the Livingstonia Mission and the early colonial era. Traditional dancing takes place in the grounds on Saturdays. (*Open Tue–Sun 10.00 16.00.*)

ST MICHAEL AND ALL ANGELS' CHURCH Chileka Road between the bus station and Grace Bandawe Hostel. This is the second oldest building in Blantyre, built by Scottish missionaries between 1888 and 1891, and well worth a visit.

CARLSBERG BREWERY (☎ *01 870222/01 820133*). Many travellers go on the free day tour offered on Wednesdays at 14.30, though it's doubtful whether the attraction lies so much in the brewing process as in the complimentary beer-swilling session at the end of the tour. It is best to arrange a tour a day in advance and to gather together a group of people at somewhere like Doogle's to split the taxi fare.

THE PAPER MAKING EDUCATION TRUST (PAMET) Chilembwe Road (☎ *01 823895; www.pamet.org.com*). This is a fascinating place where they hand-make paper and cardboard using elephant dung, grass, sisal, banana bark and recycled paper. Products such as photo albums and writing sets are available – great for souvenirs. (*Open for tours every afternoon at less than US$1 pp or only US$4 per group, Mon–Fri.*)

LIMBE TOWN is vibrant and bustling and well worth exploring. From April to September tourists are welcome to visit the **tobacco-auctioning** floors there (☎ *01 840377*). Though not as large as those in Lilongwe, they're still highly impressive and an organisational feat.

MICHURU MOUNTAIN CONSERVATION AREA The closest conservation area to Blantyre lies on Michuru Mountain about 8km northeast of the city centre, though it has to be said that all conservation areas close to the city have come under enormous pressure from people needing firewood. It protects a variety of habitats including plantation forest, indigenous woodland and open grassland. Mammals which occur naturally in Michuru include spotted hyena, leopard, serval, genet, bushpig, vervet monkey, baboon, bushbaby, bushbuck, grey duiker, klipspringer and reedbuck. Over 200 bird species have been recorded. Facilities include a basic campsite, and several day trails of between 2km and 5km in length. It is permitted to walk in the reserve at night, when a variety of nocturnal animals may be seen. There are three well-defined walking trails.

To get to Michuru, follow Glyn Jones Road west of the Mount Soche Hotel for roughly 200m, then turn left into Sharp Road until, after about 100m, you hit a T-junction where you must turn right into Michuru Avenue. About 2km along Michuru Avenue the tarmac ends; a further 6km along the road you come to a turn-off marked by a green stone reading 'Michuru Conservation Area'. Continue along Michuru Road past this turn-off, and ignore the next two turn-offs (respectively marked 'CDC Farm' and 'Michuru Office'). The road which you need to turn into is marked 'Car Park and Nature Trails'.

If you don't have private transport, you could walk to Michuru and back as a day trip, but it's close on 10km each way, which won't leave you much time to explore the nature trails. A better idea perhaps is to get a taxi to the entrance gate and then try to hitch back. Alternatively, you could camp in the reserve. For further details about walking and camping in the conservation area, contact the Chief Forester's office (☎ *01 633887/01 661471*). The Blantyre branch of the Wildlife Society of Malawi (PO Box 1429, Blantyre) funds six patrolmen, the hyena hide, trail slashing and minor road works. It has also undertaken the refurbishment of the educational centre and the toilet/ablution block.

Several of the other hills around Blantyre are protected in forest reserves, and they are popular for weekend walks with residents. With Mulanje and Zomba beckoning, these reserves are probably only of marginal interest to tourists, but if you feel like exploring, get hold of a copy of the booklet *Day Outings from Blantyre* (Wildlife Society of Malawi); it's available in most bookshops for a couple of dollars.

CHIRADZULU FOREST RESERVE Chiradzulu Mountain lies about 15km north of Blantyre. It supports the most accessible evergreen forest in the Blantyre area, though only a relatively small patch of 200ha remains, all of it above the 1,500m contour. The mountain is of particular interest to birdwatchers, as many unusual forest species are present, including a variety of robins, bulbuls, and the crowned eagle. It was at Chiradzulu in 1896 that the first specimen of the rare green-headed oriole was captured. Mammals that can be seen on the mountain include vervet and samango monkeys, baboon, spotted hyena, red duiker and bushbuck. The lower slopes of Chiradzulu, where they haven't been planted with exotic trees, are covered in thick *brachystegia* woodland.

The area around Chiradzulu Mountain has played a prominent role in the modern history of Malawi. It was near the base of Chiradzulu that Livingstone helped Bishop Mackenzie found the Church of Scotland's short-lived Magomero Mission in 1861. The largest farm in the Chiradzulu area was later bought by one Mr Bruce, a stepson of Livingstone, and was managed by another member of the clan, William Livingstone. In 1915, William Livingstone was decapitated in front of his family during the rebellion initiated by Chiradzulu's most famous son, the Rev John Chilembwe.

Getting there and away Chiradzulu Mountain can be visited either as a day trip from Blantyre or else from the small town of Chiradzulu, which is at the eastern base of the mountain. Chiradzulu Town lies about 20km from Limbe; you must first take the M3 towards Zomba, then, about 4km out of town, branch left on to the tarred S146. There are regular buses between Limbe bus station and Chiradzulu.

From Chiradzulu Town, the (unsignposted) turn-off to Chiradzulu Forest Reserve lies a few kilometres back towards Blantyre, about 1km south of the dam which lies immediately west of the S146. About 3km along the turn-off you enter a eucalyptus plantation, then about 1km further on you reach the edge of the forest. The indigenous forest is most easily explored along firebreaks, which separate it from the surrounding eucalyptus plantations.

The Providential Industrial Mission founded by John Chilembwe was forced to close after the above-mentioned incident, but reopened ten years later, and it remains today an active mission with several points of historical interest dating to Chilembwe's time. If you are interested in visiting the mission, it lies near Mbombwe trading centre, roughly 5km east of the Limbe–Chiradzulu road, from where it can be reached via a signposted dirt road starting close to Chiradzulu Secondary School.

Where to stay Chiradzulu Town is something of a backwater, with a stagnant, isolated atmosphere that is difficult to explain when you consider how close it is to Blantyre and the role it has played in Malawian history. If you have ambitions to spend the night in town, there is a very basic dollar-a-night hotel in the market, where an absence of facilities is compensated for by the friendliness of the family who own it. The hotel will boil up water for you to wash in, but unless you fancy a meal of *nsima* and boiled eggs, it might be worth bringing a bit of food along with you.

FURTHER AFIELD Still within striking distance of Blantyre are **Lengwe National Park** (see page 231) and **Nyala Park** (page 232), and **Majete Wildlife Reserve** (page 230) with its 15km of impressive cataracts as the Shire tumbles down the escarpment into the Lower Shire Valley.

The **Mpatamanga Gorge** (page 216) at the beginning of the rapids is worth a day trip out on the Mwanza Road. **Mulanje** (page 219) is now only an hour by road and makes a good day out from Blantyre. A day trip to **Game Haven** (see page 218) in Vumbwe for a walk amongst the game followed by a sophisticated lunch might also appeal. All of these are covered individually in more detail in other regional chapters.

17

Thyolo and Mulanje

Mulanje Mountain is the rugged island in the sky high above the gentle tea-growing country of Thyolo and Mulanje districts, the oldest tea in Africa. Beneath this edifice is an area which is strikingly reminiscent of the Kericho district of western Kenya: breezy, rolling hills swathed in orderly rows of tea bushes and still supporting the occasional remnant patch of indigenous forest in valleys and along watercourses. The heights of a staggeringly proportioned granite outcrop dominate the eastern skyline. This is the Mulanje Massif, the highest mountain in Central Africa, rising almost 2km above the surrounding Phalombe Plain to an altitude of 3,002m.

Tourism to this part of Malawi is inevitably, and rightly, centred around Mulanje, which arguably offers the finest hiking in the country, and is renowned among mountaineers for its exceptional rock climbing. Thyolo, too, is worth a stop, as a base from which to explore the biologically rich mahogany forest on the upper slopes of Thyolo Mountain. Visitors might hear stories of the so-called Batwa, Pygmies from Mulanje stealing pumpkins from the surrounding farmland – probably some sort of folk memory, as pygmoid hunter-gatherers vanished from this area centuries ago, though their physiology is still apparent in many local people.

Continuing beyond Mulanje is the road to the Mozambican border, leading from Gurne at the base of Mount Namule past further mountains towards the north Mozambique coast.

CLIMATE

This is a region of stark climatic contrasts. Thyolo and its surrounds have a pleasingly moderate highland climate, but temperatures climb as you descend to the Luchenza River and Phalombe Plain. Weather conditions on top of Mulanje are relatively cool, and night-time temperatures can be downright chilly, especially between June and August.

GETTING AROUND

There are two routes between Blantyre and Mulanje. With the newly tarred M4 the journey from Blantyre to Mulanje takes only 40 minutes. Unfortunately there are no villages along this road so minibuses normally take the longer M2 road. When they have to stop frequently the journey can take as long as two hours.

Shire buses leave Mulanje to Blantyre three times a day at 06.00, 10.30 and 15.00. The 15.00 express bus from the border to Lilongwe stops at Mulanje and Thyolo.

From Blantyre the buses leave three times a day to Mulanje. The morning bus arrives at 06.00 in Blantyre from Lilongwe and continues to the Mozambican border. At 12.00 there is a bus from Blantyre. The last express bus is at 18.00 from Blantyre to the border.

THYOLO AND BVUMBWE

Just before Thyolo is the market town of Bvumbwe, where on market days (Tuesdays and Saturdays) you will find one of the most impressive ranges of vegetables and fruit in the country. There's also a wide selection of clothes. Signposted on the right as you approach Bvumbwe, less than 2km from the outskirts of Limbe, the newly established Game Haven (☎ *09 962520;* e *gamehaven@globemw.net*) offers the opportunity to walk in a protected area containing all manner of game, as well as offering good birding, sumptuous food and high-class accommodation.

To the left of the road between Bvumbwe and Thyolo is the Mwalanthunzi Stone, a large meteorite steeped in local beliefs. If you are heading north, this stone will guide you safely on your journey (it doesn't work if you're going south). You must walk around the stone three times using a small stone (normally perched in a crevice at the top of the meteorite) to tap the lucky stone. Should you involuntarily whistle as you walk, then something unexpected will happen to you. When road builders decided to move the stone its wrath caused floods, destroying the new road. The stone was back in place the next day. When they moved the stone again (a further distance this time), the stone was back in place the next morning. Undeterred, they decided to crush the stone and use it in the road. The next day the stone was back in place. In the end the road builders decided to move the road a little to the right and to leave the magical stone alone.

Thyolo – pronounced *Cholo* – is the tea capital of Malawi, and one of the oldest towns in the country. The leafy administrative centre consists of a cluster of colonial-era government offices built around a rather pointless roundabout, and it is separated from the busy market and bus station by a tea field. About 1km back towards Limbe lie a string of shops, among them a PTC supermarket.

As with most Malawian towns, there is nothing much to do in Thyolo, though, if you're not in a rush and heading to Mulanje, it's a pleasant place to hang about. All Saints' Anglican Church behind the Thyolo Club is worth visiting, its unassuming graveyard serving as a reminder of how many Europeans came to settle here. If you're looking for the chance to limber up your legs before making an assault on Mulanje, the countryside around Thyolo is riddled with dirt roads which make for great rambling, with the attractive option of exploring the Satemwa Tea Estate and the remains of the sadly deforested Thyolo Forest Reserve.

GETTING THERE AND AWAY Most buses along the M2 between Blantyre and Mulanje stop at Thyolo – check which route the bus is using. Far quicker than buses are the minibuses and other *matola* vehicles which run directly between Limbe's bus station and Thyolo.

WHERE TO STAY AND EAT

Game Haven Lodge Chimwenya Estate, Bvumbwe; ☎ 09 962520; e gamehaven@globemw.net

Tione Motel About 5 mins' walk from the bus station – anybody will direct you. Far better than its faded exterior suggests and has a busy bar and a fair restaurant. *Clean dbls using communal facilities US$1.50, large, s/c dbls with hot water US$3.*

Thyolo Club ☎ 01 473259. *Camping US$3 pp, inc day membership.*

TEA ESTATES AND THYOLO FOREST RESERVE

Unfortunately, as in so many other parts of the world, Thyolo Forest Reserve on the slopes of the 1,462m Thyolo Mountain has been invaded by peasant farmers – Thyolo has the densest rural population in Malawi. In spite of the valiant efforts of the owners of the Satemwa Tea Estate, what was once one of Malawi's best-preserved mahogany forests is being chopped up for charcoal, and turned into marginal little patches of farmland.

To see the pristine remains of the forest and birds such as the green-headed oriole, white-winged apalis, Thyolo alethe, little green bulbul and moustached green tinker barbet, your only chance is to visit the rolling hills and woodlands of the adjoining **Satemwa Tea Estate**.

GETTING THERE AND AWAY To get to the forest reserve you have to pass through the Satemwa Tea Estate, which requires prior arrangement (see below for contact details). Look for their well-signposted turn-off about 4km out on the Limbe side of Thyolo. The security guard at the gate will direct you to the estate office.

WHERE TO STAY There are now two accommodation options near Thyolo Mountain, both of which lie within the Satemwa Tea Estate.

Chawani Bungalow has 4 bedrooms, each sleeping 2 people. It is set on the slopes of Thyolo Mountain, within easy walking distance of the forested upper slopes, and on a clear day it offers a great view across to Mulanje. The cost may be prohibitive to independent travellers, but would be excellent value for a group. *US$95 whole bungalow.*

Satemwa Guesthouse A colonial-era plantation house with 2 cottages (3 bedrooms each) in private gardens. Again great value for a group. Both cottages are fully furnished and have a chef/houseman available to do the cooking and cleaning. *US$90 per cottage.*

Dairy products such as milk and cheese can be bought on the estate, while a wide range of foodstuffs is avaliable at the PTC 7km from the estate in Thyolo. In addition to walking, fishing and birdwatching, the estate offers tours of the tea plantation, which is one of the oldest in the country, established in 1895. For those without a vehicle, transport to the bungalows can be arranged at the estate office, which lies a mere 500m from the main Limbe–Thyolo road.

The management recommends you make a reservation, especially at weekends. To book or make further enquiries, contact Satemwa Tea Estate (t *01 473356;* f *01 473368;* e *113213.233@compuserve.com*).

MULANJE

This attractive and spacious small town, set amid tea estates at the southern base of the towering Mulanje Massif, is one of the most picturesque towns in the whole of Malawi. Visited by most people who plan to hike on Malawi's highest mountain, it is also gaining popularity for day visits to the town itself and for day-trippers to its restaurants and Likhubula Pools. Mulanje is split into two discrete parts. Coming from the direction of Blantyre, you arrive first at the commercial centre, called **Chitakale**, where there is a PTC supermarket, a well-stocked vegetable market, a few basic resthouses and also the turn-off to Likhubula Forestry Station (the most popular base for climbing Mulanje). Mulanje itself lies about 2km past Chitakale, and it is reached by following the flame-tree-lined avenue which bisects Chitakale Tea Estate. **Mulanje Town** is where most of the administrative buildings can be found, as well as a few smarter motels. Internet services are available at Standard Holdings and InfoMulanje.

InfoMulanje Above the Pizzeria Basilica, Chitakale; t 01 466466; f 01 466241; e infomulanje@mountmulanje.org.mw or infomulanje@sdnp.org.mw. InfoMulanje is the place to contact when planning a hiking trip to Mulanje. The staff will give up-to-date information about the state of the paths, make mountain hut bookings, organise guides and porters, and can also make lodge accommodation reservations. They have a comprehensive list of places to visit, catering to all budgets and also organise tea field and factory tours around the nearby Esperanza Tea Estate.

GETTING THERE AND AWAY Several buses run between Blantyre and Mulanje every day, including two express buses. It is also possible to take one of the many minibuses from Limbe heading towards the Mozambican border. Most minibuses leave Limbe from the petrol station at the roundabout whilst others leave from the bus station and leave when they are full.

WHERE TO STAY If you want to stay near the junction to Likhubula, there are a few cheap resthouses to choose from in Chitakale, two of which are:

Happy Landing Restaurant and Guesthouse (18 rooms) Although the bar can be a little loud, the sgl rooms are clean, with communal facilities, all beds are provided with mosquito nets and the garden is tidy. *MK200.*

Chididi Motel The best of an indifferent bunch, offering clean bright rooms with three-quarter beds. *Bed US$1.40, s/c room MK400–500.*

In Mulanje

Council Resthouse Looks closed but still just about operates. Scruffy rooms using communal showers. *Rooms US$0.80, s/c dbls US$1.30.*

Mulanje Motel (13 rooms) ☎ 01 466245. Superb bar selling local Malawian lager at a good price. In addition the cosy restaurant serves both Malawian and English dishes at reasonable prices. 12 rooms with communal toilets and bathrooms and 1 s/c room. *Sgl/dbl US$4/8.*

Limbani Lodge (24 rooms) Close to the police station and the School for the Blind. Opened recently and a sister company to the Mulanje Motel. The lodge has its own bar but the restaurant is for guests only. All rooms are s/c. *MK500–1,200 per night.*

Mulanje View Motel Along the main road from Chitakale to Mulanje Boma; ☎ 01 466348. The garden looks beautiful and with the view of the mountain it is also an excellent place to enjoy dinner or drinks. The rooms and bathrooms are clean and simple. *Sgl/dbl and en-suite rooms MK650/MK750 and MK1,800.*

Camping

Mulanje Golf Club Secure and secluded camping around the swimming pool. The overnight rate includes access to sports facilities. An increasingly popular overland truck stop. The club has a restaurant and bar, and offers a full day meal and snack menu at a reasonable price. Day membership entitles access to club equipment to play golf, tennis, squash, badminton, snooker, darts, and to swim in the pool. The view from the veranda over the lush green tea fields onto the precipitous flanks of Mt Mulanje. *Camping US$5 pp. Day membership US$2 adults, US$1.50 children.*

Out of town Following the tarred road up the mountain you reach:

Kara o' Mula Country Lodge ☎ 01 466515/09 953276. A renovated colonial building with decent en-suite rooms and a bar with great sunset views of the Phalombe plains. Chalets are being built as well as a swimming pool using water diverted from the river nearby. The lodge is also the starting point for the Boma path to Lichenya Hut on the mountain, and safe parking is available here. *Sgl/shared room MK3,550/4,700.*

WHERE TO EAT

Kara o-Mula Lodge has a good restaurant with a wide range of delicious meals mostly priced at around US$3.

Tasty Food, on the Mulanje Boma Market, opposite the bus station, serves cheap and tasty local dishes run by a group of local women from Mulanje.

Pizzeria Basilica in Chitakale at the turn off to Likhubula. For upmarket pizza and pasta.

Curry Pot Restaurant, just along the Likhubula road. For a local speciality dish or something spicy, reasonably priced, often a favourite destination if you've come straight off the mountain.

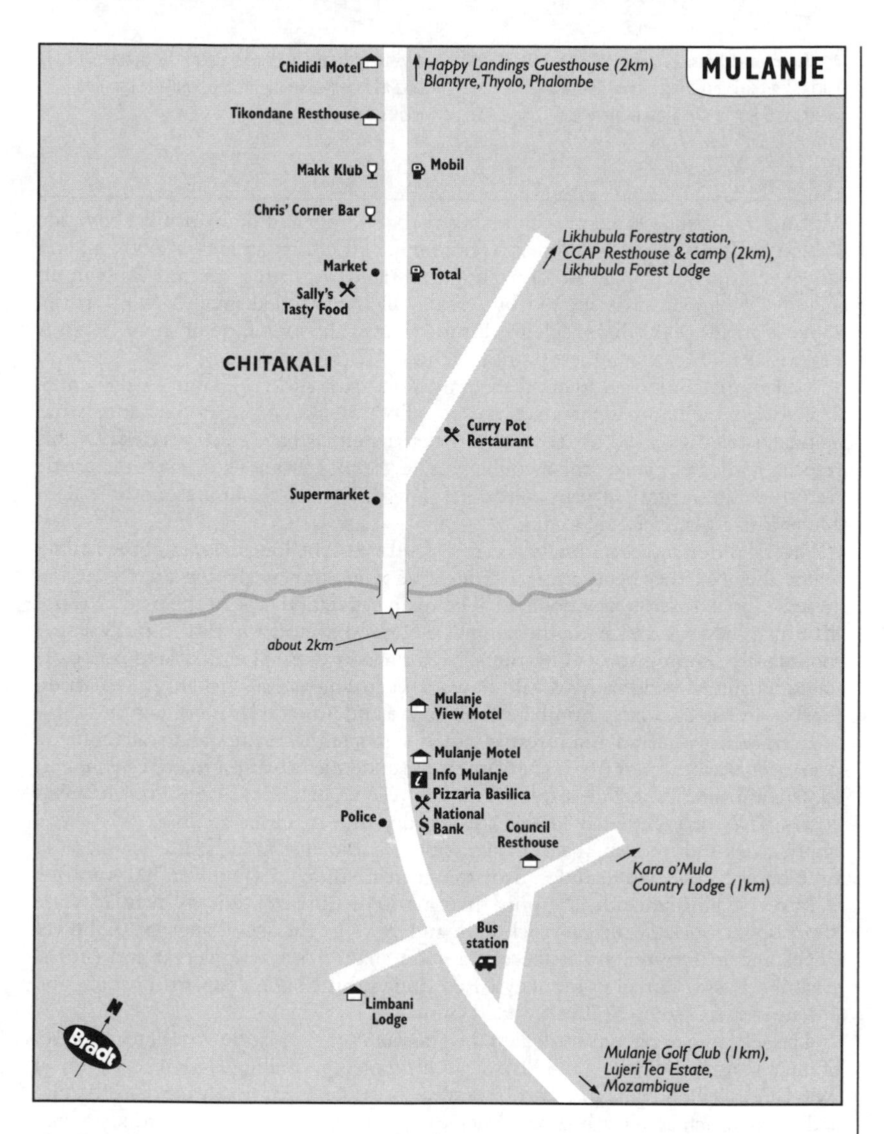

If you're heading to the Mulanje Massif, you can stock up at the **PTC** or the supermarket in Chitakale, which stock frozen sausages, fresh bread and the usual tinned goods. The **market** in Chitakale has as good a range of vegetables as any in Malawi.

TEA ESTATES Tucked away in a crescent of Mulanje Mountain towards Mozambique is **Lujeri Tea Estate** – of interest for groups wanting to relax after hiking or wanting to explore the lower slopes and tea estates. The estate has two lodges.

Lujeri Lodge (4 rooms) 01 460277/09 960344; e Richard@lujeri.com. A converted tea planter's home right in the heart of lush tea fields. 10 people can sleep comfortably and live in quite some style, and there's also gardens including swimming pool and mini tennis. *US$140 self-catering for the whole house and cook's services (US$40pp for dinner, lunch and b/fast).*

Lujeri Guesthouse (5 rooms) 01 460277/09 960344; e Richard@lujeri.com. The estate guesthouse, just a stroll away from the Lodge, has a homely living area and sleeps 10 people. *US$115 self-catering for the whole house and cook's services.*

MULANJE MASSIF

Mulanje is a vast, isolated granite massif rising sharply and dramatically above the Phalombe Plain southeast of Blantyre. The massif covers an area of 650km², and largely comprises a plateau of rolling grassland averaging around 2,000m in altitude. This plateau is incised by several thickly wooded ravines, while rising above it are 20 peaks that reach an altitude of over 2,500m. One of these, Sapitwa Peak, is at 3,002m the highest point in central Africa.

Mulanje is composed of hard metamorphic rock such as granite and syenite. The rock which forms the massif is roughly 130 million years old and it has gradually been exposed as the softer rocks around it have been eroded. In this respect, Mulanje is very similar to the granite koppies that are such a characteristic feature of the central African landscape. The difference is simply one of scale – Mulanje is a very, very big koppie.

Several different vegetation types cover Mulanje. The lower slopes of the massif, where they have not been planted with exotic pines and eucalyptus, are covered in closed-canopy *brachystegia* woodland. The main vegetation type of the plateau is not dissimilar in appearance to the alpine moorland found on east Africa's larger mountains: a combination of heathers, heaths and grasses. The moorland is notable for supporting a wide array of wild flowers, including various helichrysums, irises, lobelias and aloes, a large number of which are endemic to the mountain.

Evergreen woodland and forest is largely restricted to ravines and watercourses. The most notable forest tree on Mulanje is the endemic Mulanje cedar (*Widdringtonia whytei*), a magnificent timber tree which can reach a height of over 40m. Mulanje's cedars have been depleted in the last century due to timber felling, but several impressive stands remain, the most accessible of which lies in the saddle southeast of the Chambe Basin and includes many trees that are thought to be over 300 years old.

In the open highlands, the only mammal species seen with any regularity are klipspringer, rock hyrax, red rock hare and vole. In the woodlands of the lower slopes and in forested areas, there is a good chance of seeing vervet and (in the Chambe Basin) samango monkeys. Red duiker, bushbuck, leopard, bushpig and porcupine are also present in wooded habitats.

The selection of birds recorded on the grasslands of the plateau is not great; species of interest include Shelly's and Hildebrandt's francolin, wailing cisticola, a variety of swifts and swallows (the localised blue swallow is present from October to March), and raptors such as auger buzzard, black eagle, lanner and peregrine falcon and rock kestrel. Of more interest are the birds found in the forest and woodland, including a variety of bulbuls, robins, thrushes, flycatchers, bush shrikes and warblers.

With easy access from Blantyre, well-organised and inexpensive facilities, and some of the most dramatic scenery in the country, Mulanje is Malawi's premier hiking and rock-climbing destination, popular with tourists and expatriates alike. There are several routes from the base to the plateau, but the only ones that are used with much regularity are the Skyline Path to the Chambe Basin and the Lichenya Path to the Lichenya Plateau. Both of these routes start at Likhubula Forestry Station, which lies at the eastern base of the mountain about 10km from Mulanje Town.

In addition to there being inexpensive accommodation at Likhubula Forestry Station, there are nine huts on the plateau, connected to each other by well-marked trails ranging from three to six hours' walking duration. With 20 peaks to explore,

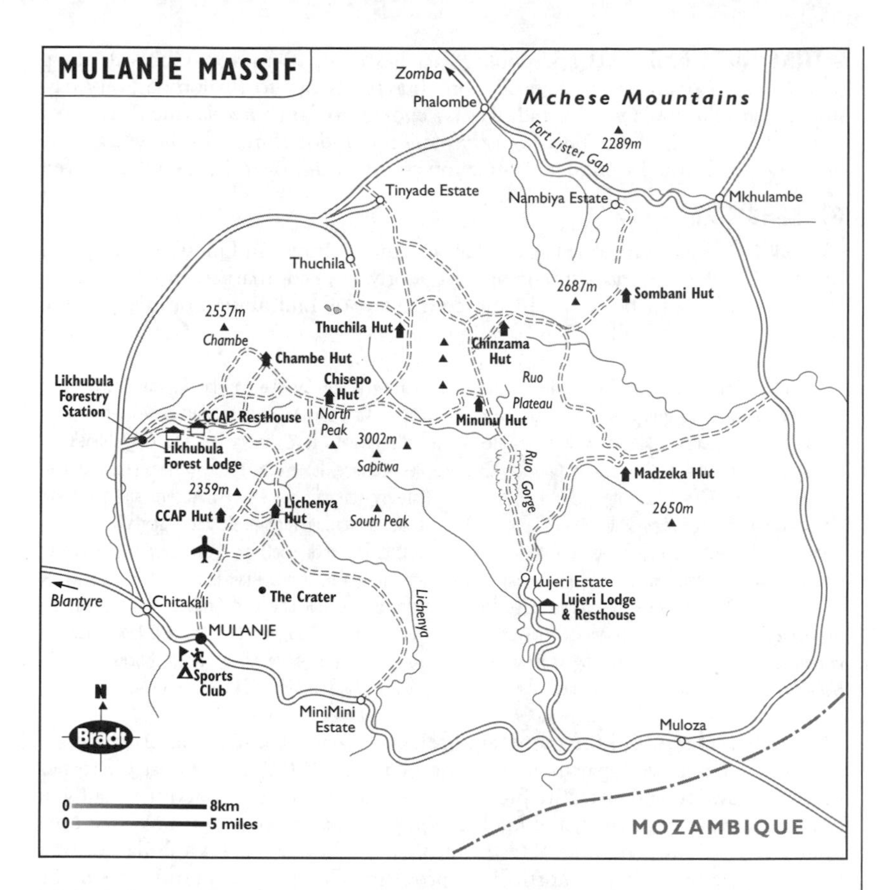

Mulanje has enough walking and climbing potential to keep anybody busy for at least a month. Frank Eastwood's comprehensive *Guide to the Mulanje Massif* (see below) covers almost every possible walking and climbing route.

Many of the streams on Mulanje are stocked with trout. Fishing is allowed with a permit, which can be obtained from the Forestry Office.

FURTHER INFORMATION For up-to-date general information on Mulanje and Mt Mulanje, as well as maps, books and postcards, **InfoMulanje** (*01 466466;* **f** *01 466241;* **e** *infomulanje@sdnp.org.mw or infomulanje@mountmulanje.org.mw*) is the place to contact. They can advise you on the routes to take, book mountain huts, organise your guides and porters, and make lodge accommodation reservations. Frank Eastwood's 150-page *Guide to the Mulanje Massif* (Lorton Communications) is *the* definitive guide to the mountain. Even a casual rambler would have to be crazy to visit Mulanje without this book, and it is absolutely essential for people undertaking lengthy hikes or who intend climbing rockfaces. The guide includes not only a wealth of background information but also detailed descriptions and times for all hiking routes and rock climbs, and maps of the more popular routes including the Skyline and Lichenya paths. *Guide to the Mulanje Massif* is widely available in Blantyre (try the tourist office if you can't find it in a bookshop) and costs around US$5.

The map sales office in Blantyre sells an excellent 1:40,000 contour map of the Mulanje Massif for US$4. It was first published in 1995, and shows all footpaths and huts on the plateau.

GETTING THERE AND AWAY Likhubula village lies about 10km from Chitakale along the Phalombe road. From Chitakale, one bus heads out to Phalombe every day, stopping at Likhubula village, and it's easy enough to find a *matola* ride. It is also a very attractive walk. Likhubula Forestry Station is about 1km from the village; the turn-off is signposted around 50m after you cross a bridge over the Likhubula River.

WHERE TO STAY

Likhubula There is only one basic dollar-a-night resthouse in Likhubula village, as well as a bottle store and a sprawling, but poorly stocked, market. More attractive accommodation can be found in the compound of Likhubula Forestry Station, about 1km from the village.

CCAP Resthouse 01 467762/09 449036. Best value and consists of a group of chalets, each with 6 beds, a shower, toilet, a kitchen with a hotplate and basic utensils, and a dining room. *Chalets US$10 pp, dorms US$5, camping US$5.*

Likhubula Forest Lodge 01 467737. An attractive old forest lodge situated near the Forestry Office in Likhubula. It has self-catering and s/c rooms. You can also book the whole lodge for 16 people for US$150. The kitchen facilities are well equipped but you have to bring your own food. The Likhubula Forest Lodge is near the starting points for the popular Skyline and Chapaluka paths to Chambe Hut as well as the Lichenya path to Lichenya Hut and CCAP Hope's Rest Cottage. It's worth spending some time at the forestry station: the setting is superb and there are some interesting rock pools and waterfalls to be visited. The rock pools are practically in the forest station, while the waterfall lies about 45 mins' walk from the station and is difficult to find without a guide. For US$1.50 per day they will look after your car while you're hiking. *Room prices US$15–35; camping US$5.*

On Mount Mulanje On the mountain itself there are ten huts, nine of which are run by the Forestry Department and one by the CCAP. All huts cost US$5 per person. Firewood and water are provided at all the huts by the watchmen, but you must bring your own food, and kitchen equipment and bedding is provided only at the CCAP Hut. The nine forestry huts can be booked at Likhubula Forestry Station: availability is not normally a problem. Camping is permitted on the mountain, but only around the huts. Staff at the huts cut firewood and light cooking fires. For Mountain Club Members pots and pans are available, but take your own candles.

The most frequently used forestry huts are **Chambe Hut** and **Lichenya Hut**, both of which lie on the eastern side of the massif, within a day's walk of Likhubula Forestry Station. Almost next to Chambe Hut is **France's Cottage**. This cottage is a more comfortable and newer version of the mountain huts. Both lie in the Chambe Basin at an altitude of 1,860m, about three to four hours' walk from Likhubula along the Skyline Path. The hut contains six hard bunks and floor space for an additional ten people. The old Lichenya Hut, on the Lichenya Plateau at an altitude of 1,840m and about five hours' walk from Likhubula Forest Station, burnt down a few years ago, but has since been rebuilt and is now even bigger and better.

The Church-run **CCAP Hut** is also on the Lichenya Plateau, about 2km from Lichenya Hut, and at the higher altitude of 1,995m. A bed at the CCAP Hut costs the same as one at the forestry huts, and bedding is provided. Beds can be booked at the CCAP Resthouse in Likhubula.

The other six forestry huts are only likely to be used by hikers who spend several days on the mountain, or who ascend by one of the more obscure routes.

Thuchila Hut lies on the north of the massif at an altitude of 2,000m near the edge of the Thuchila Plateau, about five hours' walk from Chambe Hut. There are excellent views of the peaks from Thuchila Hut, and it is the best base from which to climb Sapitwa Peak. The hut sleeps up to 16 people, but watch out for rats.

Chinzama Hut lies on the north of the plateau, at an altitude of 2,150m in the Ruo Basin, about a three hours' walk east of Thuchila Hut. It sleeps up to 12 people. Also at the north of the plateau, three hours' walk east of Chinzama, **Sombani Hut** lies at an altitude of 2,080m and sleeps eight people.

In the southwest of the massif, **Madzeka Hut** is around four hours' walk from either Chinzama or Sombani hut. It lies at an altitude of 1,820m and sleeps up to 12 people.

The smallest hut on the Mountain is **Minunu Hut**, which can accommodate up to eight people. The hut is located two hours south of Chinzama Hut.

Chisepo Hut is a newly built hut especially useful for those wanting to climb Sapitwa Peak, the highest point on Mt Mulanje. It is situated between Chambe Hut (2 hours) and Thuchila Hut (3 hours) and can accommodate over 20 people.

HIKING PRACTICALITIES To enter the Forest Reserve an entrance fee of US$1 must be paid at the Forestry Office in Likhubula. This fee helps to conserve and maintain the mountain. You can either go up one of the paths there or choose a different path altogether.

Guides and porters can be hired from all accessible paths around the mountain as they have positioned themselves at the start of all popular paths. It is mandatory to hire porters through the Forestry Office when climbing from Likhubula and Fort Lister because they are on a rotation schedule in order to provide them all with the basic amount of income, not only because it will make your hike more enjoyable. The day rate for porters is set to match those in the Himalayas. On other paths, the chairman of the local porters' group can be asked for advice on whose turn it is next to go up. Most of the guides and porters have been trained to assist tourists.

Organising a hike up Mulanje is a straightforward procedure, either through InfoMulanje or through Likhubula Forestry Station, where you can book mountain huts and arrange porters and guides as required. Guides may soon become mandatory for all visitors, and their services are inexpensive so you might consider hiring one anyway. A porter is strongly recommended, at least for your first day – the ascent of Mulanje is *very* steep. Expenses are minimal: entrance fee is US$1, huts only cost US$5 per person per night, and even a guide or porter shouldn't set you back more than US$7 or so per day. Camping is US$3 per day.

It is worth paring down your luggage to the bare minimum before tackling Mulanje; spare gear can be left at the forestry station or at Doogle's in Blantyre. What you do need is a sleeping bag or thick blanket, and plenty of warm clothing for the chilly highland nights. For those without sleeping bags, there will soon be a scheme where you can book bedding kept in each hut (book through InfoMulanje) – bliss as you won't have to carry it! You must also bring all the food you will need. The ideal place to stock up is in Blantyre, but there is a PTC supermarket in Chitakale opposite the turn-off to Likhubula and, a few hundred metres away, a well-stocked vegetable market.

A week or so would be required to do a full circuit of the huts, and you could spend considerably longer than a week on Mulanje if you so chose, but most visitors settle for two or three days, a day each for the ascent and descent, and one day for exploring part of the plateau. The most popular options are either to loop, using the Chambe Path one way and the Lichenya Path the other way, with a night each at Chambe and Lichenya huts; or else to ascend and descend along the same route, so that you can spend your free day on the mountain without being hindered by a heavy pack. If you aren't carrying bedding, the best hut to use is the CCAP Hut on Lichenya Plateau; the nearby **Sunset Viewpoint** is well worth a visit.

MULANJE PORTERS' RACE

If you're in the area around mid July, ask about the Porters' Race now an international event – organised by the Mountain Club., The Mulanje porters and other entrants race up and down 25km of steep mountain in one of Africa's maddest and most daunting fitness challenges, taking in the heights of the Skyline Path to Chambe. You're unlikely to win, but the prizes have included a bicycle, a plane ride and a night of luxury in a posh hotel. Open to men and women, the title has been held for three consecutive years by Byson Willie. For information, contact the Mountain Club (☎ *01 621520;* e *benlewis@malawi.net*) or InfoMulanje (☎ *01 466466;* f *01 466241;* e *infomulanje@sdnp.org.mw or infomulanje@mountmulanje.org.mw*).

Mulanje can be climbed at any time of year. The dry, cool months from April to September are generally regarded as the best for hiking, though there is a danger of treacherous mists (called *chiperone*) enveloping the massif between May and July. If you are caught in *chiperone* conditions, you must stay put, as walking is very dangerous, even along marked trails. During the rainy season (November to early April), many paths become slippery and some may be temporarily impassable due to flooding. The Skyline Path to Chambe is safe at all times of year as it crosses only one river, and there is a bridge.

Mulanje is not high enough for serious altitude-related illness to be a cause for concern, though people arriving directly from sea level may feel some mild effects at higher altitudes.

Women hiking alone should be careful. They, and anyone else for that matter, should consider hooking up with the Mountain Club of Malawi, who visit Mulanje, or other mountains, almost every weekend. They have a wealth of local knowledge which can save you money and trouble and enhance the whole Mulanje experience. Contact Ben (☎ *01 621520;* e *benlewis@malawi.net*).

Another option is to contact **Tiyende Pamodzi Adventures** (*PO Box 361, Mulanje;* ☎ *01 467737, or through Land and Lake Safaris*), or Look Out Tours (☎ *09 200369*) and they will tailor a hike or trek for you.

PHALOMBE AND MIGOWI

From Likhubula, a road arcs around the northeastern face of Mulanje to the small towns of Phalombe and Migowi. There is a fair amount of public transport as far as Migowi, in the form of the occasional bus and more regular *matola* rides. This link will doubtless improve, as there are plans to tar the road from Zomba through Phalombe to Mulanje.

Phalombe is the site of a rather impressive Catholic Mission, where there are a couple of basic resthouses. The major attraction is the nearby Fort Lister Pass which separates Mulanje from its smaller, more northerly neighbour, Mount Mchese. **Fort Lister** was built by Britain in 1893 to help close off the slave route between Lake Malawi and the Mozambique coast, and it was abandoned in 1902. Within the ruined fortifications lies the grave of Gilbert Stevenson, a cousin of the author Robert Louis Stevenson. Fort Lister lies 10km east of Phalombe, about 500m south of the road through the pass. Phalombe has some brilliant shop names, including the 'Slow But Sure Grocery'.

There is nothing about Migowi that invites superlatives – it's just another pleasant, friendly and totally nondescript Malawian town, no more and no less. It is, however, a potential springboard for a couple of *very* off-the-beaten-track explorations. First up is a back route across little-used dirt roads to Chiradzulu

Mountain and Blantyre. When I tried to catch a lift this way, the presence of a few hopeful locals heading in the same direction suggested that vehicles do roll past from time to time, but I had no luck and eventually returned to Mulanje Boma the way I had come. A second possibility is to continue northwards via Kalinde and Nambazo to the remote, marshy southern shore of Lake Chilwa. As with the Chiradzulu route, this isn't to be approached if you are in a hurry. If you get stuck in Migowi, there are several basic resthouses to choose from.

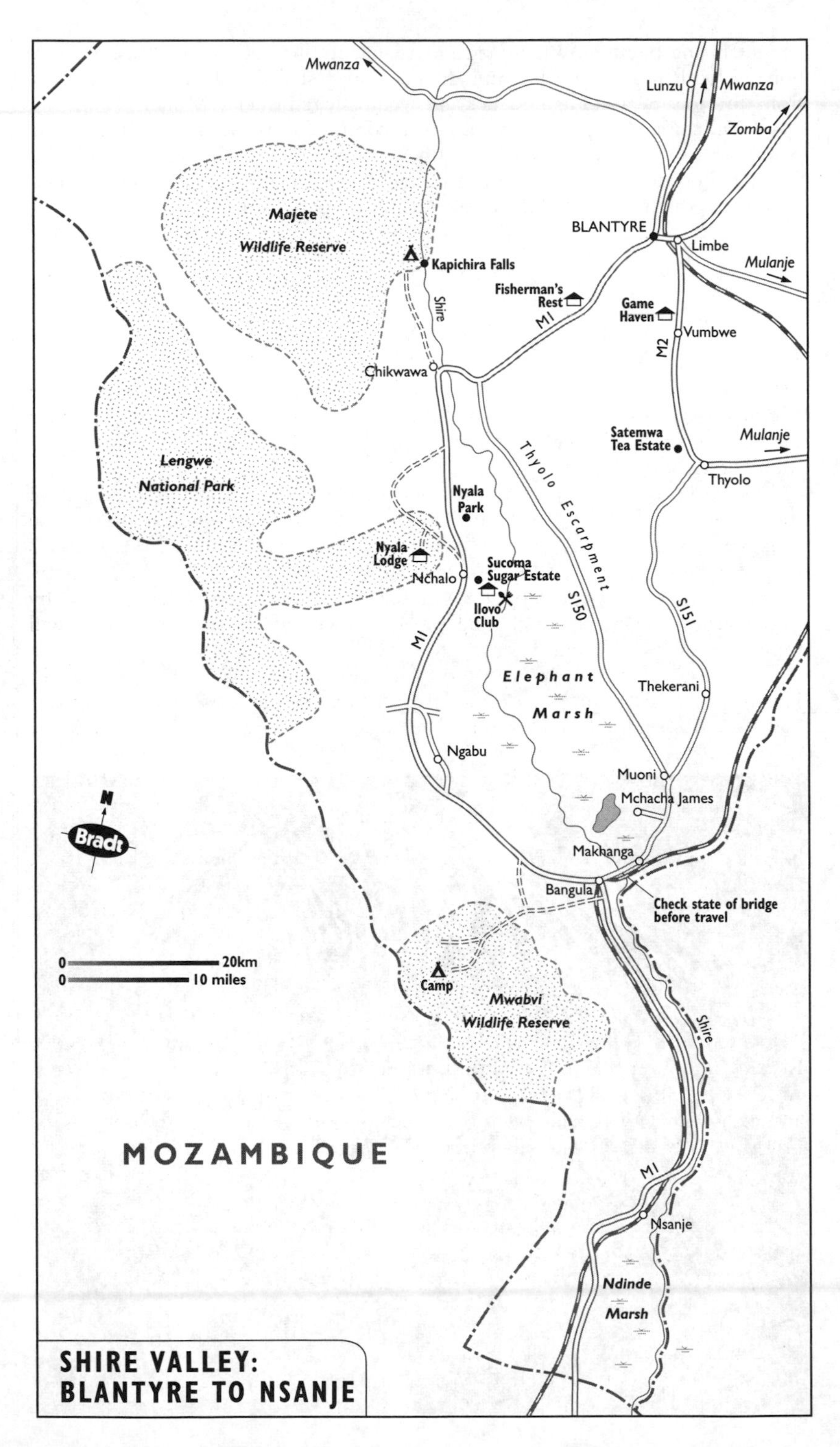
SHIRE VALLEY:
BLANTYRE TO NSANJE
Mwanza
Lunzu
Mwanza
Zomba
Majete
Wildlife Reserve
Kapichira Falls
BLANTYRE
Limbe
Mulanje
Fisherman's
Rest
Game
Haven
Vumbwe
Shire
M1
M2
Chikwawa
Satemwa
Tea Estate
Mulanje
Thyolo
Thyolo Escarpment
Lengwe
National Park
Nyala
Park
Nyala
Lodge
Sucoma
Sugar Estate
Nchalo
Ilovo
Club
S150
S151
M1
Elephant
Marsh
Thekerani
Ngabu
Muoni
Mchacha James
N
Bradt
Makhanga
Bangula
Check state of bridge
before travel
0 20km
0 10 miles
Camp
Mwabvi
Wildlife Reserve
Shire
MOZAMBIQUE
M1
Nsanje
Ndinde
Marsh

18

The Shire Valley

Southwest of Blantyre, the M1 snakes and slithers over the Thyolo Escarpment, offering awesome views across the hills of Majete Wildlife Reserve and Mozambique, before it descends to the steamy lowlands of the Shire Valley. From the lurching hairpin bends you see range after range of mountains, then finally the meandering Shire River below.

Despite a reasonably dense human population, the Shire Valley retains much of the atmosphere of wild, untrammelled Africa. In large part, this is due to the sluggish presence of the wide and lushly vegetated Shire River, still home to hippopotamus and countless crocodile. But even among the people, the Shire Valley seems less influenced by the West than much of modern Africa – if at any stage you are disenchanted with modern Africa, then a visit to the Lower Shire will remind you why you came.

The Shire Valley was the first part of Malawi to be visited by Europeans. In January 1859, Livingstone's Zambezi Expedition steamed up the Shire until its path was blocked by the cataracts that lie on what is now the southern border of the Majete Wildlife Reserve. When Livingstone travelled up the Shire again in 1861, to help Bishop Mackenzie establish the first mission in central Africa, much of the region was under the indirect control of Portuguese slavers. Worse still was to greet Livingstone on his final trip up the river in 1863 – the Shire had become, in the words of Dr Rowley, another member of the expedition, 'literally a river of death'. The banks were lined with dead and emaciated Africans; one member of the expedition calculated that a corpse floated past them every three hours.

The malaria that is hyperendemic to the Shire River claimed the lives of several members of Livingstone's expedition. In 1862, Bishop Mackenzie died on a now-sunken island at the confluence of the Ruo and Shire near Bangula. Two other clergymen, Rev Scudamore and Dr Dickinson, and the 25-year-old geologist Richard Thornton, all died in the Chikwawa area in 1863.

Today, the Shire Valley doesn't see a great deal of tourism, despite its raw beauty and many attractions. Aside from the Shire itself, a river rich in atmosphere and historical connections, with 15km of rapids before the still waters of the Elephant Marsh, this area boasts two little-visited wildlife reserves, Majete and Mwabvi, as well as Lengwe National Park and Nyala Park, the private game park at the Sucoma Sugar Estates. The Shire Valley is the most rewarding area for birdwatching. For backpackers, who may find the reserves difficult to reach without transport, there is the quite wonderful and highly accessible Elephant Marsh near Bangula.

CLIMATE

The Shire Valley is the lowest-lying part of Malawi, dropping to an altitude of 38m above sea level near Nsanje, and it is also one of the hottest. The most pleasant time to visit is from June to August, when the weather is reasonably cool and dry, and the wildlife reserves offer the best game viewing. Towards the end of the dry season and during the rains, the Shire Valley is uncomfortably hot and very humid.

The climate and altitude of the Shire Valley create ideal breeding conditions for mosquitoes. Many expatriates regard this area to be worse for malaria than even Lake Malawi, particularly during the hot rainy months between October and April, so make every effort to avoid being bitten by mosquitoes.

GETTING AROUND

The southern extension of the M1 starts at Blantyre and continues to the Mozambican border, past the towns of Chikwawa, Nchalo, Bangula and Nsanje. The M1 is surfaced until just after Nchalo. The S151 connects back round the other side of the Elephant Marsh under the escarpment (however still without a bridge over the Shire out of Bangula in 2006). During the rains you would be wise to take a 4x4, as most side roads which lead to other places of interest in the Shire Valley may become impassable in anything less after heavy rain.

The M1 between Blantyre and Nsanje is served by buses. Services are not as regular as in some other parts of the country, but if you travel early in the day you should have no difficulty getting between any two points along the M1 using a combination of buses and *matola* rides. Without private transport, reaching the reserves to the west of the M1 is rather more problematic, and even if you could get to the entrance gates, it's unlikely you'd be allowed to enter on foot. The two major points of interest which are accessible to people using public transport are the Sucoma Sugar Estate and the fascinating Elephant Marsh.

CHIKWAWA

Chikwawa is a sprawling town on the west bank of the Shire a couple of kilometres from the M1 towards Majete Wildlife Reserve. The area immediately around Chikwawa is of interest mainly to bird enthusiasts. About 1km out of town, in September, a nesting colony of carmine bee-eaters can be reached by following the dirt road opposite the police station to the west bank of the Shire River. On the M1, about 3km south of the turn-off to Chikwawa, the Kasinthula fish ponds are noted for waterbirds, particularly the large numbers of migrant waders which are attracted to the area between July and December.

WHERE TO STAY There are several resthouses in Chikwawa, including:

Machenga Motel 01 420313. Clean rooms. The motel has its own restaurant serving *nsima* and meat dishes for MK250–500. *Sgl/dbl/king size MK900/1,500/3,000.*

MAJETE WILDLIFE RESERVE

Majete Wildlife Reserve (*park entry fees are US$20 for visitors plus US$2 for the vehicle*) protects a 691km² area of hilly *brachystegia* woodland sloping down to the western bank of the Shire River. Since 2003 it has been managed by African Parks, with sister projects in South Africa, Ethiopia, Zambia and Democratic Republic of Congo. The main drive of the management is wildlife conservation and tourism is sure to follow. Already well populated with animals, including black rhinoceros, buffalo, sable, nyala, hartebeest, eland, zebra, impala, warthog and bushbuck, elephant are due to be reintroduced in 2006 (they were poached out in the early 1990s). The park now has a network of roads throughout; though please beware of tortoises crossing. The real attraction of Majete is its impressive geography, as the Shire River tears down through the steep hills along the Murchison cataracts, especially the **Kapichira Falls** near the park entrance, though these are slightly blemished by the hydro-electric scheme above them. You can imagine how depressed Livingstone felt when he saw this huge torrent of water. If you can persuade a ranger to guide you on a walk, this is exhilarating walking country, with a mass of birds in the riparian forest fringing the riverbanks. The only known breeding site of the rock pratincole is on a small island near to Kapichira Falls and the solitary grave of Richard Thornton. This rare bird is a good indicator of the biodiversity of Majete (especially after the effect of the Kapichira Dam). It is also a most inspiring conservation area. My advice is to go there before anyone else discovers it. For conservation information visit www.africanparks-conservation.com.

GETTING THERE AND AWAY Majete lies about 20km from Chikwawa along a rough dirt road. Turn into Chikwawa off the M1, then carry straight on. The turn-off to Majete is signposted from Chikwawa.

WHERE TO STAY There is no longer any accommodation or established camping facilities within the reserve, though please ask as **Majete Safari Camp**, a private establishment about 5km outside the entrance gate, may soon reopen. Camping is permitted in several areas inside Majete, often near yet another set of falls. It's likely that some accommodation will become available through African Parks (**e** *majete@mw.celtelplus.com*).

LENGWE NATIONAL PARK

This 887km² national park (*park entry fee US$5 pp per 24 hours*) lies along the Mozambican border west of the Shire River. Only the eastern extension of the park has been developed for tourism, but within this small area there is a good network of roads, as well as several viewing hides and an inexpensive camp and campsite. With a ranger it is possible to hike all day in this majestic park.

Though relatively arid, with an annual rainfall figure of well under 1,000mm, Lengwe is densely vegetated. There is lush riparian woodland along some of the watercourses, and the remainder of the park is covered in wooded savanna and dense thickets interspersed with some impressive stands of baobab and palm trees. Tourist traffic is low, and dense vegetation lends the winding roads a secluded air.

The variety of large mammals present in Lengwe isn't great, but game viewing is nonetheless good. The park supports the most northerly population of the beautiful nyala antelope, rare elsewhere but common here. Lengwe is also a good place to see samango monkeys; a troop lives in the woodland around the main hide. Other mammals you should see are impala, bushbuck, warthog, vervet monkey and baboons, and with a bit of luck buffalo and greater kudu. The only large predators in the reserve are spotted hyena and leopard. Birds are a-plenty: among the more interesting species likely to be seen are woolly-necked stalk, trumpeter hornbill, racquet-tailed roller and yellow-spotted nicator, and it's always magical to watch a heron fishing for frogs through the grass or a Boehm's bee-eater hawking for insects.

In the evening Nyala Lodge will organise a visit to Ndakwera village where you can learn all about local life, including food, beer and dancing. There are plans afoot (and part of a building) to build a heritage centre at the gate.

A useful booklet and map can be bought at the gate for a nominal fee.

GETTING THERE AND AWAY The turn-off to Lengwe is on the M1 a few kilometres north of Nchalo. From the turn-off, it's a 6km drive through a sugar plantation to the gate. It's a straight and uninspiring road through the sugar, which makes it all the more surprising when you come to the sudden trees of Lengwe National Park. Without transport, you could certainly walk to the gate, where you would need to ring the lodge to see if there is anyone who could collect you. Nyala Lodge and the campsite are only just inside, but you are not allowed to enter the park without a vehicle on account of buffalo and other animals. It's also worth noting here that there is an airstrip at Sucoma Sugar Estate should you wish to charter a plane.

WHERE TO STAY

Nyala Lodge About 1km from the entrance gate. Bookings can be made through Jambo Safaris; 08 123709/01 835356. Wonderfully sultry and an extremely comfortable place to stay, with fans or AC in each chalet. There is a small swimming pool near the bar/dining area. I can recommend an early-morning walk. Jambo Safaris will also be able to organise day trips into Nyala Park, and Majete and Mwabvi game reserves as well as the dugout tours from the east bank of the Elephant Marsh. They can also take you for an evening at Ndakwera Culural Village for $15 pp. The Sunday *brai* is a meatfest occasion that many people in the area look forward to. *Sgl/dbl US$70/120 (children 3–12 US$30) inc dinner, BB as well as one game activity.*

You can pitch a tent at the **Lengwe campsite**. *US$5 pp.*

The youth hostel is currently used by rangers during the rains and school groups and Wildlife Society students in the dry season.

NCHALO

The small town straddling the M1 south of Lengwe is, in practice, little more than an extension of the massive Sucoma Sugar Estate, the entrance to which lies in the town centre. There is no compelling reason for travellers to stay in Nchalo, though there are a few resthouses should the need arise. There is also a PTC supermarket and a good market if you're stocking up for a visit to Lengwe or elsewhere.

There is certainly a case for popping into **Sucoma Sugar Estate**, especially if you have a car. The place to head for is the Sports Club, which lies on the bank of the Shire about 6km from the estate's entrance gate. The club has pleasant self-contained single/double rooms for US$45/63 including dinner, bed and breakfast. From the grounds (and from the pontoons near the bar) you will normally see a good variety of birds, as well as hippos and crocs if you are lucky. Don't be tempted to swim here; it's infested with enormous crocodiles. The green fee on the 18- and 9-hole golf courses is US$4, while tennis, squash and swimming are covered in your day membership (US$3). The atmosphere is very friendly and the food good. Accommodation is best booked in advance (*01 425200*).

Tours of the sugar estates and the sugar factory can sometimes be arranged through the human resources manager on the estate.

The small game park on the estate, **Nyala Park** (*park entry fee US$1*) is a popular place to visit, with several non-indigenous species including giraffe, oribi and wildebeest. Even during the green season you are guaranteed to see most game. Nyala Park is to the north of Nchalo, and can be accessed through the sugar fields from the gate opposite Lengwe's approach road. Fenced and without any predators it's possible to walk here. About 12km south of Nchalo, near the township of Ngabu, is the comfortable **Ngabu Inn** which has self-contained double rooms for US$10 as well as a campsite, restaurant and bar.

BANGULA

Bangula lies on the Mozambican border near the confluence of the Ruo and Shire rivers. It is the obvious base for visits to the Elephant Marsh (though travellers without their own transport might be better staying the night at Makhanga). The best place to stay in Bangula is the **Council Resthouse** which has large, self-contained doubles for s US$2 and rooms using communal showers for US$1. There are also several private resthouses. Meals are served at **Jehova's Restaurant** (next to the PTC supermarket), but don't let the voluminous and tantalising menu painted on the wall raise your hopes too much – a fairly standard plate of chicken and rice is usually about all that's on offer.

MWABVI WILDLIFE RESERVE

This small, little-known and infrequently visited reserve lies in the far south of Malawi near the Mozambican border. The rugged terrain supports a mixture of *brachystegia*, mopane and acacia woodland. Though poaching has had a drastic effect on animal numbers, there are plans for reintroduction by Project African Wilderness, in conjunction with Barefoot Safaris and the Department of National Parks and Wildlife. Among the large mammals still to be found in Mwabvi are lion, greater kudu, sable antelope, bushbuck, nyala, baboon, vervet monkey, and leopard. The thickets protect several bird species more normally associated with coastal habitats, for instance Rudd's apalis, Woodward's batis and grey sunbird. It's the type of African wilderness that feels as if it's waiting for the world to begin and the animals to re-enter the stage.

GETTING THERE AND AWAY Coming from Blantyre, the turn-off to Mwabvi lies on the M1 just before Bangula, roughly 5km after you cross the bridge over the Thangadzi River. Turn right onto this earth road and follow the signs (and your nose) as you will need to take another right turn and then a right-hand fork. This track leads to the entrance gate of the reserve, where you must sign in.

Ideally, you want to visit the reserve in a 4x4, though a saloon with high clearance should make it through in the dry season. Mwabvi is not a practical destination without your own transport.

WHERE TO STAY Camping is the only form of accommodation at Mwabvi and you will have to take all your own provisions. The main camp is 10km from the gate. There is good water on site and an ablution block is due to be built in 2006. There is a second campsite in the bush, meaning that you can now hike between the two camps. Game rangers will normally also accompany you on walks to Ndipitakuti Gorge and a nearby sandstone pillar. For road conditions, bookings and advice, contact Barefoot Safaris (*01 707346/09 307359; e barefoot@globemw.net; www.barefoot-safaris.net*). For conservation information go to www.projectafricanwilderness.org.

ELEPHANT MARSH

This 65km long by 19km wide permanent marsh forms the eastern floodplain of the Shire River. It's a lush, beautiful area with a rich sense of place; and even if you're not into birds, this area is evidently a paradise for them. In the south of the marsh the water is thick with purple-flowered hyacinth and white lilies, and the surrounding area is studded with massive baobab trees and tall palms. The northern part is a maze of narrow channels where crocodiles slide dangerously into the water. Only some years ago this was home to one of the densest populations of hippo in Malawi, and there are hopefully still plenty secretly hiding in the reeds.

Elephant Marsh was named by Livingstone, who, on his first expedition up the Shire, recorded seeing a herd of around 800 elephants coming to drink. The elephants were mostly shot out by the early 20th century, but, although it is not protected in any way, the marsh remains a nature sanctuary of note. It supports Malawi's largest population of crocodiles, as well as hippos and smaller mammals such as otters. Of most interest, however, are the birds attracted to the marsh – they are spectacular both in number and variety

The best way to explore Elephant Marsh is by boat. Boat trips can be organised in **Mchacha James**, a small village on the edge of the marsh about 15km from Bangula beyond Makhanga. The northern section is not readily accessible, with dangerous currents. For the thrilling trip through the whole marsh, talk to Jambo Safaris in Blantyre or Nyala Lodge in Lengwe National Park; they can also arrange day trips from Lengwe.

GETTING THERE AND AWAY To reach Mchacha James from Bangula, you need first to get to Makhanga village, which lies about 10km east of the M1 along a road forking out of Bangula town centre 100m or so south of the railway crossing. There is a fair amount of *matola* transport to Makhanga, though in wet years, when the marsh practically laps the Bangula–Makhanga road, the abundant birdlife is a good inducement to walk. If the bridge is still down on the S152 to Machacha James you will still be able to take a boat across and then use a bicycle-taxi or walk up to James. The best plan is to ask beforehand if you're in your own vehicle. The other option is to use the S150 road along the bottom of the escarpment past Nsanje. This is often very corrugated in the dry, and slippery and pot-holed in the wet, but a scenic road nonetheless.

Mchacha James lies on the edge of the marsh about an hour's walk from Makhanga. To get there, don't be afraid to ask the way – 'James' is the key word. You will follow the main road out of Makhanga towards Muona, then 2km past the signpost in Makhanga reading 'Ministry of Culture and Education', an unsignposted turn-off to the left of the Muona Road leads to the village. There are several left forks in this area – if you're unsure which one to take, follow the Muona road until you notice an idiosyncratic double-storey building (signed 'Pentecostal Holiness Church') to your left, then turn back towards Makhanga and take the first turn-off, now to your right and only 100m from the church.

From the turn-off, you'll wander through a sprawling village for about 4km before you reach a mosque. The boat owners live near the mosque so just ask around: chances are they'll find you before you find them.

BOAT TRIPS At Mchacha James, you can take out a dugout (please check for stability before you go out into croc waters). The boatmen will punt through the waters, often singing or whistling gently in accompaniment. The rate for boat hire will depend on how long you want to go out for, and also on your negotiating skills: a two-hour trip should cost between US$5 and US$10 per boat.

Gliding silently along the water, surrounded by lush vegetation and with birds in every direction, is sheer visual bliss; for many it's an unquestionable highlight of time spent in Malawi. If in luck you will find a boatman articulate and knowledgeable about every aspect of the marsh, and they are usually excellent bird guides, likely to generate enthusiasm in the most aviphobic of passengers. To whet the appetite of bird enthusiasts, we saw around 30 species in two hours, including fish eagle, purple and goliath heron, glossy ibis, openbill and yellow-billed stork, malachite kingfisher and – two birds which rank highly on many birders' most-wanted list – the cryptically marked pygmy goose and the aptly named African skimmer.

If you don't have a private vehicle, it's probably wise to spend the night before you explore the marsh in Makhanga. It is possible to visit Mchacha James as a day trip from Bangula, but the marsh is ideally explored in the early morning, so it's best to overnight as nearby as possible. It would also make sense, provided that you arrive in Makhanga early enough, to do a reconnaissance trip to Mchacha James and make arrangements for a boat the afternoon before you intend to go out on the marsh.

WHERE TO STAY There is at least one resthouse in Makhanga: the **Tiyesembo Resthouse,** with single rooms for US$1 and doubles with a fan for US$2. There is no running water, and it doesn't appear to serve meals so bring some food with you from Bangula. On the plus side, the bar has a fridge filled with cold soft drinks and beers.

If you have a vehicle, it's more tempting to stay at one of the resthouses in Bangula (see *Bangula* above). As far as I am aware, there is no accommodation in Mchacha James itself, though if you have a tent you could presumably ask around for somewhere to camp free.

BACKROADS NORTH OF ELEPHANT MARSH

From Mchacha James, the S151 continues in a northerly direction to Muona Mission, where it forks along two little-used routes, both of which are often unusable during the rainy season, but which might repay exploration at other times of the year.

The S150 continues from Muona along the east bank of the marsh below the Thyolo Escarpment. This road is generally flooded after rains, as the marsh expands, but it should be passable during the dry season, and it can offer excellent birding as it sticks close to the marsh's edge.

The S151 climbs the Thyolo Escarpment north of Muona, eventually emerging at Thyolo Town. The main attraction of this road is the dramatic views back to the Shire Valley during the ascent. In a 4x4 you can normally use the S151 at any time of year. If you have a saloon car, then you should enquire about the current condition before you set off.

There is no public transport along either route, and private vehicles are few and far between, so hitching could prove very difficult.

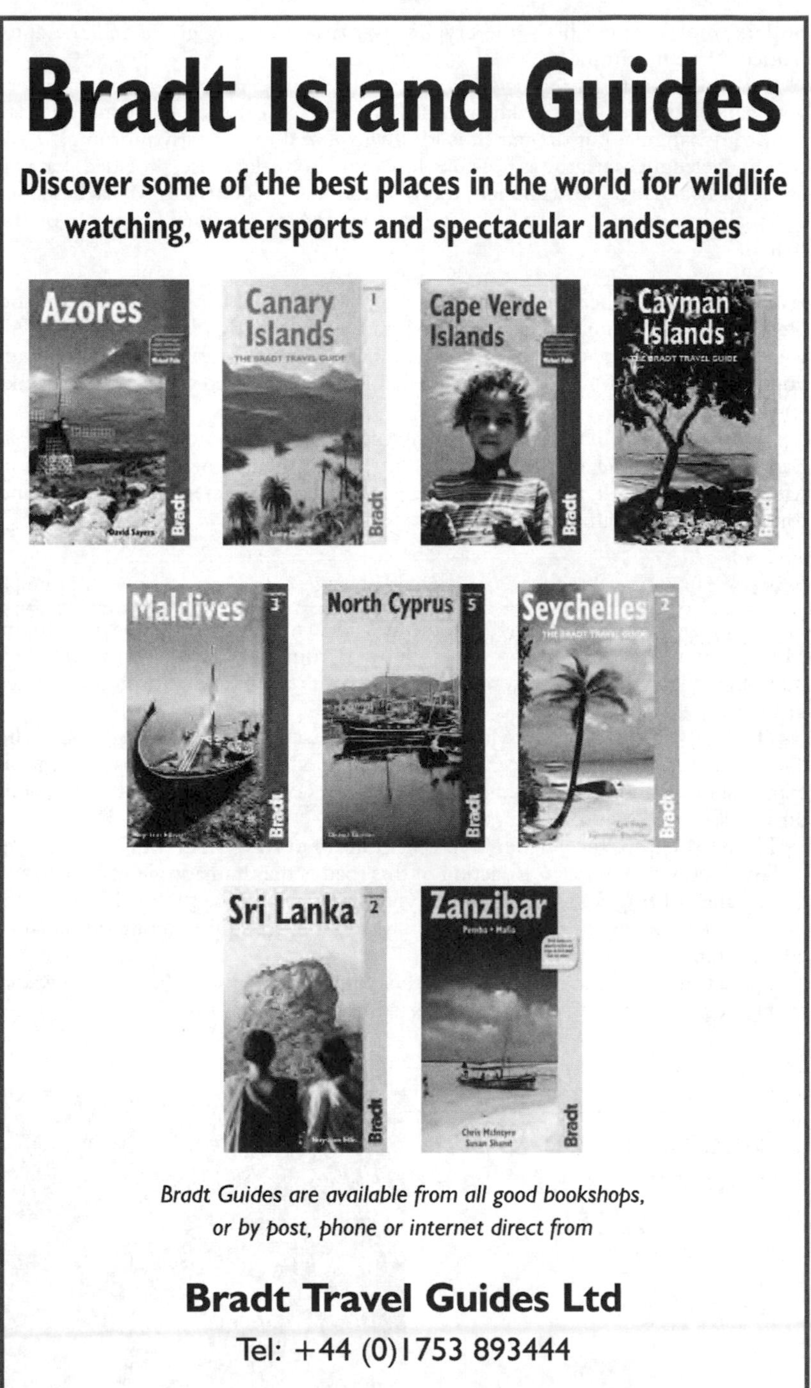
Bradt Island Guides
Discover some of the best places in the world for wildlife watching, watersports and spectacular landscapes
Azores
Canary Islands
Cape Verde Islands
Cayman Islands
Maldives
North Cyprus
Seychelles
Sri Lanka
Zanzibar
Bradt Guides are available from all good bookshops, or by post, phone or internet direct from
Bradt Travel Guides Ltd
Tel: +44 (0)1753 893444
www.bradtguides.com

Appendix I

LANGUAGE

PRONUNCIATION In Chichewa, as in most Bantu languages, almost all words and syllables end with a vowel. There are five vowel sounds, represented by A, E, I, O and U. These vowel sounds have no close equivalents in the English language; they are, however, practically identical to the vowel sounds of A, E, I, O and OU in French. Where two vowels follow each other, they are not compounded but instead each retains its pure sound.

Consonants generally have a similar sound to their English equivalent, though 'j' is always pronounced as 'dj'; 'ch' is far softer than the English 'ch'; 'ph' is pronounced as a breathy 'p' as opposed to an 'f', and 'r' is often interchangeable with 'l'. To give some examples, Rumphi is pronounced more like Rumpi than Rumfi, and Karonga may sometimes be pronounced in a way that sounds closer to Kalonga.

GRAMMAR AND TENSE The grammar and use of tenses in Bantu languages is very different from that of English or any other European language. It is not something that tourists wanting to know a few basic words and phrases need concern themselves with. People who want to familiarise themselves with Chichewa grammar and tenses are advised to buy a copy of Rev Salaum's *Chichewa Intensive Course* (Likuni Press), which was first published in 1969 and went into a third edition in 1993. If you can't find it in a bookshop, then contact the publishers directly at PO Box 133, Lilongwe (*01 721388*; f *01 721141*).

GREETINGS AND PHRASES

Hello	*Moni*
How are you?	*Muli bwanji?*
Fine (and you?)	*Ndiri bwino (kaya inu?)*
Thank you	*Zikomo (or ziko)*
What's your name?	*Dzina lanu ndani?*
How much (price)?	*Ndalama zingati?*
I don't understand	*Sindikumva*
Where are you going?	*Mukupita kuti?*
I'm going to Lilongwe	*Ndikupita ku Lilongwe*
I want .../I don't want ...	*Ndikufuna .../Sindikufuna ...*
Goodbye	*Khalani Bwino*

SOME USEFUL WORDS

animal	*nyama*	hyena	*fisi*
arrive	*fika*	journey	*ulendo*
baboon	*nyani*	large	*kula*
banana	*nthochi*	meat	*nyama*
buffalo	*njati*	milk	*mkaka*
cattle	*ngombe*	mosquito	*udzudzu*
chicken	*nkhuku*	mountain	*phiri*

egg	*dzira*	name	*dzina*
elephant	*njobvu*	near	*pafupi*
English (language)	*Chizungu*	no	*ai*
enough	*basi*	person	*munthu*
European	*Mazungu*	rain	*mvula*
far	*kutali*	salt	*mchere*
fish	*nsomba*	small	*ngono*
food	*kudya*	swamp	*dambo*
friend	*bwenzi*	tent	*hema*
goat	*mbuzi*	today	*lero*
god	*mulungu*	tomorrow	*m'mawa*
government	*boma*	water	*madzi*
hippo	*mvuu*	yes	*inde*
honey	*uchi*	yesterday	*dzulo*
house	*nyumba*		

GLOSSARY OF VERNACULAR AND SCIENTIFIC WORDS

acacia — A genus of thorny trees dominant in many parts of Africa, but not in Malawi where acacia woodland is largely replaced by *brachystegia*.

bakkie — South African word for a pick-up truck.

banda — In some African languages, this literally means home, but in hotel-speak it can refer to any detached accommodation unit.

boma — In Malawi and other parts of central Africa, the *boma* is the administrative part of town, often a discrete entity to the commercial centre of that town. Some game lodges use the word *boma* to refer to a stockaded outdoor dining area.

braai — Afrikaans word meaning 'barbecue', used widely in southern Africa.

brachystegia — The type of woodland that is dominant in Malawi, characterised by trees of the genus *brachystegia* and often referred to as '*miombo* woodland'.

buck — Any antelope.

chamba — Marijuana.

chambo — The main eating fish caught in Lake Malawi.

chiperone — Heavy mists that occur seasonally in highland areas such as Mount Mulanje.

chitenga — Sarong-type cloth worn by most Malawian women.

dambo — Seasonal or perennial marsh, normally fringing a river.

endemic — In the context of this guide, a race or species found nowhere else but in the area or country to which it is allocated.

exotic — A term that may cause some confusion as it is often abused in travel literature. An exotic species is one that has been introduced to an area; in Malawi, the pine plantations on Nyika are exotic, the palms that line the Shire River are indigenous.

koppie — Small hill, an Afrikaans term widely used in this part of Africa.

matola — A light vehicle or truck that carries paying passengers, often informally.

mazungu — Term used throughout east Africa for a white person, plural *wazungu*.

mielie — Term used throughout southern Africa for maize (corn).

nsima — Maize porridge that is the staple diet of most Malawians.

nyama — Any meat, but especially beef.

rondavel — Used by hotels to refer to a *banda* built in the round shape of an African hut.

south — South Africa – a lot of Malawians will tell you they used to work 'south'.

trading centre — Any village large enough to have a market or small shop.

Appendix 2

FURTHER READING

Please note that books can be expensive in Malawi, so it's best to get hold of them before you arrive.

TRAVEL GUIDES Several quality coffee-table books on Malawi have been published in recent years:

Johnston, Frank and Ferrar, Sandy *Malawi – the warm heart of Africa* Central Africana Ltd, 2002.
Johnston, Frank *Malawi: Lake of Stars* Central Africana Ltd, 1991. An attractively photographed and presented book, and available in most bookshops in Malawi is this updated view of Malawi.
Kelly, David *Malawi – Endangered Beauty* David Kelly, 2005. A lavish book celebrating Malawi's natural heritage with paintings by David Kelly and text contributions from conservationists around Malawi. An entertaining and informative read.

As a second source of practical travel information:

Douglas, John and White, Kelly *Spectrum Guide to Malawi* Spectrum, 2003. A lavishly illustrated and informative guidebook written by two Malawi experts.

Several guidebooks to specific regions or places of interest in Malawi are available in the country. Generally these books are inexpensive and easy to get hold of in Lilongwe and Blantyre. Absolutely essential if you are visiting the places they cover, they are:

Eastwood, Frank *Guide to the Mulanje Massif* Lorton Communications, 1988.
Johnson, Sigrid Anna *Visitor's Guide to Nyika National Park, Malawi* Mbabazi Book Trust.
Mundy, H & K *Zomba Mountain: A Walkers' Guide* Montfort Press.

The Wildlife Society of Malawi publishes a range of inexpensive booklets and bird checklists covering all the main national parks and game reserves. Also published by the Wildlife Society, and of particular interest to walkers, birdwatchers and Malawian residents, are Judy Carter's *Day Outings from Lilongwe* (1991) and Peter Barton's *Day Outings from Blantyre*, the latter updated in 1997.

HISTORY AND BACKGROUND

Ransford, Oliver *Livingstone's Lake* John Murray, 1966. One of the better general books written about Malawi. Ransford's accessible writing style and anecdotal approach to history make this book a pleasure to read, even if some of the views expressed by the author seem a little culture-bound 30 years after they were written. This book is out of print but is easily found in libraries in the UK and South Africa.

Overview of central African history

Needham, Mashingaidze and Bhebe *From Iron Age to Independence: A History of Central Africa* Longman, 1974 and 1984.

Tindall, P *History of Central Africa* Longman, 1985.

Wilson, D *A History of South and Central Africa* Cambridge University Press, 1975. All these books are slightly on the dry side; I found the most informative and readable to be the one by Needham, Mashingaidze and Bhebe.

Biographies of Livingstone and books about the Zambezi Expedition

Hibbert, Christopher and Livingstone, David *The Life and African Explorations of David Livingstone* Cooper Square Press, 2002. A first-person retelling of Livingstone's travels, a good aeroplane novel and a gripping if slightly elaborated read.

Jeals, Tim *Livingstone* Heinemann, 1973. A better book which was recently updated and reprinted in paperback.

Liebowitz, Daniel *The Physician and the Slave Trade: John Kirk, the Livingstone Expeditions, and the Crusade Against Slavery in East Africa* W H Freeman & Co Ltd, 1998. A recent biography about one of your authors' forebears.

Ransford, Oliver *David Livingstone: The Dark Interior* John Murray, 1978. Also a good read, but more difficult to get hold of.

Colonisation, politics and culture of Africa

Hartley, Aidan *The Zanzibar Chest* Harper Perennial, 2003. A passionate account of Africa's hotspots as seen by an African news correspondent, insightful and compelling.

Mandela, Nelson *Long Walk to Freedom* Time Warner Books UK, 2000.

Packenham, Thomas *The Scramble for Africa* Weidenfeld & Nicholson, 1991. You can't do better than Thomas Packenham's award-winning and wonderfully readable book.

Russell, Alec *Big Men Little People* Pan, 1999. A wry look at Africa's leaders.

Malawi

Buckley, Bea *My Malawi Journal* Athena Press Ltd, 2003. Written by a Peace Corps volunteer about her life in a Malawian village.

Morris, Brian *The Power of Animals, An Ethnography* Berg, 2000. A somewhat dense but fascinating book showing how closely Malawian culture is related to wildlife.

Ó Máille, Padraíg *Living Dangerously – A Memoir of Political Change in Malawi.* A dark but highly readable book covering Banda's last years.

Schoffeleers, Matthew and Roscoe, Adrian *Land of Fire: Oral Literature from Malawi* Popular Publications, 1985. An interesting book if you want to know more about traditional Malawian beliefs.

Shepperson and Price, *Independent African – John Chilembwe and the Nyasaland Rising of 1915* CLAIM, 2000.

Theroux, Paul *Dark Star Safari* Penguin Books Ltd, 2003. Retracing his footsteps through Africa and through Malawi, the author comes to depressing conclusions.

Gibbs, James (ed) *Nine Malawian Plays*, Popular Publications, Limbe.

King, Michael and Elspeth *The Story of Medicine and Disease in Malawi: The 130 Years Since Livingstone* Arco Books, 1992 and *The Great Rift* Arco Books, 2000. Two compelling books written by a surgeon and wife team Michael and Elspeth King about their experiences in Malawi's hospitals:

FIELD GUIDES

A number of excellent field guides to African mammals have been published in the last few years:

Baumann, Gunter *Photographic Guide to Flowers of Malawi, 2006.* Newly published glossy and informative book on Malawi's flora.

Dowsett-Lemaire, Françoise and Dowsett, Robert *The Birds of Malawi – An Atlas and Handbook* Tauraco Press, 2006. A long-awaited all-in-one comprehensive guide of birds found in Malawi.
Este, Richard *The Safari Companion* Russell Friedman Books, South Africa; Chelsea Green, USA; Green Books, UK, 1999. Rather more bulky than any of the above guides, but highly recommended if weight isn't a consideration, most aptly described as a field guide to the behaviour of African mammals.
Kingdon, Jonathan *Field Guide to African Mammals* Academic Press, 1997. For those whose interest extends to small mammals, this guide is highly recommended.
La Croix *Malawi Orchids Volume 1: Epiphytic Orchids* NFPS, 1983. For orchid enthusiasts.
Lewis, Reinthall and Trendall *Guide to the Fishes of Lake Malawi National Park* Worldwide Fund for Nature. A field guide to the fish of Lake Malawi which is comprehensive within the confines of the national park, and pretty useful elsewhere in the lake.
Moriarty, Audrey *Wild Flowers of Malawi* Purnell, 1975. Now a rare book, but the best field guide.
Newman, Kenneth *Birds of Malawi* (1999) and the same author's *Birds of Southern Africa* Southern Book Publishers, South Africa, 2002. This combination of two books includes a full checklist of every bird that has been recorded in Malawi, complete with comprehensive details of distribution and status as well as giving the page number on which the bird is described in Newman's *Birds of Southern Africa*.
Roberts Multimedia Birds of Southern Africa CD-ROM Southern African Birding, 1997–2003.
Shorter, Clare *An Introduction to the Common Trees of Malawi* Wildlife Society of Malawi.
Sinclair, Ian and Ryan, Peter *Birds of Africa – A Complete Illustrated Field Guide to the Birds South of the Sahara* Struik. A well laid-out guide with useful maps and good illustrations.
Stuart, Tilde and Chris *Southern, Central and East African Mammals: A Photographic Guide* Struik, South Africa, 1992. This is the one to go for if weight is a consideration and you're content to stick with identifying large mammals. Despite being very compact. It covers 150 large mammal species found in the region.
Stuart, Tilde and Chris *The Larger Mammals of Africa* Struik, South Africa, 1997. A more comprehensive tome by the same authors, and a better buy for those who aren't carrying their luggage on their back. *Watching Wildlife: Southern Africa* Lonely Planet.

NOVELS

Theroux, Paul *Jungle Lovers* Ballantine Books, 1989.
Theroux, Paul *My Secret History* Penguin, 1990.
van der Post, Laurens *Venture to the Interior* Vintage, 2002.

HEALTH

Wilson-Howarth, Dr Jane *Healthy Travel: Bites, Bugs and Bowels* Cadogan, 4th ed. 2006.
Wilson-Howarth, Dr Jane and Ellis, Dr Matthew *Your Child Abroad – A Travel Health Guide* Bradt Travel Guides Ltd, 2005 (2nd edition).

INTERNET SITES

Tourism sites (see also under safari companies' individual listings)

www.malawitourism.com
www.go2malawi.com
www.malawi-tourism-association.org.mw

Book sites

www.centralafricana.com Malawi-based African book specialist.
www.africabookcentre.com For all published books about Africa.
www.nhbs.com Specialist bird book distributor.

Wildlife, parks and conservation sites

www.wildlifemalawi.org Wildlife & Environmental Society of Malawi.
www.malawibirds.org Ornithological Society of Malawi.
www.malawicichlids.com Great site to find out more about Lake Malawi's unique fish.
www.wag-malawi.org Wildlife Action Group.
www.malawi.gov.mw/information1/main.info.parks Home page for the Department of National Parks and Wildlife.
www.africanconservation.org/malawi General site with links to Malawi conservation projects.
www.mountmulanje.org.mw Information on Mount Mulanje.
www.nyika.com Information on Nyika National Park & Vwaza Game Reserve.
www.projectafricanwilderness.org Information on Mwabve Game Reserve.
www.rhino-sadc.org Information on J&B rhinos in Liwonde National Park.
www.compass-malawi.com Community Partnerships for Sustainable Resource Management in Malawi.

WIN £100 CASH!

READER QUESTIONNAIRE

Send in your completed questionnaire for the chance to win £100 cash in our regular draw

All respondents may order a Bradt guide at half the UK retail price – please complete the order form overleaf.

(Entries may be posted or faxed to us, or scanned and emailed.)

We are interested in getting feedback from our readers to help us plan future Bradt guides. Please answer ALL the questions below and return the form to us in order to qualify for an entry in our regular draw.

Have you used any other Bradt guides? If so, which titles? ....

....

What other publishers' travel guides do you use regularly? ....

....

Where did you buy this guidebook? ....

What was the main purpose of your trip to Malawi (or for what other reason did you read our guide)? eg: holiday/business/charity etc.. ....

....

What other destinations would you like to see covered by a Bradt guide?

....

Would you like to receive our catalogue/newsletters?

YES / NO (If yes, please complete details on reverse)

If yes – by post or email? ....

Age (circle relevant category) 16–25   26–45   46–60   60+

Male/Female (delete as appropriate)

Home country ....

Please send us any comments about our guide to Malawi or other Bradt Travel Guides. ....

....

....

....

Bradt Travel Guides

23 High Street, Chalfont St Peter, Bucks SL9 9QE, UK

t +44 (0)1753 893444 f +44 (0)1753 892333

e info@bradtguides.com

www.bradtguides.com

CLAIM YOUR HALF-PRICE BRADT GUIDE!

Order Form

To order your half-price copy of a Bradt guide, and to enter our prize draw to win £100 (see overleaf), please fill in the order form below, complete the questionnaire overleaf, and send it to Bradt Travel Guides by post, fax or email.

Please send me one copy of the following guide at half the UK retail price

Title		*Retail price*	*Half price*
...	....	....	....

Please send the following additional guides at full UK retail price

No	*Title*	*Retail price*	*Total*
...	....	....	....
...	....	....	....
...	....	....	....

Sub total ....

Post & packing ....

(£1 per book UK; £2 per book Europe; £3 per book rest of world)

Total ....

Name ....

Address ....

Tel .... Email ....

☐ I enclose a cheque for £....... made payable to Bradt Travel Guides Ltd

☐ I would like to pay by credit card. Number: ....

Expiry date: .../... 3-digit security code (on reverse of card) .....

☐ Please add my name to your catalogue mailing list.

☐ I would be happy for you to use my name and comments in Bradt marketing material.

Send your order on this form, with the completed questionnaire, to:

Bradt Travel Guides MAL/4
23 High Street, Chalfont St Peter, Bucks SL9 9QE
☎ +44 (0)1753 893444 **f** +44 (0)1753 892333
e info@bradtguides.com www.bradtguides.com

Bradt Travel Guides

www.bradtguides.com

Africa

Africa Overland	£15.99
Benin	£14.99
Botswana: Okavango, Chobe, Northern Kalahari	£15.99
Burkina Faso	£14.99
Cape Verde Islands	£13.99
Canary Islands	£13.95
Cameroon	£13.95
Eritrea	£12.95
Ethiopia	£15.99
Gabon, São Tomé, Príncipe	£13.95
Gambia, The	£13.99
Ghana	£13.95
Johannesburg	£6.99
Kenya	£14.95
Madagascar	£14.95
Malawi	£13.99
Mali	£13.95
Mauritius, Rodrigues & Réunion	£13.99
Mozambique	£12.95
Namibia	£14.95
Niger	£14.99
Nigeria	£15.99
Rwanda	£14.99
Seychelles	£14.99
Sudan	£13.95
Tanzania, Northern	£13.99
Tanzania	£16.99
Uganda	£13.95
Zambia	£15.95
Zanzibar	£12.99

Britain and Europe

Albania	£13.99
Armenia, Nagorno Karabagh	£13.99
Azores	£12.99
Baltic Capitals: Tallinn, Riga, Vilnius, Kaliningrad	£12.99
Belgrade	£6.99
Bosnia & Herzegovina	£13.99
Bratislava	£6.99
Budapest	£7.95
Cork	£6.95
Croatia	£12.95
Cyprus see North Cyprus	
Czech Republic	£13.99
Dubrovnik	£6.95
Eccentric Britain	£13.99
Eccentric Cambridge	£6.99
Eccentric Edinburgh	£5.95
Eccentric France	£12.95
Eccentric London	£12.95
Eccentric Oxford	£5.95
Estonia	£12.95
Faroe Islands	£13.95
Hungary	£14.99
Kiev	£7.95
Latvia	£13.99
Lille	£6.99
Lithuania	£13.99
Ljubljana	£6.99
Macedonia	£13.95
Montenegro	£13.99
North Cyprus	£12.99
Paris, Lille & Brussels	£11.95
Riga	£6.95
River Thames, In the Footsteps of the Famous	£10.95
Serbia	£13.99
Slovenia	£12.99
Spitsbergen	£14.99
Switzerland: Rail, Road, Lake	£13.99
Tallinn	£6.99
Ukraine	£13.95
Vilnius	£6.99

Middle East, Asia and Australasia

Georgia	£13.95
Great Wall of China	£13.99
Iran	£14.99
Iraq	£14.95
Kabul	£9.95
Maldives	£13.99
Mongolia	£14.95
North Korea	£13.95
Oman	£13.99
Palestine, Jerusalem	£12.95
Sri Lanka	£13.99
Syria	£13.99
Tasmania	£12.95
Tibet	£13.99
Turkmenistan	£14.99

The Americas and the Caribbean

Amazon, The	£14.95
Argentina	£15.99
Bolivia	£14.99
Cayman Islands	£12.95
Costa Rica	£13.99
Chile	£16.95
Chile & Argentina: Trekking	£12.95
Eccentric America	£13.95
Eccentric California	£13.99
Falkland Islands	£13.95
Peru & Bolivia: Backpacking and Trekking	£12.95
Panama	£13.95
St Helena, Ascension, Tristan da Cunha	£14.95
USA by Rail	£13.99

Wildlife

Antarctica: Guide to the Wildlife	£14.95
Arctic: Guide to the Wildlife	£15.99
British Isles: Wildlife of Coastal Waters	£14.95
Galápagos Wildlife	£15.99
Madagascar Wildlife	£14.95
Southern African Wildlife	£18.95
Sri Lankan Wildlife	£15.99

Health

Your Child Abroad: A Travel Health Guide	£10.95

Index

Page numbers in bold indicate major entries; those in italic indicate maps